ALSO BY HILARY SPURLING

Ivy When Young: The Early Life of Ivy Compton-Burnett, 1884–1919

Invitation to the Dance: A Guide to Anthony Powell's
"Dance to the Music of Time"

Secrets of a Woman's Heart: The Later Life of I. Compton-Burnett.
1920–1969

Elinor Fettiplace's Receipt Book

Paul Scott: A Life of the Author of the Raj Quartet

Paper Spirits: College Portraits by Vladimir Sulyagin

The Unknown Matisse: A Life of Henri Matisse. 1869–1908

La Grande Thérèse: The Greatest Swindle of the Century

The Girl from the Fiction Department: A Portrait of Sonia Orwell

Matisse the Master: A Life of Henri Matisse. 1909–1954

Burying the Bones: Pearl Buck in China

ANTHONY POWELL

ANTHONY POWELL

Dancing to the Music of Time

HILARY SPURLING

ALFRED A. KNOPF · NEW YORK · 2018

12/18

THIS IS A BORZOI BOOK PUBLISHED BY ALFRED A. KNOPF

Copyright © 2018 by Hilary Spurling

All rights reserved. Published in the United States by Alfred A. Knopf,
a division of Penguin Random House LLC, New York. Originally
published in hardcover in Great Britain by Hamish Hamilton, an
imprint of Penguin Random House Ltd., London, in 2017.

www.aaknopf.com

Knopf, Borzoi Books, and the colophon are registered
trademarks of Penguin Random House LLC.

Library of Congress Cataloging-in-Publication Data
Names: Spurling, Hilary, author.
Title: Anthony Powell : dancing to the music of time / Hilary Spurling.
Description: First United States edition. | New York : Alfred A. Knopf, 2017. |
Includes bibliographical references and index.
Identifiers: LCCN 2017051875 | ISBN 9780525521341 (hardcover) |
ISBN 9780525521358 (ebook)
Subjects: LCSH: Powell, Anthony, 1905–2000. | Authors, English—20th century—
Biography. | Critics—England—Biography.
Classification: LCC PR6031.074 Z94 2017 | DDC 823/.912 [B]—dc23
LC record available at https://lccn.loc.gov/2017051875

Front-of-jacket photograph © Granville Davies
Jacket design by Chip Kidd

Manufactured in the United States of America

First United States Edition

For John, who first gave me Anthony Powell to read

CONTENTS

ILLUSTRATIONS

ACKNOWLEDGEMENTS

Anthony Powell made me his biographer long ago on the understanding that nothing whatever was to be done for as long as possible, terms that suited all parties, including his wife, Lady Violet Powell. Three decades after that undertaking, I owe by far my greatest debt to their sons, Tristram and John Powell, for their trust, patience and unconditional support. This book would not have been possible without the knowledge and archival skills of John Powell, who provided unrestricted access over the past four years to the Powell family papers at the Chantry in Somerset, as well as answering questions, supplying documents and offering unfailing hospitality.

My third great debt is to the indefatigable Patric Dickinson, Clarenceux King of Arms, former chairman of the Anthony Powell Society, whose remarkable powers of detection made him indispensable at every turn, especially in the early stages of tracking down material and mapping it out. I am especially grateful to Marion Coates's two daughters: the late Laura Cohn, who, with her husband, Stephen, talked to me at length, and allowed me to reproduce her mother's portrait by John Banting; and Catherine Chamier, who gave generously of her time and trouble.

Next I thank the many people who supplied background material and provided access to private papers: Venetia Bell for particulars about her father, Gerald Reitlinger, and for her company on an instructive tour of his incomparable collection, now in the Ashmolean Museum, Oxford; Bernard Dru for his assistance, kind hospitality and access to his father's Powell correspondence; Julia Elton for the loan of an unpublished memoir by her mother, Margaret Elton, and for an illuminating account of Eve Disher; Martha James for much information about Enid Firminger, and for lending me her own unpublished family memoir; Bryan Newman for his help, and for lending me an unpublished autobiography by his mother-in-law, Miranda Wood, née Heyward, ex-Christen; Celia Goodman and Ariane Banks for talking to me about Inez Holden; and Sir Richard Heygate for access to his father's Powell letters.

My thanks go to the late Roland Gant of Heinemann, and to T. G. Rosenthal for access to publishing archives; to my successive agents,

Bruce Hunter and Lizzy Kremer, for their help in general, and in particular for access to the David Higham Archive in the UK and at the Harry Ransom Center, University of Texas at Austin; to Michael Meredith, former College Librarian at Eton College; to Dr. Andrew Topsfield, Keeper of the Islamic Department, Ashmolean Museum, University of Oxford; to Sheila Vanker, Senior Curator of Chinese Art; to Francesca Leoni, Jameel Curator of Islamic Art; and to Bonhams Fine Art Auctioneers for photocopies of the Powell correspondence sold at auction in 2016.

I am grateful to Anne Bedish for showing me Adrian Daintrey's portrait of Varda, and to John Harris for allowing me to reproduce it; and for assistance and information to Lady Rachel Billington; Jenny Chamier-Grove; Jilly Cooper; Lady Antonia Fraser; Victoria Glendinning; Lord Gowrie; the late David Holloway; Paul and Marigold Johnson; Jonathan Kooperstein; Alison Lurie; Benedict Nightingale; the late Sonia Orwell; Thomas Pakenham; the late Henrietta Phipps; Michael Richardson of Art Space; Christopher Scoble; and Francis Wyndham.

My warmest thanks go to all the people who provided me with the peaceful and secluded places where I wrote successive chapters: Dame Drue Heinz, John and Catrine Clay, Ian Collins and Joachim Jacobs, Carole Angier, Anne Dumas, Phillida Wiggins and the late Lydia and Ian Wright.

Lastly, I thank Bruce Hunter again for reading my manuscript, and giving good advice; and Brigadier Nigel Still for checking the sections dealing with military matters in the First and Second World Wars. I am grateful to my editor at Hamish Hamilton, Simon Prosser, for his constancy, forbearance and long-term enthusiasm; to his indomitable assistant, Hermione Thompson, who prepared this book for the press with exemplary efficiency, speed and good humour; and to Ellie Smith for smoothing its path to the printers. My best thanks go to my friend and fellow biographer Carole Angier, for moral and philosophical support backed by practical assistance (including her supplementary interview of a key witness). More than anyone else I thank my husband, John Spurling, for his kindness and generosity, for never complaining in face of consistent provocation, and for giving me courage and strength throughout.

ANTHONY POWELL

I

1905–18

Small, inquisitive and solitary, the only child of an only son, growing up in rented lodgings or hotel rooms, constantly on the move as a boy, Anthony Powell needed an energetic imagination to people a sadly under-populated world from a child's point of view. His mother and his nurse were for long periods the only people he saw, in general the one unchanging element in a peripatetic existence. "All his character points to a strong maternal influence," he himself wrote long afterwards of John Aubrey, another slight sickly baby growing up in isolation without friends of his own age to become an acute and perceptive observer of his contemporaries. Both drew a steady stream of pictures in childhood, making sense of a chaotic and confusing external reality long before either learned to write. Tony pored over old copies of *Punch* with their throwaway jokes in scraps of dialogue printed as captions to crabbed spidery line drawings. Aubrey, whose biography he wrote as a kind of preliminary to his own *Dance to the Music of Time*, was an accomplished graphic artist as well as a writer. Aubrey's estimate of his own potential, and its characteristically downbeat expression, came close to his biographer's view of himself: "If ever I had been good for anything," he wrote, "it would have been a painter. I could fancy a thing so strongly & have so clear an idea of it."

"It was this powerful visual imagination which dominated his writing," Tony wrote of Aubrey, and he might have said the same of himself. As a small boy the books he read or had read to him were the standard diet of his age and sex in the decade before the First World War: the witches, sprites and hobgoblins of the *Red* and *Yellow Fairy*

*Book*s, boys' adventure stories, the knights and castles of Arthurian romance. Melancholy, observant and self-contained, he escaped like Aubrey into stories and legends of the past, "the anodyne to which he was addicted as early as he could remember, and with which throughout life he could never dispense." For company he deployed troops of increasingly battered toy soldiers and, as soon as he was old enough, constructed long chains of invisible relations. Tony was still a schoolboy when he first took up what he described as a kind of genealogical knitting. He had no home of his own, no siblings, no family to speak of except for a single aunt on each side and three cousins, sons of his father's sister whom he scarcely saw. His mother's parents had died before he was born, and for years he had no contact with his Powell grandparents either because, after inspecting him once as a baby, his grandmother refused to let him come near her again on the grounds that a grandchild made her feel old.

Genealogy joined him up to an extended family he never knew. His immediate ancestry was not encouraging. His mother's family of Wellses and Dymokes had once possessed a small country house in Lincolnshire with a modest parcel of land, both squandered in attempts by his great-grandfather to lay bogus claim to a peerage. The same man, Dymoke Wells, tried and expensively failed to seize for himself the obsolete hereditary title of King's Champion. Of his three sons, two died unmarried and the third ended the male line by producing three daughters, each of whom abandoned on marriage the name of Wells-Dymoke. Tony's Powell grandfather was less ineffectual but irretrievably unromantic. He had once dreamed of becoming a cavalry officer but his father died when he was eight years old, leaving no money to buy him a commission. Instead he migrated as a young man to Melton Mowbray in Leicestershire and became for the rest of his life, in his grandson's words, "an unappeasable fox-hunter." He funded his habit by setting up his plate as a surgeon, still a low-grade job for most of the nineteenth century, strenuous, smelly and mucky, a branch of butchery traditionally associated with screaming patients spouting blood who had to be strapped and held down on the operating table by heavyweight bruisers. Surgery had the advantage in those days that you could learn the trade on the job relatively cheaply from an older practitioner, and strike out on your own with little or nothing in the way of professional qualification (years later Tony's

Lionel Powell on the hunting field, drawn by his crony, the brewer William Adcock, with embellishments round the edges added long afterwards by their grandson, Tony Powell

mother told him that, much as she liked her father-in-law, she would do anything to avoid being treated by him).

Lionel Powell relied throughout his career on the hunting shires around Melton for a steady supply of fresh fractures. His great stroke of luck was marrying a local brewer's daughter, Jessie Adcock, an only child like her husband who, unlike him, stood to inherit a useful sum from her father. One of fourteen children of a local farmer, William Adcock had built up a successful brewery on the north-east edge of Melton, erecting a sizeable red-brick pile for himself and rising to the rank of captain in the Leicestershire Volunteers. An earlier, equally go-ahead Adcock had been the first to market the pork pies that made Melton's name (he sent them up by stagecoach to London in the 1830s). By the time Powell got there a few decades later the town had consolidated its position as the world centre of fox-hunting. Fashionable aristocrats descended for the winter season on Melton, where their needs were met by enterprising tradesmen like Adcock and Powell, the one providing beer for thirsty riders, the other patching up bones cracked or broken on the hunting field.

They made a boisterous couple. Short, tubby and emphatically bearded, Adcock was once mistaken on the station platform at Melton for the future King Edward VII (who hunted there regularly as Prince of Wales). Powell, his much younger crony and drinking companion, was a tall skinny gangling beansprout of a boy who towered over him as they plodded home together from a day's hunting, or from carousing afterwards, bedraggled, mud-plastered, clearly half-cut, the younger with one arm draped round the shoulders of his stocky friend. Hunting became a passion as well as a livelihood in a town that offered access to four packs of hounds, all based on the rolling grasslands studded with spinneys and coverts that stretched for miles in every direction: the Quorn, the Belvoir, the Cottesmore and the pack eventually known as the Fernie. The town owed its fame in hunting circles to the legendary Nimrod, whose sporting journalism had established him in the early years of the century as the father of fox-hunting in headquarters at the centre of Melton, opposite St. Mary's Church, simply known as the House. A solid and capacious hunting lodge with fifteen or twenty bedrooms upstairs, first-class stabling attached, and a long pillared portico opening at the back on to an acre of grounds, The House had belonged in its heyday to a daughter of the Duke of Rutland, and it still retained considerable splendour by 1878 when the friendship between Adcock and Powell culminated in a dynastic wedding. The bridal couple—nineteen-year-old Jessie and Lionel who was ten years older—started married life at the House, purchased presumably with Adcock money and discreetly renamed the Elms.

They put on a fine show with sumptuous hats and dresses for Jessie, luxuriant drooping mustachios for Lionel to show off the gold-braided uniform, sword, sash and plumed helmet of the Leicestershire Volunteers (he would end up as lieutenant colonel in what was essentially a predecessor of the territorial army). The spendthrift young Powells shocked their prudent and thrifty neighbours by taking trips to exotic destinations like Naples or Paris, and mollified Melton when they got back with lavish entertainment, meets and house parties ("guests came for a week and stayed two or three months, perhaps longer," said their grandson). They produced in short order two children, who inspired more resentment than anything else in their giddy young mother, and got scant attention from their fond, convivial, extrovert father, himself increasingly preoccupied elsewhere. The Elms grew more and more uncomfortable as the paths of its owners diverged, and their marriage began to go badly wrong. Old friends invited to stay, like the three Wells-Dymoke girls, found themselves making excuses to leave again almost as soon as they arrived.

Young Philip Powell—Lionel's son, Adcock's grandson—was smeared by the master of the Belvoir on the hunting field at the age of nine in 1891 with the bloody tail of a newly killed fox. It seems to have inoculated him against the sport of kings ever after, but what outraged his father was the fact that the local paper printed a picture of the boy wearing a cap instead of the correct hard bowler hat, which Lionel inked in by hand on the press cutting pasted in the family album. The affair became a family legend, turning up again (minus the hat) seventy years later in the pivotal sixth volume of *A Dance to the Music of Time*, which contains a virtually unmodified portrait of Philip Powell as the narrator's father. The Belvoir hunt went on meeting at the Elms well into the lifetime of Philip's son, Anthony, whose memories of being summoned after his grandfather's death to visit the widow at Melton were gloomy in the extreme. Long afterwards he described her house as infinitely depressing, a succession of dark, poky little rooms with an atmosphere that reminded him of a novel by I. Compton-Burnett, "nerve-wracked, despondent, more than a little sinister."

Certainly Tony's father categorically rejected his own father's horsey, hospitable way of life, and dismissed his Adcock grandfather by claiming in retrospect that he was gay. Presumably by implication Lionel Powell was too, given that the pair spent their spare waking hours together in male-orientated pursuits away from the home, out hunting or alternatively on manoeuvres followed by heavy drinking with the Volunteers. A homosexual husband might explain much about Jessie Powell's cumulative discontent with her marriage, her children and a way of life that drove her in the end to take refuge in a fantasy world of histrionics, hypochondria, ghost-raising and spell-casting based partly on folk rituals and witchcraft, partly on incessant reading of French pulp novels. Her grandson put hints of homosexuality down to envy and rancour, the punitive provincial instinct to stigmatize "an unusual man making his way up the social scale rather too rapidly in local opinion." Either way, Tony owed much to this great-grandfather he never knew. Adcock was the draughtsman in the family whose gifts—a sharp, noticing, humorous eye matched by vigorous attack and a decisive line—Tony clearly inherited. Both collected paintings, both actively cultivated the arts unlike anyone else on their side of the family, and years later Tony was more amused than dismayed to be told by a fortune-teller that Adcock the brewer was presiding from beyond the grave over his great-grandson's career as a novelist.

But as a boy it was an altogether different aspect of his family history that interested Tony. The Leicestershire Powells had long since lost sight of a Welsh connection that petered out with a Philip Lewis Powell born at the end of the eighteenth century, who squandered the family inheritance in quarrels over money and land, debts, fist-fights, lawsuits and bankruptcy. His namesake, Tony's father, was a serving soldier with no interest in his own origins or anyone else's. But genealogy became a kind of anchor for Tony himself in the years when he was growing up out of suitcases, rejoining his parents in his school holidays on their current army posting, often abroad, always in temporary accommodation, remaining so rootless that the first fixed address he ever had was his boarding school, followed later by his Oxford college. From childhood on he found his own obscure private stability in a distant heredity grounded for centuries (like John Aubrey's) in the Welsh Marches, "lands won with an admixture of force and prudent marriages by ancestors from whom the generations had left him separate and strangely remote."

Genealogy tied him securely to roots that ran deep and wide, forming a vast network to be patiently unearthed and unravelled over the next seventy or eighty years, snaking out sideways and backwards in threads that crossed, interwove and doubled back on themselves, leading eventually to Rhys ap Gruffydd, the great princely commander who drove the Norman invaders out of South Wales in the twelfth century, passing on his combative spirit to descendants including one who was the Llyr of Crugeryr in fifteenth-century Radnorshire, Shakespeare's King Lear, whose historical existence blurs inextricably into myth and legend. You could say of Anthony Powell, as he said of Aubrey and his best friend, Antony Wood, that what mattered was neither fame nor material success: "Their pleasures and their rewards were found in those shadowy and enchanted regions of the imagination where so much of their time was spent; and for both of them the past was as real—perhaps more real—than the present or the future."

Tony was unsettled and unsettling even before he was born. His mother moved house nine times in the first two years of her marriage, the period that covered her pregnancy and the first twelve months of her son's life. He was born on 21 December 1905, at number 44, Ashley Gardens, one of 159 identical furnished flats in a set of five monolithic blocks newly constructed, along with Westminster Cathedral, from glaring red brick with white stripes next to Victoria Station in London. Long afterwards Powell picked his birthplace as the home territory of by far the best known of all his fictional characters, Kenneth Widmerpool, the first person to take shape in the opening pages of *A Dance to the Music of Time*. The narrator visits him later in the Westminster flat where he lives with his mother: "the area immediately adjacent to the cathedral imparts a sense of vertigo, a dizziness almost alarming in its intensity: lines and curves of red brick appearing to meet in a kind of vortex, rather than to be ranged in normal forms of perspective. I had noticed this before when entering the terrain from the north, and now the buildings themselves seemed . . . almost as if they might swing slowly forward from their bases, and downward into complete prostration." At the time, anonymity and convenience for a quick getaway made this an ideal place to give birth, in the view of Tony's parents, who had been married for a year and a day.

Theirs was a strange romance with faintly grotesque mythical or fairy-tale overtones of a sort that strongly appealed to their son ever afterwards. Anthony Dymoke Powell was the child of Philip Powell and Maud Wells-Dymoke, the middle one of three pretty, sociable and self-possessed girls whose family had known the Powells ever since her father and Philip's grandfather married sisters more than sixty years earlier. The three Wells-Dymokes were the daughters of their father's second marriage (his first wife died childless). They were brought up mostly in Brighton, where their elderly father died when Maud was in her mid-twenties, and their mother succumbed to depression with crippling psychosomatic and physical side effects. Maud was the practical sister, some said the prettiest of the three, certainly the cleverest and by far the most dependable. She nursed her mother, managed the family's affairs and kept an eye on her sisters. Cicely, the eldest, famous for her long golden hair like Sleeping Beauty's, was too fragile and dreamy to be expected to look after

herself. Violet, the youngest, was irresistibly flighty with a reckless
self-confidence that landed her time and again in increasingly serious
trouble. Both left it to Maud to deal efficiently with doctors, lawyers,
trustees and executors, the latter including their old family friend
Lionel Powell, who tried and failed to dent Maud's composure by
playing a penny whistle throughout a key session with solicitors in
charge of the girls' trust fund.

Always more comfortably off than the Powells, the Wells-Dymokes
stayed in close contact probably because Jessie, much nearer to them
in age than her husband, enjoyed their company. Perhaps she liked
hearing about their round of dances, balls and concert parties in
cosmopolitan Brighton. Very likely she envied the lack of parental
surveillance that gave them far greater freedom than was normal
for unmarried girls at the time. Jessie's children, Philip and Katherine, were respectively four and six years old when Maud attended
her first ball aged twenty, coming home with a souvenir programme
signed by her partners for every dance. The three girls were much in
demand for their own sakes, and also as the particular favourites of
their bachelor neighbour, Lord Abergavenny, who was "rumoured
to be able to ride from Brighton to Erridge Castle [his family seat
near Tunbridge Wells] without setting a foot off his own land." All
three loved parties and dressing up. Maud's banjo solos were a star
attraction of the Ladies Mandoline and Guitar Band, performing for
charity to packed houses in the 1890s at Brighton's Royal Pavilion,
and at Hove Town Hall a few miles along the coast, once even at the
Prince's Hall in London.

The sisters were still unattached when their mother died in 1899.
Vi fulfilled her critics' gloomiest predictions by running away with
a thoroughly unsuitable man called Hodgson, who may or may not
have married her. Maud had so far rejected all proposals, claiming
improbably to have blacked the eye of a suitor who refused to take no
for an answer. Small, slender and piquant, she still looked absurdly
young, cradling her banjo or her little black pug dog, by the time
Jessie's son Phil was old enough to think of her as anything more
than an honorary elder sister or cousin. She had known him from
a baby, and must have been well aware of the maternal indifference
alternating with active dislike that made both young Powells keen to
leave home the first minute they could. Katherine, always exception-

Maud Wells-Dymoke, still looking
absurdly young at the time of her
engagement

ally good-looking, accepted what would prove to be a disastrous proposal at twenty from an apparently eligible young man who turned
up for the hunting in Melton. Phil realized his father's ambition by
joining the army, passing out of Sandhurst in March 1901, ready to
be shipped to South Africa to fight the Boers in a war that England
seemed to be winning. He returned home first on embarkation leave,
a dashing young subaltern whose dapper turnout, glossy dark hair
and trim moustache hit exactly the mood of that high patriotic and
imperialist moment.

Maud was thirty-three years old. Phil would be eighteen in April,
but something she saw in him—some urgent combination both needy
and masterful—stirred her to the depths of her being. In spite of her
enthusiastic party-going, Maud's aim in long years as her mother's
sickbed attendant and for all practical purposes her sisters' guardian
had never been to please herself. Though schooled from childhood in
Victorian notions of dutiful submission, she could not entirely stifle

the clarity and courage to recognize a chance and take it when she saw it. Things came to a head one morning over breakfast at the Elms, when Phil found someone had eaten his banana and made an angry scene that switched to tender protestations as soon as he realized the culprit was Maud. Before he sailed for South Africa in May the pair had reached an understanding that they would wait for one another, although it would be another three years before he was twenty-one, and free to marry without his parents' permission.

Having settled her own future, Maud settled her sister's. She organized a rescue operation for Vi, who had rashly accepted the advances of a senior officer in the Indian army without first securing her exit from a marriage contract, legal or not, that Hodgson had no intention of voiding. Maud removed her sister bodily to the continent, settling her safely out of reach and simultaneously negotiating at long distance the terms of Vi's release. Some said the prospective husband acted as co-respondent in divorce proceedings, others that the so-called divorce was a conventional fiction to cover an illicit affair. At all events Vi finally married Major Guy Welman Moore of the 22nd Indian Cavalry and Madras Lancers in 1902, and sailed with him for India. Cicely meanwhile, approaching forty still with a child's incapacity to fend for herself, emerged from her trance to general astonishment with an offer of marriage from the vicar of Stanway, the Revd. Oscar Worne. With one sister ensconced as a regimental wife, the other absorbed in plans for an elaborate formal wedding, Maud took steps to clinch her own future.

Phil had been posted to Pretoria to join the relatively new Welsh Regiment, a decision that had less to do with obscure Welsh origins than shrewd advice from a distant military relative, who vouched for the Welsh as reputable and relatively cheap. The Boers by this time had largely abandoned open warfare for a vicious guerrilla campaign that rendered conventional military tactics virtually useless. Phil celebrated his nineteenth birthday in April 1902, and went into action for the first time a month later. Whatever he told her was too much for Maud, who booked a passage to the Transvaal for herself and Pavey, the family's elderly housekeeper. For an unmarried woman almost twice his age to follow a man to the Cape was a flagrant, indeed ruinous violation of proprieties universally accepted and enforced at the time. Presumably Maud could not endure the prospect of losing Phil. Perhaps he begged her to come. Conceivably the fact that her father had once been his grandfather's brother-in-law meant she could pass as his cousin, but her recklessness remains hard to credit. "It would be impossible to believe in this drastic step," Maud's future daughter-in-law said nearly a century later, "if there had not survived a tiny photograph of the couple dressed for a ride across the Veldt."

In it Maud looks, as she would for the rest of her life, much the same age as her future husband. In their middle and late years she would come to seem if anything the younger of the two. At the time of their engagement she was admittedly in passionate flight from years of subjection to the iron will of an invalid in a High Victorian sickroom. Maud's mother suffered, according to Tony, from a sublimated form of the madness that also claimed her brother (who spent the greater part of his life incarcerated in an institution), and eventually her sister too. Maud's sanity was humane and robust, but the experience left her with a near-pathological hatred of doctors, hospitals and medical treatment. It also gave her an extreme sensitivity to other people's demands and needs that lowered her expectations and raised her tolerance of their behaviour to highly unusual levels.

Phil's parents categorically forbade his marriage as they had done his sister's. Katherine eloped with Arthur Bonsey in 1903, and Phil ran away the year after to marry Maud secretly in a church at Barmouth in North Wales with nobody present but themselves and the vicar. The marriage itself brought great and lasting happiness to both of them. Even the outrage of the elder Powells faded away, when Phil brought his wife back to Melton, in the warmth of an older and deeper affection for Maud. But although the couple's disparity in age proved immaterial, in practice its psychological consequences were devastating. Their union broke another ingrained taboo against a practice universally condemned in that self-righteous age as abhorrent and unnatural. Maud was acutely aware that in other people's eyes, probably to some extent in her own, she stood convicted of cradle-snatching. She saw or suspected public hostility, mockery, sniggers and pointing fingers on all sides. Her public confidence evaporated. Contact with the outside world became painful and, as she got older, excruciating. She no longer went to parties. She stopped seeing her own friends, and made no attempt to get to know her husband's. From now on she was tortured by shyness. Its shadow darkened and distorted her life, and in due course her son's.

Tony grew up in extreme, inward-looking, almost monastic seclusion. He said his mother was never really happy except alone at home with her family, occasionally admitting at most one or two of her oldest friends. Although she was loyalty itself in all that concerned her husband's career, she was never at ease with the army. She made no complaint; perhaps in some ways she welcomed the constant arbitrary disruptions and relocations that made a junior officer's life inconvenient, expensive and uncomfortable. At least they helped her avoid the kind of casual relationships she found increasingly intrusive. People who coincided only briefly between postings could never come too close. Often they hardly knew your name or your face. Regimental life was a horror she tried at all costs to avoid. Her worst nightmare was the possibility of becoming a general's wife with its demanding social calendar, and unending responsibility for innumerable staff wives. As far as their provisional existence allowed, the Powells settled into the uneventful domesticity that suited her husband as well as herself. Their son acquired as a baby the rock-bottom security that came from being unconditionally loved by his mother. He had been a puny undersized infant with such a precarious hold on life that a priest had to be fetched to Ashley Gardens to baptise him before he expired. The baby confounded his doctor by drawing on unexpected reserves of stamina, but for an elderly mother (Maud was thirty-eight years old) to come so close to losing her only child made him infinitely precious.

He was sustained by her warmth, but she also impressed on him her lack of spontaneity in even the simplest transaction with other human beings. More than anything she shrank from being singled out, or failing to conform to what was expected, and she taught him to feel the same. "I was brought up to do ordinary things," Tony said. "My parents insisted on that. I was brought up to think drawing attention was a bad thing." His social inexperience made for difficulties when he came, unusually late, into contact with contemporaries at school and university. To people who didn't know him, he often seemed cold, critical, aloof. He himself blamed a natural aptitude as an observer, forced by circumstances to make do with himself as his

Tony with Pavey and household staff

subject because there was no one else to observe: what he called "the unhappy gift of seeing oneself in some sort of perspective."

He abandoned all pretence of interest in his own story as soon as he got the chance to look outwards at other people. Human behaviour entranced him. Preternaturally alert to its subtleties and mesmerized by its intricacy, he was amazed to the end of his life by the scale of its oddity. His mother was deeply religious, nourished by an Anglican faith shared with neither husband nor son. But she did pass on to Tony as a small boy, on the one hand, her familiarity with the occult—an easy acceptance of ghosts, apparitions, fortune-telling and spirit-raising as a natural outcrop of human psychology—and, on the other, with Christian Science. Its appeal as a rational alternative to organized religion in the years leading up to the First World War meant that Powell was not the only writer of his generation—he cited Denton Welsh, Jocelyn Brooke and V. S. Pritchett—brought up by parents who subscribed implicitly to the Christian Scientist's central tenet, the primacy of mind over matter. "I have sometimes wondered," he wrote more than half a century later, "whether emphasis

At the seaside with his mother and an old
friend

on the unreality of 'matter' . . . has the effect on a child of stimulating imaginative instincts, and, as in my own case, directing them into
channels ultimately intellectual or aesthetic rather than religious."

Unlike most other children of his class and period, Tony's primary
carer was his mother, with her maid doubling as nurse. Pavey died in
the winter of 1907–78, when he was just two years old, to be replaced
by Clara Purser, a bright young woman from Gravesend, young and
energetic enough to play children's games. She took him for his daily
walks, and sometimes to the seaside on holiday while his mother
accompanied her husband on short-term postings abroad. In these
early years he had relatively little to do with his father, rarely at home
during the day and never anxious to see more than he had to of his
son in the evenings. Even as a very small child Tony must have been
aware that his demands on his mother collided with her role as a wife.

Phil was twenty-two years old when his son was born, still deeply
damaged by a mother whose default position was "a kind of innate
spite towards her children." His new wife's devotion was absolute,
her admiration always a tonic and her unfailing support balm to his
spirit, but now he found himself having to share all three too soon

with a newcomer. He responded in ways that suggest jealousy was always ready to surface. Maud's job was to see that it didn't. Both her charges required constant assiduous attention. Both reacted loudly and violently to neglect or frustration. Tony's adult relationship with his father retained all too clearly traces of a primary friction from their earliest encounters when each recognized the other as his prime rival. "My father always came first," said Tony. "My mother, throughout her life, had no other aim but to make her husband happy." That cool objective acceptance cannot have come without a degree of struggle for all three of them. As a mother Maud adored her son. As a wife she never doubted her husband's judgement, or lost her belief that his intellect ranked him among the two or three outstanding brains in the country. But in the baby's first few years it must sometimes have seemed as if she had to deal with not one but two implacable infant male egos.

Her own family experience had developed in Maud talents that perfectly matched Phil's needs. He had reacted to a loveless childhood with anger and misery. It made him a champion grudge-bearer, liable to resort at the smallest real or imagined slight in public or private to hysterical rage. She was a born peacemaker. Discord was his natural element, reconciliation her speciality. His desires were momentous and so urgent he had not the smallest ability to defer gratification. Whatever he did or wanted or felt consumed him utterly at any given moment. He seemed to himself to be dodging hostile elements bent on catching him out or taking unfair advantage. Maud by her son's account was calm, generous and open where Phil was irascible, stingy and secretive. She was lucid where he was obscure ("My father really hated clarity"). The two complemented one another with a precision that bound them indissolubly together.

After years of watching his mother "coping skilfully with my father's network of nerves," Tony came in the end to accept her view of Phil as more than capable of acute and original insight into people and things, if only he had been able to string his impressions together into any sort of coherent shape. Tony himself controlled his own careering creative instincts with strategies of discipline and restraint learned from his mother. The relatively little he said about his childhood self makes the glimpses he gave of his father in uninhibited action at home all the more startling. For all professional purposes a perfectly competent young staff officer, Phil needed—and Maud saw that he got—somewhere he could lash out with no fear of reprisal. Their son's passing references to his cruel tongue, and the fits of maniacal fury only his wife could defuse, suggest how necessary he found that safety valve.

At the beginning of 1908, when his son was just two years old, Lieutenant Powell switched jobs, leaving his regiment to start a tour of duty as adjutant to a battalion of London territorials, the Kensingtons, staffed largely in Tony's recollection by stockbrokers. Its commanding officer was Major General Alfred Turner, the same obliging relative who had recommended the Welsh in the first place, and who now inaugurated what the family ever after agreed was the happiest time of Maud's life. For once Phil was no longer in danger of being stationed overseas or (another of her most lurid nightmares) posted to Catterick. The family could count on five whole years in a home of its own, a pleasant roomy flat on three floors, picked up at a bargain rent affordable even by a junior officer: number 25, Albert Hall Mansions, part of the massive red-brick redevelopment surrounding the Albert Hall, conveniently close to territorial headquarters and opposite Kensington Gardens.

Here they would make a fresh start, far from Melton's critical eye, in a place where nobody knew them or their immediate history. Maud reinvented herself, cutting out of her life virtually everyone who had known her before, and chopping ten years off her age on official documents. She turned the former billiard room at the back of the flat into a nursery for Tony. He had a wooden rocking horse, and a plump stately Pekinese dog called Pekoe to play with. Every afternoon he went out in his pram with his new nurse Clara for a walk in the park. On rainy days they explored the three huge new department stores on Kensington High Street, or the museums going up all round them on the site of the Great Exhibition (one of Tony's favourite destinations was the Natural History Museum in bright yellow brick picked out in blue, just along the road from the Victoria and Albert in red and white). He always wanted more time than he could get to watch the Punch-and-Judy show, and he speculated furiously about the quantities of unknown children he saw bowling hoops on the Broad Walk in sailor hats and suits like his own. "A white belted (below the bottom) suit with a frilly collar, white suede boots, white socks and *white gloves*," wrote a contemporary, lovingly detailing Tony's outfit more than half a century afterwards.

As soon as he could hold a pencil he started to draw—"I cannot remember a time when I did not draw"—and his mother passed his sketches round the few old friends from Brighton who still came to tea. He had a golliwog as children did in that innocent Edwardian age before the British learned better, and the first book he read aloud without help was *Little Black Sambo*. Clara bought a copy of *Reading Without Tears* and taught him to read at four as a surprise for his mother, who was away for two months with his father on army orders. From then on he read whatever he could lay hands on, including his father's growing collection of handsomely bound, illustrated art books by art nouveau suspects like Aubrey Beardsley (the last author most right-minded parents would have dreamed of allowing a child to go near in those days). Later he learned to write with Clara ghosting his letters until, on a perishing-cold trip to the seaside just after his eighth birthday, he composed without help a letter to his mother on holiday in Florence, nicely laid out with neat spelling but no punctuation: "Dear Mummy How are you getting on how is Daddy I hope his cold is better I am getting on splendid at Brighton love from tony."

He was beginning to build up a respectable army of toy soldiers, tiny painted lead replicas of British infantry and French Zouaves from the Crimean War, West Indians from the Ashanti campaign, dragoons from South Africa, all knocking one another about in vigorous engagements on the nursery floor. He remembered once answering the door to find his own father standing outside in full-dress scarlet regimentals with sword, spurs and shiny spiked helmet, back from rehearsals for the funeral of King Edward VII. He watched the procession for George V's coronation with his mother at Hyde Park Corner, and he never forgot the handful of silent movies he saw at one of London's earliest picture palaces in South Kensington. At five or six years old he suddenly grasped his own existential basis on coming back from the park one afternoon to the dark interior of the mansion block where specks of dust danced in a shaft of sun: "Now the truth came flooding in with the dust infested sunlight. The revelation of self-identity was inescapable. There was no doubt about it. I was me."

Not long after this mental jolt the family's interlude of relative stability ran out. The time had come to move on from the enchanted hinterland of early childhood, leaving behind the wooded glades and soft grassy expanses of Kensington Gardens, the Broad Walk, the Flower Walk, the Round Pond and the Albert Memorial. More than forty years afterwards in the early stages of *A Dance to the Music of Time*, Powell invoked the memorial, absurd, majestic and impregnated with loss, as his characters pause on its wide shallow steps leading up to the bearded and gilded man in the middle, sheltered under his mosaic canopy and attended by a select group of arts and sciences in white marble with support from the symbolic Asian exiles at the south-east corner, "where, beside the kneeling elephant, the Bedouin forever rests on his haunches in hopeless contemplation of Kensington Gardens' trees and thickets, the blackened sockets of his eyes ranging endlessly over the rich foliage of these oases of the mirage." The landscape awaiting the family at Bordon Camp in Hampshire, where Captain Powell rejoined the 2nd Battalion of the Welsh Regiment in 1913, was scratchy and barren, broken only by gorse, bracken, sinewy heather and pine clumps rising from sandy ground blackened by heath fires. "Walking there was not at all like being in the country. Agriculture seemed as remote as in a London street. This waste land might have been some walled-in space in the suburbs where businessmen practise golf strokes . . . It had neither memories of the past nor hope for the future."

This passage from the last novel Powell wrote before the *Dance* indicates probably with a fair degree of accuracy how he and his mother felt as they settled into their new home, a furnished bungalow called Stonedene, isolated on top of a hill in scrubland twelve miles from Aldershot. The house, like many of the places where Tony lived as a child, was architecturally nondescript: shapeless, straggly and out of place in its surroundings, looking like "a long, low Noah's Ark, come uncomfortably to rest on a heather-grown, coniferous spur of Mount Ararat." The household inherited several cats, a large destructive brood of chickens, and a small donkey called Jock ridden without enthusiasm by Tony. He had his first lessons here from a Miss Judkins, who did the rounds of the local army children by bike. He said he learned more from reading books than from anything she taught him, and he certainly put far greater effort into the war-games that increasingly absorbed him, acted out with lead soldiers for characters in an elaborate, ongoing serial narrative.

Captain Powell acquired his first car, a fast and powerful Straker-Squire with a long gleaming bonnet that drew gaping crowds wherever it went but ended ignominiously when its owner ran it into a pond. Tony kept a photo of the car ever afterwards, and another of his father on horseback leading out the Welsh Regiment at Bordon. His own excursions took place on donkey-back, at any rate initially with his father's batman walking alongside holding a leading rein, and making disobliging comments about the military police who could be seen jogging across the heath below the house. So could the far more conspicuous Philip Oyler, Prophet of the Soil, a leading Simple Lifer based in the nearest village of Headley Down. Dr. Oyler regularly passed the Powells' gate, bearded, bare-legged and dressed, like the followers who straggled after him across Ludshott Common, in vaguely classical white drapery.

More than half a century later Powell transferred this gang of utopians wholesale, along with Stonedene itself, from fact to fiction in *The Kindly Ones*, number six in the *Dance* sequence of novels. Even the Powells' redoubtable cook, James Gomm, took on memorable new life as the sagacious and sceptical Albert Creech. When Powell eventually came to describe this period in his memoirs, he called the house by its fictional name of Stonehurst, a transposition that suggests how far by this time fiction had eclipsed its always vestigial basis in fact. He also appropriated for his novel the premonitory ghosts that haunted Stonedene, rattling the maids, unsettling the whole household, giving the author's eight-year-old self an intermittent sense of foreboding. The ghosts, or the trouble they caused, contributed to a general malaise that seems to have emanated largely from Tony's mother. Always glad to see ghosts, hoping for a chance to get to know more about them, she now found herself petrified by a nightly apparition in the shape of a household pet apparently trying to strangle her. She told Tony she sometimes woke in the morning afraid to look in the mirror for fear her hair had turned white.

For an exceptionally sensitive woman to respond with misgiving to the atmosphere in an army camp in the run-up to 1914 might seem natural enough, but Maud had more immediate disasters in mind. The marriages of her two sisters had ended catastrophically, culminating in a sensational public scandal the same year as the Powells took refuge at Stonedene. Vi had not managed to last long as the wife of Major, now Lieutenant Colonel Moore. She met a young Irish subaltern in India ("Vi has always been much too fond of people who amuse her," Maud said tartly), leaving her husband and returning alone in 1907 to England to continue her affair with Henry Inglis. When Colonel Moore himself came to fetch his wife back four years later, she agreed to give their marriage one last try, only to walk out on him again for good, at which point he demanded a divorce. To sue a woman for adultery in those days was a public assault more brutal than physical battering. Newspaper reports made the most of the case, raking over Moore's part in her previous marital break-up, and effectively shredding what little of her reputation Vi might have hoped to salvage by marrying Inglis as soon as the divorce decree became final in 1913.

She recovered her resilience with time, reverting to her old buoyant, extrovert self, "completely at ease," as her nephew said, "in ballroom or bar, palazzo or pension." But Maud could not bounce back so readily. The storm of publicity surrounding Vi touched a raw nerve, and Maud did not try to hide her perturbation from her small son in the nursery. Cecily meanwhile had given birth to a stillborn baby in 1906, and died of convulsions while pregnant for a second time the year after. For Maud, the enormity of these successive blows seems to have been literally unspeakable. She retreated more than ever from normal everyday contacts. Her son pinpointed their two years at Stonedene as the time when his parents finally narrowed down their existence to "a life entirely enclosed by their own domestic interests."

Their retreat was broken up by England's declaration of war with Germany on 4 August 1914. As a company commander, Captain Powell left with his regiment for France eight days later. His wife started packing up to return with Tony and Clara to London but already, before they left Stonedene, reports began arriving of casualties, officers wounded or killed, some of them fathers of friends who had been invited to tea, or who shared Tony's lessons with Miss Judkins. As a soldier's son Tony had a far more realistic grasp than most people at this stage, children or adults, of what war was likely to mean. "Life seemed all at once geared to forces implacable and capricious, their peril not to be foretold."

Maud borrowed a flat at 25, Berkeley Square from an old Brighton friend for the first few months of the war, moving on to furnished rooms in Sloane Street and then to a boarding house, 4, Glendower Place at the top of the Old Brompton Road in South Kensington. Her husband took part in the first heavy fighting in Flanders, marked by terrible losses on both sides, salutary defeat for the British and the deadly retreat from Mons. Well before the end of the year when the public confidently expected the war to be over, the 2nd Battalion of the Welsh Regiment was virtually wiped out in a convulsive struggle for Ypres at the end of October. One of the few officers to survive, Phil was invalided home, exhausted, traumatized, half starved and dangerously weakened by dysentery. Maud, who saw hospitals as little better than slaughterhouses, set out at once to rescue him, leaving their son with Clara. "My dear mummy," Tony wrote in what must be his first surviving typescript, posted from Glendower Place and laboriously picked out, presumably with one finger, on a typewriter with a purple ink ribbon that had cost him a fortune. "Do you think this is ripping, I got it for 10s and 6d at gamage. I hope you and Daddy are quite well, I am. Thank you very much for the cigarette cards, they were queer. I hope Tibby is quite well. With love & kisses your loving son Tony."

His father recovered sufficiently to be posted in 1915 as brigade major to the headquarters of the newly raised 95th Infantry Brigade at Sutton Coldfield near Birmingham, where his job was to oversee the wholesale recycling of civilian volunteers as soldiers to fill the trenches, now running the length of the Western Front in a stand-off that would last for the rest of the war. Brigade HQ moved up to Yorkshire that summer, relocating to Leyburn in Wensleydale, where Tony remembered the high dark stony sides of the valley, and wintry weather in his holidays in August. His father's self-control had not improved under stress. One of Tony's close friends in later life, who had been a young subaltern at this point, described Major Powell turning red when annoyed by some mishap, "standing in the middle of the road speechless with rage—almost literally foaming," a spectacle he never forgot. "That was the picture to the life," said Tony.

By this time he himself had already spent a couple of terms at Mr. Gibbs's day school, 134, Sloane Street, almost next door to the lodgings his mother had originally rented, and not far from Glendower

Place. Christopher Gibbs was one of the first to experiment with small-scale, protective, child-friendly pre-preparatory-school education, and his example would be much copied. He provided excellent teaching in a sympathetic atmosphere that made it easy for Tony to accept his discovery that he was no good at games, and to deal for the first time with something else he had not grasped before, "the unpleasantness of some boys—a necessary prelude to the unpleasantness of not a few men . . ." He himself was sufficiently inconspicuous to avoid anything like Mr. Gibbs's comment on the bumptious young Peter Ustinov, who attended the same school twenty years later: "This boy shows great originality, which must be curbed at all costs." Tony liked Mr. Gibbs, no doubt because they shared a similar sense of humour, but also because, as he said, Gibbs gave him in a relatively supportive setting at least an inkling of what to expect at the boarding school where he went next.

When Brigade HQ moved down from Yorkshire for final field training at Codford on Salisbury Plain (transformed for the duration by the military into "a kind of shanty town . . . sheds and booths set between torrents of mud traversed by duckboards"), the Powells took Tony out of school and rented a cottage in the village of Boynton. His father was back in France in action at Beaucourt by the New Year of 1916, mentioned for conspicuous courage in dispatches in April by Major General Sir Douglas Haig and shortly afterwards awarded a Distinguished Service Order. Whatever Tony had to face in his first term at prep school, his standing with the other boys must have gone up when they found out about his father's DSO.

His parents had put him down to start at the New Beacon School at Sevenoaks in Kent at the somewhat advanced age of ten and a half. He was further held up by whooping cough, missing the first half of term and arriving late, in some ways far more knowledgeable about what was going on in the outside world than his contemporaries, in others hopelessly innocent and inexperienced. Exposed to routine humiliation and bullying, he was quite without what he called "a child's . . . protective forgetfulness," writing home in evident agitation, and perhaps unwisely, to his mother in his second year to say that someone had crept up in the middle of the night and smashed the much-prized watch she had given him. He must have been all too familiar by this time with "the wickedness of boies" that had caused John Aubrey such pain and fear when he, too, was sent away to school at the same age. It was one of many points where Aubrey's experience in the seventeenth century reached out across time in a kind of posthumous sympathy to his twentieth-century biographer. Tony quoted Aubrey's account of his own childish vulnerability, and described the consequences: "'I was exceedingly mild of spirit . . . mightily susceptible of fascination. My idea very cleer; phansie like a mirrour, pure chrystall water which the least wind does disorder & unsmooth . . .' It is a striking description of a sensitive nature. For such a boy a boarding school was, inevitably, a painful introduction to many common enough aspects of disagreeable human behaviour."

Nearly all of the New Beacon's seventy-five pupils came from military families, expecting (as Tony did too at this stage) to follow their fathers into the army. The proprietor and headmaster, John Stuart Norman, had emerged from retirement in his late seventies to take back control from his two sons, both called up by the army. The rest of the staff had gone too, giving way to "an ever rolling stream of assistant masters and mistresses: the males likely to be ancient, shiftless, wounded, gassed; the females (at this school uniformly charmless) often scarcely qualified academically to do the job at all." The headmaster had a fierce temper and looked like an elderly Rudyard Kipling with "sparse grey hair, drooping tobacco-stained moustache, abnormally thick spectacles, eternally old thick tweed suit, worn whatever the climate." He taught maths (leaving Tony permanently disabled in this respect), classics and "a language that passed for French." He flogged the boys on trumped-up charges before the assembled school, and tied their legs together so they couldn't run away when he bowled a hard ball at them in the cricket nets.

Tony joined the Boy Scouts, swapped stamps and learned to accept without crying the injuries inflicted deliberately or not by the headmaster on the sports field ("nothing much short of loss of a leg would surely have been noticed"). He passed his swimming test, played cricket, took boxing lessons ("I think I bashed him," he reported proudly of an encounter with a school bully), and even managed to scrape into the rugby team in his last year. Otherwise he kept his head down, and counted the days until his mother's visits. All pupils lived under totalitarian surveillance. They were inspected for head lice first thing every morning, their letters home were monitored, they had no

Henry Yorke, who remained Tony's close friend all through their schooldays and their time at university together

keys to their private lockers, and there were no doors on the lavatories. Food was short and often uneatable. Tony's closest friend Henry Yorke remembered a stinking ham oozing clear smelly liquid, and boys so hungry they ate raw turnips and mangel wurzels from the farmer's fields (which, according to Henry, they had to hoe, loaned out by their headmaster perhaps to make up for the stolen mangel wurzels). Every child made sure he had a calendar so he could tick off the days to the end of term—"as prisoners notch the walls," said Henry.

The boys listened in chapel every Sunday to a sonorous roll-call of the thirty-seven old boys who they were constantly told had died for their sakes in the war, one for every two current pupils. "At first we paid attention," wrote Henry, "but in the end we had had so much there was no room for more." The boys themselves were drilled as replacements for their dead elders, carrying dummy rifles they made themselves in school carpentry lessons. Kent was close enough for them to hear the muffled thudding of guns in France on a clear day, and the school lay under the flight path of the first air raids in the closing stages of the war. At night the boys crouched by the dormitory windows watching bombers fly over, and next morning they picked up shrapnel in the playground. Henry claimed to have been told that enemy pilots were under special orders to target the New

Beacon. Rumours circulated about Germans boiling up corpses to eat, and generally indulging in every monstrosity the schoolboy mind could conceive. The Angels of Mons, revenants popularly supposed to have risen from the grave to watch over the troops, became in Henry's active imagination "malignant ghosts of those who had died for them drifting across their playing fields . . . Almost every night we thought we had seen them."

Henry was one of the minority of boys whose family had no military connections. Tony, whose father had survived the ordeal of Mons, knew too much for this kind of hysterical fantasy. The headmaster's tirades filled him with dark thoughts of his own. "Sometimes on icy football fields and during shifts of slave-labour when we chopped wood in his garden, I was almost inclined to doubt his oftenrepeated assertion that life was worse in the trenches." Tony spent three years at the New Beacon, and afterwards had nightly dreams of being back at prep school that continued until he reached his late twenties, when he killed the headmaster in one of these dreams. His considered conclusion at the age of seventy was characteristically restrained: "I should be unwilling to live five minutes of it again."

He said the only good thing he owed the school was his friendship with Henry Yorke. The two first met on the day the Powells came to look round, when Tony remembered talking to a chubby, dark-haired and well-behaved child exactly the same age as himself. Henry said he was habitually shown off to parents by the headmaster, fingering his plump arm like the witch in *Hansel and Gretel*, as an advertisement for the school's health and welfare. He had already been there two terms, and did not take straightaway to this quiet, watchful new boy. Henry was already a phenomenal talker, fast, fluent and funny ("he can talk like no other person I've ever met," reported the flamboyant Robert Byron, also a pupil at the same school). He liked and collected odd words and unusual books. He made up stories, like Tony, whom he came to recognize with time as an ally.

At some point they found themselves sharing the same dormitory along with eighteen other boys, who appointed the pair of them— "like professional narrators of the orient," said Tony—to entertain the rest in the dark every night for the half-hour after lights out when talking was still allowed. Tony mostly recycled the plots of popular thrillers or newspaper serials, but sometimes he tried out one of his own ("I have been inventing the most frightfully 'spooky' stories"). Once he and Henry began improvising a novel together, seated side by side on a radiator in the school gym. The novel petered out half-way down its first page but, for both of them, it turned out to be a declaration of intent. Henry was in his first year at university when he published his novel *Blindness* under the pen name of Henry Green.

Tony remained for a long time more of a graphic artist. Until he met Henry, he told his stories—to himself, and sometimes to his mother—by acting them out with lead soldiers, or sketching them in black ink. These are vigorous little scenarios, composed with an energy and panache that suggest—probably thanks to his father—a much more sophisticated acquaintance with the art of illustration than he yet had with literature. At ten or twelve he was already drawing observant and accurate sketches of fashionable hats teamed with stylish Edwardian costumes in letters to his mother, or lively miniature dramas: an eighteenth-century highwayman called Beau Brocade hanged on a gallows by jubilant troopers, a police chase in a London street, often with a cat or cats stalking along at the back. The only member of the New Beacon staff he singled out by name was the drawing master, Mr. Clarke, who was clearly impressed by Tony and encouraged him to draw.

He signed off with a flourish, "AP," adding at the bottom of one page of drawings a tiny inkwash of the artist, or possibly the author, at work with a bulging wastepaper basket behind him. His reading at this stage was still largely adventure yarns by popular favourites like Harrison Ainsworth, or Bram Stoker's *Dracula,* which he found heavy going at thirteen (he felt exactly the same when he re-read it as an adult, noting with interest this time the homosexual and Proustian overtones—"a touch of M. de Charlus"—in Stoker's bloodsucking count). Tony's first school report shows him coming bottom in the headmaster's subjects, French and maths, but first in the essay class, and sixty years later he could still dimly remember his essays being praised by two ancient masters dug up out of retirement. Still convinced at this stage that he was cut out for an army career, Tony insisted that the profession of novelist never crossed his mind, but a boy who had blued his savings at the age of nine on a purple typewriter ribbon cannot have been completely uninterested in writing.

He and Henry talked endlessly, and Tony was often invited to stay in the holidays at the Yorkes' family home, Forthampton Court, near Tewkesbury in Gloucestershire. This was not particularly grand as country houses go but it gave him his first glimpse of a family still living in a house owned by their ancestors for centuries. Where the Powells had a skeleton staff (cook, housemaid and Clara), the Yorkes kept a butler, two footmen, five housemaids and a lady's maid, a cook, kitchen maid, scullery maid and hall-boy as well as gardeners, grooms, stable-boys and farm workers. It was a more lavish complement than would have been usual even then for a minor branch of the landed gentry, but Henry's father, Vincent Yorke, also ran a successful business called Pontifex in Birmingham, manufacturing machines for filling beer bottles (another branch called Shanks, run by Vincent's younger brother, supplied the nation's growing need for lavatory bowls and cisterns). His wife Maude was a Wyndham of venerable pedigree, daughter of Lord Leconfield, brought up at Petworth House to think the less of anywhere smaller. Short and powerful, a chain smoker with a deep gravelly voice, Mrs. Yorke was witty, entertaining, well read and a keen horsewoman who taught her sons to ride, fish, shoot and follow the hounds.

"We were well brought up and saw our parents twice a day," wrote Henry, who adored his mother. The whole family breakfasted together, when the younger generation was not expected to speak, and met again for an hour in late afternoon. Tony was astonished at the easy intimacy between parents and children, especially Henry's habit of "ragging his father in a manner I should never have dreamed of using towards my own." Henry had grown up in the shadow of two older brothers, both of whom excelled at work and sport. The elder, Philip, had died at sixteen of leukaemia the year before Tony reached the New Beacon. Gerald, the middle son, debonair and athletic, winner of the school's best ever Eton scholarship, was particularly kind to the two little boys. The family even more than their home showed Tony a way of living he had never encountered before. He and Henry remained friends at Eton and Oxford, and as young novelists making their way in the 1930s, but their relationship was never again so intense as at the New Beacon, where each desperately needed the other to confirm his belief that there must be another world, and that he could one day belong to it.

Major Powell was recalled in 1917 from the maelstrom in northern

France to be posted as an instructor to the Army Staff College, currently in temporary quarters at Clare College in Cambridge. His wife
rented a set of undergraduate rooms at 4, Great St. Mary's Passage,
where Tony joined them in the school holidays, making friends with
the college porter, and taking comfort as ever in the bound volumes
of *Punch* that went back to his parents' youth in the 1890s. He knew
these drawings by linear masters like John Leech, Charles Keene,
John Tenniel and Gerald du Maurier so well by now that they acted
like a drug, "a powerful narcotic inducing reveries that shifted among
heavy swells, blue china aesthetes, lion-hunting hostesses, patriotic
Rifle Volunteers, and . . . the ubiquitous Victorian drunk." A year
later his father was back at the front, this time behind the lines on
attachment to the staff of the 95th Division, where he stayed until the
armistice was finally declared in November. The boys of the New
Beacon were given the day off to celebrate by their headmaster, who
changed his mind in the evening and made them do prep as usual.

Peacetime was not easy to negotiate for a professional soldier.
Philip Powell spent much of 1919 attending the peace conference in
Paris but, like a good many fathers of the friends Tony made later,
he never satisfactorily readjusted to the civilian world of the 1920s.
"The end of the war was the end of our generation," wrote one of
them. "We did not realise it at the time, but it was the end all the
same . . . the spirit of change was pervading every side of life, and
the traditions for which our age had stood began slowly, one after
another, to wilt and wither." In his mid-thirties when the war ended,
Major Powell returned to staff college at Camberley (standard procedure for a soldier due for promotion) in an intake that included three
future field marshals: Major B. L. Montgomery, Major John Dill and
Captain Alan Brooke. The group photo taken at the end of term was,
as Tony noted long afterwards, "an almost solid phalanx of World
War II generals." The exception was Philip Powell, whose path led
downhill from now on. His career had been very nearly derailed early
on by marriage and the birth of a baby at an age when most subalterns
were still finding their footing as adults, and in middle age even his
impressive war record could not outweigh his irrational compulsions
and lack of emotional control. "You can tell me nothing about rotten
jobs in the army," he wrote bitterly to his son at the beginning of the
Second World War.

Major P. L. W. Powell

Tony finally left prep school at Easter 1919, having secured a place at Eton like Henry (who had moved there a couple of terms earlier). Tony owed the Yorkes his first experience in close-up of a functioning family on relaxed and affectionate terms with one another, and also perhaps a first inkling that his own upbringing had been abnormal. The Powells had no house, now or in the past, and the only relations he could muster were his disreputable Aunt Vi, whose name could no longer be mentioned in polite society, his Melton grandmother who had rejected him at sight, and his father's sister Katherine, known to her nephew as Aunt Kitten, whom he hardly knew. Katherine Bonsey's life was, as a sympathetic onlooker said, a slow-moving disaster from the start. Her husband had walked out on her, leaving her with three small sons, no money and no future provision. Throughout their childhood she and her brother had stuck together for mutual protection, although Phil always came last in the pecking order imposed by a mother who disliked both her children, but marginally favoured the daughter. The only actual affection Jessie Powell showed was for Lilette McCraith, the child of the family's long-term lodger, who was also her husband's partner in the surgery, Jeremiah or "Baba" McCraith. Lilette was said to be the child of a girl he had married in Greece. Born in Smyrna, Baba McCraith lived with the

Powells at the Elms in Melton for twenty or thirty years, more or less openly acknowledged at any rate latterly as Jessie's lover, which suggests that the Greek girl was quite possibly no more than a convenient fiction.

Phil was genuinely fond of his sister, and did what he could to support her all his life, but there always remained a tinge of bitterness in the Powells' relations with the Bonseys. Tony grew up hearing them spoken of as poor relations, potentially tiresome dependants who recalled sombre memories of an earlier era. His grandmother, always blamed by his father for passing on to him her uncertain temper— fits of fury followed by depression—had never been much interested in anyone but herself. According to her daughter Katherine, Phil became more and more like his mother as he grew older. Obdurate and unpredictable, Jessie finally sent for her Powell grandson at the end of the war. Her husband had died shortly before it started, and no doubt the widow felt the time had come to see what her son could produce in the way of a descendant.

Whatever passed at that interview did not make relations with Phil any easier, and subsequent visits to Melton remained rare and reluctant. Tony, who had grown up hearing his grandmother mentioned, if at all, as a distant menace, could see nothing monstrous about her in the flesh, indeed rather liked her telling his fortune. But he had no illusions about her destructive potential, perhaps even catching a glimpse of it in action at that first meeting. In later life he often detected what he called a personal note in other writers' work, a spurt of feeling so strong that its origins remain unmistakeable, no matter how potent the creative imagination at work. Shakespeare elicited this response with, for instance, King Lear on sex, or the sadistic streak in *The Tempest*'s Prospero and the Duke in *Measure for Measure*. From the bickering Maltravers in *Agents and Patients* to the bleakly acrimonious Maclinticks and the maleficent Widmerpools of *Dance*, Powell was always good on married couples, especially where the relationship has frayed at the edges. Of them all, Audrey Maclintick stands out as prototype of the aggrieved wife exacerbating marital resentment by taking up with the handsome lodger, so much so that perhaps a personal memory underlies the whiff of neat venom released on the narrator's first visit to the Maclintick household: "When she opened the door to us, her formidable discontent with life swept across the threshold in scorching, blasting waves."

Some residual memory of the day Tony as a schoolboy of twelve or thirteen years old was finally summoned to confront his grandmother at the Elms in Melton comes over even more strongly on the narrator's second encounter, five years and three volumes after the first, with Mrs. Maclintick: "Small, wiry, aggressive, she looked as ready as ever for a row, her bright black eyes and unsmiling countenance confronting a world from which perpetual hostility was not merely potential, but presumptive."

2

1919–26

Tony was thirteen and a half years old when he became a boarder at Eton College in the summer of 1919. He was one of 1,100 boys. Almost the same number had been killed on leaving Eton in the war that had ended six months earlier. Their memory hung over the school's living pupils even before their names could be inscribed in long horizontal columns on a war memorial that ran right round the schoolyard. Nearly thirty years later, Tony came back to show Eton to his closest friend, the political journalist Malcolm Muggeridge. Another great war had just given way to a precarious peace, interpreted by Malcolm as a prelude to the imminent collapse of Western capitalism followed by Communist takeover and the final elimination of privileged enclaves like Eton. He felt confident of doom as they inspected the school buildings, yard and playing fields, where the boys playing cricket in multicoloured caps reminded Tony how passionately he had once longed to wear a cap like theirs. Malcolm said it was the power and authority it represented, in a school where sporting prowess ranked above all else, that made a coloured cap infinitely desirable.

Tony never had a hope of owning one. The cap he wore was a Scug's Cap, reserved for boys who had achieved nothing on the sports field. From the point of view of serious athletic prestige, his career ended as it had begun among the lowest of the low. If anything, it fell lower after his first year or two when, being small and slight for his age, he could usefully cox boats on the river for the bigger boys in his house. In games of Eton football on the rough ground behind the house he even played Post in a Ram, a dangerous and peculiarly painful position in a human piledriver, or ram, of boys lined up one behind the other, with the heaviest at the front and the lightest at the back, to force a goal (or Rouge) by slamming the ball into their opponents so hard it ricocheted off between the goalposts.

Founded within sight of Windsor Castle by King Henry VI in the fifteenth century, Eton had the confidence, conviction and careless indifference to outside opinion characteristic of great age. It stuck by its own rules in everything from football and fives (the Field Game and the Wall Game, both unplayable by other schools) to its uniform of top hat, white bow-tie, black waistcoat and tailcoat (small scugs like Tony wore short cropped Eton jackets until they were tall enough for tails). Other boys imposed rigorous conformity in these early years. Henry Yorke, almost a year ahead of Tony at Eton, was cruelly teased for wearing the wrong kind of overcoat, the

Tony in his first term at Eton

blunder that first made Kenneth Widmerpool notorious as a schoolboy at the start of Powell's *Dance to the Music of Time*. Henry's coat was slightly longer than the standard knee-length, which was the furthest he ever went towards a gesture of defiance. What disturbed him was not the complex code of petty laws governing etiquette and dress but the absence of more fundamental regulation. "There was far more liberty here than at the school I had left . . . probably more liberty at this public school than at any other," he wrote afterwards: "I hated the school."

By the beginning of the summer when Tony joined the year called Middle Fourth (the Fourth Form at Eton was one up from the Third, which was in fact the first year), his contemporaries had already picked friends and formed alliances. He "messed alone," in Eton jargon, meaning that he ate by himself at teatime for his first two halves, or terms. The custom of three or more boys taking it in turns to provide a hearty tea—fried eggs, sausages or chops, lobster salad and fruit cake or other delicacies supplied from home—was a way of encouraging boys to socialize within their respective houses but, although abstention was highly irregular, no attempt was apparently made to slot in the newcomer. "He does not make friends very easily," wrote Tony's housemaster, Arthur Goodhart, at the end of that first year, "and I am at a loss to know the reason." Tony's aloofness, the reserve and indefinable nonconformity that set him apart from other boys, became a regular refrain in subsequent school reports. Over the next three years Goodhart remained bemused, lamenting his pupil's inability to keep step with the rest and diagnosing diffidence ("possibly what is due to shyness may be mistaken for superiority"), or alternatively originality ("his mind and tastes are out of the ordinary"). He rapidly relinquished a faint initial hope that Tony might grow into the sort of boy who could be trusted to take responsibility, set a good example to his juniors, and end up with a job like Viceroy of India, which was the ultimate goal of an Eton education according to Tony. His own goals, which crystallized at school, were very different, and well suited to Goodhart's lax regime.

Vice-regal implications might not have come amiss to Tony's father, who had picked Eton as the best, likely to upgrade the status of all concerned as well as wiping out his own long-standing grievance at not having had a public school education himself. No more than average marks were required for Eton entry in the Common Entrance examination, and even the fees of just under £300 a year ("There was always a fuss if my own fees for a single half . . . reached a hundred pounds," wrote Tony) were not exorbitant, at any rate for an only child. The boarders were divided between twenty-five independent houses, each lodging roughly forty boys known as Oppidans, or townees (as distinct from the seventy King's Scholars, or scholarship boys, who lived in College and were generally treated with ambivalence by the rest of the school). An unpretentious house with a poor reputation and few standards to keep up, Goodhart's made no great demands intellectually or socially on its pupils or their families.

It was a large plain red-brick building standing in a field as far away as it was possible to get within the boundaries of the school from the mediaeval towers, cobbled courts and archways of the original college. Its moral tone was slack and its athletic achievements nil (Goodhart's only cup in Tony's day was won by a quartet of singers). The boys' living conditions were austere, if relatively comfortable compared to many public schools. They had separate rooms with beds that let down from the walls, heated two days a week only by coal fires in the grate ("I am having rather beastly troubles with chilblains," Tony wrote home glumly in the winter of 1920). Six bathrooms had just been installed but tin hip baths still hung outside the boys' doors. Their rooms looked out on water meadows stretching to the River Thames, which flooded the football field in winter when evening mist rose from the water to shroud the windows of the new boys on the ground floor. Beyond lay more fields, a gas works and a sewage farm. Tony flourished in this setting. "A. M. Goodhart's was not merely a 'bad' house, but universally agreed to be the 'worst' house in the school," he wrote with satisfaction.

The boys divided into two camps over Arthur Goodhart, a mildly unorthodox character with a high sloping forehead, profuse walrus moustache and an air of "being always prepared for the worst, and usually experiencing it." Many dismissed him as a dim and ineffectual crank. Discipline was never his strong point. Boys ragged Goodhart extravagantly, pelting him with missiles from behind his back, or bowling their hip baths at his closed door after lights out. One of them gave Goodhart's name to a man from Windsor who had reported his umbrella missing: when the owner arrived at the school to reclaim his property, Goodhart was first mystified, then furious, and after acrimonious investigation sent the culprit to say sorry. The boy called on the man as instructed, but told him he brought a message from his housemaster to say there must have been a mistake, as the lost umbrella had now turned up in his possession. This legendary wind-up—origin of the Braddock alias Thorne affair in the first chapter of the first volume of *A Dance to the Music of Time*—dated back to a time of rampant mayhem brought to a close by the expulsion of a ringleader the year before Tony arrived. The house had sobered up since then but Goodhart still seemed fair game to the rowdier boys, and his flounderings exasperated even the more civilized senior members, among them the notably easy-going David Cecil (who took on Tony later as a fag, or junior PA). Cecil's memories of Goodhart remained harsh and unforgiving: "a deplorable figure—perfectly futile."

Others, like Tony, remembered their housemaster fondly precisely because his standards were so far from conventional. Himself a ferocious sportsman, "an acknowledged star of all time" at the Wall Game, Goodhart rated sport well below the arts. Boys were under no pressure to put in more than the compulsory stint on a playing field every afternoon plus an hour of drill or marching in the morning with the OTC (even in peacetime Eton raised and staffed an entire battalion of the Officer Training Corps, with a regular army adjutant and ten days under canvas for the entire school at the end of each summer term). Army routines came naturally to Tony, who rose to the rank of sergeant in spite of a hostile company commander, presumably the master responsible for his final rejection of an army career at the age of fourteen. He played football when he had to on the field behind Goodhart's, even serving dutifully as captain of the junior house team. The minimum requirement was four games per week unless, like Tony, you dropped one football in favour of two runs—tedious but unsupervised and pain-free—up and down the low-lying river valley in a climate he remembered as uniformly extreme: "sleet: wind: sultry heat." In winter he followed the school beagle pack. His New Beacon headmaster had implanted in him a lifelong loathing of cricket, so in summer he rowed instead in a junior house four, sometimes sculling with a friend on sunny afternoons four miles upstream to the wooded island of Queen's Eyot, where a school clubhouse supplied food and drink.

Goodhart taught Greek, and subscribed to the prevailing mindset that had put his subject at the centre of an English education by reconfiguring the classics in High Victorian terms, a conversion neatly summarized by Tony: "Homer metamorphosed into a pre-Raphaelite poet, Plato seen as a great headmaster, Greek homosexuality merged into heroic comradeship." Romantic uplift coupled with unremitting surveillance, punitive sanctions and a gruelling workload provided the traditional solution to the problem (intrinsically insoluble in Tony's view) of controlling large numbers of adolescent boys with no sexual outlet except each other. The school timetable for lower boys began before breakfast with a first Division, or lesson, at half past seven in the morning and ended at a quarter to six. Evening prep lasted until bedtime at half past nine. But the four post-war years of Tony's schooling saw inevitable if slow and unacknowledged transition. Beatings were more tightly controlled, tolerance increased and the competitive principle slackened its harsh grip. Universal contempt was in part at least a recognition that in this direction Goodhart's led the way.

Its lack of emphasis on games was balanced by an interest in music and the performing arts, both reprehensible to the conservative, sporting and militarist diehards who were almost imperceptibly losing ground throughout the school. Goodhart had studied music at Cambridge, and never entirely relinquished his career as a composer, turning out not only school songs (including an arrangement of the "Eton Boating Song" for pianola) but music for orchestra, piano and organ, choral numbers and settings of contemporary poems as well as variations on wartime pop songs like "It's a Long, Long Way to Tipperary." As a young man, his name once headed the list of leading composers, including Elgar, Stanford, Bridge and Parry, invited to write music for Queen Victoria's eightieth birthday. In his midfifties he played and sang for the boys at communal sing-songs in his drawing room on Saturday nights, contributing take-offs of bygone celebrities like Mr. Gladstone, and encouraging oddballs—including Cecil—to experiment with theatrical production.

Goodhart was one of the first few housemasters to lift a puritanical ban on drama that had been in force at Eton for the past fifty years. In Tony's first half the house put on a performance of Marlowe's *Dr. Faustus* with Cecil as a lively, quick-fire Mephistopheles and Helen of Troy played, as the playwright had intended, by a junior boy. It was followed by an even more subversive hit the year after when Lord Beauchamp's son Hugh Lygon made a ravishingly pert and pretty Cecily in *The Importance of Being Earnest*, itself a brave choice at a time when Oscar Wilde still symbolized depravity to traditionalists who might be expected to send sons to Eton. Next came a Shavian shocker, *Arms and the Man*, the only one of Bernard Shaw's plays Tony said he ever watched without boredom. Goodhart presided in these years over a general loosening-up and broadening of horizons suggested by his kindly, if not resoundingly upbeat report at the end of 1922: "Tony's artistic tastes give me as much pleasure as his gentleness and good character."

Those tastes had been drastically expanded and updated by an eye-opening revival of *The Beggar's Opera* that Tony saw not long after its opening at the end of his first year at Eton. Staged by a new and unknown company in the slums of Hammersmith, far beyond normal boundaries for metropolitan theatregoers, it was an instant hit with London audiences just as it had been on its first night two hundred years before. Tony was entranced by its modern minimalist set, its subtly exaggerated costumes, and the gaiety as much as the casual ruthlessness of its cast of criminals, pickpockets, pimps and prostitutes. The murderous anti-hero, Captain Macheath, in a lavishly curled white wig, flamboyant hat, gold-braided and full-skirted scarlet coat with cascades of ruffled lace at throat and wrist, was the epitome of the childish highwaymen Tony himself used to sketch in the margins of letters home. Everything about Nigel Playfair's production—the originality of the young unknown designer, Claud Lovat Fraser (whose sets almost immediately revolutionized the look of the London stage), the exuberant energy of the equally young cast, the wit and savagery of John Gay's text—was a revelation.

So was its straightforward approach to sex. Polly Peachum, the scheming whore Macheath eventually marries, was played by Sylvia Nelis, who had the quintessentially English style of demure blond looks—perfect oval face, pale skin, delicate features and small curving mouth—that appealed to Tony ever afterwards. More than half a century later he described being almost literally electrified by the sexy bits, especially the love duet, "Were I Laid on Greenland's Coast," where Macheath and Polly antiphonally look forward to going to bed together. "It had an extremely emotional, not to say erotic impact," Tony said of this duet more than half a century later on *Desert Island Discs*. The couple explore the intensity of their sensations, burning hot or icy cold, in alternate lines so that the forceful throaty thrust of the tenor ("And I would love you all the day") steadily intensifies the soprano's melting response ("Every night would kiss and play"). It is a powerfully sensual evocation of the joy of sex in words that remain on the surface as innocent as the kind of romantic agitation which was the furthest all but the most reckless schoolboys of Tony's day and age could hope to go towards actual intercourse.

In theory he knew more than most, having read at an early age Havelock Ellis's *The Psychology of Sex* along with other discreet manuals and semi-pornographic picture-books kept on his father's bookshelves in a case Major Powell sometimes forgot to lock. Doodles from Tony's middle years at Eton show highwaymen giving way to scantily clad Edwardian pin-ups with tiny waists and plunging necklines. Careful study of his father's handbooks provided useful back-up at this point for an increasingly acute intuitive grasp of human behaviour. Another boy produced a photo of his mother, whom Tony came across again and recognised many years later as a diplomat's wife notorious among her circle for indiscriminate bed-hopping. "I remember thinking that's what must be happening when I was fourteen," he wrote, describing this encounter years later to his wife: "One wasted years unlearning one's instincts of this sort."

Goodhart's pupils speculated endlessly about the sex life of their housemaster, said to have remained unmarried for love of a lady pianist who jilted him to marry another Eton beak. Tony came to think in retrospect that Goodhart's bisexuality survived only in a fetishistic fixation on women's shoes. Otherwise a residue of stifled desire presumably lay behind his habit of roaming the bedroom corridors at night, hoping to detect signs of sexual activity. He delivered long rambling denunciations to the assembled house, working himself into barely controlled frenzy in pursuit of his campaign to expose and stamp out what he called "the most loathsome form of dual vice." His pupils stared blankly back like the two boys subjected to similarly interminable cross-examination by their housemaster in the first volume of the *Dance* ("At the time . . . he merely seemed to Stringham and myself a dangerous lunatic, to be humoured and outwitted").

Homosexuality was freely discussed and practised in a single-sex school where small boys acted as fags for their seniors. Fagging meant fetching, carrying and tending the fagmaster's fire with unofficial sexual services intermittently thrown in, sometimes voluntarily, sometimes not. Tony himself fagged in his second half as the junior member of a team of three or four for the formidable R. W. E. Cecil, an experienced and considerate fagmaster who had reached the pinnacle of command within the house as Goodhart's captain of games. Cecil passed him on in turn to the house captain, Arthur Peel, who supplied his fags with a contraband copy of *The Loom of Youth*, a semi-autobiographical first novel by a young author called Alec Waugh considered so sensationally frank that the Old Boys of his own public school had expelled him from their ranks a few years earlier. Waugh's account of schoolboy homosexuality, hysterically denounced in the popular press for perversion and debauch, seemed pretty much routine to Tony. He himself had a fair share of sentimental attachments but no first-hand experience of the clumsy experimental scufflings and gropings inflicted on more flirtatious or more vulnerable boys. His own approach was notably realistic, unlike the lurid projections of the masters, or for that matter his more naïve friend Henry Yorke ("Sex was a dread mystery. No story could be more dreadful, more full of agitated awe than sex"). The almost inconceivable innocence and ignorance thought to be desirable for adolescents of both sexes between the wars meant that Tony's practical experience was limited, but *The Beggar's Opera* had emphatically confirmed his preference for girls.

In his second year he fagged for David Cecil (unrelated to the games captain), chiefly memorable in Tony's recollection for letting him off a beating when the fire went out because, according to Cecil, the last boy had wept when ticked off too sharply for the same offence. This was the charming blond Hugh Lygon, a natural as Wilde's Cecily, who was a year older than Tony and would mess in his last two halves with him and a boy called Denys Buckley. A model pupil, industrious, intelligent and law-abiding, himself in due course captain of the house, Buckley gave no trouble and got none, unlike Tony's other friends. Most of them were dissidents, misfits, jokers with a taste for the kind of low-key surrealist humour personified by the three boys who found a glass of milk and a plate of cake on their tutor's desk. "One drank the milk, one ate the cake and the third broke the plate," wrote Tony, who told this story: "for some reason it has always amused me. There is something stimulating about it." The same spirit of absurdity involved an entire house turning out on parade as officer cadets in horn-rimmed spectacles, and numbering off to the bewilderment of the Guards officer detailed to take the salute:

"1-2-3-4-5-6-7-8-9-10-Knave-Queen-King-Ace." Tony never joined in this sort of thing himself but he liked the kind of boy that did.

From the beginning of his time at Eton, he found his own natural habitat in the Drawing Schools on Keate's Lane. Lower boys were normally excluded but Goodhart (whose house was practically next door) intervened in Tony's favour from his second half. This was the school's art department, presided over by another remarkable man, Sidney Evans, as independent as Goodhart and viewed, like him, with some suspicion by the rest of the staff. Evans was the last in a dynasty of art-masters that went back three generations (an eighteenth-century Sidney Evans had taught the daughters of George III at Windsor). In the course of a hundred years the Evanses had established their studio as a more or less autonomous enclave. "It was a long low room with skylights and on shelves along the wall earth-red pots, unglazed jars which generations had had to draw," wrote Henry Yorke, who belonged to a different house but resumed his friendship with Tony in the drawing school. "It was always dusk in there but it had a charm because there was no other dirty room in the whole school. Wherever a shelf ended watercolours were hung up of some of the casts and pots standing next to them and however badly these were drawn the repetition on paper and in colour of so much that was before the eye made the place amicably unreal like a living joke." Tony said it re-created as if by magic "among the byways of an English public school" the atmosphere of the kind of artist's studio on the Parisian Left Bank where painters like Evans learned their trade in the 1890s. Brushes, paints, canvases and easels jostled one another in a disorderly scrum with jugs, bowls, pans, plaster busts, fruit stands and candlesticks, the component parts of a myriad standardized still lifes.

For both boys the studio became a refuge from the shocks and strains of institutional life. "Here . . . we had what came as close to those talks which are supposed to be exchanged by undergraduates in which the course of life is plotted," wrote Henry. Tony found it a relief to have somewhere he could potter off to for Extra Drawing after tea with no questions asked. Evans did not so much attract pupils as provide them with an environment where they could meet boys from other houses—not otherwise easy outside the context of lessons or the sports field—without outside interference, and with nothing expected from them. The effect was stimulant and tonic. It figures in Henry's first novel, *Blindness*, begun while he was still at Eton.

In 1922 the boys organized themselves into the Eton Society of Arts with eleven elected members led by Bryan Howard and Harold Acton, both highly sophisticated, cosmopolitan, half-American aesthetes who drawled like 1890s dandies. So did their prime publicist, Robert Byron, said to be the handsomest boy in the school and certainly one of the most truculent, much talked about for relatively innocent stunts like pulling a toy car on a string the whole length of Eton High Street. All three of them specialized in wrong-footing the authorities. Acton said the headmaster once came into his room, picked a book at random and opened it on Picasso's fiercely erotic etching of a naked Salome high-kicking with an athlete's discipline and attack, watched impassively by Herod. Tony, who shared Acton's taste for Picasso's small expressive early etchings, retold this story more than half a century later: "'What did the headmaster say?' asked Mr. Evans. 'He smiled rather sourly,' said Harold, at his most impish." The young John Rothenstein, a future head of the Tate Gallery, came down to talk to the society, and its exhibition of members' painting was judged by Roger Fry, the man who first introduced the Post-Impressionists to London. Fry singled out A. Powell's rendering of a scene from *Macbeth*, perhaps the witches chanting spells which Tony always said was the bit Shakespeare liked writing best.

The society's magazine, the *Eton Candle*, sandwiched between shocking-pink boards and intended "to sound the trumpet of Modernism echoing through Eton's wat'ry glade," was not so much a manifesto as a shop-window for its editors, Acton and Howard. Using Acton's contacts and Howard's single-minded emphasis on self-advertisement, they attracted maximum attention by drumming up contributions from distinguished Old Etonians like Aldous Huxley, Osbert and Sacheverell Sitwell, even a posthumous, previously unpublished and predictably trite snippet by Algernon Swinburne. Otherwise the contents, mostly written by themselves, never rose much above Howard's uneasy tribute to the dead of 1914–18, its uneven lines and clumsy, cloth-eared cadences broken up by fashionable caesuras: "You were a great Young Generation . . . / And then you went out and got murdered—magnificently –/ Went out and got

"Son of the Caesars," one of the Napoleonic soldiers Tony liked to draw: he published this one in the *Cherwell* during his time at Oxford, and made decorative additions three decades later in the scrapbook he called *Dream Memories*.

murdered . . . because a parcel of damned old men / Wanted some fun, or some power, or something. Something so despicable in comparison to your young lives . . . / Anyhow, you were glorious . . ."

The *Candle*'s only attempts at art were a conventional landscape in watercolour by Acton's brother William, and an ink drawing by Tony of a rakish Napoleonic guardsman with curled mustachios, fancy frogging, sash, spurs, plumed hat and drawn sword, a slickly professional composition derived at considerable distance, as he said himself, from both Beardsley and Lovat Fraser. Imitative, immature, half-baked, the *Candle* still exudes confidence and dash. Its first and only issue was reviewed in the national press, and sold so well it had to be reprinted. Tony's father showed his copy to his former army staff captain, currently a London publisher, who immediately commissioned Acton's first book of poems on the strength of it.

But for Tony the society's appeal was not primarily literary. Sidney Evans's studio, with its undemanding drawings and its miniature version of the Apollo Belvedere, was infinitely restful to a precocious visual sensibility shaped from childhood not only by the great *Punch* satirists, but by Major Powell's extremely unchildish taste for Beardsley's arcane sexual fantasies, which had been as familiar to Tony in the nursery "as Tenniel's *Alice* or Beatrix Potter's *Tom Kitten*." So was the evil Asiatic glitter of Léon Bakst's designs for the Ballets Russes (the first sumptuous album, published in a limited edition in Paris in 1913, had been another of Tony's illicit picture-books). The studio was steeped in monochrome: a remedial diet of dim grey interiors, wintry street scenes, men in overcoats on station platforms, all rendered in the modest, small-scale, downbeat style of London's very own Camden Town group. A Sickert man himself, Evans talked about Matisse and Picasso to his pupils without either marked enthusiasm or the insular complacency of the average British patriot who wanted them hanged or shot for subversion. Tony's own aesthetic horizons would never reach much beyond Evans's studio, which he remembered fondly ever afterwards. He had a good eye, refined and sharpened by long practice, and was well on the way to reviving his old plan of being a graphic artist when Evans retired prematurely at the age of fifty-six in 1922. "It was nothing less than a disaster for me," Tony wrote, "when Sidney Evans retired before I left Eton."

He was beginning dimly to envisage a future bound up at some level with art or books. He won a minor prize for English literature at fifteen, and tied for the same prize a year later, but the subject was too humble a component of a classical education to count in its own right at Eton. So far as literature went, Tony educated himself in solitary school holidays spent reading, drawing and roaming the streets. His mother still moved constantly from place to place, knowing no one and rarely staying long enough to make contact with the neighbours, even supposing she had wanted to. In these years Tony could never be quite sure where he would join her at the start of his holidays. "I hope Daddy will get back soon," he wrote in November 1920: "It will be exciting to know where we are going."

His father was in fact stationed in Dublin with the 2nd Battalion of the Welsh Regiment as part of an occupying British army in Ireland. November marked the start of a major escalation in sectarian violence as the country moved towards partition, and civil war between republicans and nationalists. Savage attacks met with bloody reprisals from the British. Small towns were ransacked and city centres burnt out. Martial law was imposed in southern Ireland. The republicans responded with guerrilla warfare modelled on the Boers' campaign of terror in South Africa: bombing, kidnapping, coercing civilian informers, raiding British barracks and ambushing British patrols, all familiar tactics to Major Powell, whose military career had started in Pretoria.

With no immediate prospect of joining her husband, Maud Powell rented a small villa in London's St. John's Wood, and took her furniture out of store for the first time since leaving Albert Mansions, a sure sign that she expected an extended stay. This interlude of two or three years at number 1, Melina Place was the first time Tony had ever lived with his family in a whole house behind their own front door. Their space was marked off by a small paved courtyard at the front, and a sheltered garden at the back in a neighbourhood expressly designed for privacy. It had originally been laid out north of Regent's Park as an area where high-class tarts could receive the visits of their rich protectors in discreet seclusion within easy reach of central London. Tony liked the louche tone, left over from countless shady assignations in Victorian brothels, that added a surprising twist to his mental picture of crusading knights from the Order of Saint John who had once owned the wood.

But his increasing understanding of how other boys and their families lived contrasted sharply with the reclusive isolation he shared with his mother. "She and I . . . seem to have been much alone at Melina Place," he wrote, looking back. "We got on well together but I was often bored while growing up." Tony's mother read little, and did not share her husband's taste for art nouveau illustrated books. When she wanted a present for him, it was Tony who picked out a rare or curious item from the catalogues—"arriving at the house in shoals"—that relieved the tedium of Melina Place. Antiquarian book catalogues remained favourite reading ever afterwards ("more calming than wine lists," Tony said cryptically). Another thrill was the arrival of a real live author, moving into a house a few doors down from the Powells soon after they moved in themselves. Arthur Machen, who wrote for the *Evening News* and had once been an actor, played his part with a panache not lost on his teenage devotee: "the occasional sweep of an Inverness cape, surmounted by a broad black-brimmed hat, with the sound of a throaty cough, made him seem all a bohemian author should be."

The 1920s saw something of a Machen boom, with an eclectic mix of literary and art-world celebrities—Wyndham Lewis, Jerome K. Jerome, Augustus John—attending parties at his house, and a string of successful novels issuing from it. *The Secret Glory*, *The Home of Souls* and *The Hill of Dreams* were precursors of magic realism (Jorge Luis Borges was an admirer, and so was T. S. Eliot) with mystic and cabbalistic overtones, deeply rooted in the wild Welsh landscape from which the author came. Machen dramatized his own story in *The Secret Glory*, revisiting his younger self as a lonely fifteen-year-old schoolboy, reasonably adept in class but useless at games, entirely lacking in team spirit ("not the type which the Public School exists to foster") and further handicapped by antiquarian interests, a romantic passion for Welsh history and an ironic sense of humour. By some mysterious process this aloof unpromising outsider mutates into a prodigy at work and games whose brilliance dazzles the Oxford dons when he sits the Balliol scholarship examinations that Tony himself would take the year after the book came out. Machen's hero promptly throws away a triumphant Oxford future in favour of the writer's path of penury, solitude and rejection ("Don't you know that the populace always hates the artist?"). *The Secret Glory* was heady stuff for any boy facing the same choice at the same age in 1922, the year it came out.

But it was a decidedly less glamorous neighbour who first opened the door to the world Tony longed to enter, "the kingdom of art and letters that lay beyond the hills." Christopher Sclater Millard was an antiquarian book dealer, a literary type at the opposite extreme to the flamboyant Machen. Tall and cadaverously thin, he wore a uniform of old grey flannel trousers, faded cotton shirt and patched tweed jacket with an air of melancholy distinction. He had a deep musical voice, an impressive presence and a lively energy that greatly impressed Tony, who said that in his early teens anyone over thirty seemed on the brink of decrepitude to him. Millard, who was almost fifty, treated him as a fellow collector, encouraging him to specialize in Lovat Fraser, building up his confidence ("I assure you I know very little about Fraser's work save from what you tell me"), and deferring to his knowledge ("I . . . passed it over as 'doubtful' but I would trust your judgement better than mine"). It was a characteristically generous, scholarly and entertaining education from one of the most distinguished bibliophiles of his generation. "He was the first grown-up person to treat me in conversation on absolutely equal terms," Tony wrote long afterwards.

He could never quite remember how they met, except that it was through his mother, probably ordering a book, and that her description made Tony set out himself to inspect Millard's headquarters a few streets away at the back of number 8, Abercorn Place. It turned out to be not much more than a garden shed subdivided into two tiny rooms. One was a bedroom and the other, where Millard did his business and entertained his friends, brimmed and bulged with books stacked on and underneath the furniture, in boxes and on shelves from floor to ceiling. It was a treasure trove to Tony, and so were the stories told him by his host. As a young man Millard had been appalled by the protracted trials and brutal punishment of Oscar Wilde for homosexuality. For the next seventeen years he laboured to salvage Wilde's reputation by producing what is still the definitive bibliography of his work. He showed Tony two drawings said to have hung in Wilde's drawing room (classical studies by Simeon Solomon, who featured long afterwards in *A Dance to the Music of Time* as the master revered by Edgar Deacon), and a manuscript in purple ink of the *Ballad of Reading Gaol* with Wilde's handwritten tag across the top: "For those who live more lives than one, more deaths than one must die." It was still unusual in the 1920s to talk unselfconsciously and seriously about Wilde as a man and a writer, rather than a shameful memory so vivid, even quarter of a century after he had left prison, that the trustees of the National Portrait Gallery had just turned down a full-length oil portrait of him as a successful playwright in his prime. "I should have thought they might have been able to find space for it in the lavatory," said Millard, showing Tony the canvas.

This was literary gossip of a high order, and Tony reciprocated with news of the Eton Arts Society. Millard bought a copy of the *Candle* to put in his catalogue, and was immediately intrigued by Bryan Howard ("an exceptionally talented young man"), who reminded him of another precocious schoolboy from an earlier generation, Charles

Scott Moncrieff, still often to be found feeding crumbs to the birds in the garden round Millard's shed. Moncrieff's life work was his translation of Marcel Proust's *À la Recherche du temps perdu*, the sequence of twelve novels that would in due course shift the foundations of the English novel. His choice of title, *Remembrance of Things Past*, came under attack with news of the first volume, *Swann's Way*, due out in the autumn of 1922. Tony, listening to "Millard's talk about books, authors, people he had known," was entranced.

So was Millard. "You are a great temptation, you know," he said suddenly one day over tea. At the time his declaration made so little impression that Tony simply assumed it was a joke and thought no more about it. But for all his charm and openness, Millard had a different side, "something wan and starved, as if the shadow of calamity had dimmed him," said another young admirer. When he met Tony he was in fact barely two years out of gaol himself, after serving twelve months in Wormwood Scrubs for illicit sex with boys. He had served an earlier prison sentence before the war, and must have known that this new friendship could flourish only on borrowed time. He and Tony continued amicably exchanging letters, visits and useful bibliographic tips until Major Powell's former staff captain, the publisher Thomas Balston, made an unexpected connection in the spring of 1922, presumably while browsing through Millard's catalogue, and promptly reported his suspicions to his old company commander. A painful interview followed between Tony and his father. Visits abruptly ceased, letters were intercepted, and all contact with Millard was broken off. The whole episode upset Tony deeply. He had liked and looked up to Millard and, although he understood the reasoning behind his father's verdict, he could not accept it. "I was brought face to face with the difference between schoolboy sentiment . . . and the whole force of society lined up to threaten a reputation. It was hard to experience no misgiving." The last lesson Millard taught him was a sobering one about adult use of power, and the ambiguity of weakness.

The Powells left London almost at once on army orders. Millard, who might surely have expected worse, wrote philosophically to Tony to say he had spotted a removal van outside 1, Melina Place, and received in return a letter from Mrs. Powell, explaining gently that her husband had been posted out of London. "I am glad that my mother, who understood things by instinct rather than by any other means, behaved as she did," Tony wrote forty years later. What mystified him in retrospect was the behaviour of his parents. Having no companions of his own age, Tony had started talking at home about Millard and his books with an enthusiasm that might have made many parents think twice about their son spending so much time at such close quarters with an evidently lonely and markedly attentive older man. Tony's upbringing had been in some ways exceptionally permissive. Neither parent apparently saw anything odd about their small son's fondness for the naked eunuch making frantic love to the heroine in Bakst's *Shéhérezade* ("to me a picture of incredible beauty"), and the same laxity allowed him to associate later with a convicted paedophile. Tony put their incomprehension down to limited experience of what went on outside their own domestic backwater.

Although Tony's friendship with him lasted eighteen months at most, Millard left an indelible impression. He was one of those characters too highly flavoured and too fully realized in themselves to transfer to fiction, but traces of him linger throughout the *Dance* in the person of Mr. Deacon. Both were eccentric antiquarians, food cranks with strongly held progressive views, no apparent means of subsistence and a surprisingly broad range of acquaintance: when Millard died in 1927, delegates from the Marylebone branch of the Labour Party sang "The Red Flag" at his graveside. But Deacon belongs to a world of robust and rackety comedy that could accommodate neither the authority and weight, nor the genuinely tragic side, of C. S. Millard.

After nearly two years in Dublin, Major Powell had been transferred to Southern Command Headquarters at Tidworth Camp on the eastern edge of Salisbury Plain. His family rented successive furnished houses in the close and on the green, both dominated by the bells and by the grace and bulk of Salisbury's great Gothic cathedral, but Tony's anger and distress at what had happened over Millard settled into an epic gloom that seeped out in his memory over the whole city. All he could remember afterwards was a pair of simpleminded brothers trundling a barrel organ around the streets, and his own aimless solitary rides along newly tarmacked roads on a horse supplied by the army for his father's use. Once it ran away with him. Both the bolting horse and the barrel-organ brothers would reappear in his third novel, *From a View to a Death*, which also reflects the kind of difficulties he was having at sixteen with girls. These had become an elusive species, difficult to track down, let alone get near: "even tennis parties seemed mostly to consist of majors, colonels and their wives." Tony's father's attempts to tease him out of it only intensified his adolescent boredom and resentment: "My father used to say: 'Of course you're not the sort of chap who likes to take a gun, and get a bit of rough shooting.' This was patently true; but, if it came to that, neither was he."

Tony got through the holidays thanks to his mother's subscription to Boots circulating library. He read hungrily through the fiction section, devouring in great gulps the standard authors of the day—John Galsworthy, Hugh Walpole, Somerset Maugham and W. J. Locke. All of them would soon come to seem to him terminally old-fashioned, but at the time his expertise was so extensive that he won a Galsworthy competition in the *Morning Post*, and got a pocket set of the collected works inscribed: "For A.D.P., with the wonder and admiration of John Galsworthy."

It was the famous first number of T. S. Eliot's *Criterion*, published in October 1922, that alerted him to an alternative approach. Eliot had taken over and translated a lengthy assessment of James Joyce's *Ulysses* from the *Nouvelle Revue française*, a shrewd move from a born literary politician aiming to point a whole generation in new post-war directions. *The Waste Land* first appeared in the same issue. Tony read it in the school library at Eton, and registered an impact he could not yet fully absorb. This was his final year at school, a time of prestige and privilege when boys could take liberties with their uniform, keep sherry in their rooms, and go drinking at a specially designated pub in town with a barman so professional he had no problem recognizing Tony on his return with Muggeridge quarter of a century later.

Goodhart remained dubious about Tony's social skills ("It's all very like reviewing, I suppose," said Tony, coming across his dismal school reports as an adult only too familiar by then with the routine drudgery of the weekly fiction round-up). But at this point even Goodhart conceded a marked increase in confidence. Against stiff opposition from his father, Tony secured a place to read history at Balliol College, Oxford. He also won an Oppidan prize in the July examinations taken by all Eton's senior pupils at the end of each school year (Tony came third, or ninth including King's Scholars, out of the whole school). Goodhart reported that he had finally found congenial company within the house: "he is a great friend of my captain Duggan, for which I am glad . . ." A year older than Tony, Hubert Duggan was already captain of Goodhart's house when he replaced Lygon in the mess with Buckley (who would in turn succeed him as head of house), and established an immediate rapport, especially with Tony. All three were members of the library, the Eton equivalent of senior prefects responsible for house discipline, and their first move under Duggan's leadership was to abolish the beatings traditionally administered by prefects. A rapid return of anarchy and chaos forced the reformers to backtrack, a rare defeat for Duggan, who had set about liberalizing the regime at Goodhart's with an innate authority that came in part at least from experience of being out of control himself.

A prime troublemaker for much of his school career, Duggan found in Tony a detachment that matched his own. He had a subtle wit with a strong streak of melancholy combined with the dash, elegance and fine-boned good looks of a young man in an Elizabethan miniature: "lively, obstinate, generous, not very happy, and quite relentless." Tony predicted he would end up, when he was slightly older and less tentative, looking exactly like the Emperor Alexander in Veronese's painting in the National Gallery. He was sceptical, self-contained and, like Tony, exceedingly well-read. Books brought them together from the start, and so did the protective habits of laid-back behaviour and cool ironic understatement each had developed early in response to pressure at home. Duggan's background was cosmopolitan, turbulent and well-heeled. His father, descended from an Irish-Argentinian landowning family, had died supposedly of drink when Hubert was eleven. The son became a disturbed and disruptive teenager in perpetual conflict with his autocratic mother, a beautiful American heiress who promptly secured the power to match her wealth through an ambitious second marriage to Lord Curzon, best known of all India's viceroys, subsequently foreign secretary in Lloyd George's government, and widely expected to succeed him as prime minister.

Hubert and his even wilder elder brother Alfred grew up between their stepfather's palatial London home at 1, Carlton House Terrace, his crusaders' castle at Bodiam in Sussex, and his family estate of

Kedleston in Derbyshire. Hubert's looks, his charm and his casual offbeat humour reappear in Charles Stringham, the narrator's closest friend in the early stages of the *Dance*; and in his public and professional life Curzon certainly inhabited those chilly regions of power and will associated with Stringham's stepfather, Commander Foxe: "Like a man effortlessly winning a walking race, he crossed the carpet with long, easy strides: at the same time separating from himself some of the eddies of cold air that surrounded him, and bequeathing them to the atmosphere of the room after he had left it."

In fact both Duggan brothers got on unexpectedly well with their stepfather, who treated them with a resigned and humorous tolerance that was, as Tony said, probably the only feasible response to Alfred's escalating lawlessness at school and university. By this time Curzon's career had taken a steep dive, starting in May 1923 when to his astonishment he was passed over as prime minister in favour of Stanley Baldwin. Eight months later Curzon lost his post as foreign secretary. After seven years of trying, his wife abandoned hope of giving him an heir (Curzon had three daughters by a first marriage), and embarked in her mid-forties on a series of affairs. His elder stepson was sent down from Oxford (as chancellor of the university, Curzon managed to get the sentence altered from permanent to temporary exclusion). Hubert, who had nearly died of appendicitis at the time of his stepfather's public humiliation, had to be removed from school, reaching Oxford only in the summer term of 1924. Tony found him one morning in his rooms at Christ Church, still in bed and talking to an unassuming middle-aged man in grey, apparently a tradesman "come to deliver some goods, measure the window for curtains, possibly press that a bill should be paid." The visitor turned out to be Lord Curzon, who died less than twelve months after this encounter.

The only other close friend singled out in Tony's recollection came from F. E. Robeson's house, a relatively dissolute establishment with a reputation for gambling and loose living, where he messed with Robert Byron. John Spencer, who unlike Duggan had barely read a book (except for lurid yellow novelettes, the 1920s equivalent of the gutter press), epitomized a decidedly more raffish style of Eton chic. A sleek, urbane, all-or-nothing character, his jokes were as throwaway as his paperbacks. He dressed immaculately, and amused himself by ordering a suit of plus fours for Byron cut from rare Scottish tweed ("the stuff is like autumn leaves with the sky showing through") that fitted its short, plump, tubby owner like a glove. Apart from his "indefinable air of being up to no good," Spencer made few concessions to the fact that he was still at school. His father was a successful City stockbroker, and he himself was already adept in all the ways that Tony wasn't, most of them strictly prohibited by the authorities. His time was spent smoking, drinking, dancing, flirting openly with girls and disappearing as often as he dared on illicit undercover trips to London. Notorious in his house as the accredited lover of an Eton shop assistant, he was probably the boy spotted by an awestruck Henry Yorke "letting himself out of a suburban villa where I was told he was supposed to have a mistress." It was Spencer who initiated Tony into the mysteries of London nightclubs, escorting him on a tour that ended with Mrs. Meyrick's Forty-three, in practice as much a brothel as a club in Gerrard Street to the east of Piccadilly, an area renowned between the two great wars for the unrivalled density of its prostitute population. At the end of his final year Spencer was expelled for getting blind drunk at the OTC summer camp on Salisbury Plain.

Tony disgraced himself too, on what was presumably the same occasion, turning out for 6 a.m. inspection on his last day at school with a devastating hangover after over-enthusiastic celebrations the night before, collapsing on parade, and having to follow in an open cab at the tail of the column of a thousand boys marching up Windsor Hill to the train station: "The pinnacles, the turrets, the incomparable elm-trees were left behind. My schooldays were over. I paid off the cab and, more dead than alive, trailed along the platform. I found the compartment somehow, and my disappointed section, who had hoped that I had been left behind permanently . . ."

Tony claimed later that this was the last time he ever raised his voice, a rare indication of the horror he felt at his father's habitual hysterics, and the price he paid for his own phlegmatic calm. Spencer (whose parents promptly packed him off with a one-way ticket to Australia) was the model in both character and appearance for Peter Templer, who presides with Stringham over the narrator's worldly education in the opening stages of the *Dance*.

Looking back, Tony came to feel that his personality had been formed and his future shaped more than anything else before or afterwards by "days at school where so many forces, hitherto unfamiliar, had become in due course uncompromisingly clear." Eton, like most schools, offered the full range of human behaviour in embryo to an attentive observer. It also provided Tony with what he needed at a more basic level: the underlying stability and continuity that came from a sense he had never known before of belonging to a community that accepted him, the nearest thing to a place where he felt at home. The school became from now on a kind of virtual extended family whose members—however rebarbative, reluctant or remote—stood in all his life for the actual relatives he hadn't got.

Oxford, when he reached it in the autumn term of 1923, inspired no such affection. After Eton's broad open spaces, large free-standing houses, and schoolyard designed to hold a thousand boys or more, Balliol's small mediaeval front quad seemed cramped and poky, the whole college awkwardly hemmed in by Trinity College to the east and St. John's to the north. The advantages that struck other undergraduates fresh from school—relative freedom from regulation, historic architectural and intellectual traditions, even the privacy and independence of a room of one's own—had all been anticipated for Tony at Eton. The exuberant attention-seeking of his contemporaries left him unimpressed. Byron covered the eighteenth-century panelling of his rooms at Merton in duck-egg-blue paint, hung up coral curtains and imported enough gilt-edged damask chairs to invite thirty people to lunch at a time. Harold Acton at Christ Church painted his sitting room lemon-yellow, and declaimed his own poems through a megaphone from the balcony. Tony did nothing special to his own small, dingy pair of rooms above Balliol's back-garden quad.

Much of his time at Oxford passed by his own account under a dark cloud of listlessness and depression. He was dismayed by the undergraduates' relentless snobbery and unremitting emphasis on money. Neither had apparently impinged at Eton, ostensibly a still more sheltered enclave where even the humblest pupil could hardly avoid contact with power and wealth (among the boys Tony came across, Buckley ended up a high court judge, Lygon and the two Cecils belonged to the hereditary peerage, the elder Duggan had already been earmarked by his stepfather for Cabinet office). "Money did not come into it at school," wrote Henry Yorke: "At Oxford money was everything." Tony, who had none of Henry's social standing, and got an annual allowance from his father of £300, which was substantially below the norm, could not run up debts on the traditional lavish scale of other undergraduates for fear of detonating explosions at home.

Raucous high spirits were the trademark of a generation that grew up, as a friend of Tony's said, "too young to enter the war, too old to inherit the peace." It was a way of turning their backs on a disjunction they could do nothing about. They were the first to come up to the post-war university with no ex-soldiers in their ranks, and they were acutely conscious of what Tony called the age gap of the 1920s: "Men and women grown up before 1914 were not only older, they were altogether set apart; and thus they remained throughout life. *You never caught up with them.*" Although the war was rarely mentioned either by its survivors among the younger dons, or by the older men who had dispatched their pupils to the front for four successive years, its impact hung heavy on Oxford's more or less enclosed, still largely monastic male society. The authorities tolerated inordinate alcohol consumption, but drew the line at sex. In his third week at Balliol, Tony supplied an alibi for Alfred Duggan (whose chauffeur drove him up to London most nights to enjoy both wine and women) by swearing he had seen him lying dead drunk on the floor all night. Another time Tony used his Old Etonian scarf to lower Alf over the college wall: the scarf tore in two, which didn't stop the night's excursion, but this time Alf returned too drunk to climb back in again and was sent down for good.

Homosexuality was not surprisingly endemic, especially at Balliol. Tony himself was very young (seventeen years old on arrival) and strikingly good-looking in an ingenuous blond way. He was also relatively innocent in a society where pretty boys were open to every sort of predatory advance. One of his bitterest complaints, at a time when women were at best grudgingly tolerated in the university, was the lack of female company. It is probably impossible to pin down at this late stage what, if anything, actually happened. All that can be said for sure is that Tony's subsequent accounts of his personal experiences at Oxford are both vague and uncharacteristically harsh. He certainly refused all invitations to take part in the summer reading-parties organized for favoured youths in his Swiss chalet by Balliol's elderly dean, F. F. Urquhart, better known as Sligger, a mild, teetotal bachelor who, like many if not most dons, was gay.

Tony was briefly taught by Urquhart, and liked him well enough.

But he reserved far greater respect for his principal history tutor, Kenneth Bell, a bluff, extrovert ex-gunner with a Military Cross, a hard-drinking habit, and a love of women strongly deprecated in that misogynist environment. Bell was an outstanding and original teacher, and Tony worked steadily for him, if with decreasing enthusiasm. Intellectually as in every other way at Oxford, Tony was on the defensive, perhaps because of over-exertion the year before, perhaps because of some more specific incident. In states of adolescent gloom bordering on adult depression, academic history sometimes seemed to him as pointless as the undergraduate scrum endlessly jostling for position, advantage and profitable connections ("I think Byron scarcely knew anybody there, or throughout his life, he did not think would ultimately be of use to him"). Spencer had given university a miss altogether. Hubert Duggan took one look and left Oxford at the end of a single term. Tony plodded on, making few if any new friends, falling back on more or less casual acquaintances, people he never got to know well and had no plans to see again.

He spent the long summer vacations touring Europe with one or other of these random companions, generally better-off than himself, not always as keen as he was on picture galleries and assorted cultural phenomena. Between school and university he had put in some weeks learning French, a traditional rite for successive batches of Eton leavers placed with the family of a Mme de la Rive in Touraine, whose household Tony later faithfully described in the first volume of the *Dance*. After he left Touraine, he took the train down via Switzerland to Italy. A year later he pressed further into the countries of central and eastern Europe, still pocked and scarred by recent battles, their borders newly curtailed, extended, reassigned or invented altogether at the Paris peace conference his father had attended. He travelled with a New College boy called Archie Lyall, Tony's third choice for this grand tour after the first two candidates dropped out. They met up in Venice and parted in Prague, stopping off in between at Belgrade (shabby, untidy, full of fancy-dress soldiers and gypsy music), Budapest (lively and assertive with traces of its pre-war glitter), and newly dispossessed Vienna, where the ragged soldiers of a once great army begged for money on the streets.

A decade later in his second novel *Venusberg*, Tony revisited the unreality of this trip, its atmosphere of Edwardian musical-comedy shadowed by only too real and unmistakeably sinister undertones. Venusberg itself with its green Lutheran spires and red-and-gold Russian cathedral was based on Helsinki spiced by a dash of the ancient Hansa city of Tallin in Estonia (the two capitals were then still known respectively as Helsingfors and Reval). Tony had paid at least two visits to Finland, staying with his parents at Christmas 1924, and again the following Easter, at the mighty Hotel Fenner in Helsinki, where Major Powell had been posted for six months on attachment to a British Military Mission. Scores of visiting cards pasted into Tony's photograph album testify to a lost world of minor diplomats and dignitaries, army officers, polyglot officials, assorted princelings, counts and barons. Helsinki astounded Tony. It was the real-life equivalent of a world he had only glimpsed in imagination up to then. The people he met, and whose visiting cards he kept for the rest of his life, belonged to the wholly unfamiliar society depicted in Russian novels: Dostoevksy, Turgenev, Tolstoy, even Chekhov's plays, all of them only just beginning to infiltrate English consciousness for the first time in translation in the early twentieth century.

Finland had declared its independence five years before Tony got there. He would set his own third novel in the small, inward-looking foreign community of an invented and newly liberated Baltic state complicated, like Finland, by Scandinavian allegiances and by a large Russian community, itself heavily reinforced by exiles in flight from the 1917 revolution. The plump, brilliantined Count Bobel, who sells face cream in *Venusberg*, was based on a commercial traveller in cosmetics encountered on the train to Budapest; and the prototype of the melancholy migrant Count Scherbatcheff was a Russian travelling by Danube river-boat. Perhaps one or other of Tony's dancing partners in Helsinki—the Baroness Aminoff for instance, or Frau Lixxie von Schkopp, geboren von Hofstetter xu Platxoll—contributed something to the local siren who seduces the young English hero in *Venusberg*. Tony travelled home via Scandinavia with his parents at the end of their Finnish posting, reaching Hamburg towards the end of April 1925, at the same time as news that Hindenburg had been elected president of Germany: a development that would lead directly eight years later to the accession of Adolf Hitler as chancellor. Finland's brief interlude of peace and independence would end in 1939 with invasion by the armies of Soviet Russia.

In the summer of 1925 Tony set out again for a central Europe still best known abroad as the setting of countless carefree comic or romantic operettas. This time he travelled in a small Vauxhall car owned by Romney Summers, a boy he had known at Balliol who invited him and a friend called Geoffrey Allen to make the epic journey by motor-car to Vienna. They worked their way through France, crossing the Swiss Alps and continuing down through the former territories of the defeated and now dismantled Austro-Hungarian empire, a gruelling route on what were as often as not in those early days still unmade roads. For an inexperienced nineteen-year-old driver, even with two others to take turns at the wheel, it was a rough induction. Somehow they reached their destination, where the victorious British pound, riding high against most other currencies, meant they could treat themselves to the pre-war luxury of the Sacher Hotel. Happy to welcome English tourists at this juncture, no matter how hard-up and bedraggled, Frau Sacher herself personally presented them with slices of her legendary chocolate cake.

Fifty years later Tony chose "Tales from the Vienna Woods" on *Desert Island Discs* to commemorate this trip whose climax, as he turned a corner in the Kunsthistorishes Museum, was a sudden, astounding confrontation with Bruegel's *Hunters in the Snow*. The painting's scale and reach, its breath-taking structural perspective, the vitality and immediacy of its human personnel in both close focus and longshot shattered all preconceptions. Allen, who held Tony's personal record ever after for being less interested than anyone else he ever met in art or books, had had enough by this time. He returned to London alone by train, leaving the other two to drive back turn and turn about, a thousand miles across the great European plain.

Tony's meagre holiday allowance of £50 meant that, even with a favourable exchange rate, he could not splash out as his companions might sometimes have liked on drink or girls. He certainly could not afford to patronize places like Chabanais in Paris, a classy and expensive brothel where most of the boys he knew claimed to have lost their virginity. Many had been sent there expressly for the purpose by their parents. Several of them afterwards described the excruciating embarrassment of these encounters. Abysmally ignorant, terminally inhibited, physically inept British boys found themselves confronted with almost infinite opportunities for misunderstanding and cross purpose. Henry Yorke was not alone in discovering he could do no more than talk to the prostitutes he met in Paris. Even Cyril Connolly—a figure of such worldly eminence at Eton that nothing in later life ever quite matched the grandeur of his schooldays—emerged at eighteen from one of these establishments miserably aware that his virginity remained intact. Tony, in Paris with his parents for his twentieth birthday in December 1925, had the practical mechanics of sex laid out for him at last by an obliging young tart called Lulu, whom he had quite innocently picked up while taking tea on the Champs-Elysées with a boy from Trinity called Marcus Cheke. Lulu, who worked for Zelli's, an undistinguished nightclub-cum-whorehouse in Montmartre, pointed out that she had in fact been touting for custom, and sidestepped Tony's defences by seducing him with competence and speed.

Back in England the prospect of any genuine contact with women seemed as far away as ever. He could no longer count on even low-grade diplomatic hops now that his father had returned to regimental headquarters at Tidworth. Already a connoisseur of boredom, Tony extended his acquaintance with Salisbury's furnished lodgings and the cheap residential hotels of Andover. Oxford by now seemed scarcely more inviting. If the university's social side repelled him, so did its crude and cocksure attitude to the arts. The headquarters of bohemian Oxford in his day was a rowdy hangout called the Hypocrites Club, named for its Greek motto from Pindar: "Water is best." It consisted of two clubrooms with a dartboard and a tinny piano above a bike shop opposite Christ Church, where vast quantities of strong dark beer were consumed by boys unused to drinking on this massive scale. In his first week Tony had been asked to lunch there by a semi-sober Alf Duggan, whose standard lunchtime order was a pint of burgundy in a beer tankard. Drunken, crowded, noisy, a kind of parody of an adult pub, the place smelt of fried onions and specialized in aggressively bawdy talk and intellectual pretension. Tony found small consolation at the Hypocrites in the interminable stretch that had somehow to be got through before life itself could begin. "How little I liked being at Oxford. I longed to get it over and go down."

It was in this mood that C. M. Bowra found him early in the summer vac of 1925, holed up at the Knoll Hotel on the outskirts of Andover. Bowra was twenty-six years old, and already the most talked-about young don in the university. He belonged to that generation Tony could never hope to catch up with, having been called up straight from school and spent two years on the French front. Although Bowra never spoke of what he had seen or done there, Tony came eventually to feel that its memory was always with him. It gave him a prodigious appetite for all he might have lost, and an imperative need for human company. He had a vigorous, incisive mind, lightning wit, and a mesmeric personality. Isaiah Berlin found his conversation incomparable, and Noel Annan compared meeting him to downing tumblers of brandy ("One left reeling"). Elected a fellow of his college on graduation, and appointed dean shortly afterwards, he taught classics, passing on his ways of thinking and speaking, even his distinctive intonations and turns of phrase, to generations of impressionable young men.

Bowra was short and stubby with a head so big Tony said he looked like Humpty-Dumpty, but nobody noticed any more than people in the eighteenth century paid attention to Dr. Johnson's stammer. Tony first met him in his third term and made an immediate impression ("He passed all Maurice's tests," wrote Bowra's biographer approvingly). He became almost at once a member of the Bowra circle, calling him by his first name and regularly included in hilarious, drunken dinners in his rooms at Wadham. What impressed and startled Tony from that first meeting was Bowra's modernity: "Everything about him was up-to-date." Where his academic elders were stuffy, authoritarian, portentously high-minded and invincibly mealy-mouthed, Bowra was frank, matter-of-fact and casual. He not only recognized the actualities of ordinary human behaviour, but saw them as perfectly natural: "open snobbishness, success worship, personal vendettas, unprovoked malice, disloyalty to friends, reading other people's letters (if not lying about, to be sought in unlocked drawers)—the whole bag of tricks of what most people think, feel, and often act on, yet are ashamed of admitting that they do, feel, and think." For Tony it was an unexpected liberation to find Bowra articulating things he was only obscurely conscious of himself. In a sense it launched him on the lifelong study of the ways ordinary people act, feel, think and above all manipulate each other that would eventually culminate in the *Dance*.

Tony had originally been introduced to Bowra by a Balliol contemporary called Piers Synott, who was also present a year later on that unexpected visit to Andover. The couple were by this time more or less inseparably involved in a passionate, platonic friendship (Bowra dazzled and seduced undergraduates verbally though never physically) and, since Piers was due to spend the rest of the summer on his family estate in Ireland, Bowra urgently needed company. They had made what was presumably a considerable detour on the off chance of collecting Tony, who proved only too happy to exchange his current tedium for a few days in Bowra's rooms. All might have gone well if Tony, finding himself once again terminally bored during his host's daily absence on college business, had not blurted out his feelings about Oxford one evening over dinner. Bowra was appalled. Oxford was the professional and emotional centre of his being, and Tony had struck at his tenderest and most vulnerable part. Although the two continued to meet on friendly terms after that dreadful night, in retrospect Tony reckoned that it was another thirty-five years before the wound was fully healed, and their relationship could resume on the same terms as before. Bowra had taught him much about human relations, honesty and power, lessons Tony absorbed and understood only long afterwards. As an adult looking back he blamed himself severely for the adolescent egoism whose effect on Bowra had simply not occurred to him: "The idea that Bowra himself was a young man with a career ahead of him, about which he no doubt suffered still all sorts of uncertainties, even horrors, never even crossed my mind."

By far Tony's happiest memories of Oxford came from his last year, when he got away from college to share lodgings with Henry Yorke. The two had rooms next to one another on the top floor at number 4, King Edward Street, where they held lunch parties that must sometimes have given the hosts more anxiety than pleasure (once they invited a girl, and were incredulous when she accepted; another time they asked both Bell and Bowra, two rival magnetic fields of force not easy to combine in the same room). But they increasingly inhabited a world of their own, recapturing the intent, exclusive and absorbing intimacy of their years at prep school. Now as then they talked books. Together they discovered Marcel Proust, reading, exploring and endlessly discussing each new volume of *Remembrance of Things Past* as it came out. Tony devoured the first three books while he was still at Oxford and realized, like Henry, that the novel as they knew it could never be the same again. They were caught up in a rage that gripped the whole of literary Oxford, not only for Proust but also for Eliot's *Waste Land* and "Prufrock," which looked set to do for poetry what the Frenchman was doing for fiction. The post-war tide of radical innovation made the previous century's writers suddenly look musty, ornate and hopelessly outdated. New angles, fresh perspectives and the merciless undercutting of pretension were an immediate priority. Ronald Firbank seemed the funniest author alive, Aldous Huxley operated at fiction's cutting edge, and the three Sitwell siblings led the way.

Tony admired them all, but he and Henry were unusual, if not unique, among their fellow undergraduates in simultaneously gulping down the Russians, coming hot from the presses in those years in English translations by Constance Garnett. Henry was bowled over by *Crime and Punishment*: "a most awful, dreadful, supremely great book," wrote his alter ego, the excitable schoolboy hero of his novel *Blindness*. "What a force books are! This one is like dynamite!" Tony himself was not so keen at that stage on Dostoevsky although he would in the end rank him above all others, citing *The Devils* as "perhaps the greatest novel ever written." Both of them read Turgenev ("the unadorned style then rather above my head," said Tony).

Both also read the earliest available versions of Chekhov's plays, which would exert marked influence on each of them as writers. Initially dismissed as incomprehensible, if not actually meaningless, Chekhov had seemed unworkable on stage until a production of *The Cherry Orchard* in January 1925 at the Oxford Playhouse. Although many of the actors (including the twenty-year-old John Gielgud as Trofimov) remained as baffled as their audiences, its transfer to London in May proved to be a turning point that launched Chekhov unstoppably on the English theatre. The two young sages in King Edward Street had already grasped in essence a literary revolution that would not be generally accepted for another twenty years or more. "Irrelevancy means so much," wrote Henry at nineteen, "it shows you what a person is and how he thinks, and conveys atmosphere in a way that is inconceivable if you haven't seen Tchekhov's *Cherry Orchard*."

For Henry as for Tony the opening up of these new worlds easily outclassed academic work, the company of fellow undergraduates or political turmoil in the country at large (Tony spent the ten days of the General Strike in May working in a kind of emergency post office set up in Reading Gaol). No other occupation could command the energy and purpose they brought to literary experiment and discovery. Whether or not they recognized what they were doing—and Tony certainly did not, or not at any rate with his conscious mind— each was laying the foundations of a novelist's career. Tony worked hard on the intricacies of construction. Growing indifference to the academic ramifications of nineteenth-century

The publisher Thomas Balston, Major Powell's former staff captain, who shaped Tony's career

diplomacy (his special subject was the Congress of Vienna, chosen perhaps for the Proustian aftertaste of Frau Sacher's *Schokoladentorte*) was offset by increasing interest in the practicalities of how to shape and flavour any given piece of writing. For Tony the question had been raised in his first term by a tutor who objected to the first sentence of his first essay, making him think about writing in an entirely new way: "*I now saw in a flash the importance of structure.*" That first intimation was broadened and deepened in tutorials with Bell, and refined at second hand in Tony's last year by professional advice from Constance Garnett's husband Edward.

One of the great editors of his generation and an outstanding talent-spotter, Garnett earned a modest living as a publisher's reader. The manuscript of Henry's novel, completed in the spring of 1925, had been submitted first to Chatto and Windus, and then on Tony's suggestion to his father's former second-in-command, Tom Balston, now the editorial director at Messrs. Duckworth. Both Balston and Chatto's reader turned it down. That autumn, when Henry moved into King Edward Street, his book was finally accepted by J. M. Dent on advice from the reader overruled at Duckworths, who was Garnett. For all his enthusiasm, Garnett had serious reservations too, and all through the winter he and Henry wrestled with the text in what became for Tony an extended vicarious tutorial on creative writing. Henry accepted Garnett's cuts, incorporated many of his changes (which included rewriting the entire last chapter), and passed on his "invaluable hints about novel-writing." In December he travelled up to London to meet the venerable old man face to face. By this time novel-writing and reading had superseded all other considerations for Henry, if not for Tony, whose final examinations were due round about the same time as printers' proofs from Dent. *Blindness*, scheduled for publication in the autumn of 1926, transformed the standing of the ménage at King Edward Street, in their own eyes and other people's. "A published novel could not altogether be laughed off," said Tony, whose involvement was strictly editorial.

His own future remained a blank that was only finally filled in by another of Balston's drastic interventions. It was Balston who had persuaded Major Powell to send his son to Balliol in the first place, and now he suggested taking Tony on as an apprentice publisher, in practice office dogsbody, at Duckworths. The proposal was accepted with alacrity by Major Powell, and also by his son, failing anything better in prospect. Coasting along on the strength of encouragement from Bell, Tony confidently expected a respectable second-class degree in his final exams. Bowra, possibly less sanguine, was among the first to see the list of results that summer. "I feel you need a word of congratulation on Tony's third," he wrote sardonically to Henry. "I had no idea that this was what you had worked for all these years. It will be interesting to hear his line on it."

Whatever that may have been was swamped by the overwhelming relief of an escape so long and urgently awaited. In a back room at Duckworths a few months later Tony discovered Robert Burton, whose *Anatomy of Melancholy* would become, like the *Brief Lives* of his contemporary John Aubrey, a lifelong companion. Dr. Johnson said the *Anatomy* was the only book that ever made him get out of bed in the morning two hours before he wanted to, and Tony might have said the same. He copied out a favourite passage in his notebook at the time, and used it almost fifty years later to conclude the twelfth and final volume of the *Dance*. In the autumn of 1926, the new world about to open for him meant freedom, autonomy, the end at last of being pushed around, in short the start of life itself together with the hope of meeting girls. Tony reached London with the sense of joyful anticipation described in that torrential passage from Burton's *Anatomy*: "Now come tidings of weddings, maskings, mummeries, entertainments, jubilees, embassies, tilts and tournaments, trophies, triumphs, revels, sports, plays: then again as in a new shifted scene treasons, cheating tricks, robberies, enormous villainies in all kinds, funerals, burials, deaths of princes, new discoveries, expeditions; now comical then tragical matters . . ."

3
1926–29

"All publishing houses are scenes of violent internal struggles for power," Tony wrote more than half a century after joining Gerald Duckworth & Co., by which time he knew more than most about the rough roads of the book trade. But nothing had prepared him for what he found on arrival in the autumn of 1926. He wore a natty plum-coloured suit, double-breasted with a lapelled waistcoat (an outfit never forgotten by Duckworths' admiring office boy), and was put to work copying out invoices on a high stool at the trade counter on the ground floor of number 3, Henrietta Street. Outside, a turbulent traffic of porters, delivery men, barrow boys and horse-drawn lorries filled the street, which formed the south-west boundary of Covent Garden vegetable market. Inside, the premises had a distinctive atmosphere of "decaying fruit and veg, the dusty mustiness of ceiling-high packed bookcases, the stale sour smell of packers' paste."

Duckworths' street door stood open all day, giving access to a shabby uncarpeted stone passage lined along one side by small offices housing low-grade workers: the surly and secretive accountant Mr. Child, the downtrodden lady book-keepers, the one-man packing department, and the three breezy young invoice clerks who cheerfully instructed their latest recruit in a pithy streetwise vocabulary of cockney invective, lewd jokes and bawdy songs. Steep stone steps at the back end of the passage led up through a swing door to a set of slightly less cramped but not much grander offices on the first floor, where the firm's three partners and their managing director would shortly be joined by Tony.

Rifts between opposing factions took precedence upstairs. "Dust was everywhere, disorder infinite," said Tony, describing the partners' office. Far from offering instruction, his employers treated him with a suspicion that ranged from passive reluctance to explain even basic publishing routines to active hostility from the head of the firm. Large, taciturn, slow-moving, Gerald Duckworth saw himself as an Edwardian clubman. He smoked foul-smelling cigars, enjoyed a bottle of claret a day over lunch at the Garrick, and was often half tipsy in the office. He disliked books and those who wrote them, an attitude not at all uncommon in a generation of gentlemen publishers who found their own comfortable autonomy threatened by the author: "a natural enemy against whom the publisher must hold himself arrayed for battle," wrote the head of Chapman and Hall, a rival concern a few doors along on Henrietta Street.

Duckworth had originally founded his firm for reasons hard to fathom, perhaps as an act of sublimated spite against his more illustrious relatives (his stepfather was the doyen of Victorian men of letters, Sir Leslie Stephen, and his half-sister was Virginia Woolf). Thirty years in the business had brought him, by the time Tony got there, "close to detesting books with all his heart." He had already sacked the firm's rising star, a brilliant young entrepreneur called Jonathan Cape who left in 1920 to found what soon became a publishing powerhouse. At this point even Duckworth grudgingly admitted that his own outfit was moribund. He brought Tom Balston in as Cape's successor to revitalize the firm, but his own hostility to books and authors now extended to anyone who tried to promote or publish them, especially to Balston, and by association to his new sidekick, Tony Powell.

Duckworth blocked Balston at every turn. All efforts to bring the firm into line with changing post-war markets, to modernize its policy and ginger up the book list were suspect. Warfare between the two camps affected the entire workforce, including the managing director, A. G. Lewis, a resilient and resourceful character whose extensive contacts and knowledge of production complemented Balston's editorial efficiency and flair. The two had worked together at Fisher Unwin before the war, and between them they kept Duckworths going under steady fire from Gerald. Neutrality was not an option. "Even to a boy's ears the planning conference was in the nature of a conflict," wrote Tom Bishop, who had arrived a few months before Tony as a fourteen-year-old office boy, "it being apparent that Duckworth and sycophant Child were allowing no proposals from upstarts Balston and Lewis to carry very much weight."

When Tony eventually graduated to a first-floor desk, it had to be inserted along with two broken-down armchairs into the small room occupied by Lewis, himself chronically overworked and far from anxious to spend time initiating a technically inept trainee. Balston was no help either. He was old enough to be Tony's father (and had indeed stepped in more than once to take over the parental role Major Powell couldn't or wouldn't play) but, once his protégé was safely installed, he showed no further interest. He had joined the firm on the understanding that Duckworth would be only too glad to give up running it, which meant a free hand for Balston, especially since the only other partner, George Milsted, was thought to be terminally ill. When both assumptions turned out to be false, Balston was too busy fortifying his own position to consider other people's. Tony got no guidance beyond a vague sense that he was expected to resuscitate Duckworths' ageing list with fresh recruits from among his own contemporaries. A solid team of pre-war talent—headed by Hilaire Belloc, W. H. Hudson, Charles Doughty and Ford Madox Ford—had barely been updated since Edward Garnett left with Cape. Change meant decay to Duckworth, faithfully seconded by Milsted, who was more at home on the racetrack than in literary London, dressing like a bookie in aggressive checks and brown bowler hats, seldom dropping in at Henrietta Street, and taking next to no part in the publishing process when he did.

Both senior partners judged writers much as they might horseflesh, by the money they brought in. Neither felt comfortable except with seasoned performers turning out reliably undemanding romances on an industrial scale to service the mass circulating libraries in an age before radio, TV or digital media. Top of this list was Elinor Glyn (a brisk and likeable redhead in Tony's recollection) backed by the young and pushy Barbara Cartland with an even younger Godfrey Winn snapping at her heels, pursued by more sluggish sellers like Eric Muspratt and Hector Wintle. Duckworths specialized in the kind of author who, as Tony said, allowed himself a good deal of platitude. His former special subject, John Galsworthy, "one of the firm's most lucrative properties," had long since come to seem the epitome of banality, self-satisfaction and fake sentiment to Tony, who watched him make an entrance, hovering silently in the office doorway as he waited with ill-controlled impatience for Lewis to look up from the estimates on his desk in shock and awe: "Galsworthy stood there smiling with boundless condescension; the smile became increasingly fixed as Lewis continued to ponder the estimates. Finally Galsworthy gave it up as a bad job."

It took time for Tony's seniors to realize that much of the repetitive and mechanical drudgery of publishing—composing advertisements and blurbs, assembling catalogue copy, correcting proofs—could usefully devolve on him. But he was deployed from the beginning to deter and repel all comers at Duckworths' open door, a steady flow of prospective, dissatisfied or discarded authors together with the usual flotsam still peopling the book world today: "literary agents, gossip writers, professional seducers, philosophers, thaumaturges," as Tony put it in the notebook he used at this point for jotting down impressions. Much time was spent standing in the draughty stone passage, or sitting on hard upright chairs in a cubby-hole upgraded to waiting room where, as Tom Bishop reminded Tony long after-wards, "you patiently interviewed so many callers." Similar ordeals would recur in his first and fifth novels, each in its way a hymn to the superlative powers of endurance developed by its hero as various customers rehearse their grievances, outline their projects and retail their plots in remorseless detail: "He did not listen. He knew that the best he could hope for was that he should avoid hearing it all more than once . . . He swayed slightly, an apparent vision of trellis-work before his eyes. His mouth was curiously dry . . . he wondered how long it was going on."

When not confronting authors head on, Tony passed long hours with his feet up on the desk riffling through their unsolicited manu-scripts. He said nothing taught him more about the technical side of writing—not so much what worked as what didn't—than reading and assessing up to fifty bad novels a week. Any spare time was spent exploring the book-stacks in the "mice- and beetle-infested basement stockroom" at Henrietta Street. Tony read Joseph Conrad, Henry James and August Strindberg for the first time in Duckworths' unsold popular editions as well as discovering future standbys like Robert

Burton's *Anatomy* and Casanova's *Memoirs*. But the evenings after he left the office remained for most of his first year in London hard to fill.

He lived in Shepherd Market, a sleazy spot twenty minutes' walk away from Covent Garden, chosen because it was the setting of a notorious seduction scene in the first chapter of Michael Arlen's *The Green Hat*. This was Major Powell's favourite novel, a book that had caused a sensation in 1924 and made enough in royalties according to its author to earn him £120,000, or roughly £3 million in today's money. Arlen (who was in fact an Armenian called Dikran Kouyoumdjian) had written it in a couple of rooms "above a mean lane in a place called Shepherd Market . . . bounded on the north side by Curzon Street, on the south by Piccadilly, on the west by Hertford Street and on the east by Half Moon Street." Tony's own two rooms were on the ground floor of number 9, Shepherd Street, a dilapidated house on a dingy thoroughfare round the corner from an all-night garage. The Market itself was a small surviving pocket of cobbled streets and archways, little shops and unassuming pubs tucked into modern Mayfair in the angle between Park Lane and Piccadilly. Many of its inhabitants worked locally as pickpockets, touts peddling illegal betting slips, and Piccadilly prostitutes with rented rooms in the only modern block: "a kind of tarts' barracks," said Tony.

He got used to being woken in the small hours by whores, drunks and hustlers trying to get in at the nailed-up street door that formed one wall of his tiny bedroom. His flat was roughly the size of "an airing-cupboard divided into two compartments." The whole building was so rickety that his living room had to be held up by a massive wooden prop to stop the upper storeys collapsing on him. The space that remained was almost entirely taken up by a glass-fronted bookcase, a miniature sofa and an upright chair. A small flimsy table folded flat against the wall could be opened out if necessary, but reading and writing were not possibilities envisaged by his friendly landlady, a Mrs. Williamson, whose generous hospitality sometimes almost overwhelmed him.

With time he got to know a neighbour the same age as himself called Bumble (short for Beatrice) Dawson, an art student who lived above the butcher's shop at number 13a. Most nights he dined alone at a communal table in the pub opposite, the New Chesterfield Arms (2s 6d for three courses). Although he preferred not to admit he'd picked the place for its dubious literary associations, Arlen's recommendation served Tony well: "the Market's air of seedy chic perfectly suited my own post-Oxonian mood."

Seedy chic was the point of *The Green Hat*. It offered an exhilarating mix of cynicism and the higher tosh dispensed with humour and a dazzling modernity that took in everything from the sexual revolution to narrative experiment and cutting-edge technical advances like electricity, telephones and the cinema. Its doomed heroine Iris Storm, a boyish beauty with short, cropped hair, small, neat breasts and blazing blue eyes, became an immediate icon. Promiscuous and déclassée, Iris has her cake and eats it too in a hectically daft denouement when she redeems her life by dying "for purity." *The Green Hat* set the tone for a disaffected generation that liked fast cars (Iris drives a long low yellow Hispano-Suiza convertible), American jazz, crowded parties and casual sex. Part Edwardian male fantasy ("She was a woman until she touched you. Then she became woman, and you water"), part post-war feminist with a good mind and active sexual appetites, Iris appealed to all ages and both sexes. Women might have liked to be her, men to stumble with her "in the burning darkness of the vile rubbish-heaps of desire."

Shepherd Market's rubbish-heaps reappeared a few years later in Edward Burra's painting *Saturday Market*, featuring a fearsome tart with luminous yellow skin and cavernous dark eyes wrapped in a grey-pink negligée, blowsy above, skimpy below, its trailing drapery outlining the curve of one hip and revealing a shapely calf as she picks her way on three-inch heels across a wasteland of discarded cabbage leaves, offal, trash, phosphorescent puddles and a scavenging dog. Burra's sordid scene lyrically evokes the urban landscape Tony knew when he first started scribbling down potential book titles (*Naughty Figs, Landscape with Ruins, Dignity and Impotence*) in his notebook along with names for characters (Nunnery, Fosdick, Chipchase) and snatches of dialogue. He met Burra only after he had moved elsewhere but the Market's louche potential stimulated them both. "I liked living there," Tony wrote, "because . . . the neighbourhood still hinted at Green Hats and deaths-for-purity. I was twenty and had just come down from Oxford."

Much of his behaviour in this first year was aimed at what he called "de-Oxfordification," a kind of personal detox programme that meant positioning himself as far away as possible from the snobbery of undergraduate contemporaries, their childish posturing and intellectual pomposity. Duckworths' general shabbiness and the Market's garbage were capped by an even more drastic measure in the summer of 1927, when Tony joined a Territorial Artillery Regiment. This was a move he kept dark if he could at the time and afterwards. "I felt that if the Gunners were good enough for Tolstoy, they were good enough for me," he explained defensively in his memoirs half a century later. The military setting had been familiar since childhood but there is a punitive edge to Tony's subsequent accounts. He trained two nights a week in the outhouses and drill halls of a battery headquarters in South London, reached by a long bus ride with two or more changes on the way, and a ten-minute walk at the far end. Here he was instructed in cavalry techniques ("impelling an iron-mouthed horse round a dusty shed under glaring electric light bulbs can be a thankless, if not humiliating, occupation"), and how to wipe out an enemy with maximum economy and precision by shellfire.

The place was dismal, the manoeuvres often exhausting, and the weekend social round of golf and bridge almost more than he could bear. What appealed to Tony was the efficiency and discipline, the sense that individual eccentricity could flourish within a sharply defined and regulated setting. He particularly liked the regular army adjutant, Captain Bloodworth, a man with a loud voice who wore loud suits and yearned for less prosaic, spiritual or aesthetic realities he could not articulate ("I should like to meet writers who really count, like G. K. Chesterton, Belloc," he confided wistfully to Tony). Bloodworth's sympathetic character and modest literary aspirations would be passed on a decade later to the central character in *What's Become of Waring*.

Tony's social life at this stage was arid, sometimes non-existent, apart from the odd dinner party for elderly Duckworths' authors in Balston's Victoria mansion flat, and occasional invitations extended by the mothers of boys he had come across at school or college: Anthony Russell, Matthew Ponsonby, Richard Plunket Greene, Rupert Biddulph and others. He dined at their houses and danced with their sisters, some as restive as he often felt himself ("I used to wonder if I was boring him as much as I was boring myself," one of them wrote about her typical partner, "and, when it was his turn, I speculated whether it was possible that he was boring himself as much as he was boring me"). Much as in the army, uniformity and conformity were paramount in a world whose strictly chaperoned inhabitants performed the same handful of unvarying routines night after night. The girls, who drilled themselves to look in Arlen's phrase "bored with boredom," all had the same shingled hair, short skirts and sleek tubular silhouettes. The men wore tailcoats, black trousers and white gloves. Everybody knew everybody else in places like the Pall Mall clubs, and the Cavendish Hotel on Jermyn Street.

Tony had been put down for the Travellers at twenty by the dean of Balliol. An Oxford acquaintance introduced him to the Cavendish, where the rooms had the shabby comfort of a run-down country house and the stern, white-haired proprietor, Rosa Lewis, a charismatic beauty in her Edwardian past, seemed to have known not only the current generation's fathers, but often their grandfathers as well. "In her day she must have been a kind of nanny," Tony wrote in retrospect, "a faintly sinister one, to a lot of rich, raffish, but perhaps ultimately rather lonely young men . . ." The forbidding, even faintly macabre undertones he sensed at the time vividly convey the impact of both the Cavendish and its proprietor on a poor, wary and extremely lonely young man in the late 1920s. It was only long afterwards that Tony, far less naïve and a great deal more confident, came to see the Cavendish as a modern equivalent of the tavern at Eastcheap, Falstaff's favourite pub in Shakespeare's *Henry IV*.

Most of Tony's dancing partners he never saw again with the exception of Adelaide and Mary Biddulph, Rupert's sisters, distant cousins and country neighbours of the Yorkes at Forthampton, where he probably first met them. He took Mary out to dinner from time to time in London, but more often it was her elder sister Adelaide, always known as Dig, who dined with him after a visit to the ballet, the cinema or a show at the Royal Academy. The two kept up their conversation when she was in the country in an exchange of letters, swapping gossip and comparing notes, Dig capping Tony's complaints of tedium at work with her own lively accounts of rustic futility and depression. Their correspondence suggests the easy, flirtatious terms of a relationship that he at least would have liked to take further, if they hadn't belonged to irreconcilably different worlds.

The constraints of his working week and exiguous pay were meaningless to Dig ("*Why* aren't you going? It's *too* sickening," she wrote when he refused an invitation because he had to go to work in London). Hostesses like Maude Yorke and Mary Biddulph included Tony on their long lists for the kind of large-scale ball or scrum where there was a chronic shortage of presentable spare men, but he seldom made it on to their smaller lists for more select parties. The problem was that Tony was basically ineligible. He had no prospects, no connections, nothing to inherit and he wasn't related to anyone people had ever heard of in the world of debutante dances and court presentation. A job in the City or the Foreign Office, even at a pinch the BBC, might have been acceptable but girls like Dig Biddulph did not marry boys with dead-end day jobs in small unstable concerns like Duckworths. "Do write and tell me how you are getting on in the 'office'!" Dig wrote helpfully.

Tony's false position was made unequivocally clear to him. He never forgot being snubbed as a young man by hostesses as different as Lady Ottoline Morrell at Garsington ("an ordeal of the most gruelling order"), and Georgia Sitwell at Renishaw. Even Hubert Duggan, who had joined the Household Cavalry on leaving Oxford, left him in no doubt that their two paths had ceased to intersect. Henry Yorke, who ticked all the right social boxes, had admittedly also taken a job on leaving Oxford, going to work as a labourer for his father's firm in Birmingham as soon as his book was published at the end of 1926. He moved up through the iron foundry and the brass foundry to the coppersmiths' workshop, complaining bitterly in his letters of privation and discomfort. Tony kept him posted on the London scene in breezy bulletins with an undertow of dismay. "Hopeless inferiorities," ran a postscript that suggested each was more than familiar with the other's problems. "I still can't understand Henry and the Birmingham job," Dig wrote severely to Tony, "but one thing I do know is that it doesn't make me have what you call inferiorities and it shouldn't make you either."

Tony understood only too well what Henry was doing in Birmingham. He was researching a novel. By the time he went down from Oxford, he had not only published his first book but completed twenty thousand words of another, which he continued in Birmingham every evening after work. He read extracts from the manuscript to Tony on occasional home visits, explaining that his plan was to

accumulate sufficient material to complete this second novel about
working men before moving back to the family's Regency townhouse
in central London. Tony himself had little progress to report from
Duckworths or the dance floor. He shuttled between the two, making
notes in a small grey cloth-bound publisher's dummy (the kind of
mock-up with blank pages produced to show what any given book
will look like). His entries included glimpses of the social round—
garrulous hosts, insincere butlers, expressionless girls comparing him
unfavourably to their fiancés—as well as imaginary book titles, suggestive names and remarks overheard at the office: "Publisher talking: 'I understand he has written a book of the bitter-sweet variety.'"
Tony had no novel in hand himself, nor any but the vaguest intention
of ever writing one, but increasingly he included putative subjects,
scraps of plot, even whole passages of narrative easily recognizable in
retrospect as try-outs for one or other of his early novels. "Ah, you're
buying experience, young man," said an observant hostess, or perhaps one of the "courtly old bores" who also figure in this notebook.

Its pages offered an escape from social constraint, sexual frustration and the consistent discouragement he received at work. "I am
so bored I can knock my head against the wall," Tony wrote on the
second page, quoting a line from Chekhov's *Ivanov*. He said much
the same in his own words to Dig and others in the summer of 1927.
An outburst to Henry at the end of August lamented "the dreadful
monotony of life" with all his friends out of London: "It does not
contain a single soul I know . . . And no one seems to be coming back
until well into September. Meantime I suppose I shall die of boredom." His attempt to fill the blank by joining the Territorials only
made him feel more frantic. Dining with Robert Byron that August
to discuss the possibility of Duckworths publishing a travel book,
he found himself confessing his horror of the narrow claustropho-
bic vistas that stretched ahead of him in all directions. Shocked by
the genuine despair behind Tony's "almost suicidal" eruption, Byron
said he felt friendlier towards him afterwards than he ever had before.
"The last thing on earth I should like is to be young again," Tony
himself said grimly more than seventy years later.

Things began to look up in October 1927, when Balston sent
him to learn printing at the Holborn Polytechnic (also known by
its grander title as the Central School of Arts and Crafts). Tony

resigned from the Territorials to take evening classes at the institute on Southampton Row, which turned out to be full of "the most *ravishing* young women," none of them, unfortunately, enrolled on the printing course. "I shall have to take up art needlework or something of that sort in order to make some friends," said Tony. The friend he made that autumn at the Poly was Evelyn Waugh, who was studying carpentry. The two had first made contact earlier in the year when Tony arranged for his new acquaintance (whom he had known only by reputation at Oxford) to call on him as a prospective author at Duckworths, where Balston promptly commissioned the biography of Dante Gabriel Rossetti that became Waugh's first book. He worked on it intermittently, often overtaken, like Tony, by fits of deep depression. A brilliant Oxford career had ended three years earlier in collapse when he lost his scholarship, took a third and started drinking heavily. Two brief penitential stints as a prep-school master had got him nowhere. His future remained a source of constant anxiety to his family, especially his father Arthur Waugh (who ran the rival publishing firm of Chapman and Hall on Henrietta Street), and his elder brother, the successful novelist Alec Waugh ("those years seemed marked with a steady retrogression," Alec wrote of his unlucky sibling: "I would not care to re-live the November and early December of 1927"). Duckworths' advance of £50 on royalties—double Balston's usual sum—had come as a relief but neither Evelyn's brother nor his father believed in his capacity as a writer. "Balston will never see that book," Waugh senior predicted glumly: "I suppose I'll have to make it good."

By the time of his chance meeting with Tony on 25 October at the Poly, Evelyn was drinking again, still hard up and living at home on a modest allowance from his father, supplemented by a part-time job that he was "too ashamed to mention" teaching at a school in Golders Green. His plan was to be a craftsman or a carpenter ("Oh, Tolstoy and all that," was his explanation when Tony asked him why). With *Rossetti: His Life and Works* scheduled for delivery in the spring of 1928, he had already begun a novel called *Picaresque: or the Making of an Englishman*, reading the opening chapters aloud to Tony and posting off further instalments as he wrote them ("I have done another chapter & am getting near the end now"). Evelyn claimed to have burnt the manuscript at the end of 1927, but Tony said that not a word

Tony drawn by Nina Hamnett at the start of their affair

had changed when it was published the year after as *Decline and Fall*. The handwritten inscription in his copy suggests the friendship had been a lifeline to them both: "For Tony who rescued the author from worse than death."

The two spent much time together walking and talking, and Tony was often invited to cold Sunday suppers at Evelyn's parents' house in the North End Road on the outskirts of the newly emerging Hampstead Garden Suburb. He and Evelyn sat up long after the older Waughs had retired to bed, once so late that Tony missed the last bus and had to walk home in the small hours to Shepherd Market. This was the first genuinely literary household he had ever encountered ("books—their writing, editing, printing, advertising, marketing—a normal way of life"), and he liked the whole family, including Evelyn's father, whose old-world approach to publishing made Balston seem by comparison "a thrusting youngster of alarmingly modernistic tendency." Arthur Waugh, himself a colleague and contemporary of Gerald Duckworth, clearly approved of his son's new friend, encouraging their relationship and taking a keen interest in Tony's professional progress. "This was the period when I knew and liked Waugh best," wrote Tony.

However much Evelyn complained then and later about his father, the Waughs, like the Yorkes, basically got on well together at home, in sharp contrast to the Powells. Catastrophe overtook Tony's father at the end of 1927. His confident expectation that he would take command of the Welsh Regiment's home battalion foundered when it was posted to Shanghai as part of the British Defence Force, shipped out to contain fighting in China between Communists and Nationalists. Major Powell was still in his mid-forties when, after serving briefly in that torrid climate, he fell ill and came home to convalesce, afterwards refusing to return to the Far East, which meant he had no option but to resign his commission and leave the army. Whatever may have happened in China—whether it was a purely physical collapse or a moral breakdown, perhaps the cumulative result of years of attrition—it was, as Tony said, "a shattering blow." Anger, frustration and bitter disappointment now compounded his father's existing problems. The Powells found what turned out to be a permanent home at number 3, Clarence Terrace in Regent's Park, where their son regularly dined with them, although it seems to have been tacitly understood that there could be no question of inviting friends like Evelyn or Henry.

A sketch of Tony reading in the winter of 1927 shows a self-contained character in a collar and tie with neatly brushed hair, clear-cut regular features and long slender sensitive fingers. The artist was Nina Hamnett, with whom he embarked on what an Oxford contemporary called "his first grown-up affair." Nina was knowledgeable, cosmopolitan and experienced in the ways of many different worlds. An unmistakeable presence in artistic and literary London, she was at this point more at home in Paris, especially the shadier parts of Montmartre, where hard-up foreign artists hung on by their fingertips. A friend of Ossip Zadkine and the Bulgarian Jules Pascin, sculpted nude as a girl by Henri Gaudier-Brzeska, Nina knew Brancusi and had shared Modigliani's studio. At home she had been painted by Sickert, Augustus John and Roger Fry, himself one of her many former lovers, much influenced when young by her originality as a painter, enchanted by her boyish charm and chutzpah, but defeated in the end by the kind of promiscuity that would barely have caused comment in a man: "*elle est vraiment putain* [she's a real whore], but a nice one," he wrote ruefully to Vanessa Bell.

In a painters' world, where girls featured more or less exclusively as mistresses and models, Nina operated on equal terms with men.

She had a broad and multifarious acquaintance on both sides of the Channel ranging from Jean Cocteau and Princess Eugène Murat to Nancy Cunard, Gerald du Maurier and the sinister wizard Aleister Crowley. She was by choice and force of circumstance a displaced person. An army child, like Tony, brought up in an environment where girls counted for nothing, Nina had retaliated early by refusing out of hand to be "the same kind of gutless half-wit as the rest of the sex." Her father, Lieutenant Colonel Hamnett of the Army Service Corps, was cashiered for embezzlement, becoming a cab-driver himself and turning his eldest daughter out at sixteen to pay her own way as best she might. Reluctance to marry or go on the streets left unrelenting poverty as her only option.

From the age of twenty-one, Nina had an income of 2s 6d a week, settled on her by two aunts, and supplemented by what little she could earn from the sale of drawings. Sex played little or no part in her economy: she could take it or leave it, like most men, as casually as having a glass of wine with a friend. "I let them get on with it," said Nina briskly. Tall and slender, with small breasts and long slim legs, she had the same well-toned, athletic body in Gaudier's *Dancer* of 1913 as in John Banting's surrealist nude painted almost two decades later in 1930, shortly after her affair with Tony: it shows Nina sprawling backview in an armchair, characteristically alert with one foot braced against the floor, the emphatic curves of shoulder blade and buttock set off against the long taut curving sweep of hip, thigh and calf.

What made Nina unique in the rackety circles she moved in was her manner and appearance. She looked, dressed and sounded all her life like a product of the ultra-respectable Royal School for the Daughters of Army Officers in Bath, as indeed she was. Fellow painters found her impossible to categorize. Ahead of her time in this as in much else, Nina did not so much transgress as fail to recognize boundaries of class, race, age or sex. She combined absolute recklessness in her personal life with tight professional discipline, a rare combination that appealed to Tony, who in turn touched and intrigued her. For most of 1927 her centre of operations was still the Café du Dôme in Paris, where she described picking up a boy she called "my little Etonian," and taking him to a party in the Latin Quarter along with three black girls from Montmartre and another from the north

Nina painted by John Banting soon after she and
Tony split up

known as *la fille du curé* (the curate's daughter), famous for stripping
off her clothes in public. Nina's pick-up was "a well-dressed young
Englishman who had just left Oxford . . . He looked so respectable
that we made him dance a tango with *la fille*. I think he felt that he was
really starting out on a career of adventure." This was Tony, in Paris
to celebrate his birthday and attend what Dig called "murky shows"
at New Year, 1927.

The two met again apparently by chance that summer in Duckworths' office in London. Nina had been commissioned to illustrate
a book with text by Osbert Sitwell, who had seen her drawings on
show at Claridge's gallery in July, and proposed they work together
on a subject of Nina's choosing. *The People's Album of London Statues*
was one of the first books Tony saw through the press from start to
finish. Delivering her completed batch of drawings long before her
co-author got round to producing words to go with them, Nina suggested drawing Tony too. He sat for her in a squalid rented studio
in Thackeray House (named for the novelist, who set part of *The*

Newcomes in the studio above Nina's) at 35, Maple Street, just south of Fitzroy Square. Tony was twenty-two to Nina's thirty-eight years old at the start of their affair. She opened the door to a milieu he had so far only read about in novels of romantic bohemian poverty. When Nina complained of mice in her studio, a friend advised her to skin and eat them. She introduced her new young man to favourite pubs, the Fitzroy Tavern, and the Plough in Museum Street, where an Oxford contemporary, Peter Quennell, was amused to find Nina exuberantly drunk with Tony sitting shyly by her side. Alcohol, which would eventually claim her for its own, was already beginning to limit her concentration and restrict the quantity if not the quality of her work.

But Nina's magnetic personality was one of the key factors that popularized this run-down area north of Soho as an alternative to Chelsea. Fitzrovia, bounded on the west by Fitzroy and Charlotte streets, would be home territory for Tony's generation long after he left Nina. For the moment she was still in her prime: sleek, debonair and purposeful, riding high on sales from two successive London shows, categorized by bewildered gossip columnists as a dashing if decidedly risqué young thing, and admired by fellow artists for what Augustus John called "her light, savant and malicious touch," the equivalent in graphic terms of Tony's ironic wit. He was largely responsible at any rate initially for her transfer of headquarters from France to England in the course of their affair. His reserve suited her extroversion. Something about her imperturbable young publisher detained Nina long after the *People's Album* was eventually published in the autumn of 1928. "It seems that Nina Hamnett . . . remains in England," Aleister Crowley wrote crossly the year after, "on account of a young man who is employed in an important position with Duckworth the publisher."

Involvement with Nina—"a liberal education" in the words of Alec Waugh—was precisely what Tony needed at this stage. She was a regular at Collins's Music Hall, and at the Comrades Hall in Camden Town on Sunday afternoons to watch the kind of boxing match he later described in detail in his first novel ("Finding a way of killing Sunday afternoons is half the battle," said Nina, whose conventional upbringing had left her with a dread of stagnation and inertia). She introduced him to old friends up and down the social spectrum from the ethnographer T. A. Joyce at the British Museum to the Comte de Malleissy, a virtually destitute French aristocrat and opium addict of great charm and disruptive potential, staying at the Cavendish with his pet monkey and his Pekinese. One night Nina and Tony dined at the Savoy with Rosa from the Cavendish as guests of an American millionaire, who tipped the cloakroom attendant with a £5 note (well over £100 today).

Nina recommended Tony to her friend and rival Betty May, whose memoir, *Tiger Woman*, he published with considerable success in spite of Balston's well-justified misgiving. A favourite model of Augustus John and Jacob Epstein, Betty was a tiny tough East Ender with the dramatic looks of a gypsy doll and a ferocious temper masked by an air of melting sweetness. She had served her time in the criminal as well as artistic underworlds of London and Paris, but it was her public feud with Crowley, the Great Beast himself, that brought her fame and fortune. She had married in 1922 as her third husband a brilliant boy called Raoul Loveday, newly graduated with a First in history from Oxford when he met Crowley, who offered him a secretarial post. The Lovedays travelled out to join the new community set up in Sicily to further Crowley's cult of sex, drugs and his own supremacy as leader. Raoul, formerly known as Fred, had been a popular secretary of the Hypocrites, whose members (among them Alfred Duggan) were on the point of setting out to rescue him from the lair of the Great Beast when news came that he had died suddenly not long after his arrival. Rumour said Crowley had sacrificed or strangled him. By Betty's scarcely less sensational account, her young husband had in fact been forced to perform the ritual killing of a cat, and afterwards to drink its blood, a shock so great that he collapsed a few days later, drinking water from a polluted stream and dying of enteric fever.

The ensuing scandal gave Crowley for the first time what he craved, a national and international reputation for depravity. Labelled the Wickedest Man in the World by the right-wing magazine *John Bull*, he was enthusiastically built up by the press with the aid of Betty's revelations as a cannibalistic, sex-and-drug-addicted monster of perversion. Loveday's fate and other lurid episodes recounted with knockabout gusto in *Tiger Woman* (largely ghosted by an obliging journalist called Bernard in collaboration with Tony) marked a startling new departure for Duckworths' list. It also put a certain strain on both sides. No stranger to violence and intimidation, more than capable as Tony said of handling artists, addicts, gangsters and necromancers, Betty met her match in Duckworths' misogynist managing director, Mr. Lewis, himself no doubt equally alarmed by her. "Please, please, never, *never*, make me talk to that *thin* man again," she begged Tony: "I fear him. I *fear* him!"

In 1928 Tony seriously considered commissioning a novel from Crowley himself, perhaps a sequel to his *Diary of a Drug Fiend*, only to be flatly overruled by Balston. "We are taking no risks," Tony reported to Henry, "& I am looking forward with some pleasure to seeing Jonathan Cape & Victor Gollancz turned into guinea pigs or homunculi, after some difference of opinion about royalties." Crowley promptly offered his memoirs instead. "This sounds the sort of rubbish which should sell," wrote Henry helpfully, adding that the outraged proprietor of the *Daily Express*, Lord Beaverbrook, threatened a personal vendetta: "A campaign by Beaverbrook might be the making of the old man's memoirs, on the other hand it might be the end of the firm which published it. You will know which . . ." Balston declined to bet on Duckworths' future, and turned down this offer too.

Crowley's next move was to invite Tony to lunch with him at Simpson's in the Strand. Loveday was by no means the only bright boy from Oxford or Cambridge to be flattered and intrigued by the offer of a job over lunch with Crowley. Other recent candidates included Tony's Oxford contemporary Tom Driberg, and Henry's older brother, Gerald Yorke, who had been Tony's contact in dealings over the memoirs. Crowley told each of them (as he had told Loveday) that he was looking for someone to take over as his magical heir. Driberg pocketed the drugs Crowley supplied as sweeteners, but had sense enough to reject his proposition ("the wildest stories . . . circulated . . . some may have been spread by himself to frighten those in the strange, closed, credulous world of occultism who had crossed him"). Gerald, who had left Cambridge with the best degree in an outstanding year, accepted with alacrity the post of Crowley's official agent, which turned out to mean in practice his minder, his go-between in negotiations with Scotland Yard and the Home Office over a possible return to England, above all his fundraiser and principal backer.

For four years Gerald poured his family's money into Crowley's bank account. He arranged an annual income, stumping up £800 (well over £20,000 today) out of his own pocket to pay for publication of *Magick in Theory and Practice* and, when Tony could not be won over, a further £1,000 to bring out the first two of six volumes of *Confessions*. Henry endlessly discussed his infatuated brother with Tony, both of them worrying away like a couple of disapproving elderly aunts, exchanging notes on symptoms, proposing strategies and predicting madness for "poor Gerald," who cut loose from Crowley in the end at considerable emotional as well as financial cost to himself. A succession of young secretaries who failed to get away all came to more or less miserable ends (Loveday's successor, Norman Mudd, eventually killed himself).

Primed in occult lore from childhood by his mother, Tony not only accepted Crowley's luncheon invitation but looked forward to returning the correct ritual response ("Love is the Law, Love under Will") to his host's expected greeting: "Do what thou wilt shall be the whole of the Law." To his disappointment the Great Beast turned up in a shabby brown suit and grey homburg hat in place of necromancer's gear, projecting an aura of bleak and brutal authority purely by the chill force of his personality. He seemed more grotesque than awesome with mottled yellow skin stretched taut over a massive, misshapen bald skull and clownlike features, "strangely caught together within the middle of a large elliptical area, like those of a horrible baby." Something about Tony's alertness (he was, perhaps unconsciously, storing material at this meeting that would come back to him half a century later when he wrote the final volume of the *Dance*) put Crowley on his guard. Whatever his original intention, he thought better of it, offering no explanation for his summons beyond a rambling rigmarole about "the hard life of a mage, its difficulties and disappointments, especially in relation to the unkindness and backbiting of fellow magicians." What had clearly been intended as an exploratory lunch led nowhere, nor did Duckworths have any further dealings with the Great Beast.

If Tony's wilder schemes for livening up the list fell through, one of his earliest and most ambitious coups was to bring out at intervals over two years the collected works of Ronald Firbank: ten slim, eye-catching, unmistakeably contemporary volumes known as the Rainbow Edition because each was bound in a different, brightly coloured cloth. Although Duckworths could have sold twice as many copies as they were prepared to print, Tony had secured agreement in the first place only because costs were covered by a bequest in the author's will. But Firbank represented as far towards modernity as the firm could bring itself to go. Tony put out feelers towards several of his most remarkable contemporaries, few of whom at that stage could meet Balston's criterion of popularity without risk. Robert Byron caused such ructions over his first book ("they do not like or understand the book," he complained furiously to his mother: "It shall come out only over my dead body") that Balston gave up editing it, and *The Station: Mount Athos: Treasures & Men* appeared towards the end of 1928 with a touching dedication: "For Tony with bitter remorse for his sufferings—Robert."

Tony brought out his own first published work at the same time. *Barnard Letters 1778–1824* is a collection of lively, gossipy family correspondence that he came across through a descendant called Rosamond Barnard, "a rather amusing young woman . . . with a singularly obscene mind." Editing her manuscript helped fill the many empty hours of his apprenticeship at Duckworths, and he planned to follow it up with a book about Stendhal, who had a powerful grip on him at this point: a project soon abandoned, surviving only vaguely in his fifth novel as the narrator's unwritten thesis, *Stendhal, and Some Reflections on Violence*. He read Lermontov's *A Hero of Our Time* for the first time this year in a new translation by Reginald Merton, and was so overwhelmed by something he never fully managed to pin down that he immediately re-read the whole book twice more, becoming increasingly mesmerized by its ambitious scope and extraordinary clarity. Looking back afterwards at the end of his long career, he would recognize Lermontov as the strongest single influence on him as a writer.

He started a diary, and swiftly abandoned that too. At some point he began pasting bits and pieces into a scrapbook called *Dream Memories*. It opens with a surrealistic title page—faded family photos and Boer war mementoes caught up in a patchwork of wildly disparate images—and builds to climactic end-papers: a sensuous riot in sober colours of rococo lovers enlaced in pairs and threesomes, ripping off shirts, bodices and garters, writhing bodies and flailing limbs emerging from or subsiding into waves, draperies and bowers. Hunting and drinking scenes by Tony's great-grandfather Adcock (see Chapter 1, p. 5) alternate on the intervening pages with exuberant, eighteenth-century sexy pictures apparently collected by Major Powell. The first faint outlines of the kind of pattern traced later in the *Dance* go back to the jostling mob of strangely juxtaposed material in *Dream Memories*: jowly men and plump cushiony beauties, the meaty male images that dominated Tony's Edwardian childhood, interspersed at intervals with his own lively adult sketches of dashing, skinny little figures, diminutive observers, early prototypes of the narrator of the *Dance*, watching attentively from the sidelines.

Novels now interested him analytically, rather than for their characters or stories. He was thrilled on re-reading Wyndham Lewis's *Tarr* by "his luminous brutal prose, blocked in with a painter's eye," and correspondingly bored by the conventional plotting of James Joyce's *Ulysses* (he had to smuggle a copy back from Paris because the book was still banned as obscene in England in 1928). He re-read Hemingway's *The Sun Also Rises* and realized that it changed for ever the way novelists use dialogue, a naturalistic revolution already pioneered by Chekhov, and at the opposite extreme by Firbank: "purposeless exchanges that are their own purpose, on account . . . of an undercurrent of innuendo and irony." Most electrifying of all was E. E. Cummings, whose novel *The Enormous Room*, about life in a military prison in France in the First World War, made even Aldous Huxley and Norman Douglas seem out of date. "*The Enormous Room* seemed infinitely strange . . . an extraordinary mixture of violence, humour and moving observation," he wrote of the revelation that knocked him sideways when the book first came out in England in 1928: "Cummings really opened my eyes to the new demotic style of writing . . ."

New writing increasingly preoccupied Tony, but publishing it was uphill work. He would eventually build up a strong contingent from his own generation in spite of Balston's innate caution and Gerald Duckworth's unconditional resistance, which made it almost impossible at first to recruit unknown talent. The rising stars he recommended were regularly snapped up by other publishers, starting with Henry Green, whose *Blindness* had been rejected by Balston even before Tony joined the firm. The manuscript of Evelyn Waugh's *Decline and*

Fall, delivered as work in progress chapter by chapter to Tony (who found it extremely funny), was also turned down by Balston in 1928, ostensibly because the author declined to make changes to his text. In fact the reason was that Gerald Duckworth's niece, Evelyn Gardner, had infuriated her aristocratic family that summer by secretly marrying the author, at that point a penniless young carpenter with no family connections and no apparent prospect of ever earning a serious living. Tony, who had got to know and like Evelyn Gardner in the months when Waugh was courting her, commissioned a novel from her flatmate, Pansy Pakenham, and another from Pansy's sister Mary. Waugh's own novel, published later the same year by his father at Chapman and Hall, was an immediate hit ("For Tom Balston," he wrote sweetly in a presentation copy, "the stone that the builder rejected"). So was Antonia White's *Frost in May*, another manuscript Tony tried and failed to smuggle past his superiors.

One of the few finds Balston thoroughly approved was a friend Tony met through Waugh, a beautiful and brilliantly funny young journalist on the *Daily Express* called Inez Holden. Duckworths published her first novel, *Sweet Charlatan*, followed by *Born Old, Died Young*, a scathing indictment of the world she came from with herself as the hard-boiled, unsentimental, resolutely post-war heroine maltreated by her aristocratic mother, a heavy-drinking, horse-riding Edwardian beauty of considerable wealth and relentless egotism. "We were at the Holdens the other day," Evelyn wrote to Tony, "& Mrs. Holden asked how Inez was & I said rather ill last time I saw her & living on cachets de Faivre. Mrs. Holden said 'I don't think I know the de Faivres.'" Inez was a drop-out long before it was fashionable to be one, living on her wits and charm, always desperately hard up, excellent company and a first-rate gossip whose stories, though perfectly true, became weird and fantastical as she told them. An adventuress like the heroine of her novel, she was probably the first girl Tony came across to embody in fact a type he would re-create in fiction with particular relish ever afterwards, "the sort of woman who, if she had been taken in adultery, would have caught the first stone and thrown it back."

She had wangled her way on to Duckworths' list by bewitching Balston, "a nature altogether unused to adventuresses," said Tony: "It would not be going too far to say that for a time she made hay of him." Inez would cut a dashing figure as one of the models for Roberta Payne in Tony's fifth novel, *What's Become of Waring*, a book about a publishing house that might be said to have made hay of the Duckworth office and its personnel. Balston himself modelled for Roberta's slavish suitor, Hugh Judkins, a deeply repressed ex-school-teacher struggling to regenerate the ailing firm of Judkins & Judkins. "I must not be misunderstood, of course, when I say I have known him well . . . ," wrote Edith Sitwell, another of Duckworths' authors, congratulating Tony when the book came out: "I know those sudden bursts of temper and argumentativeness, the laugh, and the feeling of a blackboard as spiritual background."

Edith had a special relationship with Balston. She and her two brothers marked his first and most dramatic publishing coup in 1926, when he had swooped down on all three of them on holiday in Italy, seizing his chance to cut out their previous publisher by signing them up on the spot. At the time they represented the exuberant public face of contemporary writing, and a signal defeat for Gerald Duckworth. Edith was in her fortieth year and her brothers in their thirties but they were still by far the youngest authors on Duckworths' list, and for almost a decade Balston brought out nearly everything they wrote. "Every time the public thought they had vanished from sight they popped up again," wrote Nina Hamnett, who came between Edith and Osbert in age: "new poems, new books. They were like corks floating; every time you tried to push them down they came up and floated on the surface."

Like the rest of literary and artistic London, she had watched their post-war transformation into a kind of triplicate celebrity with fingers in every pie, unpredictable and irreverent, radiating energy and high spirits, promoting feud and vendetta for the hell of it. "They exult in a scrap," said Arnold Bennett: "Battle is in the curve of their nostrils." No aesthetic controversy, cutting-edge concert, first night or book launch was complete without the Sitwells dressed in eye-catching outfits under identical black capes and high Spanish hats, "tall fair attenuated courtiers from a mediaeval tapestry," said Tony, himself by this time a cog in the Sitwell publicity machine.

He liked them all, especially Edith, who was an old friend of Nina's, and Osbert, who had unwittingly initiated his young editor's affair with her, and presided benignly over it ("Give my love to Nina

should you see her. It's a lovely book," Osbert wrote from Italy when the *People's Album* came out with a highly successful launch at Tooth's gallery in November 1928). The Sitwells' relentless self-promotion was matched by the kindness and imaginative encouragement they gave a younger generation starting out immediately after them on the same stony path. They had invited Tony that summer to a wildly dysfunctional house party at Renishaw, their long dark crenellated house in Derbyshire built directly over the coal-pits that provided the family fortune. An elaborate system of terraces and topiary gardens, lit at night by flares from the mine and the glare from local iron-smelting furnaces, was currently under demolition as part of their father's unending programme of renovation. Sir George Sitwell, who looked and acted like a Renaissance tyrant, had given his life to gran-diose building schemes on the one hand, and tormenting his children ("after us like a fox after chickens," said Edith) on the other.

Tension and disturbance ran beneath the surface of this large and lively house party. Tony put the shadows in the background down to Sir George's scandalous treatment of his wife, Lady Ida, who had fallen into the hands of swindlers after running up large debts that her husband refused to settle, even when she was tried for non-payment in 1915 and sentenced to three months in prison, after which she took to drink. Sir George, who was teetotal, banned alcohol from the house. As adults the children reversed their roles, mocking their father relentlessly behind his back and taunting him at mealtimes to his face. Tony, still a diffident twenty-two-year-old, was reduced by his host to uncontrollable nervous laughter. Edwin Lutyens, another Sitwell guest in the summer of 1928, said it was like living on a volcano. Georgia Sitwell, married to Sacheverell, the youngest and least flamboyant sibling, made things worse by dismissing Tony as a kind of upper servant—"a colourless young man with some humour who is employed by Duckworths"—and insisting there was no room for him when the car came to collect guests for sightseeing. Always peculiarly attuned to mad and malevolent fathers, Tony later came to think that the Sitwells' tendency to reinvent Sir George as a comic monster played down the extent of his actual derangement.

It was at Renishaw this summer, with the whole family assembled for a month to entertain guests and snipe at their father, that Edith wrote her macabre and sonorous poem "Gold Coast Customs." Its Ashanti setting came from a visit to the British Museum with Nina, whose friend Thomas Joyce brought out masks and totems from the ethnographical collections. The poem's incantatory rhythms, combining jazz syncopation with a steady undertow of drums, surge and recede like the sea bearing flotsam on its swell: scraps of African imagery, memories of jobless workers on contemporary London streets and hunger marchers the year before, compounded by a personal bitterness still so raw that, when Edith read her new work aloud to selected guests, she broke down in tears. "Among the writings of the three, hers make pain the most explicit," wrote Tony, "Gold Coast Customs especially conveying a sense of horror and squalor that recalls Hood." He was moved and impressed by Edith, who always responded enthusiastically to the company of bright young men. "I wish you were not going today," she wrote when he left Renishaw: "It has been great fun, your being here."

Duckworths published *Gold Coast Customs* the following January, with Tony supervising production. The Sitwells lent the firm a prestige out of all proportion to the minimal sums their books brought in. Osbert, whose income ranged from £1,500 to £2,000 a year in the late 1920s and '30s, earned less than £50 of it from poetry. He entertained young writers, artists and composers to lavish dinners at the house he shared with Sacheverell in Chelsea, keeping an excellent cellar, first-rate cook and Jeevesian manservant ("just the bare luxuries of life, not its necessities" was Osbert's motto). Edith, who lived on an allowance considered more appropriate to her sex of £100 a year, provided tea and buns at her small shabby flat in unfashionable Bayswater. Both were exceptionally generous and insatiably demanding friends, especially to their publishers. Edith took tea, dined and went to parties with Balston, who was tirelessly attentive, returning her long chatty letters, exchanging family histories and personal confidences, reading every word she wrote, and responding with patience and tact even when refusing her most importunate demands.

Osbert did business with Balston but, like his sister, relished Tony's company. He liked to spend much of the day at Duckworths in the run-up to a book, swapping jokes and gossip, keeping a disgruntled eye on rival authors, grumbling furiously about their superior treatment, bigger advances and better-looking books. Osbert "could feel competitive about the most insignificant of writers," said Tony, thinking of Osbert's particular bugbear, Godfrey Winn, just twenty-two years old when Duckworths brought out his first novel in 1928, and already a rival in the publicity stakes while clocking up far larger sales. Like Shirley Handsworth in *What's Become of Waring*, Winn was the rising star of the women's list, prolific, touchy, on the make, a specialist in dishevelled boyishness with doggy eyes and a permanent set smile.

His winsome portrait filled the dust jacket of *Dreams Fade*, bound in grey linen with gold lettering (Osbert's first novel, *Before the Bombardment* in 1926, had run-of-the-mill red cloth binding with the title in drab black). At the New Year Tony wrote to warn Osbert, wintering at the Hotel Cappucini Convent in Amalfi, that Winn was planning to work on his second novel in the same hotel on Balston's advice. "If I had not known I might very well have been carried up to heaven in the chariot of my own fire," wrote Osbert, preparing a chill reception ("An atmosphere as of an unseen hip-bath of cold water about to fall"). After a long campaign of slight and stand-off, Winn eventually left with his completed novel ("at least 800 pages long," Osbert reported cattily: "Tom ought to be delighted").

He himself was having trouble with bankers and lawyers. "Each set frightens the other about my affairs, and then charges me for it," he told Tony, adding cheerfully: "My father has been ill, and I am just writing to him to say I have been offered a Labour peerage." Presumably the problem worrying Osbert's lawyers was his next book, *Dumb-Animal & Other Stories*, dedicated when it came out in 1930,

"For dear Tony, who always does his plucky worst under adverse circumstances, from Osbert Sitwell." The circumstances could hardly have been trickier in this case, since the book, based entirely on real people, provoked a disastrous libel suit, settled only when Duckworths agreed to recall all library copies, pulp the remainder, and lend Osbert the money to pay damages and costs. Balston was keen to hang on to the Sitwells, who were becoming steadily more restive on account of measly pay and even measlier print runs. They had two assets he could not afford to lose: the conviction and panache of a triune performance that mesmerized the public, however reluctant it might be to buy their books in bulk; and their invaluable ability to spot the potential of young writers and musicians, sometimes almost before they were fully aware of it themselves.

Constant Lambert, Tony's exact contemporary and for the next twenty years his closest friend, was one of them. A boy of precocious brilliance and slender faun-like beauty, he had been Osbert's protegé even before he won a scholarship at seventeen to the Royal College of Music, and was commissioned at nineteen by Serge Diaghilev to write a ballet score. Brought up in south London, son of an Australian painter born in St. Petersburg, he had been gravely ill as a child, emerging after many years bedridden with a damaged foot, a perforated eardrum and a passion for life, "preferably in a form twice as large and six times as outrageous." He educated himself musically as a schoolboy at the London Proms, and found his bearings in contemporary literature through *Wheels*, the magazine edited by Edith Sitwell. "At seventeen or even earlier he had the mind and interests of a well-informed adult," said Michael Stewart, a contemporary at Christ's Hospital (and later foreign secretary).

While Tony was still at school, Constant had made friends with the Sitwells, worked with Diaghilev in Monte Carlo and Paris, published his first articles in the London press, made his first radio broadcast and become a public performer with a reputation for innovation and iconoclasm in the avant-garde art world. In 1926 Edith invited him to share the narration at the triumphant second showing of *Façade* (which she dedicated to him), a sequence of poems delivered through a megaphone at the Chenil Galleries with music by the Sitwells' other schoolboy prodigy, William Walton. Diaghilev's *Romeo and Juliet* set to Lambert's music provoked a surrealist riot the same year, afterwards playing to packed houses in Paris and the West End. By the time he and Tony finally met in a London pub the following autumn, Lambert had become, with Walton, one of the country's two outstanding young composers. Tony asked him for a musical contribution to an anthology of young movers and shakers, a book (eventually abandoned by Duckworths) that marked the start of their lifelong friendship.

They were both twenty-one years old. Voracious and sophisticated readers, individualistic and discerning, allergic to pretension, neither quite managing to fit in with the majority of their contemporaries, each responded to something deeply congenial in the other. "Lambert was the first contemporary of mine I found, intellectually speaking, wholly sympathetic," Tony said in retrospect. They came from very different disciplines—Tony was intrinsically unmusical—but they shared a practitioner's attitude to the arts, at once pragmatic and exacting, at the opposite extreme from the aesthetes of Tony's Oxford generation ("With them there seemed always an amateurishness, a narrowness of view, a way of treating the arts as if they were a useful social weapon"). Tony and Constant were more at home with the prosaic bar-crawlers of Fitzrovia than with Bloomsbury and its ethos, which seemed to them, as to many of their contemporaries, "no less elderly, stuffy, anxious to put the stopper on rising talent, than the staunchly anti-avant-garde Duckworths." Constant was as passionately interested as Tony in other people, an accomplished mimic and first-class raconteur, full of stories about the Sitwells ("Sir George is the strangest old bugger you ever met," their butler told him confidentially, "and as for poor old Ida, she doesn't know whether she's coming or going"), and his own fractious relationship with Diaghilev (the two disagreed on everything from surrealist ballet decor to the Russian's trick of welcoming guests with "Will you have one drink?," a greeting that as Lambert said "always got the evening off to a bad start").

There was something magical about Constant. "He carried about with him the aura of a conjuror," according to his second wife, and already as a young man he generated a repertoire of tall tales among friends and acquaintances bemused by his exotic background

MR CAN + MR CANT

Tony with Constant Lambert: "He carried
about with him the aura of a conjuror."

and multiple talents. He claimed to be "the only francophil English
composer from St. Petersburg who worked on the Trans-Siberian
railway, who himself can play 'God Save the King' literally by ear"
(Constant's characteristically dangerous party trick was to hold his
nose and play tunes by forcing his breath through his punctured eardrum). He was beginning to thicken out at this stage, drinking more
and developing a pronounced limp, which did not prevent him and
Tony talking for hours on end on marathon walks all over London.
In the evenings they carried on talking in pubs, or dropped in on the
music hall at the old Shaftesbury Theatre, where Tony became a regular for a time. One of their longest walks ended up on the Thames at
Wapping in the bar of the Prospect of Whitby, a favourite pub with
Nina, who had been a student of Constant's father, George Lambert
("the best professor I have ever had," she said). She shared his love
of Victorian melodrama, organizing a party to watch a revival of *The
Executioner's Daughter* from two stage boxes at Collins's Music Hall

where the murderous villain was mesmerized by Constant, shoving his black head with big bushy mustachios into the box to glare at him from fiery eyes in close-up.

Perhaps it was through Nina that Tony first met Constant. It was certainly Nina who introduced him to Adrian Daintrey, the hard-up young painter who rented the next studio to hers in the shabby house on Maple Street where Tony had once sat for his portrait. Daintrey, who had known and disliked Nina in Paris, resented what he thought of as her patronizing manner, a resistance intensified by the fact that he could not conceal from her experienced eye how urgently he needed money at this point. A solicitor's son, educated at Charter-house, he had given up all prospect of a regular job on the strength of his first show with Paul Nash in 1928 at a chic but short-lived gallery lined with coffee-coloured velvet on Maddox Street. Its owner was Dorothy Warren, a niece of Ottoline Morrell, charming, stylish, inexperienced and experimental (she caused outrage the year after by showing D. H. Lawrence's erotic paintings). Daintrey's was her first show, and he characteristically improved the situation by sleeping with her. "I take women as I find them," runs one of many remarks clearly made by Daintrey in the early pages of Tony's notebook, "the latter is usually more difficult to achieve than the former."

In this as in much else, he modelled himself on Augustus John. Astute and discriminating, a shrewd judge of both people and paintings, Daintrey never in the end consolidated his own ambition as an artist, seeming content with an undemanding, hand-to-mouth career aimed at nothing much beyond sub-Impressionist oil sketches of London streets and a handful of portraits for quick sale to rich clients. An accomplished serial womanizer, often combining business with pleasure, his finances remained at best precarious. Henry Yorke never forgot being frogmarched by Nina into Daintrey's studio with a view to buying a drawing, an episode that would resurface along with much else Tony first encountered through Nina in his fourth novel, *Agents and Patients*.

Daintrey's spontaneous wit and worldliness, his pithy and peremptory speech, the imperturbable manner he had evolved early to cope with all eventualities, were precisely what Tony needed at this point. The world represented by Daintrey and Lambert released him for ever from the "eternity of boredom" that had yawned before him on leaving Oxford. He spent hours gossiping in Daintrey's studio, comparing notes on people as much as painting, surrounded by a companionable clutter of canvases stacked against the walls with brushes, paint pots, unwashed glasses and half-drunk bottles of wine littering every available surface. Successive studios over the next fifty years remained the same in the smallest particular, all of them based, like Daintrey's dress and outlook, on a bohemian era slightly before his own.

He shared both Lambert's love of France and his practical, workmanlike approach to the arts. Tony spent a Christmas holiday walking the streets of Paris with Lambert, and an Easter break with Daintrey exploring the painters' territory around Le Havre in Normandy. At Daintrey's insistence they sampled sailors' brothels, and were taken aback by the priggishness of the other customers. It was one of several tests Tony had to pass, starting on their first night in a cheap French hotel when "Daintrey suddenly rapped out, 'What do you think of Bonnard?' 'I like his pictures very much.' 'I'm glad about that,' said Daintrey. 'Otherwise I don't think we could have continued the trip together.'" That night they dined, again by Daintrey's demand, at the Ferme Saint-Simon, once a simple hostelry selling basic meals to Impressionists, long since overrun by tourists prepared to pay astronomical prices for gourmet spreads with leather-bound menus handwritten on parchment: "These we studied with sinking hearts. There was a long pause. Daintrey said: 'You ought never to have allowed me to come here.'"

Daintrey was the first of many painters of Tony's own generation with whom he felt instantly at home as he had with Nina's friends, especially the English surrealist, in some ways more of a post-war punk, John Banting. Tony became a familiar figure at their raffish parties in and around Charlotte Street. The crowd he met there was a subsection of the horde of party-goers who turned up night after night, in fancy dress as often as not, at private houses and in the countless ephemeral little nightclubs springing up all over London where you could dance the Charleston and the Black Bottom, or simply sway slowly from side to side on tiny close-packed dance floors. "The band should be coloured, the room dark," wrote Henry Yorke, who said he found it impossible to go longer than a week without the "sort of blood transfusion" represented by well-played dance music.

At first Tony combined attending deb dances with the other kind of party, sometimes changing into white tie and tails halfway through the evening so as to commute straight from one world to the other. Outmoded and inflexible, hard going as he often found it, the hierarchy of the ballroom had taught him much: "I do not regret (from a writer's point of view) having served my turn there," he wrote later. At the time, he moved with alacrity into the peculiar underworld inhabited by painters, writers, poets and performers, a scavenging crowd initially as hard to penetrate as the debs' lists. Many of them congregated after hours at the Varda Bookshop on the ground floor of Constant's lodgings at 189, High Holborn, "a Comus-like rout," according to Peter Quennell, who found evenings at the bookshop altogether too strenuous. "The party that followed, with occasional expeditions to lively Soho pubs, often lasted till the small hours; a homeless guest . . . could sometimes be discovered next morning fast asleep among the bookshelves."

Quennell soon left to be succeeded in his rooms on the top floor by Nina, shortly before or soon after she finally parted company with Tony in the winter or early spring of 1929. After a loose and by her standards uncommonly long attachment, she took a young black boxer as her lover and started work on a book of her own, the observant energetic painter's memoirs, *Laughing Torso*, eventually published by Constable. In a sense it was Tony's parting gift. She had given him both pride and pleasure ("He built her up as a romantic *femme de trente ans*, a Bohemian mistress," said Quennell), launching him in the process on a course from which he never again deviated. Their affair was one of several loose ends tied off that spring. "Just a line to tell you that my engagement to Dig comes out on Monday," Henry wrote on 18 April after a long silence, adding as a postscript: "I hear you don't approve." It had always been understood between them that Henry was Mary's suitor and, although Tony could never have been seriously in the running for either sister, this offhand letter dealt a blow, perhaps more on account of his old friend's treachery than Dig's defection.

Henry's second novel, *Living*, was about to come out, and a further postscript to his letter announced a reissue of *Blindness* in a new popular edition. Evelyn Waugh, capitalizing on the huge success of *Decline and Fall*, had nearly finished *Vile Bodies* (an even more rapturously received bestseller on publication nine months later). That spring Tony could no longer put off a decision that had been creeping up on him for some time. When the house in Shepherd Street came so near collapse that a second massive wooden bulwark had to be erected in his tiny living room, he found a basement flat at 33, Tavistock Square on the outskirts of Fitzrovia. He signed a three-year lease on three small empty rooms at an annual rent of £110, roughly a third of his income, and furnished them with bare necessities borrowed or bought from junk shops. "*Barnard Letters* out of the way, the basement more or less habitable, I took a firm hold on the question of what sort of a novel was to be written—an extension of that enigma—in what style?"

The style he finally settled for was what he called urban pastoral, and this first novel came to seem to him in retrospect a dry run for the *Dance*. He saw its theme as unrequited love, although when he first started he had barely set eyes on, let alone been turned down by, the girl who would disrupt his life and haunt his work long after their ways had parted. He met her at a Chelsea party soon after he moved to Tavistock Square. Her name was Enid Firminger, and he fell deeply in love with her at sight. She was small, white-skinned and slender with dark eyes in a perfect oval face, short sleek dark hair, and an air of almost childish innocence combined with innate sophistication. A former student at the Slade a year or two ahead of Daintrey, Enid knew many painters and had been a close friend from childhood of Freddie Mayor, well known for his convivial parties in Cork Street, where his gallery was fast becoming one of the few places in London to see avant-garde English and French art. Freddie was a lifelong gambler, encouraged as a boy by Enid's father, James Poole, himself a racing man forced to throw up everything and leave the country after a betting scandal. Enid and her younger sister Joanne grew up as wards of their mother's second husband, a successful businessman called Reginald Firminger, who turned out to have been a husband in name only when he left the girls' mother to marry a younger woman in 1923. Their mother died a year later and the two girls left home, aged twenty and fifteen years old, taking with them only a suitcase each, to make what they could of the future on their own.

Both were exceptionally good-looking. Enid, generous, poised and protective of her younger sister, was the more stable and by far

Enid Firminger, the girl who disrupted Tony's life and haunted his work

the more practical of the two. She had studied piano under Gustav Holst at St. Paul's Girls' School, and shown considerable talent as a painter. Now that she had to earn a living, she became a top model for magazines like *Vanity Fair*, and for both French and English *Vogue*. Enid was easily the loveliest of the famous model pool of girls who congregated with artists at Maresfield, the hospitable country home of the painter Edward Wadsworth. A favourite with *Vogue*'s house photographer, Maurice Beck, she posed with Joanne for his *Danseuses*, an art deco frieze of two lithe leaping nudes exhibited at the first Salon International du Nu Photographique in Paris. The two Firmingers embodied, indeed helped to create, the 1920s fashion for cool, self-possessed girls, swan-necked and long-waisted with shingled hair and smooth streamlined silhouettes. There was never any shortage of eligible young men competing for Enid's attention. One who hoped to marry her—probably Jimmy Patino, heir to a Bolivian tin mine—wooed her with a racing car so she could try out the newly opened Grand Prix circuit at Brooklands in Surrey.

When Tony met her at the end of the 1920s she was the presiding girlfriend of the fastidious Dick Wyndham, a painter and prodigious party-giver who had inherited Clouds, the Wyndhams' great house in Wiltshire. Joanne's lover was Tristram Hillier, a banker's son turned painter currently studying in Paris. The two sisters, both very much at home on the Parisian Left Bank, made their London headquarters in a flat at 243, King's Road, entertaining friends in an atmosphere more like a French *salon* than a standard Chelsea party. Osbert Sitwell, who knew them both, told a story of one scruffy young literary type saying to another, as they walked down the King's Road, that the two prettiest girls in London lived on the top floor of number 243, and he hadn't a hope of meeting either. The types in Sitwell's story were Peter Quennell and Cyril Connolly, both rising stars of literary London, but neither remotely eligible in King's Road terms.

Nor was Tony. Whether or not he actually took her out to dinner, Enid, who could not enter a room or a restaurant without turning heads, would have produced much the same effect as Susan Nunnery, the unattainable heroine of his first novel, *Afternoon Men*, on a first date with that book's central character: "He hoped that lots more people would come and sit at the table and talk and drink and make assignations with Susan and give him good advice and argue with each other, because then it would become funny, and he might be less angry." For at least a year their affair remained tenuous and problematic, ending presumably with something like the real or imagined exchange at a boxing match in *Afternoon Men*, when the hero's half-hearted comments on substandard bouts gradually lend momentum to Susan's sad, reluctant, realistic insistence that for all their mutual attraction their affair has no future. "Fear has much in common with jealousy in the sudden violent unexpected realization that you are not loved by someone you adore," Tony wrote in his notebook. Enid caused him perhaps for the first time the stabbing jealousy that seemed to him ever afterwards the most fearful of all emotions. "A most violent passion it is where it taketh place," wrote Burton in his *Anatomy of Melancholy*, "an unspeakable torment, a hellish torture, an infernal plague, as Ariosto calls it." One of Tony's distractions in 1929 was a joint party he gave with Lambert in the last week of June at Tavistock Square, lasting from six o'clock in the evening until three the next morning. They asked new friends and old, Constant bringing in musicians and Tony a fair sample of the book world. A strong contingent of painters included Lambert's friend Edward Burra and another former art student turned dancer, William Chappell, with the future choreographer Fred Ashton. The two young Waughs, who had been to all appearances happily married for exactly twelve months, arrived separately and left early. Tony had met a contemporary called John Heygate at their flat earlier in the year, and asked him to the party without noticing that he was on the brink of an affair with young Mrs. Waugh.

She and Heygate had a lovers' tiff that evening and, running across each other again by chance later the same night, made it up over dinner at Boulestin's. Two weeks later Tony left London on a motoring holiday in Germany with Heygate, again without apparently realizing that the night of his party had marked a stage of no return in the break-up of the Waughs' marriage. The trip was disrupted in Munich by a telegram from the wife asking Tony to send John back to London. Heygate set out at once, anticipating a confrontation with the angry husband and taking the precaution of buying a revolver on the way. Tony finished his holiday alone, and realized with surprise when he got back that the first person to spot signs of strain between the Waughs had been Tom Balston.

By this time Tony himself had tacitly abandoned publishing as anything more than a useful day job. His three-year probationary period with Duckworths ran out that autumn. The original agreement between his father and Balston had stipulated a subsistence income of £300 for Tony to be paid over three years in a decreasing ratio by Lieutenant Colonel Powell (like all army officers, he took automatic promotion on retirement), who agreed to invest sufficient capital at the end to make his son a partner in the firm. In the event no money was forthcoming, and no explanation was given either. Perhaps the wreckage of his own career made Tony's father feel he had a right to ruin his son's too, or perhaps he simply could not bring himself to offer a leg-up to a former subordinate. This was a completely unexpected blow from Duckworths' point of view. When an incredulous Balston finally grasped the trick that had been played on him, there was a showdown in Henrietta Street that ended with the chief executive pursuing his old commanding officer out into the road and along the pavements as far as Saint Martin-in-the-Fields, where the two shouted abuse at one another across Trafalgar Square.

For Tony it was the last in the long chain of his father's private and now public rejections. He accepted it, as he had schooled himself to do from boyhood, without comment or visible reaction, knowing that from now on he was on his own. He came eventually to believe that Duckworths had been no more than a convenient way of shelv-

Tony drawn by Adrian Daintrey, who, like
Constant, opened up a new world: "I don't
think there was ever a period where I learnt
more in a short time."

ing the problem of his future, and that Colonel Powell had never had
the least intention of handing over the final payment that would have
made his son a partner. Tony was now stuck in an ill-paid job with no
prospect of promotion. He negotiated terms of his own with Balston,
who reluctantly agreed to continue paying £300 a year, which, even
with his father's annual allowance of £150, was barely enough to see
him through as he worked on his first novel.

The transition Tony had undergone since he reached London is
plain to see in a pair of drawings made four years apart. Nina's portrait head of 1927 (see p. 79) shows a serious, clean-cut, ingenuous
and conventional youth on the verge of the break-out described long
afterwards in the third volume of the *Dance*, and in Powell's early
memoirs. A later drawing by Daintrey suggests a decidedly more sardonic and altogether cooler character with watchful and observant
eyes under the tilted brim of his slouch hat. *Afternoon Men* was pub-

lished in 1931, the year of this second drawing. If Enid Firminger modelled for the heroine, there are traces of Nina Hamnett, too, in the overwhelming personality of Naomi Race. The hero William Atwater, "a weedy-looking young man with straw-coloured hair and rather long legs" (Tony's relatively short legs were never a strong point), was a projection of the author as a junior curator in the ethnographical department of what is clearly the British Museum. Said to be one of the best books ever written about museum curators, *Afternoon Men*, like Edith Sitwell's *Gold Coast Customs*, owes a debt to Nina's ethnographical friend, Mr. Joyce. Touched up perhaps with hints of Duckworths' Mr. Lewis, he supplied the prototype for Atwater's senior colleague, Mr. Nosworth, who urged his superiors to keep their more suggestive exhibits locked up, and spent nine years agitating for a revolving office chair.

The title came from Burton's description in *The Anatomy of Melancholy* of the kind of crew Tony now found himself among, "a company of giddy-heads, afternoon men," in other words, as he said, people who spent their mornings recovering from the hangover of the night before. Two of the main characters are painters (Barlow and Pringle, based respectively on Daintrey and a contemporary of his at the Slade called Gerald Reitlinger). The novel's lack of illusion about either the literary or the art world suggests an author only too familiar with both. Certainly Powell is unusual among English novelists in that his imagination remained to the end essentially pictorial. Long afterwards, he described the basic training he had picked up at first hand in artists' studios: "These meetings with painters made a strong impression . . . As in a vision, the professional necessities of painting were all at once revealed. I don't think there was ever a period where I learnt more in a short time."

4

1930–32

I always rejoice in the bland cruelty of Mr. Powell's style," wrote Harold Nicolson, expressing a common view that baffled Tony. "I thought I had written a quiet little love story with a contemporary background," he said of *Afternoon Men*, "and was astonished when it was greeted as a slashing satire." He saw the novel as a fairly accurate account of the kind of life he was leading when he wrote it. Its high points—the shambolic opening party with its memorable drunks, the dismal routines of office life or perfunctory sex, and the climactic discomfort of the final weekend in the country—are all absurdly funny precisely because they are so excruciatingly authentic. Written fast, catching the distinctive tone and rhythms of its day, this is high comedy with a bleak undertow that comes at least in part from the fact that—like all Tony's early novels—*Afternoon Men* was produced against a background of political disruption and incipient economic chaos, both endemic in Europe after the collapse of the US stock market in the autumn of 1929. England's newly elected Labour government was powerless to contain raging unemployment. In the German general election of September 1930, Adolf Hitler moved in from the fringes of dissent to make his National Socialists, or Nazis, the country's second largest political party with a power base that leaped from twelve to one hundred and seven parliamentary seats.

Tony was on the beach at Toulon in the south of France that summer. He arrived there alone in August, bringing his manuscript on the advice of Constant Lambert, who had completed his piano sonata a few months earlier at the Hôtel du Port et des Négociants on Toulon's sheltered inner port. Tony moved into a small, hot room under the roof looking out on one side over the town's naval dockyards, and on the other at sailors' bars and cafés lining the quayside. Plans to spend the next three weeks working solidly on his novel were almost immediately disrupted by four more of Lambert's friends already installed at the hotel: Ed Burra and Billy Chappell with a couple of girls they had known from art school, Irene Hodgkins and Barbara Ker-Seymer, always known as Hodge and Bar.

The quartet had been inseparable since they first met in their early teens, and started constructing a collective identity from adolescent dreams of urban chic fed by films, fashion magazines and travel posters ("the people are so glorious so chic," the young Burra wrote enthusiastically to Bar from Paris, "500 miles of lip stick 60 gallons of fleshing 40 tons of eye black & 17 miles of false lashes are used in Montmartre alone every day I'm certain"). Make-up, morally repugnant in the conservative small-town and suburban settings they had left behind, stood for provocation and defiance in their brave new post-war world. Their tone was comical and camp. Hodge, who got her first job in Nigel Playfair's upmarket cabaret, *Midnight Follies* at the Metropole Hotel, was unambiguously straight. Bar was bisexual, Chappell had recently acquired a first boyfriend called John Lloyd (always known as the Widow, one of Tony's wilder contemporaries at Oxford), and Burra was gay in spirit although in practice probably more or less inactive (homosexuality remained a criminal offence in England for nearly another forty years). Virginal if not exactly innocent, far less sophisticated than they looked or sounded, the four had amused themselves for years by impersonating crooks and gangsters, "hardened hustlers, prostitutes and alcoholics." In the summer of 1930 they were still, like Tony, in their early twenties but they shared a quick, streetwise intelligence and a flamboyant visual wit unlike anything he had come across before. It was as if the London cast of a contemporary *Beggar's Opera* had descended on Toulon.

All of them were seduced by the strong colours and clear shapes outlined in Mediterranean sunlight so theatrical that, as Tony said, even the railway station "appeared neatly arranged as for the opening act of a musical comedy." Senegalese soldiers in exotic outfits, baggy-trousered Algerian Spahis and French sailors with red pom-poms in their caps strolled about the streets. A seafaring port equipped with an immense natural harbour, Toulon was unused to tourists but well accustomed to supplying the navy's off-duty needs for drink, drugs and whores of both sexes. It was a heady environment for visitors as responsive as Burra and his friends. They bought sailor suits—wide-legged white trousers with striped tops and blue berets—and joined in the parade.

Hodge, who was ravishingly pretty, surprised Tony long after-wards by claiming she had always fancied him. She was engaged to be married at the time, and in any case he favoured Bar, "a small, sleek and vivacious figure in a matelot's jersey," who exemplified for him ever after the archetypal 1920s girl. More than fifty years later she drew a series of these flappers for him as try-outs for the cover of his last novel but one: decorative young women with flat chests and shingled hair, clutching cocktails in one hand and cigarette-holders in the other. Bar had known Tony since they were both twelve years old (their mothers had met as fellow fans of Christian Science). As observant as he was himself, she was well on the way to becoming one of London's most up-to-date photographers, "busy photograph-ing Miss Modern washing her panties in Trex," as Burra put it drily.

Burra was the group's imaginative driving force. "He spoke rarely, but always with devastating aptness," said Tony. Anaemically pale, prematurely old, chronically unwell, he seldom joined the others out of doors, preferring to spend his days drawing and painting ("always his deepest pleasure," said Chappell) at the shady end of his hotel room. Chappell was the funniest of the four, and the one Tony found most sympathetic. He organized their daily excursions to the nearby bathing beach of Les Sablettes, and kept watch for the local gen-darme, who patrolled the sand with a pistol to make sure no visitor of either sex violated the moral code by stripping off the top of his or her regulation one-piece bathing costume.

Tony had by this time abandoned any serious attempt at work, breakfasting with the others at the Café de la Rade and catching the paddle steamer most mornings to spend the day with them at Les Sablettes. He was an appreciative audience, and they never tired of performing for him. Slight, supple and energetic, Chappell had trained with Marie Rambert's ballet corps, and spent the previous year dancing in Ida Rubinstein's company in Paris for Bronislav Nijin-ska. Once he danced for Tony as he lay stretched out on the sand. "Salome dancing before Herod" was Hodge's caption to a snapshot of Chappell twirling gracefully with a towel on a beach empty except for that single sunbather. Tony's habitual watchfulness, so different from their own, intrigued and puzzled all of them. "Nobody could get the wrong impression of you," Bar wrote ruefully, "because you don't give anything to go on!"

Tony himself paid particular attention to Burra, whose single-minded concentration seemed like a reproach. Burra painted the hotel's window grilles and balconies, the house fronts along the quay, the fountain spouting greenery on the Place Puget, and of course the sailors. A year later he used Toulon as the setting for *Rio Grande: A Day in a Southern Port*, the ballet he designed to Lambert's music for Freddie Ashton as choreographer. Chappell danced the key role of the Creole sailor with Alicia Markova as his pick-up (replaced later by Margot Fonteyn, appearing as a principal for the first time aged fifteen). Burra painted Toulon's brothel quarter on the drop curtain, and Ashton remembered audiences responding to the tarts posed suggestively at every open window with "the same kind of buzz—slightly startled, half affronted, half delighted—as greeted Picasso's front cloth for *Le Train bleu* at the Coliseum in the 1920s."

On a rare expedition beyond Toulon, Tony watched Burra at work on *Dockland Café, Marseilles*, a beautiful, sombre composition of interlocking strips and curlicues in brown, black and grey with pink highlights, organized around a gay assignation between two young sailors in a harbour bar. What impressed Tony was Burra's working method, "one of the most unusual I have ever observed in any painter." There is something faintly eerie about the account he wrote nearly fifty years later, as if, looking back as an old man at the end of his career, he saw his own younger self reflected in Burra's mirror:

He would sit in a hotel bedroom on a rickety hotel chair at an equally rickety hotel table—possibly even a dressing table—dozens of extraneous objects round about him (including the remains of petit déjeuner) while he executed his pictures. What was always an immensely complicated design would be begun in the bottom right-hand corner of a large square of paper; from that angle moving in a diagonal sweep upward and leftward across the surface of the sheet, until the whole was covered with an intricate pattern of background and figures. If not large enough, the first piece of paper would be tacked on to a second one—in fact would almost certainly be joined by several more—the final work made up of perhaps three or four of these attached sections.

In practically every detail this passage describes the way Tony himself worked for quarter of a century on the *Dance*: the cluttered bedroom, the flimsy chair, the improvised work surface that might have been a dressing table, and the design itself steadily taking shape on paper, a design so immensely complicated that its scope and scale had to be revised at intervals and regularly extended, sheet by sheet and volume by volume, "until the whole was covered with an intricate pattern of background and figures." Tony and Burra were too different ever to become close friends, but perhaps each recognized an imaginative affinity in the other as well as the same stubbornness of character and uncompromising purpose.

Towards the end of the month Burra and Chappell returned to England, leaving Hodge to wait for the arrival of her fiancé, Dennis Cohen, publisher and founder of the surefooted little Cresset Press. Cohen would have made an ideal husband—charming, considerate, witty, considerably older than she was and decidedly better off— except for a sudden Mediterranean storm the day before he reached Toulon that knocked both Hodge and Tony off course. A battered sailing boat, blown in from Cassis, crept into port, manned by two handsome desperados who claimed to have survived mortal danger by lashing the helm so that the boat ran all day before the wind, while they lay in the stern drinking red wine and declaiming Paul Valéry's *Eupalinos* aloud to mountainous waves. One was a young Greek artist called Jean Varda, the other was the English painter Tristram Hillier. Barefoot, in torn singlets and patched pants, "caked with seasalt spray, bearded and deeply burnt by the sun and wind after several days at sea," both were electrified by Hodge. Hillier said she was "so astonishingly beautiful that I could not refrain from gazing at her in constant wonder." Varda whispered to him that she was a goddess. The upshot was predictable. At the *bal-musette* or local hop that evening, it was obvious that Hodge and Hillier (who had just been dumped by Joanne Firminger, and was still smarting from her rejection) had eyes for no one but each other. By the time the visitors sailed away again next morning, Hodge had promised to follow Hillier to Cassis as soon as she could break off her engagement to Cohen. "At Victoria I lost my umbrella," he said philosophically afterwards, "at Toulon my fiancée, at Monte Carlo my money, and on the return journey my ticket."

Hillier had brought his model with him in the boat, an old friend from the Slade who turned out to be none other than Joanne Firminger's sister Enid. Her arrival put paid to any lingering hope Tony might have had that she could ever be more than a dream for him. Perhaps he watched her dancing that night with a stranger, as the hero of *Afternoon Men* watches Susan, in a passage so thick with jealousy that the reader can almost see her partner's lumbering footwork and hear his laboured breath: "He circled round her heavily, his hand on her back, spread out like a pachydermatous growth or alien bunch of fruit." At all events it seems to have been at Toulon that Tony finally accepted his loss emotionally as well as rationally, feeling, like Atwater in his novel, as if the pit had dropped out of his stomach. He left the others dancing and returned alone to the hotel, staying just long enough to forward Hodge's post and commiserate with Cohen before packing his bags for home. He caught a plane to London from Marseilles, a form of transport still so novel that he had to ask the man in the next seat whether or not to tip the driver.

Falling profits and rising costs made Duckworths in the slump even more dispiriting than usual, Gerald's rancour and resentment, Balston's lack of thrust all the more pronounced. Months of stress proved too much for the accountant, Mr. Child—a doggedly obstructive man nicknamed by Tony the stunted troglodyte—whose muffled shrieks could be heard from time to time behind the closed door of his office. Tony rang round his friends, drumming up contributions for a bare-bones operation initiated by Balston, a pop series of potted biographies called *Great Lives*. He had already fixed up Charles I with Pansy Pakenham, the flatmate who had urged Evelyn to marry Waugh (a move she bitterly regretted), and whose second novel he was about to publish. Now he extracted bids for lives of Byron, Beethoven and Thomas Gray respectively from three Oxford contemporaries, Peter Quennell, Alan Pryce-Jones and Wyndham Ketton-Cremer. Afterwards he relieved his feelings by putting Balston's brainchild into his novel as the Keynote Series of *God's Failures*. When Elinor Glyn delivered yet another overblown romance, he asked Bar for a dust

jacket, explaining frankly that she was the only person he knew "who could do anything awful enough."

He returned to his own unfinished manuscript, stepping up the pace and writing non-stop all through one weekend to make up for time lost at Toulon. *Afternoon Men* was finished by the beginning of 1931 and passed for publication by Balston, whose best offer was £25 advance on royalties. Tony, already saving up to buy a car on Heygate's advice, blued £100 on a Morris Minor, a grey two-seater with red upholstery, bucket seats and a top speed of 50 mph. It was cramped and jerky, the smallest and cheapest car on the market, but it changed his life. He bought a typewriter to put in it, and bumped about the country to the consternation of his friends ("This driving complex must be exorcised," Heygate wrote sternly: "You put the wind up Evelyn by appearing nervous").

At Duckworths, Tony switched roles, becoming his own editor, organizing production and marking up the script. He picked Misha Black—at that stage still an unknown designer even younger than himself—to execute his plan for an unmistakeably contemporary, elegantly stark jacket, using simple lettering and an arresting backlit image of a jointed wooden dummy with a wineglass in its hand. Mr. Lewis took over at the printers and the binders. Operations were held up in March when the deteriorating financial situation, or corrosive inner gloom, finally unhinged Mr. Child, who locked himself in the lavatory, cursing and howling like an animal. Although Duckworth himself supervised the rescue, it took an hour before the door could be forced open and Child packed off in a waiting ambulance (he ended up incarcerated in an institution, making occasional reappearances at the office in lucid intervals).

When *Afternoon Men* came out that spring, it produced the same half-affronted, half-delighted buzz as Burra's drop curtain in reviewers easily shocked by its world of short skirts, cocktails and casual sex. Among fellow novelists, Heygate was enthusiastic, Henry Green, with two novels currently in circulation, was condescending ("I suppose I am generally recognised now as being as good as any novelist can be," he told Tony grandly round about this time). Evelyn Waugh (who still published non-fiction with Duckworths) dedicated his next travel book to Tony "from his brother of the pen," a generous gesture, given that Tony remained friends with Waugh's newly divorced wife as well as with the treacherous Heygate. The two of them were currently installed in the Waughs' old Canonbury flat, planning to marry and both working hard on novels of their own. "The trouble with your novel is that I can't stop reading it," wrote the future Mrs. Heygate: "The moment it arrived I read it, & now I'm reading it again, & I expect I shall read it tomorrow too."

A problem that would crop up in one form or another for the rest of Tony's career surfaced for the first time when two acquaintances he barely knew complained about being cast as minor characters in his novel. One was Humphrey Pease, an urbane old Etonian who withdrew his objection when someone pointed out that Verelst, his fictional double, ends up in the last chapter seducing the hero's girlfriend. The other was Bobby Roberts, a friend of Waugh's, only too recognizable as the portly, pink-cheeked, almost permanently tipsy Fotheringham, sub-editor of a spiritualist paper ("the aura of journalism's lower slopes clung round him like a vapour"), who had already figured unflatteringly in Heygate's *Decent Fellows* the year before. "I am fortunate to have got away with it," Heygate wrote cheerfully: "I only warn you that you apparently haven't." Roberts was genuinely hurt, a reaction anticipated in *Afternoon Men* in a musical exchange of pure Powellian melancholy, when the drunken Fotheringham wonders why any of his friends still bother with him:

"My dear Fotheringham."
"I mean it."
"You can't."
"Yes, yes, I do."
"Don't say so."
Fotheringham picked up the two glasses. He said:
"I shall say it and I shall repeat it."
"No, no. Don't repeat it."

Roberts was eventually mollified by a review that quoted Fotheringham's drunken ramblings to show this new novelist's mastery of speech patterns. He had met Tony through John Heygate, who liked to end a heavy evening's drinking with thirty or forty verses of an old comic standby, "The Hole in the Elephant's Bottom," performed as a double act with Roberts. Both of them had started out as subversive young employees in the news department of the infant BBC under its puritanical director general, Sir John Reith. Bobby had extravagant ambitions but drink stopped him ever rising much above subsistence journalism or short-term jobs, often with fly-by-night publishing ventures, none of which dimmed his exuberant personality and groundless faith in his own career prospects. He touched a novelistic nerve in both Heygate and Powell. Over the years Heygate built him up into a semi-mythical figure, a preposterous alter ego who took on outsize proportions in both conversation and correspondence. Tony used him as a launchpad for two seedy journalists, Lushington in *Venusberg* and Lindsay (Books-Do-Furnish-a-Room) Bagshaw in the *Dance*. For the next two or three decades Bobby had a knack of turning up at irregular intervals in both their lives, still with his old expansive swagger, still floating new schemes each more implausible than the last, still touting for work to tide him over in the meantime: "Some sort of beachcombing bagmannery," as he said himself with the shrewd self-knowledge that always touched Tony's heart. Writing in 1977, the year of Roberts's death, Tony summed him up as "a richly comic figure" with a streak of tragedy, in effect a job description for a minor character in the *Dance*.

Becoming a published author was a step up on the social scale, and Heygate urged Tony to make the most of it, explaining his own scheme for using his next novel to advertise its author's availability to girls ("Could one introduce one's address and telephone number into the hero's story?" he asked hopefully). Without going as far as Heygate recommended, Tony had his admirers too. "Dear Mr. Powell," wrote one of them soon after *Afternoon Men* came out, "I and my husband would be so pleased if you could spend the weekend with us at our tiny cottage." Her name was Juliet O'Rorke and, like so many of Tony's friends, she turned out to be an accomplished artist. She gave him one of the first luxury books produced by Cohen's Cresset Press, the *Chelsea Song Book*, illustrated by herself with twenty chromolithographs in pale clear colours, as witty, stylized and offbeat as the folksongs they accompanied. Juliet was a favourite with Cohen's cousin, Michel Salaman, a lavish party-giver who liked to mix pretty girls from the art schools and the big West End shows with the playwrights, painters and musicians he and his wife regularly entertained at their big house in the country (Juliet said weekends at the Salamans' felt like stepping into a real-life version of Noël Coward's *Hay Fever*).

Quick, sharp, stylish and inimitably funny, she was four years older than Tony, a native of the Chelsea art world, tirelessly alert for anything fresh, smart and up-to-date. In the spring of 1931, Tony was all three. She amused him, and he made her laugh. They started meeting in galleries, going for walks together, lunching or dining at expensive restaurants. Soon talks and walks were not enough. Their affair seems to have started in early August, and been temporarily interrupted almost at once when Tony left to spend his annual holiday in the south of France again. He settled first at Sainte-Maxime, taking the manuscript of his new novel with him, determined to work this time without distraction from anyone he knew. "It seems quite a hundred years since I had dinner with you & I don't suppose you will ever come back from Sainte Maxime," Juliet wrote on 7 August in a letter that ended with a typically tart pay-off: "Did you miss me you swine." Tony promptly moved on round the coast, posting Juliet a letter of suicidal depression. "Darling—what is the use of my writing long letters to Ste Maxime if you go flouncing off to Toulon?" she asked crossly in her next bulletin of London gossip, signing off with a piece of curt advice: "Don't cut your throat."

Juliet had been married for two years to an up-and-coming young architect from New Zealand, whose ultra-modern interiors for the Orient Line were about to revolutionize the style and content of the great ocean-going cruise ships. Juliet contributed hand-coloured menu cards, and crystal light-fittings in the shape of seahorses for the first-class dining room. The O'Rorkes had a nanny to look after their small son and a pretty house in Upper Cheyne Row, but Brian's laconic Antipodean manner and insatiable appetite for hard work made him difficult to live with, at any rate for anyone as fun-loving and as easily bored as Juliet, whose zip and dash depended on high levels of maintenance and attention.

The slender narrative thread of Tony's second novel starts with a chance encounter between the central character and a young married woman, neglected by a husband largely consumed by his own work. Admittedly the setting is the under-employed, inward-looking, more or less enclosed diplomatic community of a small, newly liberated Baltic capital, based on memories of the Powells' circle in Helsinki with a dash of Tallin thrown in. Ortrud Mavrin, an academic wife with unmistakeably Slav looks, is terminally bored like Juliet with the same tart way of talking, a "rather sparkling hardness" that gives an edge to everything she says. Older and far more sophisticated than her inexperienced lover, Ortrud seduces him, after a first tentative advance on his part, with a practised speed and skill that leave him "surprised and rather shaken."

Re-creating the chill Nordic townscape of *Venusberg* in the glare and heat of a Mediterranean high summer cannot have been easy. Tony had brought copies of his first novel with him, writing on the flyleaf of the one he gave Billy Chappell, "In memory of Toulon and the boys and girls" with a postscript underneath: "Alas, all ageing rapidly." Chappell was twenty-three that summer to Tony's twenty-five. Among the boys and girls at the hotel were Chappell's lover, John Lloyd, and Lloyd's brother Wyndham, himself also in keen pursuit of what the brothers called "boys and booze." Word of Toulon's laid-back culture had got back to Paris, bringing Jean Cocteau and his current boyfriend, both mostly too drugged to leave their hotel room. Bar was there as well as Chappell's fellow dancer, Freddie Ashton (nicknamed Hotsy Trackles by Burra), both with their respective partners. Tony's old neighbour from Shepherd Market, Bumble Dawson, came too. So did Dorothy Varda, the proprietor of the bookshop in High Holborn where so many of Tony's friends had found lodgings. She turned out to be the troublemaker responsible for tipping off both Pease and Roberts when *Afternoon Men* came out ("in the war she would have been rightly shot as a spy," Heygate said indignantly). Always known by her surname, like a man, she had once been briefly married to the sailor from Cassis, Jean Varda, himself a surrealist painter and printmaker.

A whole stretch of the French coast was beginning to resemble a crowded arty party in Fitzrovia, as Lambert had warned Tony the year before ("the only difference between Marseilles & a Great Ormond Street party is one of expense"). There were so many visitors that Burra threatened to run away and join the Foreign Legion if any more turned up. For Tony that Toulon summer of 1931 served as prototype for the many hectic gatherings that would punctuate the *Dance*, where coincidence regularly assembles a disparate bunch of people, shakes them up together and deposits them at the same party, art gallery or coffee shop. After two weeks he left for Arles, where the girls were said to be the prettiest on the coast, and got a shock when he recognized the one who turned and waved at him as Enid Firminger. Back in London by the end of the month, he found a postcard waiting for him with a glitzy girl on one side, signed on the other by practically every guest at Toulon's Hôtel du Port. "I was so sorry to miss you—we are just going to be drummed out of town by the horrified proletariat," wrote Burra. "My tummy is black best news I know," reported a triumphant Chappell. Varda sent "all the love in the world," underlining the next word of her message with two emphatic slashes: "<u>You</u> are my nervous breakdown."

If this was a declaration of intent on Varda's part, Tony was too preoccupied elsewhere to take action. He began lunching regularly with Juliet, who, like Ortrud Mavrin, needed somebody to take her out, and notice the outrageous things she did and said ("I didn't play tennis at the party because I was afraid of saying bugger," she confided after a week in Scotland, where Brian was doing up a castle for the grouse season). Meetings were not always easy to arrange. "Who is that very good looking gentleman who came to lunch the other day?" asked the O'Rorkes' sharp-eyed nanny after one of Tony's visits. Juliet told him to contact her at a friend's address, and took to telephoning him from dress shops, and scribbling notes in the writing rooms of the classier department stores. Secrecy lent adultery an extra thrill. "It is awful ringing you up at Swan and Edgar," she wrote happily, "and writing to you at Harrods doesn't really seem to be much better."

Tony reported the stages of their affair in characteristically bittersweet letters to Heygate (who read them aloud to Evelyn), at the same time plotting the rise and fall of a parallel affair in *Venusberg*. Ortrud Mavrin and her lover snatch meetings at her house, sometimes under the baleful stare of her small son, more often in the presence of her cowed and ineffectual husband whose only recourse is to escape back to his study. As Lushington in the novel grows cooler and more detached, Ortrud becomes more fractious, treating her husband in public with a brutal asperity that dismays her lover. There is no way of telling if life was imitating fiction, or the other way round, as Juliet too grew moodier, more demanding and increasingly resentful of time Tony spent with Varda. "I hope your dinner with V wasn't as nice as your dinner with me at Rules," she wrote jealously, demanding details when Varda moved out of London and invited Tony down to stay for a weekend on the south coast. She described the failure of Michel Salaman's attempts to marry Varda off, adding a pointed warning—"perhaps he will insist on your marrying her after all so there."

Juliet's letters had never made any attempt to hide her disillusion with her husband, and now she began talking openly of separation and divorce. Evelyn Heygate, newly married to John and only too aware of the misery of the divorce courts, wrote anxiously in the New Year to say she had dreamed of Tony and his difficulties with Juliet: "I hope this isn't so . . . Anyway, if you *are* seeing her, give her my love." It seems to have been the threatened break-up of the O'Rorkes' marriage—perhaps especially Juliet's hints that Tony could be cited as co-respondent in divorce proceedings—that finally made him put a stop to their affair. "You are tramping through the marshes and ticking Varda off about the dog," Juliet said accusingly, when he told her they should stop seeing one another. Her last letter was as down to earth as ever: "Well, I have had a reconciliation instead of a separation after all. I really couldn't imagine myself . . . living alone in a squalid bed sitting room. I must say there is nothing more boring than either leaving home or being unhappily married."

Venusberg, "that wry Baltic idyll," as Elizabeth Bowen called it, is the nearest Tony ever came to writing a novel about politics. It takes place in a country fought over by rival factions—Nationalists, Social Democrats, Fascists, Jesuits, Agrarians—and riddled by conflict between Nazism and communism, the two great utopian dreams that ravaged Europe in the aftermath of the First World War. The narrative is interspersed with muffled shots, street protests, rumours of terrorist bombs and assassination plots, culminating in the final random shooting that leaves Ortrud Mavrin lying dead on the street alongside her new lover. Her death abruptly terminates an affair that had been at best scrappy, disjointed and provisional. But it is Frau Mavrin's edginess that gives the book its ironic core, adding human warmth and feeling to the general sense of chaotic disintegration embodied in a scene where the lovers inspect the toppled and dismembered body parts of a colossal bronze statue:

> Lushington was examining the head of the statue, which lay with its heavy Roman nose buried in the grey brittle grass. Contact with the earth had given the potentate's face an agreeable patina. Beside it was an arm and a hand holding an orb. Farther off, an immense top-boot . . . [Ortrud] put one foot on the statue's ear under its wig and tried to rock the head backwards and forwards. It moved slightly, nuzzling into the frozen grass . . .

Written fast like its predecessor, and finished in late spring or early summer, *Venusberg* was scheduled for publication in autumn 1932. This time Tony celebrated by driving his car the wrong way along the Great West Road ("My misadventures show how dangerous it is to be sober in charge of a car"). He had grown so attached to his bumpy little Morris that, when Salaman offered him a flat high up on London's Haymarket looking directly out over Piccadilly Circus, he refused on the grounds there was no parking. In spring and summer he drove out to spend weekends with friends in the country. He had been one of the first visitors Varda invited down to stay when she left town the year before, renting a series of flats, cottages and houses on the Sussex coast, or inland on the downs, where she kept a goat and the un-house-trained dog that Tony found so tiresome. Like him, she had been writing a novel, submitting the completed manuscript that spring to Tony, who returned it politely with comments and suggestions. It was called *Faces* (*Faeces* was its author's pet name for it), and privately he thought it disappointing, shapeless and insipid.

Varda was an ambitious reader, especially of contemporary avant-garde French authors, several of whom she knew in person. Her first long-term lover, when she was still barely into her twenties, had been John Rodker, a young modernist poet with a tiny one-man press in Paris on which he printed oddments in the 1920s for friends like James Joyce, Ezra Pound and Wyndham Lewis. This was when Varda first contacted Tony, sending him a letter in 1927 to ask if he would publish her translation of Raymond Radiguet's *Le Diable au corps*, another first that Duckworths automatically turned down. So for that matter did T. S. Eliot, then editor of the *Criterion*. It was left to *Vogue* in its brief modernist heyday under Dodie Todd and Madge Garland to introduce Radiguet to an English public who, as Eliot rightly pointed out, were not remotely interested in obscure French experimental novels. Varda's credibility as Radiguet's translator cannot have been helped by the fact that *Vogue* was simultaneously promoting the cool English style epitomized by girls like Hodge, Firminger and the most glamorous of them all, featured in a full-page studio portrait above the caption: "The celebrated West End mannequin, beauty and stage star, Dorothea Varda, wearing stockings stitched with jewels."

If Varda had what her condescending male friends called a masculine intelligence—Lambert even claimed she had a man's sense of humour too—her looks were literally stunning. She had golden hair, blue-green eyes under elegantly arched brows, delicate colouring and fine bones. Adrian Daintrey's portrait shows her as a ravishing curly-headed blonde in the early 1930s, but a portfolio of photos taken as professional calling cards a decade or so earlier show a sterner, almost Roman profile emphasized by a short sleek bob with a kiss curl on each cheek. In a full-length study Varda looks slender and severe,

The beautiful and stormy Varda, who longed
to join the world of books

an unsmiling young beauty in a floor-length, long-sleeved, scoop-
necked velvet gown posing with a cigarette between long tapering
fingers.

By 1924, when this photograph was taken, she had been appearing for six years on the Variety stage in smash-hit shows with stars
like Alice Delysia and Douglas Byng (both favourites with Tony at
school and university). Born Dorothy Stewart in America in 1901,
the third of four daughters of an English electrical engineer, she had
followed her eldest sister who ran away at nineteen to go on the London stage. Dorothy was handpicked by C. B. Cochrane as one of
his Young Ladies, the famous Edwardian chorus line that regularly
creamed off the West End's top talent. Even by his exacting standards
she was outstandingly lovely, carrying herself with such exquisite
grace and poise that some said Cochrane had plans to promote her
as the most beautiful woman on earth. Certainly he billed her as the
Beautiful Varda in at least one of his most successful musicals at the
London Pavilion. But, unlike her sister Marjorie (who, as Madge Stu-

art, went on to become a star of the first silent films), Dorothy always had her eye on another world than theatre. If she played a Moorish harem slave in Cochrane's spectacular *Agfar*, she also appeared three months later in a one-off matinee production of *Ordo Virtutum*, a liturgical drama from the twelfth century by Abbess Hildegarde of Bingen, translated by Arthur Waley and performed in plainchant. It was part of a remarkable triple bill at the Haymarket in December 1919 that included a ballet duet to music by César Franck, danced by Marie Rambert and the handsome young Greek Jean Varda.

Pregnant at twenty, Dorothy fled to Paris after a hasty marriage to the child's father, who was Jean Varda. Like most girls of her class and period, especially those without family support or backing, she had neither formal education nor career prospects at a time when in any case the only professions open to her, other than the theatre, were teaching or nursing, both in practice reserved for celibate single women. The majority settled for a husband in the end but, in spite of the many eligible men who tried to change her mind, marriage was a yoke to which the young Varda could not submit. Her forced union with Jean lasted a few months, long enough for him to leave her with a baby daughter and an introduction to his friend John Rodker. Involvement with Rodker, who had himself already fathered and abandoned two infant daughters by different mothers in Paris, was a salutary experience for any girl whose intention was to operate on equal terms with men. Varda responded eagerly to the world of poets and writers that he opened up but, unlike him, she kept the baby.

Back in England nearly a decade later, Tony remembered a small daughter in the background, Domenica or Minka, generally away at boarding school or being looked after by a young minder from Universal Aunts. By this time Varda had solved the practical problems of existence—hotels, restaurants, foreign travel, no doubt rent and household bills as well—by acquiring an escort or titular fiancé, bluff, long-suffering and discreet, who could be relied on to foot bills and follow orders without question or complaint. Captain Turle was a naval officer, always referred to as the Admiral by Tony and his friends (he would in due course end up a rear admiral in the Royal Navy). But the company she enjoyed was still the arty crowd of hard-up writers, artists and musicians, the kind of people who congregated on the beach at Toulon, or in the Salamans' hospitable house in Surrey. Tony called her "the beautiful and stormy Varda" and, although she was only a little older than either himself or John Heygate, both treated her defensively, with a faintly wary respect, as if she were an animal that might bite back if provoked.

Certainly Varda's comments could be caustic, and her wit cruelly near the bone. She was the same age as Juliet O'Rorke, slightly older than Firminger and Hodge, just old enough to have appeared at seventeen before audiences of young soldiers on leave from the Western Front, an experience that might explain the consolation she found later in the company of sane, undamaged young men with their lives still intact before them. Either that exposure, or hard times in Paris, or perhaps some earlier family trauma had left her so badly maimed that she could never coordinate her considerable forces, or bring them to bear for long on any particular purpose. For all her brilliance and beauty, her effortless ability to light up any room she entered, Varda remained a constitutional malcontent, restless, hard to please, subject to sudden destructive spurts of rage or despair. "She was unfortunately incapable of finding tolerable any known pattern of existence," wrote Tony, who probably understood her in the end as well as anyone ever did. "Neither simple nor complex paradigms of life suited her, nor were effective in casting the devils out."

On her return to England in 1926, at or near the end of her affair with Rodker, it was Michel Salaman who hit on the inspired solution of buying her a bookshop. The premises stood out, like their owner, on Holborn's drab grey pavements with a shop-sign painted by Edward Wadsworth that read "varda bookshop." Wadsworth's daughter, Barbara, remembered it as absurdly out of place, "as though with its pale pink, blue and white colouring, and its complete simplicity of lettering, it had dropped there by mistake on its way to Cannes." Above the bookshop was the flat where Varda lived and entertained her friends. Two more tiny flats on the top floor provided her with an income from lodgers, who paid part of their rent in practice by minding the till in her absence. Behind the shop there was a backyard used by local tarts to relieve themselves when the pubs closed.

Surrounded now by books, and by the crowd who hung out at the shop—gossiping, drinking, flicking through their own and other people's titles on the shelves—Varda conducted a nightly running party upstairs, and put in daytime appearances downstairs when she could find the time. Tony remembered Lambert in his brief stint as her tenant complaining that "all the lunatics in London were let out to buy their books" whenever it was his turn to take charge of the shop. Varda's lodgers became more restive as her absences grew longer. Eventually she lost interest altogether, moving out to a flat in Mecklenburgh Square and leaving the bookshop to go rapidly downhill, losing money, piling up debts and running out of stock. By 1934 its affairs had reached a state of such catastrophic disarray that, although the shop itself continued trading at different addresses under one of Varda's brothers-in-law, the Varda Bookshop company ended inevitably in liquidation.

Varda had long since left London, taking a house next door to Bobby Roberts's father at 67, South Terrace in Littlehampton. "I laughed for the first time in years at your letter," she wrote, arranging a visit from Tony in January 1931, soon after her move to the seaside: "I think I can never return." Tony gave her a blank publisher's dummy to use as a guest book, and for the next two years she switched addresses, dotting about the southern counties—from Littlehampton to High Halden in Kent, then back to Fletching Common in Sussex, followed by an oast house at Five Ashes—remaining always within easy reach of London by the Brighton line. She and Tony swapped news, jokes and literary allusions on postcards, Varda's from an extensive feminist collection of Edwardian bathing belles, society ladies, once a hefty French bruiser all belly and buttocks with beefy arms and legs, another time a galloping centaur (also unmistakeably French), half horse, half woman in diaphanous muslin with a jockey astride her back. On 7 April 1931, Tony presented her with a reissue of the book that changed his life, Cummings's *Enormous Room*, dedicated "For Mrs. V with love from Tony" on the flyleaf with a jingoistic jingle by Oscar Wilde paraphrased below: "Set in this stormy Northern sea,/ Queen of the restless fields of tide!/Varda! What should men say of thee,/Before whose feet the worlds divide." A month later he gave her a copy of his own first novel, inscribed again "for Mrs. V," this time with a verse from what soon became their Tennysonian signature tune: "Out flew the web and floated wide,/The mirror cracked from side to side/'The curse has come upon me', cried/The Lady of Shalott." They both spent holidays in France that summer, Varda and the Admiral showing signs of stress by the time they briefly caught

IT TAKES ALL SORTS TO MAKE A WORLD: Page from Tony's album showing Evelyn Heygate and Constant Lambert (*top left*), Varda, and John Heygate (*middle row*) at Thornsdale with newly published copies of *Afternoon Men*.

up with Tony at Toulon. "Still not looking more than a day ahead & longing for home and peace!" she wrote, announcing their arrival: "I shall like seeing you again love D.V."

Varda dropped in on Tony from time to time in London, but more often than not they met at Thornsdale, the oast house at Iden near Rye in Sussex where old friends from the bookshop crowd still congregated at weekends. It belonged to Gerald Reitlinger, a Slade contemporary of Bar, Burra and Chappell, himself a highly unsuccessful sub-Impressionist painter. Reitlinger could have been a character out of Dostoevsky, according to Tony, who put him into *Afternoon Men* instead as the painter, Raymond Pringle. He was a tall, clumsy, shambling figure with thick spectacles and the double-jointed walk that always made Pringle look as if he were about to topple over. Reitlinger was once stopped in New York by two girls who asked if he was Groucho Marx. "Yeah," he answered, adding out of the side of his mouth with a leer, "but incognito." Reitlinger's family circumstances—he was sixth of the seven children of a Jewish banker from Vienna, currently living in St. John's Wood—had left him with a comfortable income and an insecure personality. In some ways, he and Varda were ideally suited. Both were sardonic souls with the deep-seated habit of self-deprecation perhaps inbred in the younger members of large families. He was happiest with a crowd round him, she could generate light and warmth in any gathering if she chose. She liked parties, and he liked giving them.

Reitlinger had been known even as an art student for his wild Chelsea parties (he gave the legendary Sailor Party, described at the time by Billy Chappell as "bugger heaven & no mistake"). Now that he had a house in the country, he invited friends down to stay instead. The only snag was that, although he had the instincts of a host, he had neither the human warmth nor the basic housekeeping skills that might have smoothed his path in practice. His house, made from two converted labourers' cottages on marshland outside Rye, was isolated, uncomfortable and inadequately heated. He paid a girl from the village to clean the place, and hired a succession of plain cooks but rarely provided anything to drink. Pringle's house party in *Afternoon Men*—with canvases in the bath, empty bottles on the piano, scratch meals, faulty plumbing, no hot water and no means of escape except a car with a defective starter—gives a fairly accurate impression of Thornsdale hospitality. Reitlinger had an adequate income from his family but nothing like the bottomless wealth his cash-strapped friends assumed. They mocked his stinginess and social ineptitude, circulating stories about his grotesque behaviour that were energetically embroidered and enriched, relished, repeated and passed round, each new version outdoing the last in a kind of larger-than-life oral fantasy that Reitlinger himself if anything encouraged. "He was intended by nature to be gold-dug," as someone says of Pringle in *Afternoon Men*.

In his London years, Reitlinger had pursued some of the prettiest girls of his art-school generation, including Hodge and Bumble Dawson. One of his former girlfriends, finding herself stranded alone with him for a weekend in the country, claimed implausibly that she'd had to send for Burra to protect her. Varda, too, once arrived to find she was the only guest with Reitlinger hovering at her side, "enquiring if *I had* everything I wanted & was I *sure* I preferred to sleep alone. He was nature's gentle (afternoon) man all the weekend," she told Tony. Varda was the model in *Afternoon Men* for Pringle's fiancée, the attractive, forceful and high-handed Harriet Twining. When angry villagers waylay Pringle outside the pub at closing time to protest about the immorality of his house party, it is Harriet who defuses a potentially nasty situation by forcing him to double the maid's wages. Varda had done much the same for Reitlinger in real life, and Tony thanked her for it at the front of her copy of *Afternoon Men*: "I am especially indebted to Mrs. Varda for the unfortunate episode described on pages 199–202." Varda was apparently also behind the encounter in Chapter 22, where Atwater sleeps with Harriet, an agreeable, almost accidental interlude on a sunny cliff-top above the sea, when perhaps art imitated life.

Both Varda and Reitlinger were prime examples of Tony's rule that characters who were fully realized in fact left nothing much over for the novelist to do in fiction. Both would play key roles in his life, and make occasional, sometimes unexpected contributions to his work. Even at this early stage when Tony did not know either of them at all well, he was one of the few to have at least an inkling of a side of himself that Reitlinger kept dark from his friends. He may have been a figure of fun to the artistic riff-raff he so freely entertained, but serious scholars—archaeologists, historians, connoisseurs, specialists in Persian porcelain, experts in art-market economics—rated him on a very different scale. He had collected Islamic and oriental pots assiduously and with expert discrimination from an early age, building up over four decades what eventually become one of the finest collections ever put together, in the UK or anywhere else. He was a member of the archaeological expedition to Mount Athos described in *The Station* by Robert Byron, whose vindictive and virulently anti-Semitic portrait of him as Reinecker was typical of the reception Reitlinger got from his contemporaries at the time.

Unlike Varda, he managed in the end to work out a way of life that suited him reasonably well, relying almost exclusively on friends for human contact, and sublimating his craving for sensual beauty and physical perfection through the gorgeous colours, shapes and textures of his porcelain jars and platters. He kept most of them locked away upstairs, probably a sensible precaution given his guests' ignorance and indifference to aspects of their host that didn't fit their reductive preconceptions. In 1932, four years after he published Byron's book, Tony brought out Reitlinger's account of his own travels in Iraq and Asia, *The Tower of Skulls*. Travel books had always been one of Duckworths' strongest lines, a perennial standby that the firm depended on more than ever in time of general retrenchment. Even so, Tony can't have found it easy to induce Balston to take on this dry, matter-of-fact handbook with no colourful descriptions, no narrative grip and none of the easy flow of gossip and personal reminiscence that might have made it easier to sell.

Duckworths came closer to extinction than it ever had before in 1932 with staff cutbacks all round, directors' salaries halved and the mortgage on the property in Henrietta Street drastically extended to cover the bank overdraft. At the beginning of June, in a confrontation of what Tony called unambiguous menace, Balston told him that the firm could no longer afford to keep him on, even at the absurdly low salary it had always paid. Balston's letter, probably as humiliating to write as it was to receive, explained that the best he could offer was part-time work in the mornings only, guaranteed for no longer than twelve months, at a reduced salary of £200. He said nothing about *Venusberg*, due out that autumn with no one to oversee its progress if Tony left in the crucial run-up to publication, even supposing that publication went ahead at all. "It seems to me that you put much more energy and initiative into writing than into publishing," wrote Balston, warning Tony that he had no aptitude for a publishing career while at the same time proposing terms he had no choice but to accept.

The new arrangement started on 1 July. Tony had just moved house, leaving his Tavistock Square basement shortly after its three-year lease ran out for a flat high up with a view a few minutes' walk away at 35, Brunswick Square. It contained a "long rickety blue sofa" on which he lay full-length and pondered plots, characters and settings, the looming shapes and patterns of the third novel that had been tugging at the back of his conscious mind for years. He said that his first three novels all came easily: "The dammed up reserves of twenty-five years were there to be drawn on." In retrospect he sometimes made it sound as if he had transposed people, places and events virtually unchanged from the world about him, calling up the past in what was apparently a steady stream rising from inchoate depths of memory as fast as he could write it down. The rickety sofa played a key role in this imaginative process. From now on for the rest of his life, wherever he lived and whatever he was writing, there would always be a sofa on which Tony could lie and think about his next book.

In 1932 presumably he also pondered how to pay the rent. *Afternoon Men* sold around three thousand copies, including a second impression and cheap popular reprints, a highly satisfactory total for a first novel, but an income from writing looked as uncertain as publishing had now turned out to be. Even the inordinately prolific Sitwell brothers, both now threatening to leave Duckworths, earned miserably small sums out of all proportion to their literary celebrity. Most of Tony's friends faced similar problems. Reitlinger had no job to lose but Heygate had lost his, having been forced to resign rather than be sacked when he married Evelyn, because Reith refused to tolerate anyone tainted by divorce at the BBC. Heygate's uncle, who owned the family estate in Ireland with his nephew as his heir, tried to disinherit him, and his parents cut off his allowance. He and Evelyn retreated to cheaper lodgings outside London and turned to jobbing journalism, sending off stories and articles on anything from antiques to travel, shopping or shipping lines.

To the surprise of both, Evelyn turned out to be the better earner of the two with a radio play under discussion and a wildly enthusiastic fiction editor at *Harper's Bazaar*. Slender and slight with bobbed hair, short skirts and a passion for speedway racing, she personified every modern trend that dismayed an older generation and delighted contemporaries: "little Evelyn seemed so roguish in those days," John wrote wistfully in retrospect, "with her made-up lips & her combination of scarlet & black leather." Although their finances still fluctuated wildly, John blued everything on an MG sports car as a birthday present for his wife, who nearly wept for joy, and urged him to splash out again the year after on a Wolseley Hornet for himself at the mind-blowing price of £240: "we have got about that as overdraft," Evelyn wrote happily to Tony.

In the summer of 1932 John landed a job with the Gaumont-British Picture Corporation as part of an economy drive promoted at the time as the cinema's next great leap forward. It entailed working in collaboration with Germany's state-funded film company, UFA, which owned the continent's largest state-of-the-art film studios, and had plans to revolutionize the European industry by making imitation Hollywood movies, each screenplay to be shot simultaneously in two or three different languages by the same director using different casts of German and English actors, in some cases French as well.

John's job was to supply idiomatic dialogue for the English team in return for a princely salary: "more money to spend in a week than I'd been accustomed to in six months." Leaving Evelyn behind to recover from a strained patch in their marriage, he travelled out to Berlin in late July.

Tony saw him off in a first-class carriage on the train from Liverpool Street Station, and joined him a month later, arriving in a torn and grease-stained motoring coat after driving nearly eight hundred miles with overnight pit stops in his trusty Morris Minor. The journey was perhaps a necessary displacement in response to upheaval at Duckworths, and possibly Tony felt an urge to discuss with Heygate what he saw as a basic realignment of his life. The two had made a habit of walking and talking on weekends in the country, tramping over the South Downs behind the Heygates' flat in Brighton, as Tony did with Lambert in London. "I can see you both climbing over some barbed wire," wrote Evelyn, "without a hesitation in what you were saying, just discussing whatever it was as though there wasn't any obstruction there." By Heygate's own account, they took up their non-stop discussion again in Berlin. Their staple subjects were the books they were writing, and the girls they were pursuing, especially the girls, a topic of which Heygate never tired before, during or after any of his marriages. One of his running jokes in Berlin was that Tony's monologue on his own love life, interrupted in mid-sentence as the train pulled out, had resumed smoothly a month later in the middle of the same sentence as if nothing had intervened to stop it ("I knew that he was going to continue his conversation exactly where it had been suspended by the train's departure from Liverpool Street . . .").

Tony spent his first day or two entertaining Heygate with a dispassionate assessment of the relative good and bad points of the extras, dressers, camera assistants and other girls on the film lot. In return Heygate filled him in on his recent affairs, starting with a girl on the train, followed by another on arrival in Berlin, and a whole succession of Trudis, Hannis and Maggis once he reached the studio. This was clearly a familiar routine for them both. The son of an Eton master universally disliked by the boys, Heygate had responded by taking after his mother, who was used to turning heads and had conducted a long affair with the art master, Sidney Evans. Her handsome, debonair and seductive son eyed up every girl he met, and slept with a fair number from an early age. He had a casual sexual confidence he did his best to instil in Tony too. On their first visit to Berlin together three years earlier, it was Heygate who picked up inside information from the hotel's gay barman, and led nightly expeditions to the bars, cabarets and clubs of the city's western pleasure district from which both returned bemused by the prodigious scale and scope of talent on offer.

Now there were more prostitutes than ever, swarming in the streets, hanging round restaurants and lodging houses, often waiting outside the hotel bedroom door with a descending tariff ("They bid each other down to five marks, four marks . . . three marks— three English shillings"). But by 1932 most of the girls were amateurs, clumsy, ignorant and frightened, driven in from small country towns and villages by hunger and the need to eat. "They were afraid of disease," said Heygate, "afraid of having babies. But there was one thing they were more afraid of, and *that was of starving*." He and Tony attended a cabaret, "an absolute Royal Academy of nakedness," where the girls' pneumatic breasts contrasted sharply with their lean thighs and stick-thin arms: "AP and I came out. We had seen enough for one evening . . . We were ashamed. We felt depressed and sober."

Other changes were noticeable by day. Tony said he had seen no Nazi marches in 1929, and very few individual Brownshirts on the streets. Now the atmosphere was heavy with violence and tension. Unemployment had reached six million, the government was close to collapse, lawlessness could barely be contained. Enormous banners signalling general elections at the end of August confronted one another from every hoarding and house front in the Nationalists' black, white, red, and the Social Democrats' black, yellow, red, both outnumbered by the hammer-and-sickle of the Communists and the Nazis' black swastika enclosed by a white disc on a red ground. Ugly street fights broke out at intervals between Nazis and Communists. Even foreign tourists were aware of larger forces on the move: "two great bodies of troops," wrote Heygate, "the one in greeny-grey, the army of the state, the Reichswehr . . . and another trained army in brown shirts and breeches, the army of Adolf Hitler, both waiting in the city's outskirts for orders to march."

It was a relief to escape to the fantastic unreality of UFA's studio at

Neubabelsberg. The film company had installed Heygate in a luxury hotel near the cathedral, and Tony found a room on the top floor of a cheap pension with an outside lift that was his only way to reach the ground. Each morning Heygate drove them both in the company's Mercedes along the racetrack and past the Wannsee deep into pine forests at Potsdam where UFA had set up its headquarters in a clearing. The rearing windowless walls of the vast studio complex looked like a fortress. "When you approach the main studios you expect to be shot from above," said Heygate's English boss, Bob Stevenson (who made his name three decades later as director of *Mary Poppins*). The whole place was manned and run by Prussians with military discipline and precision. Inside was a microcosm including every conceivable place and period, reconstructed with meticulous banality in canvas, lath and plaster. The pair threaded their way through the ballrooms of eighteenth-century Vienna and the dug-outs of a First World War battlefield, to the location where Heygate worked, "a series of derelict streets and houses through which the wrath of God had swept like a tornado, carrying off the interiors and back premises."

His first film was *Happy Ever After* (Heygate's rendering of *Ein Blonder Traum*), a forgettable fairy tale about two window-cleaners in love with the same girl, starring Jack Hulbert and the bilingual Lilian Harvey. John spoke German (he had spent six happy months in Heidelberg on leaving school), but his attempts to inject throwaway English humour, speed and sexiness into a slow and stolid German script made little headway. Tony kept his end up by making friends with the director's former girlfriend, a girl called Thea Struve, exploring his strange surroundings, and watching Heygate struggle with an impossible task in an atmosphere that alternated between frenetic action, apathy and stagnation. Brief glimpses of the city itself, together with the film company's surrealist sets, confirmed the view formed on his previous visit to Berlin: "infested with prostitutes of both sexes, beggars, pimps, freaks, eye-glassed duel-scarred ex-officers, this macabre city presented a monstrous vision of life . . ." In election results announced just before Tony left for home, the Nazi Party more than doubled its total of parliamentary seats, returning 230 candidates who settled down to wait, like their army in the suburbs.

Venusberg was published at the beginning of October. Tony dedicated a copy to Constant Lambert, who had written to him in Berlin to explain that he would be away at the time of publication on tour with Sadler's Wells Ballet. As their newly appointed musical director, he had just received sailing orders for Copenhagen: "they read like the more depressing patches in *Venusberg*. I go in a small boat which takes about 3 days & arrives in the small hours. The right Nordic note is struck, I think, by the sentence 'Captain Nellemose—whom you will know by his scarred face—will meet you.'" Nellemose turned out to be the man in charge of the company's travel arrangements, but his sinister aspect in this letter typifies Constant's knack of making unexpected, always mysteriously apt and timely interventions in Tony's life.

Constant had married a very young and striking wife called Florence Chuter the year before, while Tony was in Toulon. Her beauty, intelligence and wit were quite exceptional, according to Tony, who had been one of very few people to know of their romantic story from the day they first met by accident in 1929, when Constant called on a Russian pianist whose door was opened by Flo, then a fourteen-year-old housemaid. The couple soon became inseparable. Flo's origins remained uncertain: she was the child of an East End mother and an unknown father, possibly a Javanese or Arab sailor who gave her the exotic oriental looks and small, neat, catlike features that had always appealed to Constant. She was largely uneducated and infinitely receptive. He filled her up like the blank pages of a book, taking her to concerts and the ballet, playing her music and advising her what to read. His gifts as a director released an innate assurance in Flo. By the time she started appearing with him in public, and meeting the wide circle of his friends, she was a creature of fastidious finish and perfection. Tiny, elegant and exquisitely composed with almond eyes, high cheekbones and glossy black hair drawn smoothly back, she once told Tony that whenever she felt dishevelled or off colour, she had only to look at the portrait in his flat of his grandmother's friend, Lady Cardigan, whose stern expression and straight back never failed to give Flo back her balance.

Varda was fascinated by her, recognizing in Flo something of her own inborn flair and chic. Tony himself seems to have been dumbstruck at this point. Varda sent him a card, when *Venusberg* came out, showing a curly-headed child in Regency costume pestering his mother: "Mama don't make me beg in vain, / Read that pretty book again." The message on the back said simply: "Need I add anything? but my undying love V." Tony gave her a presentation copy with a formal inscription on the flyleaf: "For Mrs. Varda with the author's love, Tony Powell. Oct 16th, 1932." Underneath he drew a heart pierced by an arrow, adding what sounds like an almost involuntary exclamation: "God! It's good to be alive." Perhaps it was the book itself, or the change it made in Tony's status, that shifted their relationship on to a new footing. "Send me news of Varda," wrote Heygate, detailing his own recent conquests in a bulletin from Berlin, "you and your fiancée, as we say in this delicate trade . . ." She and Tony started exchanging notes, hasty scribbles sometimes no more than a sentence or two long, the 1930s equivalent of tweets. Only Varda's side of this correspondence survives, undated, with no superscription, address or envelope, often on scraps of paper torn off larger sheets, folded over and apparently dropped through Tony's letterbox by hand. She encloses painkillers, asks to borrow a book, apologizes for not phoning, promises she won't be late, and wonders why he hasn't come to see her. These are unimportant, inconsequential little messages, quite different from her other letters, saying nothing in particular but unmistakeably conveying intimacy and trust.

If Heygate knew that something had changed between them, so did Reitlinger, who invited them down to Thornsdale together. In London they dropped in and out of one another's flats (Varda in Mecklenburgh Square lived opposite, separated only by the width of Coram's Fields from Tony in Brunswick Square), and they had each other's keys. They went to parties and visited friends together. "I thought Varda was looking particularly beautiful at the Wadsworths," Heygate wrote on 6 December, back in Berlin after a brief trip to London, "& later at the Café Royal & I wonder that you are not married to her seriously." Marriage was not an outcome that occurred to either of them, but Varda's notes suggest that for a short time she was happy, at peace even with herself, enjoying a contentment she had rarely known before.

She called herself "Olga," apparently a private joke between them (Olga is the name of one of Pringle's unsatisfactory ex-girlfriends in *Afternoon Men*). Her extreme sweetness and sharpness, the perils of coming too close to her, were summed up by one of the Lloyd brothers on a postcard of a carved wooden tip-up seat from Gloucester Cathedral, showing a mediaeval maiden skilfully inserting a phallic instrument between the jaws of a small horned demon. Wyndham's caption ran: "Picture of Olga extracting pleasure from a tooth." She and Tony speculated with interest about a manuscript Reitlinger left lying about, a semi-pornographic fantasy judging by the extract they read, describing a Javanese girl being beaten by an older woman. One of Gerald's elder brothers had once produced something similar, a book called *Slavey*, published in France under the pseudonym Captain Teach and featuring scenes set in the whipping parlour of a New Orleans brothel.

Tony's own new novel was already well in hand. In it he looks back to his Powell origins on the hunting fields round Melton Mowbray, and to the time he served in the strange world of debs' dances, dining in their families' Mayfair houses, and spending weekends at their places in the country. The central driving character in *From a View to a Death* is a pushy young painter, an irrepressible opportunist of colossal nerve and cheek called Arthur Zouch, easily recognizable to friends as Adrian Daintrey. Invited down to paint portraits by the Passenger family at their big house in the country, he erupts into their peaceful rural neighbourhood, seducing the eligible girls, infuriating their parents, and generally causing mayhem until Mr. Passenger eliminates him, mounting him for a final memorable hunt on an unmanageable horse that bolts and breaks his neck in the last chapter but one.

Unlike Tony's first two novels, both preoccupied with unrequited love, this one squarely confronts marriage, treating it unromantically as a necessary but painful solution to the universal problem of how to survive without being wholly engulfed by boredom, loneliness or insanity. Betty Passenger's brief union with a homosexual Italian pseudo-duke ends in divorce. The elderly hypochondriac Mrs. Brandon lives for memories of the love match that left her a grieving widow (she and her husband squabbled and fought throughout their time together, according to local gossip). Two recklessly unsuitable engagements fall through, and a third is broken off by death. Up at the big house the megalomaniac Vernon Passenger has long since settled humbly for a truce on terms dictated by his wife, who is by far the better-tempered and more intelligent of the two. Major

Fosdick in the village avoids domestic conflict by locking himself in his study to smoke his pipe, dressed in a sequinned ballgown and an elaborate Ascot hat. Even the Brandons' cook has indelible memories of her departed husband: "it seems only yesterday that I was married to him. I shan't forget that day in a hurry. *Day of Wrath! O day of mourning! See fulfilled the prophet's warning!*"

In the autumn of 1932 Tony had not yet picked a title for his book—Varda called it *Drag Hunt Ball*—but he said its basic material had lain at the back of his mind for years. He remembered writing a first draft several pages long, and discarding it again before he had even started work on what turned out to be his first novel. *From a View to a Death*, as the third was eventually called, is an absurd observant throwaway farce on the sombre themes of failure, madness and the marital problems of the middle-aged. Its preoccupations might seem premature for a young man still in his mid-twenties, but a mood that darkens towards the end accurately reflects the author's state of mind as he wrote it. Things had soured between himself and Varda. Their affair had lasted no more than a couple of months when, sometime in mid-December, it came to an abrupt end. The last of Varda's flurry of notes to Brunswick Square, undated but delivered formally this time in an envelope by post, suggests that the break-up followed some sort of lapse on her part. A few years earlier she had slept with Evelyn Waugh after a party ("both of us too drunk to enjoy ourselves," Waugh noted in his diary), and possibly it was another casual betrayal that lit a flame of jealousy in Tony. Whatever the cause, the parting was definitive. "Tony dear," she wrote miserably: "I love you very much, for being so nice to me, & making me feel ashamed of myself. Please, go ahead being nice to me, don't give me up as a bad job. That experiment certainly was not a success as I felt so ill. Ring me sometime this week, so that I will know you are not too mad. Yours Olga."

Both of them retreated out of London, Varda to spend Christmas with Reitlinger at Thornsdale, Tony to Ireland, where he had accepted an invitation from an old Etonian acquaintance, an Ulsterman and officer in the Life Guards called Pat Herdman, with a thriving family linen mill outside Strabane in County Tyrone. Pat and his new wife Mary ran a hard-drinking, fox-hunting, bookless household that could not make head or tail of Tony. His only congenial companion was Mary's silent schoolgirl sister Pam (who intrigued him so much he turned up in the New Year at her boarding school in Hastings, claiming to be an uncle come to take her to the cinema). At the Boxing Day meet Tony rode to hounds with the rest of the house party on a horse from Pat's stable that repeatedly threw him off.

That day's work afterwards became a legend in the neighbourhood, where feeling ran high against the British. Tony put it straight into his novel, killing off Zouch by mounting him on a notoriously vicious horse in a scene that gave considerable satisfaction to his hosts when they received a copy on publication. *From a View to a Death* was probably the only novel Pat Herdman ever read with pleasure. Jasper Fosdick, a jug-eared ex-army oaf, unemployed and unemployable, already sacked from nine jobs in three years, sounds as if he might have struck a chord. So does Betty's daughter Bianca, a mute angry child, at six years old already a prime troublemaker and dry run for Pamela Flitton in the *Dance*. The settling of minor scores, always an enjoyable sideline in these early novels, takes on particular relish with the Passengers' butler, Marshall, an adept (like *Venusberg*'s obsequious Mr. Pope) in the art of unnerving new arrivals: "The butler stood stock still, seeming to consider whether or not to throw back Zouch's suitcase on to the drive . . . For a moment Zouch thought he was about to spit, such a look of distaste passed over his face."

By the time Tony got back from Strabane to London, Varda had left again with Reitlinger for a winter break in Italy, returning only briefly at the end of the month before setting off with him again. Quite how they broke their news to Tony is hard to guess. He was apparently not invited to the brief ceremony at Kensington Registry Office where Dorothy Varda married Gerald Reitlinger on 26 January 1933. Four days later Adolf Hitler became chancellor of Germany, shortly afterwards abolishing all other political parties to make himself dictator. The markedly mixed response of the English upper and middle classes was summed up in the sixth volume of the *Dance* by the narrator's Uncle Giles: "'I like the little man they've got in Germany now,' he would remark, quite casually."

5

1933–34

On sleepless nights in Tavistock or Brunswick Square, Tony filled the time by making up rhyming couplets. A kilted Scotsman playing the bagpipes in the small hours on the street outside his flat started him off on what eventually grew into a hymn of hate against the Scots, ". . . a Race whose Thought and Word and Deed/ Have made a new INFERNO *North of Tweed,*/ Where they can practise in that chilly HELL/Vices that sicken; Virtues that repel." Tony recited his exuberant farrago bit by bit as he wrote it to friends over lunch in Soho, widening his scope to incorporate side-swipes at popular targets like the prime minister, Ramsay MacDonald ("Fewer such statesmen ENGLAND might be better for/Confused of Mind; no less confused of Metaphor"), and Heygate's old enemy at the BBC:

> *. . . cheerless REITH, unparalleled Enormity*
> *Of* Scottish *Prudery and* Nonconformity;
> *Of all his race scarce one can we desire less,*
> Teetotal *Despot of the ambient* Wireless.

This sort of thing went down well with the regulars at Castano's in Greek Street, then one of the cheapest places in London for a good Italian meal. Tony met friends there every day for lunch, or at Maxim's Chinese establishment in Wardour Street, moving on afterwards for coffee at Legrain's in Gerrard Street, and stopping on his way back to the office to watch the buskers on a patch of open ground at the top of the street behind the old Shaftesbury Theatre. Here he and Lambert first heard the blonde girl on crutches with the voice of an opera singer, who would resurface thirty years later halfway through the *Dance*. Three transvestite male dancers, high-kicking on the same spot, wore sequinned ballgowns like Major Fosdick in *From a View to a Death*. A man with a drawn sword prodding another man, lying gagged and chained on the ground behind the theatre, went straight into Tony's fourth novel, *Agents and Patients*.

Tony came across the bondage merchants with Heygate, who said ominously that was how he felt about his marriage. He was back in London with Evelyn by February 1933, writing up his experiences at the film studio in a second novel, and picking up old friendships over lunch at Castano's. It was a convivial meeting place, with ten or twelve tables on the ground floor, an upstairs room for cards in the afternoon, and an Italian proprietor who clearly found his core customers highly entertaining. They included the Heygates, Lamberts, Daintrey and the Lloyd brothers, the last two preparing as they neared thirty to ditch their disreputable past and become model citizens instead. John went home to Wales, where he was promptly elected mayor of Montgomery. Wyndham, round-faced, sedate and sweet-natured, less flamboyant but as sharply funny as his elder brother, stayed on in their old flat in Queen Square, practising as a doctor and writing a book for one of Duckworths' pop series, *A Hundred Years of Medicine*. Tony dedicated his diatribe against the Scots—improvised, updated and often chanted aloud at Castano's—to the Lloyds with acknowledgements to Lambert, who had contributed some scurrilous lines of his own about Scottish composers. *Caledonia* in its final draft ended with a call (still echoing today) to disband the Union, rebuild the old Roman wall, and "Replace this Race with others, all too few/ The honest *Welshman*, or the worthy *Jew* . . ."

This was an implicit tribute to Reitlinger, whose fondness for fiercely competitive sessions of *bouts-rimés* had made Tony a dab hand at rhyming couplets. Weekends at Thornsdale generally wound up after dinner with poker and parlour games, or attempts to raise the dead with the help of ouija board and planchette, popular post-war pastimes that Tony knew more about than most, thanks to his mother. In their mid- to late twenties, Reitlinger and his guests still had the insatiable appetite for jokes and clowning of a generation overshadowed for much of their childhood and adolescence by war and its aftermath. They dressed up, improvising storylines or cinematic clips (Tony was still an addict of early-afternoon film showings) in the garden where basket chairs and a makeshift wooden gibbet provided endless scope for ambushes and hangings. Tony documented proceedings, sticking photographs into an album and adding wonkily typed-out captions underneath. "He had the option between the Hangman's Rope and Poison," ran a headline clipped from a newspaper to go with a snap of Tony himself strung up on the gibbet. In another, his ex-neighbour, Bumble Dawson, swings from the crossbar with Tony presiding as her executioner above the caption: "Mrs. GERALD CORCORAN (formerly Miss Bumble Dawson) hanged for adultery at Thornsdale in the County of Sussex." Reitlinger was an ex-suitor of Bumble, herself now married to a tall handsome guardsman who had left the army to start up a business with her making fashion accessories, and later dealing in contemporary art (Burra was the first artist the Corcorans represented).

Reitlinger and the Lloyds, all three excellent photographers, worked overtime on weekends when the arrival of the Lamberts made things livelier still. A serial adultery scenario featured Tony and Flo, surprised in various compromising positions by an outraged Constant, who effortlessly dominated Thornsdale theatricals, at one point even upstaging the heroine in the "Burning of Joan of Arc" by kneeling purposefully in front of her with his back to the camera. Escapades like these scandalized the village, and so did the quantities of pretty girls Reitlinger invited to stay: Flo Lambert, Bar Ker-Seymer, Evelyn Heygate in her biker's leathers, as well as socialites of the day like Mamaine Paget and her twin sister Celia, or Joanne Firminger and her two pretty sisters-in-law, Elspeth and Gwyneth Lloyd. What seems to have been a one-off attempt at nude bathing in the muddy stream that ran through the grounds at Thornsdale was still vividly remembered by elderly parties in Rye half a century later, when Billy Chappell retired there. Burra reported threatening remarks made at the time by the cook's husband, rolling home drunk from the pub ("this place is nothing but a br—but a br—but a bloody brothel"). Prurient speculation was exacerbated by the host's habit of photographing his female guests in suggestive, even mildly erotic poses, and carefully pasting the results into his album.

Even his marriage failed to suppress the gossip entirely. From a strictly practical point of view it had obvious advantages on both sides. Reitlinger could hardly have hoped to secure a lovelier or more sophisticated mistress for his house and himself. Varda for her part seems to have reckoned their union would give her the kind of base for entertaining friends that she had once briefly enjoyed at the bookshop, a chance to offer lavish hospitality against a stable background to a witty and fascinating literary salon. "I hope it will be nice for all of us," she wrote, explaining the marriage to Tony. But the letters she sent him from honeymoon in Morocco that February were far from reassuring. In Tangier she claimed to have appendicitis, threatening "to spend the rest of the honey in a nursing home." Whores of both sexes swarmed round them in Casablanca and Marrakesh. "I think you would adore the women," she wrote, sketching an egg-shaped bundle with an eye-slit at the top, and two feet protruding from the bottom, labelled in brackets: "this is a woman." Varda was drunk—"sick & unconscious the whole time"—in Rabat. An Arab in the desert dropped a stone on her index finger, bruising it so badly she could hardly hold a pen. "Really I am having a most interesting and pleasant h--n," she wrote from Fez, where she ended up in bed again with a pain.

The situation scarcely improved after the couple got back to Thornsdale in March. Varda felt herself a failure as a hostess from the start, weighed down by the demands of her household ("Perhaps I was right to avoid possessions all my life"), and finding its smooth running almost more than she could manage. Staff gave notice, plumbers cut off the water ("I seem to have made Thornsdale even more uninhabitable than ever"), and Gerald's elder brother ruined a weekend with Tony by behaving like "a scabrous old bore." Possibly, Henry Reitlinger felt entitled to cut up rough, given that his fellow guest had so recently been the lover of his new sister-in-law, a fact that Varda at least was not inclined to conceal. Her letters alternated between apologies and urgent requests for Tony to come back again. "Goodnight my precious," she wrote after their initial reunion in March, "I adore you & perhaps when we have both married & divorced a few more people & at ninety I have a *dot* & put an ad in the matrimonial *Times* you will answer it. V."

The atmosphere at Thornsdale grew strained and irritable. Varda took no part in the usual charades, appearing only once in Reitlinger's album in a rare wintry snapshot of the couple taken in the garden together shortly before their marriage. Dressed for the part of lady of the manor in a double-breasted overcoat of country tweeds, she looks uncharacteristically ill at ease. Reitlinger's caption—"Trilby and Svengali"—invokes a famously hypnotic relationship, one of the great seduction sequences of High Victorian fiction in a bestselling novel by Gerald du Maurier. In the summer of 1933 the tension between the Reitlingers became unbearable, and their rows increasingly dramatic. The couple split apart in July, having managed to stay married for less than six months. Tony, chosen by Varda as confidant, now found himself cast as the solution to her problems. By the end of the month she had commandeered his three-week annual holiday abroad in what seems to have been a contest of wills, with Varda as keen as Tony was reluctant to restore their relationship to its former footing.

He insisted on separate hotel rooms, and made sure their travels were chaperoned by the Corcorans, when they finally set out in Varda's car for a motoring holiday in Spain. The four of them drove down through France at the beginning of August in summer rain and sweltering temperatures that steadily rose as they approached the Roussillon and the border with Spanish Catalonia. They headed for Barcelona, where all four visited an imposing whorehouse whose inmates in long floaty white dresses reminded Tony of the slope-shouldered, full-bosomed, wasp-waisted ladies in pen-and-wash brothel scenes by Constantin Guys. They struck inland to Saragossa and on through the mountains to Madrid, covering close on a thousand miles in just over a week. They visited the Escorial and watched a bullfight, mesmerized wherever they went by bandits and beggars who seemed to have stepped straight out of *Carmen*, or Goya's *Disasters of War*.

Varda sent a triumphal postcard to Wyndham Lloyd (who had joined his brother in Wales), showing Goya's sunny painting in the Prado of acrobats walking on stilts: "Here is an idea for next year's mayoral fiesta at which if Tony & I are alive we shall hope to assist. At the moment he is sweating out his last breaths in a neighbouring room [the word "bed," scratched out underneath, remains clearly visible]. The heat is appalling & the itinerary one that would normally take 6 months." Heat worse than anything known even in Madrid for nearly twenty years—so brutal that it sapped the will to move, let alone try and get away from the capital—was compounded by political chaos. "A strong and threatening tide of history meets you at the frontier," wrote Tony, quoting Wyndham Lewis. Simmering unrest on the streets, anarchist uprisings and vicious reprisals had weakened a Republican government about to be undone by the formation of the fascist front that swept the parties of the right to victory in general elections at the end of the year. The violence that would erupt in civil war just under three years later was already palpable.

On their last day in Spain, the party reached San Sebastián, driving for hours in drenching rain from one hotel to the next in search of a vacant room, and finally settling after midnight for a luxury honeymoon suite at an extortionate cost none of them could conceivably afford. Varda's unrivalled capacity for causing disruption, held uneasily in check for too long, broke out in force soon after they crossed back into France in a reckless confrontation between her and Gerald Corcoran. He and Bumble left immediately for Paris, a defection that rankled with the other two, now faced with paying over money they hadn't got for double their anticipated share of fuel costs on the journey home as well as for the Channel car ferry. Duckworth was still paying Tony a part-timer's pittance. Varda depended on a meagre allowance irregularly doled out by an unwilling Gerald. "Has either of them thought of having the other certified?" Heygate wrote at the end of August to Tony: "It should be painfully easy." Fractious, explosive, tormented by demons, Varda cannot have been an easy companion on the eight hundred miles back to London. Her marriage was a sham, her relations with Tony beyond repair. Constant Lambert, accidentally encountered with Flo in Saragossa at the start of the trip, summed up the situation in a pertinent jingle:

It's no good escaping your doom
By taking a ticket to Spain;
The bulging portmanteaux of gloom
Will arrive by a later train.

Tony was back in London in good time to oversee production of *From a View to a Death* for publication in mid-October. His plan was for the expressionless wooden doll that had figured on the dust jackets of his first two novels to be mounted this time on a rearing horse, clearly a mechanical fake with clumsy articulation and absurd dangling hooves that somehow made the finished design more menacing. Misha Black's jacket, like his variations on the same theme for subsequent novels, conveyed precisely the nuance of impersonal, unmistakeably contemporary unease the author had in mind. But, though Black himself went on to become one of the twentieth century's great industrial designers, his book covers found little favour with Duckworths. Nor did the books themselves, judging by the dedication of *From a View to a Death*: "For Tom Balston with an author's condolences, 17 October, 1933." Tony's contemporaries shared none of his publisher's misgivings. Evelyn Waugh picked Powell as the only novelist of his generation worth watching on the strength of this latest book, and John Betjeman wrote to say he couldn't remember anything that had made him laugh so much, adding a wistful postscript: "I would rather like to dress up in sequins on the quiet." Edith Sitwell urged everyone she knew in Paris to get hold of a copy: "It is the kind of wit the French really understand," she wrote firmly to Balston.

Heygate reacted competitively, threatening to parody Tony as Rightlaw in his current novel, the barely fictionalized *Talking Pictures*: "I am afraid you are for it in the part when you come to Neubabelsberg . . ." This was the beginning of a kind of literary leapfrog between them. When he started writing his own next novel, Tony cast Heygate on the first page as Peter Maltravers, the nefarious conman whose irrepressible charm and energy drive the plot. Oliver Chipchase, Maltravers's sardonic sidekick with a weakness for amateur psychoanalysis, is a projection of Tony himself. The title, *Agents and Patients*, came from John Wesley's division of the human race into those that do things, and those that have things done to them. The book's central duo—"post-war types, already perhaps a little dated"—are Wesleyan agents. Hard-up, unscrupulous, manipulative, surviving hand-to-mouth on odd jobs in the film industry or low-level journalism, they pick up a gormless dupe called Blore-Smith with more money than he knows what to do with, and proceed to relieve him of it.

Comprehensively diddled, disillusioned and fleeced, Blore-Smith finally escapes their clutches, ending up far better equipped than before to deal with the world and its ways. His rehabilitation takes the form of a tour of Paris, Berlin and London, conceived—like the

John Heygate, modelling as Maltravers to Tony's Chipchase in *Agents and Patients*, "post-war types, already perhaps a little dated"

lewd murals in a Parisian brothel sampled on the way—"in a spirit of complete moral detachment." A high point is his encounter in a gay nightclub on the Kurfürstendamm with the querulous, high-handed but ultimately irresistible enchantress, Mrs. Mendoza, herself an affectionate tribute to Varda. Another is the scene in a West End art gallery where Blore-Smith—dizzy with excitement at his own daring—decides to buy a modern painting. Watched by Chipchase and the astounded gallery owner, Reggie Frott, he shells out an exorbitant sum for a canvas picked out at random ("one of the worst paintings I have ever hung in my gallery," Frott confides frankly to Chipchase, "and between you and me, that's saying a good deal").

Frott and his gallery were easily identifiable as Freddie Mayor and his outfit in Cork Street, both undergoing a startling modernist conversion in the summer of 1933 ("Tell me about Freddie's gallery," asked Heygate, accustomed like Tony to treat the place as a congenial party joint for himself and his friends: "is it serious, on his part at least?"). Encouraged by the success of contemporary art in Paris, Freddie had secured financial backing from Fyfe Duthie, a Scottish shipping magnate now married to Enid Firminger, and commissioned Juliet's husband, Brian O'Rorke, to carry out a gallery make-over. Velvet drapes, dim background lighting, plushy seats and dark panelling gave way to white walls and simple tubular furniture in a light-flooded space that looked to incredulous gallery-goers as if the pictures had been hung in a hospital. Battle stations for the modern movement in Britain were drawn up by Paul Nash, announcing in *The Times* the formation of his combative Unit One with an operational base in the Mayor Gallery. Headed by Burra and Wadsworth, Nash's list of revolutionaries included Henry Moore, Ben Nicholson, Barbara Hepworth and an ambitious young Canadian architect, Wells Coates, currently making a name for himself with his Isokon building, a block of flats on Lawn Road in north London that proposed a revolution in urban living.

Coates's wife Marion worked as an editor for the Nonesuch Press, and as publisher's reader for Jonathan Cape. Tony met her perhaps through mutual contacts in publishing, or more probably at one of Freddie's parties since she and Wells were essentially part of the Charlotte Street art scene. He was a glamorous figure with Hollywood-style good looks and a taste for snappy dressing, fast cars and pretty women, but his consuming desire was to propel England towards the kind of futuristic transformation already envisaged on the continent by Corbusier and Gropius. In 1933 he founded the radical think tank MARS (Modern Architectural Research Group) with Maxwell Fry and others for this purpose. Marion remembered him ever afterwards as he had been in those days, "young and poetical and earnest," not so forceful as he later became, "but more mysterious." She said at the time, when he outlined his overall plan to her, that it would be a Napoleonic campaign.

The Coateses had started married life six years earlier in Wells's first shot at a wholly modern interior, a streamlined and elegantly functional first-floor apartment in Doughty Street with murals painted by John Banting, and minimalist armchairs from Heal's. Wells's Lawn Road Flats would become the first major building in the UK to apply modernist principles with anything approaching such style and authority. Their completion in 1934 shifted the parameters of British architecture, but it also destroyed Wells's marriage. Problems with builders, contractors, workmen, clients and neighbours preoccupied him for three years to the exclusion of virtually everything else. What little energy he had left went on designing the first recording studios for the BBC's new building in Portland Place, and simultaneously conducting an affair with Molly Pritchard who, together with her husband Jack, had commissioned the flats in the first place. By the time Tony met Marion Coates in the late autumn or winter of 1933, she was living with a small child and a semi-detached husband a few streets away from Lawn Road in an unreconditioned basement flat at 12a, Belsize Park Gardens.

She was gentle, self-contained and demure with a softness and sweetness of manner that hid a cool analytical brain and a streak of unexpected toughness. In a portrait of her with her baby daughter Laura, painted by Banting shortly before she met Tony, she has short, roughly cropped fair hair, classically regular features and a sad expression. She wears a severe dark polo-neck jersey, the sort of thing that exasperated Wells, who could never understand her refusal to show off her singular beauty by dressing more elegantly. Marion had pale porcelain skin, a fashionably slender figure and lovely legs but no interest whatsoever in looks or clothes. She read greedily—"I am a gobbler of print," she said—and with discrimination. Her gravity and composure, sharp judgements, cool wit, unexpected sensuality and delicate English-rose looks, even her occasional awkwardness captivated Tony. Looking back half a century later, he said she was someone "for whom I once had a great passion." If Marion's rational and restful temperament made her the opposite of Varda, Tony was her antidote to Wells. She had loved her husband for his stubborn visionary spirit and crusading zeal, but she had had more than enough by this time of his domineering egotism, his constitutional irresponsibility and compulsive self-aggrandisement. Tony's self-deprecating humour was a powerful corrective. So was his laid-back, low-key approach, and his overriding interest in other people. She recognized underlying scepticism, and a strength of purpose at least as uncompromising as her own. Her childhood, like his, had been abnormal. Born in China to British parents—Daisy and Frank Grove, a concert pianist and an engineer in charge of the original Kowloon–Canton railway—she had been sent back to school in England at five or six years old, making the long journey by rail and ship alone except for a slightly older brother. For the next twelve years she attended St. George's, Harpenden, the only boarding school in the country prepared to accept pupils of all ages and both sexes, including children

Marion Coates: "Someone for whom I once had a great
passion," said Tony.

from abroad with nowhere to go in the holidays. It taught Marion
never to expose her feelings, and to trust nobody but herself.

Her response was to become a doctrinaire idealist, rejecting the
bourgeois affluence of a conventional middle-class background,
turning her back on her parents, and replacing the emotional stability
they had never given her with ideological commitment. She studied
political science at the London School of Economics under the young
Harold Laski, and joined the Communist Party. These were heady
days at the LSE. Laski himself was a hugely popular lecturer, one
of the key intellectual players of the 1920s and '30s who steered a
whole generation in a surge to the Left. Marion's particular friend
and mentor was the charismatic young physicist J. D. Bernal, a Jewish Italian from Tipperary, also a practising Marxist who confidently
predicted war between the capitalist West and Soviet Russia. Bernal's
manifesto, *The World, the Flesh and the Devil*, found a ready response
among post-war optimists, especially students, who saw their noblest
dreams for the future coming true in Russia with its promise of cul-

tural progress, scientific planning and social justice for the workers: "Under capitalism the inescapable impoverishment of the masses, in the Soviet Union joyous work on the clearly outlined road to a classless society . . . In science, in education, in religion, in the family, in the prisons, the USSR gives practical embodiment to the progressive ideas of the nineteenth and twentieth centuries." These remained Marion's core convictions for the rest of her life.

She was twenty-two years old when she married Wells in 1927 to the horror of her parents, who had returned to London by this time to settle in a large comfortable house on Holland Park. Marion said that Wells gave her the most joy anyone ever had, and also the most pain. He seems to have been silent, abstracted or absent much of the time. A letter she wrote him long afterwards paints a bleak picture of their time together: "I have been angry about it . . . that you were never there, that you never said 'Poor darling!' when you might, that you let me see how uncomfortable it was to be clung to." Wells's obsession with Lawn Road Flats shut her out even more effectively than his serial affairs with other women. For all practical purposes the marriage disintegrated with the birth of a baby in 1930, leaving Marion face to face with the realities of survival as a single mother on a shoestring. Barely able to support himself, let alone a wife and child, Wells sent her every so often a few notes in an envelope—£3, rarely as much as £5—but the regular allowance they had agreed she would need (£2 10s a week) was beyond him. Forced reluctantly to rely on parental support, Marion responded with rage and despair as the domestic trap closed round her. She felt herself fading in her mid-twenties into a "grass-green-greying widow," her courage and energy draining away, her individuality sapped. Five years into the marriage, she took a secretarial job in the Cape office, found a flat for herself in Belsize Park and hired a Swiss girl to look after the baby. "Do not imagine I shall dash off & have a lot of lovers," she told Wells: "I feel incapable of any emotional power for a long time."

Wells had knocked her off balance, and drastically reduced her faith in herself as an autonomous being. Accustomed to being highly attractive to men, loved and envied by women, Marion had for once lost her nerve. When she met Tony, he set himself to restore it. He said she reminded him of Rubens's *Chapeau de paille* (*Woman in a Straw Hat*) in the National Gallery: "There was that same sugges-

tion, though only for an instant, of shyness and submission . . ."
Certainly the girl in Banting's portrait has the smooth pale forehead,
straight nose, small sweet mouth and faintly quizzical cock of the
head that characterize Rubens's sitter. By January 1934, Tony and
Marion were regularly spending evenings together, and by the end
of that month he had apparently broken off his novel because of her.
"I am glad to hear you are in such an amorous mess," Heygate wrote
enviously from his parents' house in Hampshire: "As usual I suppose
your state of feeling makes work & the need for work entirely super-
fluous & trivial." Tony wrote back a fortnight later asking where to
go for a quiet weekend in the country with no fear of being disturbed
by inquisitive friends. Heygate suggested a pub called the Swan at
Lymington on the edge of the New Forest: "on re-reading your letter I must observe that the Swan is not very romantic & only fairly
secluded. However none of 'us' are likely to find our way there . . .
why not go to the St. Pancras Hotel?"

One of the things Marion minded most about her husband's defection was enforced celibacy. She needed both tenderness and sexual
satisfaction, as she explained frankly to Wells, who seems to have
rated quantity over quality in sexual matters. Unusually direct in
this as in much else, Marion had apparently discussed sex with Tony
over lunch the first time they met. If she reminded him of Rubens's
plump pretty young matron, he said she also had something of the
most voluptuous of the three girls lounging on harem cushions in
Delacroix's *Femmes d'Alger* (*Women of Algiers*), the one on the right
in a loose baggy white top with a rose in her hair and her bare leg bent
at the knee. The first six or seven months of 1934 were a time of acute
happiness for both of them. Unlike any of Tony's previous affairs,
this one seems to have been conducted well away from parties, public
meeting places and the company of friends. Perhaps the intensity of
their feelings blocked out awareness of anything else, or maybe they
simply couldn't bring themselves to waste precious time together.

They had after all much to say to one another. Whether or not they
discussed the books they were respectively writing, editing and publishing, Tony had work in progress to read aloud to her as he often
did to his friends. Maybe Marion read hers to him. The only book
she ever compiled and wrote herself came out that year, an original

and imaginative *Sea Sequel to the Weekend Book* covering every conceivable topic from Mutiny, Piracy and Shipwreck to Small Boat Seamanship and Sea Stories (an impressive list of contributors headed by Columbus and Hakluyt veers off in surprising directions, ending up with Ivan Turgenev and Stephen Crane). The exchange between them was all-absorbing that spring. "Do write me 500 words on being in love . . . ," wrote a disconsolate Heygate, whose marriage to Evelyn had fallen catastrophically apart: "Is it really better than not being in love? Can you write better? See more jokes?" Tony's response, if he sent one, has disappeared, with the rest of his letters to Heygate, although with time he repaired that omission in ways neither could have foreseen. Few writers have ever given a more poignant, persuasive, ultimately devastating account of being in love than Powell in the *Dance*, where the narrator finds himself haunted over nearly fifty years and twelve volumes by an affair in his twenties with a girl called Jean Duport. His memories take on a disturbing life of their own: stated, restated, reflected, refracted, at one point violently twisted and wrenched into hideous new shapes that continue to return and re-form, as in a fairground mirror, so that recollections become monstrous distortions of themselves, secreting a poisonous power as concentrated as the pure potent essence of those few far-distant months when, as a young man, his life had been briefly lit by the radiant, cool, clear presence of Jean herself.

Marion left no record of what she thought of this extraordinary transposition, although she undoubtedly recognized her portrait in the mirror of the *Dance*. Their affair was as brief as it was passionate, and seems to have more or less run its course by the late summer of 1934. Her priorities and Tony's had proved to be too far apart, their very different understanding of human behaviour in each case too deeply held, the angles from which each approached life itself too sharply opposed to leave much room for manoeuvre. But throughout the 1950s, '60s and '70s, long after Marion had finally parted from Tony, her daughter remembered a change in the atmosphere at home whenever a fresh volume of the *Dance* came out, and her mother rushed off to the nearest bookshop to buy a copy.

In August 1934, Tony's attention was violently jerked back to Duckworths by an internal explosion. A routine board meeting between the three directors on 18 August erupted without warning over some issue so footling that afterwards no one could remember what it was:

> all Gerald Duckworth's pent-up rage over the years on the subject of the Sitwells, Waugh, Beaton, other modern abominations forced on him by Balston, broke out; while, at the same instant, Balston gave voice to his equally powerful resentment of what he had long regarded as Gerald Duckworth's obstruction and inertia.

The upshot was that Milsted voted in Duckworth's favour, and Balston walked out. Far from inheriting Duckworth's position as head of the firm in natural succession as he had every reason to expect, given that the chairman had for years been drinking himself to death (he succeeded three years later), Balston left the firm for good the same day. Gerald Duckworth sank back satisfied into his customary torpor. Milsted took advantage of the situation to double his own salary, but lack of inclination or practical expertise prevented his pursuing a more active role. From now on Mr. Lewis, the formidable managing director, kept the office ticking over and production lines moving with his customary efficiency, but that was as far as he was prepared to go. Balston's latest protegé, Alan Harris, an able and agreeable newcomer recruited from the academic firm of T. G. Bell, had no experience of general publishing.

That left Tony, at twenty-eight, to take over editorial control of a broken-backed and much shrunken concern rapidly returning to the state of ossified conservatism Balston had been hired thirteen years earlier to remedy. Osbert Sitwell promptly moved to Macmillan. His brother Sacheverell had already decamped, complaining that a charwoman earned more than he did. Their sister Edith said that Balston's resignation marked "one of the worst days in our lives." Certainly he left small pickings behind him. Current turnover—"reprints of a few staples, a series of historic lives and some miscellaneous travel and adventure books"—barely covered expenses. Typical titles of the kind of work that won Mr. Lewis's approval, and made Gerald Duckworth feel comfortable, were *Love Is Too Young*, *Youth on the Prow* and *Fly Away Youth*. Tony had a copy of the last with a double-edged inscription by the author, whose steady output and satisfactory sales

Pakenham Hall

were one of the firm's few plus points: "For Tony Powell from God-frey Winn, or from a lowborn to a highborn."

Tony's first move a week after Balston's departure was to leave the country for three weeks. He had been invited for a fortnight's holiday to a castle in Ireland by the owner's sister-in-law, whom he had met at a party given by one of his authors. Pakenham Hall, when he finally got there, after a miserable overnight sea crossing from Liverpool, was a great grey sprawling pile with Victorian crenellations, turrets and moat, "an enormous gothicky castle in the dimmest bogland in the middle of Ireland," said an inmate. It stood surrounded by gardens and ornamental lakes in nine acres of parkland in County Westmeath. Tony was initially dubious, remembering the Herdmans of County Tyrone, but friends assured him he had nothing to fear from his hosts. The 6th Earl of Longford and his countess ran an outfit as far removed as it was possible to get from the hunting, fishing and shooting regimes of neighbouring castles.

Edward Longford (who had been three years ahead of Tony at Eton) had inherited his title at thirteen and repudiated it as soon as he came of age, calling himself Eamon de Longphort and turning his house into a Nationalist bastion. He flew the flag of the Irish Free State from his tower, and sang rousing Fenian songs to his house guests in the evenings round the piano. He had met and married his wife Christine at Oxford, where she too prudently converted to the Nationalist cause. They were both very young when they moved to Ireland, hired a butler accustomed to castles, and painted the dark panelling of their baronial hall bright red, blue and lime green. Tony had never met either of them.

His visit was clouded from the start by the fact that Christine Longford was also a novelist whose astute and witty first novel, *Making Conversation*, had caused considerable stir when it come out in the same year as *Afternoon Men*. Hailed as a modern Jane Austen, she had made slightly less of a splash with a second book, *Country Places*. Elizabeth Pakenham, the sister-in-law who asked Tony to stay, had optimistically assured Edward and Christine that he would give their house party "the right sort of sparkle," while simultaneously informing him that they were "thrilled at the prospect of your coming." Neither turned out to be true. Tony arrived a day late, having missed his connection in Dublin and had to catch a bus next day. Christine, who had read *Venusberg*—"it might be about Dublin"—was not looking forward to being upstaged in her own home by a supercilious rival from London with three published novels to his name, and a fourth under way. She had never in any case much liked Elizabeth, the wife of Edward's brother Frank, who had been not only younger, trendier, better connected and quite as clever as Christine at Oxford, but a celebrated beauty as well, which her hostess was not.

"I could fill a book (and no doubt shall one of these days) with what is happening here," Tony wrote after five days to his mother, describing the electric undercurrents generated between Christine and Elizabeth, who had stirred things up just before his arrival by warning the rest of the house party that he was "4 feet 3 inches high & had very broad shoulders & always carried a gun." Metaphorically speaking that was perhaps how Christine herself was inclined to see him. Although heavily dependent on London contacts to keep her in touch with the latest developments—Waugh, Betjeman, Tony himself and many other ambitious young writers all stayed at the castle—she made it clear she would stand no nonsense from pretentious metropolitan imports doing their best to make her feel like a provincial nobody. Tony had enjoyed *Making Conversation* and looked forward to meeting its author, whose sarcastic comments and dismissive laughter soon let him know he'd made a mistake.

It was only much later that he recognized Christine's response as defensive, fuelled by bitter resentment at being cut off by her own choice from the literary world that should have been her natural habitat. Unlike her husband, who in his early thirties was growing stupendously fat, Christine was small, skinny and wiry with what the

Lord Longford with house guests: his mother-in-law, Mary Manning and Tony

painter Henry Lamb (another of her brothers-in-law) called an Aztec look. Watchful, inquisitive, as sensible as she was sharp, Christine dealt with her own equivocal reaction to Tony by writing a play about him. *Anything but the Truth* was performed at Dublin's Gate Theatre in May 1937 before a gossipy inquisitive audience who knew or suspected it was based on a particular house party at Pakenham Hall. It plots the attempts of a houseful of weekend guests in the remote Irish countryside to impress a visiting London celebrity, who turns out to be no help whatsoever in furthering their respective careers, being solely interested in pursuing, or being pursued by, all the available girls.

The Longfords' guests in August 1934 consisted of Elizabeth and Frank Pakenham with two close friends of theirs, Anne and George Martelli, and Christine's mother Mrs. Trew. The only unattached girl was a fellow writer called Mary Manning: exuberantly charming, highly competitive and fiercely determined, she was the same age as Tony and a great deal more famous than he was in Dublin. She had made a hit at the Gate with her first play, bypassing the popular vogue for fey, sub-Yeatsian tributes to Mother Ireland by speaking directly to her own sceptical urban generation. *Youth's the Season* was adroit, apolitical, sexually experimental and wholly free from nostalgia, like its author. Micheál MacLiammóir played the lead, and the cast included an enigmatic silent character called Horace Egosmith, based on an old boyfriend of the author by the name of Samuel Beckett. The part was played by Beckett himself with such relish that he wrote a speech of his own for Egosmith (the author made him drop it, but not before it had sparked his interest in playwriting). Arty intellectual Dublin had no trouble recognizing itself in this snapshot. Mary was a journalist by profession, a natural critic and reviewer, so accustomed to taking other people's work apart that, much as she liked Tony, she couldn't resist giving him a whole page of sharply critical notes on *Afternoon Men*. "But O Tony," she added, almost in spite of herself, "your dialogue is gorgeous. I've never read such dialogue before or since. You must write a play."

Mildly allergic all his life to anything to do with the theatre, Tony was already having a hard time at the castle, where Edward and Christine's mutual passion for theatricals in general, and the Gate in particular, meant that most conversations revolved around choosing, writing, casting and directing play scripts with occasional breaks for backstage rumour and intrigue. His hosts were about to set up a rival group of their own called Longford Productions, and Tony was embarrassed to discover that their company secretary was a distant cousin of his mother, Lionel Dymoke. The connection was almost too much to bear. Mary was his only consolation, and they arranged to meet in Dublin as soon as he could get away and carry on where they left off, while she showed him round the town. The relationship went so well that Christine began dropping hints about how far it had actually gone, a situation that suited Mary, who clearly had no objection to its going a lot further. "You're an awfully companionable cad, rather a loveable swine!" she told Tony, who was enjoying their encounter as much as she was. By the time she left at the end of his first week, Dublin gossip rightly suspected the start of an affair.

A general changeover of house guests at that point meant that everyone departed except Tony, who had almost another week to fill in before he could decently escape to spend the last two days of his annual holiday with Mary in Dublin. He particularly dreaded Elizabeth Pakenham going, and leaving him with no one to stand between him and his hostess or for that matter his host, clearly no more enthusiastic than his wife about having people he didn't know foisted on him as guests. "I have taken a tremendous dislike to the Irish," Tony wrote gloomily to his mother on 30 August, explaining that the fresh contingent contained several people he already knew, among them Edward's sister Pansy Lamb with her husband Henry, and another younger sister he'd never met.

Pakenham Hall was the family home of Edward's five younger siblings, who treated it as their own, coming and going as they pleased with friends, spouses and children, sometimes not even bothering to announce their plans to their hostess in advance. Christine accepted without protest a tidal wave of her husband's relations rolling in every summer as predictably as the sea, while Edward largely blotted out their existence by immersing himself in one of his various obsessions (Irish Nationalism, the Gate Theatre, food or, failing these, anything Chinese). Visitors read or wrote books, and played games according to castle rules: joke tennis, and a variant of billiards called Slosh. The hardiest picked their way over knife-edged stones to bathe in the beautiful chill waters of Lough Derravaragh ("the shock of the icy water almost anaesthetised the pain in the bather's feet"). In a photograph taken by Tony, Edward lies like a beached whale on the grassy bank of the lake. He has the look of an outsize schoolboy with scarlet cheeks and stripy jumper in his portrait by Henry Lamb, who was steadily working his way through the Pakenham family, painting them one after another in successive summers.

Henry, who was nearly twenty years older than his wife, belonged to an earlier generation than the rest of the household and dealt with the age gap by commandeering a bedroom as studio where he could set up his own self-contained enclave. This year it was Tony who sat for him, wearing bold strong holiday colours. "The coat was pale-ginger, collar blue, tie dark blue and there was a red pullover," wrote Henry, who eliminated the pullover and lowered the tone of the shirt and tie so as to produce a canvas in his favourite monochrome browns and greys. Finding Tony a fidgety subject, he picked the youngest member of the household, his wife's sister Violet Pakenham, to keep the sitter's mind on the job. She seemed just as jumpy as Tony at first, distracted and restless, more interested in trying to make out what it said on the newspaper Henry used for cleaning his brushes than in entertaining the model. Tony took up a standard pose for his portrait, facing forward, head tilted slightly to one side, unsmiling, preoccupied, both eyes swivelling to his right as if he had caught sight of something or someone that made it hard to sit still. Perhaps he was thinking about another portrait session in his last novel that ended unexpectedly with a proposal. He said the whole atmosphere of the house had been transformed for him by Violet's arrival.

At some point he caught her attention. By the end of the week both recognized a mutual change of direction. "There was something in the air between you two," a fellow guest said afterwards. As soon as the portrait sittings were over the pair of them moved to the library, where Tony read aloud from the half-finished typescript of *Agents and Patients*. Forty years later Violet described with a poetic intensity unlike anything else in her published writing what happened when she took Tony outside and picked him an apple, like Eve, in the kitchen garden, then set off to show him the sheets of white bog cotton flowering in the bog garden, finding that something had distorted her sense of time and distance:

> never did we reach the Float Bog . . . but on these walks we began a conversation which has continued unabated until this day. To me surroundings known from childhood, and perhaps blurred by familiarity, came into focus as though I had been given new spectacles of a magical clarity. Looking down from a hilltop, it seemed that the white horses on Lough Derravaragh had never before galloped so dazzlingly over the steely blue water. Indoors, in the library, the leather backs of books collected two centuries before had never glowed so golden in the morning sun, as I sat in a window-seat and Anthony read aloud from the novel that was, at that moment, growing under his hand.

Pakenham Hall held unhappy memories for Violet: terrifying journeys as a small child in wartime across the Irish Sea for Easter and summer holidays, always expecting the boat to be hit by German torpedoes; merciless bullying in the nursery by her big brothers; shouting matches at mealtimes when the family split into opposing camps on the Irish question. That summer the panics and discomforts of her childhood were finally exorcized by Tony. He sent her a letter as soon as he reached Dublin, and she wrote back at once: "Darling Tony . . . My Spies Inform Me that Dublin is full of Dym & distant relatives of yours & that you sit in corners taking notes. All very sinister . . ." She was cheerful, chatty and circumspect, describing the jokes he'd missed and the games they'd played in his absence ("By the way the habit of potting the wrong balls at Slosh is now known as Powell's disease"). Tony took Mary out to dinner on his first night in Dublin and made love to her next day, an impromptu coupling at the back of a shop, made awkward by Dublin censoriousness and Tony's change of heart in the days they'd spent apart. Violet had already fixed up a visit to friends, but she ended her letter with a tentative proposal to meet on the boat crossing back to England on Sunday night, 16 September: "If however it's a bore don't bother . . . I will try not to take it too badly, still I shall probably tell half Bloomsbury & all Chelsea the plot of your new novel with jokes."

But Tony had to catch the Liverpool boat the day before Violet so as to be in the office on Monday morning. On Wednesday he dined with John Heygate, who put what sounds like a direct transcript of their conversation into his next book, *Motor Tramp*, which once again features Rightlaw and his love life: "Now take my case—would you say I was the sort of man to get married? Exactly! No one would! . . . You are absolutely right. In principle. But . . . this girl is different." Tony dined twice with Violet the following week on 25 and 29 September. Next day he asked her to marry him, having made sure in advance that she would be alone at teatime in the house she shared with her sisters in Rutland Gate. Violet, who knew perfectly well what was coming, accepted his proposal. They had known each other for three weeks, not counting the few days Tony spent without her in Dublin. "Undoubtedly it was rash," he wrote nearly half a century later: "On the other hand, there is absolutely no way of knowing what being married to someone is going to be like, short of marriage to that person."

Violet was twenty-two years old, lively, funny and pretty with a pink-and-white complexion, brown eyes and brown hair, but it was her extraordinary openness to experience, her voracious hunger for life and the energy she put into it that made her different from the other girls Tony knew. She was inquisitive, observant and smart with an intuitive understanding of people, and a consuming passion for parties. Unlike her two older sisters (both authors of Tony's at Duckworths at one point or another), who had fled the debutante world in disgust at the earliest possible moment, Violet could not have enough of it. She loved deb dances, hunt balls and receptions, moving on impartially afterwards to continue dancing into the small hours at one or other of the hundreds of sleazy nightclubs, open "midnight to the milkman's round," dotted all over the bottle-party belt in and around Piccadilly. Once she and her current boyfriend agreed to pool invitations and see how many parties they could clock up between them in a single night: by the time the sun rose over Battersea Bridge, their joint total came to eleven.

Always amply supplied with escorts and dancing partners, Violet's life in these years was far racketier than Tony's had ever been. She went to the Café de Paris for Douglas Byng, Nana of the Manor, Vivette the Vestiaire, "the melancholy songs of Chic Endor and Charlie Farrell." She hung out by day at the Savoy Grill or the Berkeley Hotel, by night at the relatively innocuous Blue Lantern in Ham Yard but more often at joints like the Bag o'Nails, or what Tony described as the inconceivably squalid 43 in Gerrard Street, both in fact semi-brothels as much as clubs. Violet favoured the Slippin' with its glass dance floor and louche waiters serving smoked haddock, bacon and eggs all night, but even she drew the line at Smokey Joe's, a sordid Gerrard Street cellar eventually closed down by the police. "Violet went to nightclubs and bars and seems to have done anything she chose," said her mystified sister Mary, who never forgot or forgave her own dismal years as a miserable and mutinous debutante.

On horseback in the country Violet was as fearless as she was inexperienced, borrowing a horse to go hunting, riding point-to-points whenever she could, learning in painful practice the risks and perils of jumping fences she knew nothing about on horses she had never ridden before. In 1933, the year she turned twenty-one, she played for the London Ladies, the winning team in the first all-women polo match ever held in the capital, at Ranelagh (one of her team mates was Muriel Wright, later Ian Fleming's girlfriend, in some sense the first Bond girl). Photographs show her wielding her mallet, looking slender, dashing and dishy in breeches and boots.

No aspect of Violet's chosen way of life had been easy to achieve. She may have seemed to others enviably free from parental or any other control, but she was still shadowed by a strict conventional upbringing based, perhaps even more than for most girls of her class and age, on discipline and repression. She could scarcely remember her father, the 5th Lord Longford, who had been killed commanding

London Ladies polo team (Violet is second from left)

his regiment at Gallipoli in 1915 when she was four. Her early years had been governed by her mother according to the rules and assumptions of her own Victorian girlhood, "a . . . way of life which, as far as I was concerned, had evaporated like the dew of the morning," said Violet. She and her younger sister Julia, always known as "the babies," lived in isolation at the top of the house with their minders ("Lady Violet's bad enough," said a nursemaid, "but Lady Julia's a thousand times worse"). Up until puberty and beyond they wore ribbed woollen stockings and buttoned boots with long hair cut in a fringe and tied back on top by a ribbon bow. Longing desperately to look and behave like other girls of their age in the 1920s, they had to scheme and beg for the right to wear shoes and short skirts, bob their hair, and even to go to school.

Every concession that the two youngest girls managed to wring out of their mother seemed an inconceivable privilege to their elder sisters, whose response to the regime at home had been to leave altogether as soon as they legally could. Under their father's trust fund, each of his daughters received at twenty-one an annual allowance of £400, enough to fund at least a degree of independence and choice. Pansy married Henry Lamb. Mary studied at art school, and moved into a Chelsea studio where Violet posed for her naked, watched with interest through the window by men from the Alvis car factory on the far side of the road. Having closely observed her elders' escape routes, Violet picked a different course, remaining under the family roof but treating her mother's prohibitions (drink, boys, make-up, smoking) as house rules that did not apply outside the front door. As an alternative to art school, she enrolled at the LSE, regarded by her mother as a rabid revolutionary outpost. Julia escaped to read philosophy, politics and economics at Somerville College, Oxford, and stayed the course, but Violet lasted only one term, fully agreeing with her tutor who suggested she was wasting her money and the school's time.

On 13 March 1933, she gave her own twenty-first birthday party at the Berkeley Hotel without telling her mother, whose idea of a suitable function for young girls was sedate and carefully chaperoned with a select list of guests and soft drinks (Lady Longford had never tasted wine in her life), preferably served by powdered footmen. Violet painted her nails scarlet and wore pink orchids at her party, invited whoever she liked and danced to the hit tunes of 1933: "Hello Beautiful," "Ooh That Kiss," and Oscar Hammerstein's catchy little number "I've Told Ev'ry Little Star." By this time Lady Longford had taken a short lease on the house in Rutland Gate for herself and her three unmarried daughters. Mary took over the attic, Violet and Julia lived downstairs with their mother who, still only in her mid-fifties, was becoming steadily more incapacitated for reasons she would never discuss. In fact she was dying of colon cancer but, since she refused to allow any mention of the disease or its symptoms, or even the fact that she was ill at all, her daughters found it hard to respond. A stern pretence of normality was kept up to the end in spite of two professional nurses moving into the house. These were the years when Violet was out every night, often returning only with the first signs of dawn in the sky. She appeased her mother by constructing an elaborate system of alibis and excuses, explaining that she had been visiting former schoolfriends, catching up with cousins, staying with Pansy, or spending the evening with Frank and his new wife Elizabeth.

At the end of 1933 Lady Longford finally died, releasing all the emotions rigorously suppressed for so long by her bewildered daughters. Violet was still absorbing the shock of her death when she caught pneumonia the following spring, and very nearly died herself. She recovered slowly, spending the weeks of her convalescence stranded in a seaside hotel on the south coast, an experience that if anything intensified her desire to dance every night until three or four in the morning. She and her sisters went on living together at 12, Rutland Gate, now an adult-free zone, liberated entirely from unwanted interference or supervision. For the first time in their lives they could openly entertain friends, and go where they wanted without asking permission. Tony spent much time there that autumn, beginning the long process of getting to know Violet and the vast extended family network of aunts, uncles, cousins and siblings to which he was about to belong.

It was an environment—especially strange to an only child—where individuals struggled to assert themselves against the collective identity. "I took my place . . . between two cousins," Violet wrote, describing her birth, "like a puppy newly entered in a pack of hounds." Her mother had had little time or attention to spare for any of her children except the eldest. Edward, singled out as his father's heir, set apart from the others by his mother's devotion, was always addressed within the family by his courtesy title, Lord Silchester. He was thirteen when their father died. Violet remembered their mother making a rare trip to the nursery to announce to her and the two-year-old Julia that from now on they must call him Edward, not Silchester. It felt to her, even as a four-year-old, as if "a semi-stranger was being replaced by a complete stranger."

Affection or intimacy played little part in her childhood. Lady Longford, for a long time very nearly unhinged by her husband's death, remained ever afterwards emotionally tight-fisted. All her children were afraid of her. The younger ones knew her only as a forbidding figure, crippled by arthritis, walking with a stick or on crutches, "the neurotic, semi-invalid whom I occasionally saw in the distance," said Mary. Violet said she never realized there was anything odd about the "skull-cracking collisions" exchanged by her family as greetings until a friend, watching them kiss, said he pitied any husbands the sisters might pick up later.

Strong attachments were discouraged in a childhood that had been as rootless as Tony's. Even in her father's lifetime, Violet's family had constantly switched houses, and as a widow Lady Longford retained a compulsive need to be on the move. At least twice a year she uprooted her entire household to make the long journey by land and sea with maid, nannies and baggage to Pakenham Hall, a place she had always detested. Her release from this annual self-imposed obligation came only with Edward's early marriage and move to Ireland (where an equally uncritical, no less adoring wife completed the process of his permanent infantilization). Lady Longford never saw Pakenham again. "My mother closed that chapter of her life with an almost audible slam," said Violet. The family had no other permanent base. Often parked with relatives as a young girl, spending the London season in leased or borrowed accommodation, Violet grew up in two successive, large, cheerless, rented houses in the Home Counties whose chief advantage, from her point of view, was being within easy reach of her maternal grandmother at Middleton Park in Oxfordshire. Her grandmother gave lavish children's parties at Christmas, welcoming her eight small grandchildren into her bedroom to play on the floor while she underwent the protracted ritual of being dressed by her maid every morning.

Violet's grandmother was Margaret, Countess of Jersey, former chatelaine of Osterley Park just outside London, a great beauty in her day, wife of a Tory statesman, legendary party-giver and -goer, celebrated above all before the war as the friend and patron of writers. Rudyard Kipling, Robert Louis Stevenson and Henry James had all been her friends, correspondents and guests at Osterley. Violet with her passion for parties, her sociable instincts and delight in other people was a throwback to Lady Jersey, who warmly approved. Well aware of her own daughter's shortcomings, she had always paid particular attention to Violet and her sisters, sending letters, invitations, presents and books (handy cheques as they got older) to compensate for the situation at home. "Grandmamma was a mother to me," said Violet.

As soon as they had settled their engagement, Tony introduced Violet to his parents, who were predictably charmed, especially Colonel Powell, always a soft touch for young girls. Tony in turn was presented to Lady Jersey and received with unexpected kindness, given that a boy without connections, prospects or viable income was by no means an ideal husband. Including both their allowances and

Duckworths' minimal salary, the young Powells could count on considerably less than £1,000 a year (a third of the sum needed to manage modestly in London in the early 1930s, according to Evelyn Waugh's brother Alec). Admittedly none of Violet's siblings had married for money or status: Christine's mother took in paying guests, Elizabeth's father though a Harley Street surgeon had nothing but his salary to show for it, and Pansy's husband was a worse than dubious earner. Lady Jersey's own three daughters had made far from brilliant matches to men who rated, by aristocratic standards, as dim Celtic peers: Lords Longford, Dunsany and Dynevor.

Possibly she reckoned any shelter for her grand-daughter better than none at a time when the country's political and economic future looked unequivocally bleak. The depression of the last four years showed no signs of lifting by 1934, when unemployment figures reached new and terrifying highs in the UK, while Germany under Hitler was well on the way to becoming a menace again. In any case this was the kind of literary affair calculated to appeal to Violet's grandmother. Perhaps she recognized a vigour and wit in Tony's three published novels beyond anything Henry Lamb could bring off on canvas. A writer herself as well as the friend of writers, she encouraged similar interests in the young Pakenhams, who nearly all grew up to write as well as read books. "In my family at that date there were at least four novelists, like volcanoes in more or less active eruption," said Violet. Tony had courted her with a half-written manuscript, and confirmed her interest by the impression he gave, even as a tourist in Dublin, of turning life into literature, taking notes as he went. If Lady Jersey backed her own (or Violet's) literary judgement at this point, she was on to a good thing in the long run, and besides she loved her grand-daughter.

The engagement was announced in *The Times* on 8 October, and the wedding scheduled for seven weeks later. Tony used the interval to extricate himself from previous entanglements. For six months and more he had been in the habit of spending at least one or two evenings a week with Marion, right up to the last time they dined together on 22 August, three days before he left London for Pakenham Hall. On his return they met once more for lunch in late October. Marion accepted Tony's explanation of what had happened with her habitual lack of fuss, observing tartly to one of her daughters long afterwards

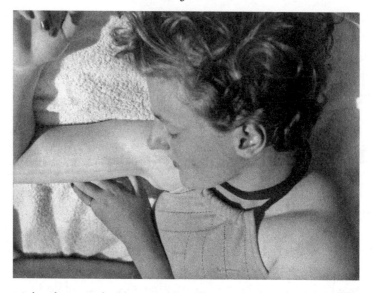

Violet photographed by Gerald Reitlinger: "This girl is different,"
said Tony.

that she could quite see why he preferred to leave her for the daughter
of a belted earl. She herself went on to have an affair the year after
with Bernal's close friend, another outstanding young scientist with
an influential future ahead of him called Solly Zuckerman. She followed it up by attempting a reunion with Wells that ended in divorce.
Two decades later when Tony revisited their affair in the *Dance*, he
equipped Jean Duport with a husband and two lovers, a dodgy trio
of coarse, brash, cocky opportunists (one was a racing driver) who
between them personified his incredulous distaste for Wells Coates.
Marion for her part formed a long-term partnership far more suited
to her principles with an Irish electrician, a shrewd humorous working man who cherished her for the rest of her life.

Like Marion, Mary Manning took the news of Tony's defection
in her stride. She sent a photo of herself with him ("where you can
behold what never was to be"), and some bracing advice: "Get down
to it now & write something terrific, staggering, a knockout, anything you like, but disclose the bleeding heart shamelessly." Tony had
published a novel a year for three years running but the fourth, due
out in theory that autumn, had to be put on hold while its author
dealt with wedding preparations, and made the rounds of his future
in-laws. Violet introduced him to her maternal Aunts Markie (or

Margaret) and Beatrice, the Ladies Dynevor and Dunsany, and to her favourite Aunt Cynthia, the lively, sociable and very pretty widow of the Earl of Jersey who had shocked the family by making a second marriage to her son's handsome young tutor, Rodney Slessor. The 9th Earl, Cynthia's son and Violet's cousin Grandy (short for Grandison), deputed his Uncle Arthur to lunch with Tony and look him over on behalf of the Villiers family.

Failing relations of his own, Tony provided a hectic tour of his friends instead. Violet got on easily at once with Constant and Flo Lambert, and captivated Reitlinger, whose photographs of her were ethereally beautiful, far more so than the relatively conventional professional engagement portraits taken for the society papers. She had already met the Heygates as the bickering Maltravers in the pages of *Agents and Patients*, and she had known Evelyn even before that from her days as Pansy's flatmate. The couple had begun divorce proceedings by this time but, in spite of a tricky start, the young Powells remained on good terms ever after with both of them. Tony's high spirits spilled over that autumn into his review of Heygate's *Talking Pictures*, letting rip when he reached Rightlaw:

> There will be few readers who do not succumb to Rightlaw's charm, even though he appears for a few pages only. His considered brusque remarks, followed by equally brusque questions about other people, make us feel at once that we have been privileged to meet a really delightful person, intelligent, sensitive and reserved. If there were more Rightlaws about, the world would be a pleasant place to live in; if there were more characters like Rightlaw in literature, novels would be a joy to read . . .

When the same character turned up again in a first draft of *Motor Tramp*, Heygate's typist advised him that Rightlaw was so much more interesting than he was himself that the whole book should be recast with Rightlaw as hero. "While not believing this I am going to write a lot of episodes . . . specially to reintroduce this beastly fellow," he warned Tony: "Everything you have ever written or mean to write about my driving is to be repaid in advance by Rightlaw."

Lambert published *Music Ho!* the same year, a brisk, fierce, entertaining survey of the contemporary music scene that deflates the pretensions of twentieth-century modernism, with special reference to Schönberg's Krafft-Ebing touch ("Jung at the prow and Freud at the helm"), and Hindemith's drab bland repetitive scoring "with its evocation of underground railways and hygienic tiling." You can hear the kind of quick sharp one-liner that amused him and Tony in his pithy dissection of the contemporary pop scene, already beginning to infiltrate everywhere with the invention of the gramophone and the wireless: "It is a Psalmist's nightmare." Constant, who had heard all about Tony's dim view of Ireland, sent Violet a postcard of Burne-Jones's *Love and the Pilgrim*, showing the luckless pilgrim being extracted from a bramble bog by the winged figure of Love. Constant's caption underneath ran: "Lady Vi [R] introducing Mr. Powell the well-known Welsh novelist [L] to the beauties of the Irish landscape."

Lady Vi herself filled a whole photo album at this point with the society weddings of her cousins and friends. Tony kept his end up with an invitation in November to the most theatrical wedding of the year, sumptuously staged by Cecil Beaton, one of his more successful Duckworths' authors. Beaton's sister Baba was the bride, dressed in sexy skin-tight silver lamé with long swirling skirts and a gossamer train the size of a small ornamental lake borne by tiny red-velvet bridesmaids, an outfit that would be admired, envied, photographed, copied and talked about to the day she died more than sixty years later, and beyond. Violet herself had been one of eight bridesmaids at Frank's marriage to Elizabeth three years earlier. She was so much in demand that the *Daily Sketch* had published her photograph the year before with the caption: "Three Times a Bridesmaid, never a Bride."

The article was probably written or prompted by her sister Mary, who had two columns of her own, on gossip and shopping respectively, in the London *Evening Standard* under the name of Mary Grant (she said she got all the tips she needed for both of them from her two "mysteriously well-informed younger sisters"). Lord Beaverbrook took such a fancy to Mary that he made her one of his chief reporters, leaving Violet to take over the Mary Grant columns, which brought in a useful ten guineas a week at the start of her marriage. The wedding itself on Saturday, 1 December, at All Saints, Ennismore Gardens, a few hundred yards from Rutland Gate, was in every respect the opposite of Baba Beaton's. Violet had no bridesmaids, no wedding reception and the plainest possible high-necked, long-sleeved wedding gown. Wyndham Lloyd was best man, and Lady Jersey gave the bride away, signing the register with Tony's parents and leaving the church on the arm of Colonel Powell.

Many of the wedding guests behaved strangely on account of a party at Rutland Gate given for all their friends the night before by the bride and groom. Tony remembered somebody playing "If You Were the Only Girl in the World" on the Pakenhams' old school-room piano, and gin was poured the whole evening like water by a couple of inexperienced young maids sent round to mix the drinks by Violet's grandmother. The party got so out of hand that several of the guests were still half drunk next day. Constant, who had arranged music for the wedding, was too hungover to come to the church. Henry Lamb was tipsy but came all the same. As a friend of both bride and groom, John Heygate threatened to disrupt proceedings by changing his seat from one side of the aisle to the other at intervals throughout the service.

Heygate had booked the bridal pair into the Bridge Hotel, Newhaven, for the wedding night, which they spent in "a poky little room looking out on a wall," supposedly once occupied by the exiled French King Louis Philippe. The hotel was conveniently close to the Channel ferry terminal for the crossing next day, three hours to Dieppe in calm weather, six or seven in a small steamer buffeted, tumbled and deluged by the mountainous seas of a winter storm. Tony said it was the worst crossing he ever experienced. Violet, newly recovered from pneumonia, still had a streaming cold. They spent the next three days and nights recovering on the Orient Express, travelling south by sleeper via Paris, Vienna and Belgrade. On the fourth day they reached Athens, then still a small, cheap, run-down Balkan capital, ill adapted to tourists, especially in winter.

They contacted a Greek schoolfriend of one of Violet's uncles, Alexander Pallis, and visited the Acropolis in wintry sunshine. They explored the little temple of Poseidon perched on the steep rocky tip of Cape Sounio before moving westwards to Delphi. On Mount Parnassus they were the only visitors walking the Sacred Way to the temple of Apollo, zig-zagging upwards from one level to the next in a great arc round the sheer sides of the mountain with eagles soaring above, and as yet no buildings to block their spectacular view of the plain and the sea far below. Next they found a boat to Crete, a trip so far from any standard tourist trail that it needed all Tony's considerable determination to organize. In Heracleion, where they were pleased to find you could buy two glasses of ouzo for a British penny, they took a room at the small, mosquito-ridden King Minos Hotel ("little developed since the days of the minotaur," said Tony). What chiefly interested him was not the classical or Hellenic glories that were Greece but the much older ruins of the great Minoan palaces, Knossos, Phaistos and Agia Triada. All three sites were still in process of excavation, not yet infested by tourists, all three opening up for the first time a world, at once ancient and pristine, that matched the Powells' own magical sense of discovery as they drove on honeymoon "across the island in that incredible Cretan light, which, especially towards sunset, turns the mountains into every colour of the spectrum, the sky all but black in one direction, dull gold in another."

Back in London by the end of the year, they squeezed themselves and their possessions temporarily into Tony's attic flat in Brunswick Square. Their wedding presents included a coffee pot from Pietro Castano in Greek Street, reminding them to drink coffee at his place next time instead of moving on to Legrain's round the corner. Adrian Daintrey sent a sketch in brown ink of the pair of them side by side on a sofa, presumably the blue one in Tony's flat. An Irish friend, Desmond Ryan, printed off a whole edition of *Caledonia* on a private press, bound between tartan boards with a frontispiece by Ed Burra. Tony collected snaps of his wife taken on their week together at Pakenham Hall, and pasted them into his album under a headline clipped from a newspaper:

VIOLETS GROW LIKE WEEDS

6

1935–39

Sometimes in the summer and autumn of 1935 Violet took the bus up to Hampstead to set up her easel alongside a new friend, the painter Eve Disher, tiny, sharp and bird-like with a formidably intelligent eye and a subtle feathery brushstroke. Eve's studio just behind Heath Street was as small and unmistakeably feminine as she was herself: "all silver grey and rose pink with many bowls of flowers," said the model, who posed naked for 2s 6d an hour. Her name was Miranda Hayward, and she never forgot the "tall blonde girl" whose newly married husband came to fetch her after the painting sessions: "a thirtyish man of medium height in a light-coloured suit and brown suede shoes—a rather flamboyant touch at the time. I studied him surreptitiously with the awe and reverence reserved for authors." Mr. and Mrs. Anthony Powell were both snappy dressers. If Tony was rightly pleased with his new ginger outfit, Violet wore an even more dashing black-velvet pantsuit that made an indelible impression on Miranda at a time when nicely brought-up girls from provincial England did not wear trousers.

Plain, plump and powerfully determined, born and brought up in Birmingham, the only child of working-class parents who had named her Beryl and insisted she better herself by acquiring secretarial skills, Miranda had marked time in low-grade typing jobs until she was old enough to run away from home, change her name and re-create herself as a writer in London. It was John Heygate who first came across her in June 1935, the summer she turned twenty-one, in a pub outside Birmingham where he had gone in pursuit of his prospective second wife, Gwyneth Lloyd. Gwyneth's brother Seton had his eye on Miranda too, but got nowhere once she realized Heygate was a writer, the first "living breathing author from London" she had ever met (Tony was the second). By her own account, she talked and he listened in a conversation that lasted the rest of the weekend. On the point of leaving with Gwyneth for a premarital honeymoon in Germany, Heygate read Miranda's unpublished novel and forwarded it to Tony, predicting that his "Birmingham discovery" would in the end "put all us writers in the shade."

He sent Eve money from Germany to tide Miranda over as a part-time model in her first weeks in the capital. Tony in turn was so struck by her manuscript, *Girl Gone Wrong*, that he recommended it to his own agent, Cyrus Brooks at A. M. Heath, putting her forward meanwhile for the job of secretary at Duckworths (the sudden death that autumn of the previous secretary had left the firm without a typist). For a girl who had spent her teenage years daydreaming about the London book world, this was a heady initiation. Miranda left a vivid account of her first visit to a publisher's office for a job interview with the head of the firm:

> an old man sat at a roll-top desk awash with papers and . . . lurching columns of books, flanked by an unframed life-sized portrait of a lady in a droopy lace dress that was propped up against a chair [this was Gerald Duckworth's half-sister, Virginia Woolf] . . . The publisher blinked at me blearily from beneath bushy white eyebrows . . . I would have guessed him to be about 80 [he was in fact 65], possessing all the peculiarities of advanced age—rheumy eyes, shambling gait, asthmatic breath.

After three gruff barks ("Can you type? Write shorthand? File?"), Miranda got the job. As the firm's only secretary, tapping out letters for both partners, the managing director Mr. Lewis, and two general editors—Alan Harris and Tony himself—she had unrivalled access to Duckworths' financial affairs, dealings with authors and internal politics, all digested with Tony in "our daily conversations about life and letters." He had fixed her up with the previous secretary's vacant flat while Violet kitted her out in a smart secretarial dress and coat, but from the start both accepted Miranda on equal terms as a fellow

Tony and Violet, drawn by Adrian Daintrey

author, a hard-up, ambitious freelance like themselves, in need of an initial leg-up on the precarious lower slopes of the writing profession.

Like her sister before her, Violet herself was starting out at this point on London's *Evening Standard*, scouring the shops for the consumer column, now retitled "A Woman's Point of View": "the less make-up the better is a golden rule at point-to-points" was her advice, followed later in the season by "What to Wear on the Beach." She toured the sales, picking out fishnet gloves at Swan and Edgar, South American skunk cravats at Gorringe's, novelty woollens at Dickens and Jones, and—for draughty country-house weekends when an entire house party might easily find itself queuing for the single bathroom—"the £1 dressing-gowns at Fenwicks in natural shantung or brown crêpe with dainty checks."

Violet and Tony had found a poky little flat on the two top floors of 47, Great Ormond Street, a small Georgian tradesman's house at the opposite end of the street from the more fashionable section near Queen Square, where Tony's wealthier Oxford contemporaries carried on the Hypocrites' tradition of lavish heavy-drinking hearty parties. The Powells entertained old and new friends on a more modest scale warmly and often. Marion Coates was their first dinner guest on 21 January. Varda came later with her current escort, Dennis Proctor, a Treasury official generally agreed to be the most boring man anyone they knew had ever met, barring only his friend and work colleague John Bullard, who occupied the first-floor flat immediately below the Powells.

Their parties mixed the usual crew of jobbing writers and painters with so many dancers from the Sadler's Wells Theatre, ten minutes' walk from Great Ormond Street, that the top flat at number 47 became almost an unofficial annexe for the ballet crowd in the next few years. Once the Powells served so much mulled claret to the chorus line and principals—including Freddie Ashton, Billie Chappell and the ebullient Australian Robert Helpmann—that the matinee next day was punctuated by "heavy thuds on the boards of the Sadler's Wells stage." The company had started out in 1931 with six girls, joined the year after by five men, performing one evening and one afternoon a week. Lambert as principal conductor and composer was part of the triumvirate with Ashton and Ninette de Valois who transformed an insignificant, semi-amateur, part-time outfit into what eventually became the Royal Ballet. Tony's old friend Bobby Roberts was house manager, tipsy more often than not but for once holding down a job that suited him, and only too glad to boost attendance by handing out free tickets. The Powells became regulars in these years when the young company came together, and set about discovering what it could do.

Lambert had his first major orchestral triumph in March 1935, soon after the move to Great Ormond Street, with a revival of the *Rio Grande* featuring Chappell as the coloured sailor, and Margot Fonteyn in her first starring role as the tart he picks up on the port. She was just fifteen years old. "When the little, golden-skinned Fonteyn fell so gaily into my arms in *Rio Grande*," Chappell wrote long afterwards, "she was too young to understand life's potentiality for happiness and despair." Flo Lambert had been fourteen or fifteen when she first met Constant. Now she was twenty, heavily pregnant with a baby due in May, isolated, apprehensive and still painfully ignorant in a way that was beginning to seem more tiresome than touching to her husband. The couple still rarely missed a party, but Constant's attention was slowly shifting to Margot, as innocent and eager as Flo had once been, and almost equally uneducated.

He lent her records and a copy of *Ulysses* together with a modernist reading list. A few months later he sent the Powells a postcard

Tony and Violet photographed on their rounds by his friends
and her family

from Blackpool, altering "t" to "w" in the last line of the printed caption: "A simple message here I send,/A dainty picture too/To let
you know just where I am/And what I think of you." In his next bulletin, on tour with the company in Edinburgh (where his hotel pad-
locked the bathroom taps "in case anyone steals a bath on the sly"),
he claimed gloomily to be starting to gibber in the streets with mysterious drops of blood appearing on his hands: "Do you think I am
going to get stigmata? I shouldn't be surprised." As Margot eluded
him, Constant started drinking heavily, finding relief in the sombre
cadences of Thomas Nash's lines about the plague years in sixteenth-
century London, *Summer's Last Will and Testament*, which he set to
music for orchestra, chorus and baritone solo.

Chained to his desk all week as usual, Tony proposed a whirl of
country weekends that summer for himself and his wife so she could
get to know his friends, and he could meet her family. Destinations
ranged on his side from Evelyn Heygate's modest thatched cottage
at Little Crittenden in Kent to Cecil Beaton's extravagantly done-up

house at Ashcombe near Salisbury with its dramatic interiors and pro-liferating statues. Violet's contributions included visits to Osterley, to the Dunsanys in their rustic Palladian retreat at Dunstall Priory near Shoreham, and to the cottage at Coombe Bissett on the edge of the Wiltshire Downs where Pansy and Henry Lamb were now living with two little daughters.

The Powells spent a couple of weekends with Gerald Reitlinger, who had moved to a new house as comfortless as the first but roomier and slightly nearer London. Woodgate was an unimpressive red-brick Sussex farmhouse with a Regency stucco facade and a large dilapi-dated garden just outside Beckley, where the village people referred to the new owner quite unselfconsciously as the squire. He relished the absurdity of his position, signing one of his first letters from Wood-gate: "Yours Gerald (quasi-colonel, pseudo-yeomanry)." A snapshot shows his disembodied head in wire-rimmed spectacles: unsmiling, thin-lipped, grizzled, but evidently pleased, looking absurdly like an actual bust set down at the top of a flight of stone steps. "From now on they call me Squire" ran the caption in Tony's album, and the tag was so absurdly incongruous that for the rest of his life Reitlinger was invariably known as the Squire by all who knew him. Woodgate's pillared portico, its gravel terrace and the back lawn below, the gar-den shed and the gibbet brought along from Thornsdale, all took on new life as an endlessly adaptable stage set for his friends' amateur dramatics. A snap from June 1935 shows Tony strung up on the gal-lows again. In another, Reitlinger wearing a judge's wig admonishes Violet, caught embracing a portly gent sculpted in stone: "Go sin no more."

In August there was less energetic entertainment at Felbrigg Hall near Cromer on the east coast. The Powells set out on what they called "Mr. and Mrs. Sponge's Sporting Tour" until they ran out of money to pay bills, and had to be rescued from a pub in Diss by one of Tony's authors. Wyndham Ketton-Cremer, an Oxford contempo-rary who had inherited his father's estate while still at Balliol, turned out to be only too pleased to invite his publisher to stay. Duckworths had just brought out his elegant brief life of *Thomas Gray*, which starts with a kind of delayed detonation, quoting as its first sentence Dr. Johnson's crushing verdict on the poet: "Sir, he was dull in company, dull in his closet, dull everywhere. He was dull in a new way, and that

Edward Burra's *Saturday Market*, with its scurf of rubbish and its urban tart, was largely based on Shepherd Market, the seedy backstreet off Piccadilly where Burra's dealer lived, and where Tony spent his first years in London.

Anthony Powell (left) and Evelyn Waugh
(below) soon after the start of their long
friendship, both painted by Henry Lamb

Constant Lambert (left), painted by
Christopher Wood, shortly before he
became Tony's best friend

I don't mind if I do

Postcard altered by Tony to make the man on the barstool
look even more like his old friend Gerald Reitlinger

Nina Hamnett (right, painted by Jacob Kramer), who picked Tony up in Paris, seduced him, and showed him a world he'd only read about in books before

Dorothy Varda (left), painted by Adrian Daintrey: "You are my nervous breakdown," she told Tony.

Marion Coates (right) with her baby daughter, painted by John Banting in 1933, just before she and Tony first met

Violet Pakenham, painted by Eve Disher: "This girl is different," said Tony.

Gerald Reitlinger, painted by Eve Disher, with three Iznik plates from his collection

Page from a scrapbook marking the start of the *Dance* with a miniature version of Tony in the middle, presiding over a performance of *Powell's Puppet Show* (presented by an eighteenth-century namesake, Martin Powell), against a background of sexy pictures from Colonel Powell's collection

Another page from the same scrapbook, showing Tony's photographs of Normandy after the Allied invasion of 1944, pasted in above *The Masque of Cupid* by John Hodgson Lobley (himself an official war artist in the First World War)

A Dance to the Music of Time by Nicolas Poussin in the Wallace Collection

made people think him great." Ketton-Cremer's refutation was cool, crisp and firm, infused with a sympathetic understanding based on the author's personal regard for his unassuming subject whose entire output barely exceeded a thousand lines, and who remained throughout his short, inactive, unadventurous career "well content to drift on in a life of deep but completely aimless study."

Tony said that already as a young man Wyndham looked as if he should have worn an eighteenth-century tie-wig. He was not yet thirty when he wrote what was clearly in some sense a blueprint for the life he himself intended to lead, alone except for his dog Sailor in his big bare barn-like Jacobean house with its spectacular floor-length windows, ancient plumbing and complete lack of all mod cons including electricity. Self-contained and superlatively well-behaved, Wyndham maintained an invincible sobriety that baffled even Tony: "To the end of his days, an additional glass of sherry before dinner, one of port after, represented the height of his indulgence . . . One longed for him to get drunk, swear, fall down, break a window, even if he remained (as he always did) uncommitted as to sex." In fact he was discreetly gay, and quickly grew sufficiently attached to Violet to be frank and funny with her about his preference for boys, even if he never mentioned it to Tony. This visit marked the start of a lifelong friendship with the Powells, who paid annual visits from now on to Felbrigg in August. Wyndham grew close to both of them, eventually becoming one of the small group of regulars who read and corrected the *Dance* in proof. Tony took a characteristic snapshot of him that first summer with his face almost completely blacked out by the photographer's shadow, captioned "Man in the Iron Mask."

Violet slipped effortlessly into the heterogeneous interlocking circles of Tony's friends. She gave up dancing, riding, polo apparently without a pang to plunge into a shabby, rootless urban world unlike any she had known before, a world where people made or failed to make their own money and connections, and women like Eve Disher or Miranda Hayward operated freely without any of the social and financial safety nets enclosing Violet and her sisters. She too was now an inmate of the seedy freelance book world and, like her husband, scarcely less familiar with the sub-sect of musicians congregating round Constant. She married Tony too late to meet their figurehead, the esoteric composer Philip Heseltine (known professionally as

Peter Warlock), a tall, deliberately satanic figure in flapping cloak and big black hat, adept of the occult, often drunk or drugged and always ferociously destructive. Heseltine killed himself in his Pimlico flat in 1930, but Violet must have met his sidekick, Gavin Gordon, who sang and acted as well as composing music for Sadler's Wells' *Rake's Progress* in 1935 (it was during rehearsals for Gordon's orgy scene that Constant revived his flagging orchestra with the memorable ditty: "Oh dearie me,/I do want to pee/And I don't much care/If the audience see").

She certainly knew Heseltine's biographer and disciple, the *Manchester Guardian*'s music critic, Cecil Gray: "a distinctly uncomfortable character," said Tony, "who saw himself as the hack in the presence of creative genius." Taciturn, morose, occasionally manic, Gray was another heavy drinker, a Calvinist Scot and practitioner of black magic with a colossal ego and a cocaine habit. Like many misogynists of his self-destructive sort, he devoted disproportionate amounts of time to the pursuit of women, or in his own words "painted and powdered whores, and perfumed bitches." The first of his three wives had been a mannequin for Patou in Paris, a beautiful Russian exile whose mother lived openly with the younger brother of the tsar, and who had herself divorced John Gielgud's brother Val to become Mrs. Gray. His second marriage in 1934 was to a startlingly lovely Scottish ballerina who left him, like her predecessor, after sticking it out for six years. The third wife lasted only five. "While I do not defend the practice of wife-killing," Gray wrote shortly before she died, "I can understand better than most the state of mind which leads to it."

By the time the three weeks of Tony's annual holiday came round in September, Violet was probably ready for a break from prolonged and concentrated exposure to the phantasmagoria peopling her husband's life and work. Perhaps he was too. They stayed at Cascais on the rocky Atlantic coast of Portugal, finding a room in an English boarding house run by a gay couple escaping from the punitive laws against homosexuality at home. Tony had first met Philip Sainsbury with Varda in Littlehampton, when he was producing classy little editions of arcane and amusing texts on his private Cayme Press. Now in his forties, he was a relaxed and expansive host, known as "Aggie" to guests treated by him and his boyfriend George Eley more like members of their house party than hotel residents. The holiday suited both Powells: sun and sea in scenic surroundings with easy access to churches, museums and picture galleries in Lisbon, a formula they followed with minor variations for much of their married life.

At the end of the month they returned in high good humour. Violet was pregnant, and Tony was about to deliver the completed manuscript he had abandoned part way through twelve months before. John Heygate, who, like Violet, had heard bits of it read aloud by Tony, wrote to say he had finished reading the manuscript in a dream, transforming it in his fantasy into a journey through a cosmic landscape with himself at Tony's side: "A sort of modern Vergil and Dante?" *Agents and Patients* was by far the most ambitious and assured of Tony's first four novels, but the future was not looking good for an apolitical, humorous narrative with Germany on its itinerary. Heygate, travelling that summer with Gwyneth through his adopted country, sent a reassuring report from old haunts in Berlin: "Nothing has changed. Nothing . . . Piety & prosperity. Americans shooting dice in the Eden bar. Same old storm over the Rhine where I am sitting . . . Nothing changes." Unlike Tony, he still shared the widespread optimism peddled in these years by the British fascist Oswald Mosley, and the credulous Mitfords. Heygate, who had sat next to Unity Mitford at the Nuremberg Rally in July, now urged the Powells to join him, bombarding Tony with postcards of Nazi stormtroopers, squads of Hitler Youth ("the Hitler Jugend are the boys"), photos of Horst Wessel and the vicious anti-Semite Julius Streicher, whose cartoon drawings of Jews even Heygate didn't find funny: "But Aryans needn't be. It's only the persecuted races that have to make jokes."

At some point in late November or early December, Violet miscarried her baby. "The news of your tragedy . . . is altogether desolating," wrote Henry Lamb, who had not yet found time to send congratulations on the pregnancy: "And now, alas poor Violet & poor Tony, your infernal luck just fills me with gloom and tears." Well-wishers reminded her that she was still young and healthy with plenty of time to try again in future, but Violet wept uncontrollably. Her state of mind was well expressed by Constant, conducting the first performance in January 1936 of *Summer's Last Will and Testament* with its plangent laments and rollicking macabre death-rattles, and its climactic "Dies Irae [Day of Wrath]" composed in honour of Heseltine.

Agents and Patients came out the same month. Both events were more or less completely upstaged by the illness, death and lying in state of King George V, marked by tolling bells, muffled guns and a dirge of pipes as the coffin made its way through the capital followed by an apparently endless procession of men from the army, navy and airforce slow-marching between vast crowds in silence in one of the most theatrically extravagant funerals ever mounted in Britain or any other country. Perhaps this public act of grief had a subconscious undertow, a kind of collective acquiescence in the seismic social shifts inevitably approaching with the imminent collapse of empire as Europe prepared to tear itself apart again. There had been no threat of military intervention from the Allied powers in 1935 to check German rearmament, explicitly forbidden by the peace treaty less than twenty years before. No move would be made in March 1936 to prevent Hitler's armies reoccupying the Rhineland. Incipient unrest had brought Spain to the verge of the civil war that broke out in July between Republicans and Nationalists.

By publication day history was overtaking *Agents and Patients* at a cracking pace, at any rate in the central section set in Berlin. On re-reading the book half a century later, Tony was startled to find how many of his characters he had lifted straight from life. At the time he was perhaps surprised by the enthusiasm of friends who recognized themselves in its pages. Heygate was delighted with the urbane Maltravers in his flashy gangster outfits ("I am advertising you daily by my check overcoat," he wrote exuberantly to Tony), and his ex-wife ruefully accepted the portrait of her marriage—"though I must say I think it was I who was gagged & bound & he who jabbed at me with a sword."

Even Varda was happy to take credit for the fearsome Mrs. Mendoza ("isn't it funny, I could have sworn that I didn't pat my hair," was her breezy comment). The book was probably never read by her former escort, Captain Turle, faithfully transposed as a strong, silent naval commander struggling for words when he finally got the push: "He could only stare in front of him with steel-blue eyes that seemed to have sunk far back into his head from the strain of scanning immeasurable tracts of sky and sea . . ." This sombre sequence takes place at the Berlin zoo, where the vague sense of foreboding hanging over the central section of the novel crystallizes in a memorable image as Maltravers and Chipchase join the crowd watching the great apes confront their public:

> The male gorilla was swinging on his trapeze, very slowly backwards and forwards, facing the people with an expression of hatred and contempt. He had caught something of the national character of the race he found himself among, and his demeanour suggested a Prussian captain of industry at his morning exercises.

Tony's narrative was sown with private jokes like the fast car he gave Maltravers—"a torpedo-shaped gamboge machine"—in memory of long hours spent hunched at ground level in the cramped passenger seat of Heygate's first MG. The book ends with a grand finale on location in the country where Maltravers triumphantly achieves his ambition to make a film, and Chipchase as his cameraman gets to shoot the entire cast. Evelyn Waugh had been paid substantial money for a Hollywood film script (never used) in 1935, and Tony contemplated something similar himself. Duckworths was becoming intolerable. Given that his weekends were fully taken up elsewhere, he must have written most, if not all, of the last part of *Agents and Patients* in the office, but now that it was out he no longer needed a writing retreat. Seeing the firm's endemic torpor from outside through Violet's amused and observant eye gave him a jolt, and so did Miranda, who made it clear that nothing had changed in the past decade: "It sometimes looked as if the old man preferred not to publish anything at all. Mr. Milsted promoted books about big game hunting, exploration and other virile pursuits. Mr. Lewis yearned only for runaway best sellers, however lustreless. The younger men were uncompromising highbrows. Wars of attrition surged . . . beneath the glassy surface."

Tony had had enough. Never one to counsel caution, Violet agreed. In August he formally announced his resignation to a "more than orientally" uninterested Gerald Duckworth. Tony's last move before he left the office was to order copies of the *Shorter Oxford Dictionary* and Burke's *Landed Gentry* on trade terms. Only Edith Sitwell mourned his going, but she also saw it as a chance to replace him with a needier

The Lamberts play-acting with Tony at Woodgate

protegé, the twenty-two-year-old Dylan Thomas. "I believe him to be the coming poet . . . ," she wrote in her job application: "it would be a turning point in the boy's career . . . to have the *discipline* he'd have in your office." Duckworth ran true to form in the curt reply that reached her by return: "There is no possible place here."

Tony and Violet celebrated by sailing from London docks on 29 August for Leningrad on the Soviet ship *Smolny*. Tourist trips to the USSR, briefly fashionable in the early 1930s, could be booked through London's new branch of Intourist, an outfit staffed by Stalin's secret police, or NKVD, that seemed more despotic but otherwise much like any other inefficient tourist agency ("I'm going into their office . . . and break up the place in protest," said Tony). It sent relays of curious Westerners to marvel at the results of Stalin's first Five-year Plan: collective farms, heavy industry, the abolition of corruption together with the land-owning kulaks that went with it, power and progress for the workers, all ushering in a new, free and equal future for mankind. Teams of young film-makers, headed by Sergei Eisenstein and V. I. Pudovkin, exported brilliant experimental works as revolutionary in technique as in idealistic content. At Woodgate, the Powells and Lamberts devised their own agitprop scenarios, acting out the *Liquidation of the Kulaks* (they were slaughtered in Reitlinger's summerhouse by a bearded member of the Komsomol, so heavily disguised he could be identified only by his shoes and his flannel trouser bottoms). In *THE FIVE-YEAR PLAN*, Tony took the wheel of a heroic Soviet tractor plastered up to its wheel-tops in Sussex mud. Constant brandished a scythe as a *Discontented Peasant (Pudovkin Productions)*. Flo was the *Discontented Peasant's Wife (Gaumont British)*.

These antics reflected the general friendly, if faintly sceptical attitude to what was happening in Russia. Malcolm Muggeridge, reporting at first hand from Moscow on the famine that followed Stalin's widely publicized plan in 1933, had been largely ignored or disbelieved by the few who read him. Tony had not yet met Muggeridge but, like most people in literary London, he knew Prince Mirsky, an elegant and erudite lecturer at London University, tall, genial and shabby, who had published books on Pushkin and Lenin, disowning his own Tsarist origins to become in exile an increasingly convinced Marxist. The Powells were dazzled by the water-borne beauty of Leningrad, Dostoevsky's city—"the pellucid northern light gives an amazing radiance to the pastel shades of stucco and sparkling onion domes"—and not surprised by the drab squalid hinterland that was, as Tony said, no more than any lover of its literature might expect. They explored museums and galleries before taking the train to Kiev, a trip chiefly memorable for the wild scene on the train when Violet gave one of her old jerseys to the rugged crone who checked their tickets, and was astounded by her passion of gratitude in return. In Moscow they met Mirsky, who had been officially allowed home four years earlier: "He seemed much the same; somehow not quite like the rest of the people in Moscow, any more than he had looked like the rest of the people in London."

He gave no inkling that prospects were poor for people like himself in Russia. The first of the great Moscow show trials had ended a few days before the *Smolny* reached Leningrad with death sentences for Grigory Zinoviev, Lev Karmenev and fourteen others accused of plotting to kill Stalin. The wife of one of them had been a fellow passenger on the *Smolny* with the Powells, who had grasped the extent of her distress, and her terror of being seen in contact with Westerners, but realized only much later that the trial had provided Stalin's pretext for launching a murderous initial purge that autumn. Mirsky's arrest as a British spy followed a year later after a second chance encounter on the street in Moscow with another of his London friends, the historian E. H. Carr. By the time Mirsky died in a labour camp at Magadan in 1939, Stalin had killed about a million people. The Powells had been among the last Westerners to visit Russia before the campaign of terror that became, in Tony's words, "one of the great slaughters in the history of the world."

None of this was evident at the time in Britain to relative conservatives like Tony, still less to the many on the left of the political spectrum who supported Stalin's regime more or less uncritically to the end. Most people were more concerned by developments in Germany and Spain than in the Soviet Union. Back in London on 19 September, Tony had other problems now that he was out of work. He had to wait another month (his first break of more than three weeks in ten years) before his agent finally fixed him up with an opening at Warner Brothers' Teddington Film Studios.

Easy money from films was the dream of virtually every ambitious young writer at the time, but the best Brooks could find him was a foothold on the lowest and most menial rung of a notoriously slippery ladder. Tony was hired to manufacture scripts for the fixed percentage of essentially unwanted British films that had by law to be produced by any American company keen to get a grip on the British market. The results of the government's attempt to boost its ailing infant film industry were called quota-quickies, a dispiriting name that suggests why British films were widely agreed to be unwatchable at that stage. Nearly everything about his new job dismayed Tony, starting with an elaborate commute involving multiple trains and trolley-buses, or alternatively dual daily car journeys through central London traffic at rush hour. He clocked on at Teddington on 19 October, working strict office hours six days a week in a strip-lighted cell under close supervision on a production line churning out stories more likely than not to end up being junked. His first assignment was scrapped after four weeks and nine storylines laboriously wrung out of the same uninspiring subject. The second was an obvious nonstarter. "Teddington seemed to combine some of the dreariest aspects of office life with making demands on the machinery of creative invention in a manner that was at once superlatively exhausting, yet wholly unsatisfying," he wrote angrily looking back.

Warner Brothers offered an unspecified probationary period leading with luck to a six-month contract on the princely salary of £15 rising to £20 a week (Duckworths had paid £5). The pay was one consolation. Another was the company of two much younger fellow scriptwriters, Terence Rattigan and Tommy Phipps. Rattigan at twenty-five was a smooth customer. His first play, written with a friend while still at Oxford, had transferred to the West End two years earlier. His second, *French Without Tears*, opened on 6 November to rave reviews. Tony witnessed the almost fairy-tale arrival of overnight celebrity with a speculative eye. In the few weeks they spent together concocting abortive stories, each capping the other's daft suggestions with even wilder absurdities of his own, the two had laughed a lot. They also discussed the mechanics of their trade, debating whether or not popular acclaim was the most a writer could desire or get. Tony liked and was faintly unnerved by Rattigan, diagnosing the deep inner bitterness he came to associate later with too easy acceptance of limited goals (he saw the same combination of outward success with "ghastly interior misery" in Somerset Maugham).

Tommy Phipps was another charmer, a tall, big-boned, jug-eared boy with the same disarming breeziness and toothy good looks as his elder sister, Joyce Grenfell (whose public debut in revue was still three years ahead). Children of an outstanding American beauty—one of the five famous Langhorne sisters—the pair had been largely brought up after the breakdown of their parents' marriage by the eldest of the Langhornes, their aunt Nancy Astor, in her great Italianate house at Cliveden on the Thames near Taplow. Tommy, who had fled to California as a teenager, now returned penniless at twenty-three, bringing with him a pretty wife even younger than himself and a baby son. The marriage started to come to pieces during his stint at Teddington, when the toddler had to be sent away to Cliveden to be looked after by Aunt Nancy. Knocked off balance, unable to cope, badly in need of a role model, Tommy latched on to Tony, pestering him with endless personal questions. Embarrassed, at times appalled

The Powells posing in front of their own front door

by this "terrible fascination with my life," Tony recognized it later
as the price he paid for what Tommy gave him in return. Accepting a lift home one night in his young admirer's rusty banger with
its unreliable gears, dodgy brakes and beat-up engine, Tony watched
three larger and more powerful cars bear down apparently abreast in
the middle of a particularly narrow stretch of the Great West Road:
seizing the hand-brake as they sped towards what seemed imminent
collision, Phipps muttered to himself, "This is just going to be a question of upbringing." Recognizing a good book title even as he diced
with death, Tony pocketed it mentally to await retrieval fifteen years
later for the opening volume of the *Dance*.

After serving two months of his sentence on the "weariest of treadmills," Tony saw in the New Year with Violet at Woodgate, perhaps
testing out in practice some of the film treatments he and Tommy had
cooked up at Teddington. His thirty-first birthday ten days earlier,
coinciding for once with financial solvency, put a serious new slant on
his and Violet's future as a married couple. The prospect of starting a
family meant a home to put it in, and the Powells found one that Jan-

uary just to the north of their regular Bloomsbury beat. Number 1, Chester Gate formed half of a pair of nondescript houses that had been squeezed by some nineteenth-century developer into a gap at the back of John Nash's terraces, lining the eastern edge of Regent's Park with monumental simplicity and sobriety. The Powells' new house had seven rooms on five floors, counting the basement. After the cramped attics they'd lived in up till now, it gave them a miraculous sense of space and privacy.

Neither of them cared at that stage about the inconvenience of so many little rooms supplied by a clumsy service-lift, creaking up from the kitchen below the pavement to the dining room on the ground floor that was to double as Tony's workroom. What seemed innumerable flights of narrow twisting stairs led up to the drawing room, and up again past the main bedroom on the second floor to two small rooms at the top. The exterior badly wanted painting, and the elderly fabric was in need of serial repair. Luckily Tony had no book in hand for the moment, because a study next to the front door with the telephone in the hall meant constant traffic of people calling, knocking, talking on the doorstep or tramping along the passage outside his closed door.

But advantages far outweighed the drawbacks. The sitting room on the first floor looked out on to a small communal garden in the square behind, with the park itself a few minutes' walk away at one end of Chester Gate. At the other end lay Albany Street, running due south from Camden Town to Fitzrovia. The cheerful competent cook who had come daily by bus to Great Ormond Street agreed provisionally to keep coming to the new house, and as soon as they could afford it they took on two young maids, Doris and Irene Mears, who had worked for the Pakenham sisters at Rutland Gate. The Powells moved in with Tony's sofa, accumulated books, a refrigerator that had been a wedding present (still a relatively unusual acquisition in the 1930s), and whatever furniture they could scrounge, borrow or buy from junk shops and auction sales. They also brought their first cat with them, an intelligent and observant Siamese called Bosola after the multiple murderer in John Webster's play *The Duchess of Malfi*. Tony rounded up surviving family portraits of relatives and connections (including the painting of Lady Cardigan that always fortified Flo Lambert). He particularly liked cheap unfashionable

French Empire furniture, and developed a knack of spotting chairs, consoles and side-tables with chased gilt banding and spindly legs. Violet planted petunias in the window boxes.

Tony's parents had settled in a flat a short walk away at Clarence Terrace, a dubious blessing in their son's view, but a long lease on the new house would scarcely have been possible without help from his father. "I suppose one oughtn't to grumble as he does cough up quite a lot of the necessary," Tony eventually conceded, "but he has a wonderful air of conveying that he is a mixture of General Gordon and Saint Francis of Assisi and that one is a compound of King John and Titus Oates." Although the antagonism between father and son had been to some extent defused by Violet's arrival, nothing could repair the damage done by the public repudiation Tony had undergone at Duckworths. Colonel Powell for his part had never got over leaving the army ten years before. He studied law, taking a creditable second-class degree in his late forties but making no further plans to join the Bar. He was now drifting through his fifties in retirement on distant, if civil terms with the young Powells.

He treated Violet with a flirtatious gallantry that did not entirely hide a bullying undertow, but he had no power to hurt her as he had once tormented Tony. On the contrary, she and Tony systematically re-created him in these years as a comic monster, a defensive device that turned his behaviour into no more than a routine aggravation like boredom or bad weather. "He wasn't actually at his worst but about the worst-but-two," Tony wrote of a brisk spat that ended with Colonel Powell agreeing to pay for the repainting of the house at Chester Gate. He grew increasingly subdued as Tony learned, under Violet's tuition, to treat his father's tantrums, obstructiveness and conviction that everything he did or said was invariably right as absurd, at times almost more pitiful than provoking.

Violet herself was still writing for the *Standard*, and painting in the Hampstead studio where Eve Disher entertained her with racy stories of the many lovers picked up in the course of an adventurous career. Nearly twenty years older than Violet, she had grown up in the war, running away from home in 1918 to make a disastrous marriage to the theatre critic Maurice Willson Disher. They spent their brief married life in a rented flat in one of the Stracheys' houses in Gordon Square (Eve claimed in old age that the love of her life was Lytton Strachey's youngest brother, James), where Eve breathed deep and early the heady air of Bloomsbury. Independence was the first principle she learned there, sticking with it ever after in both her private and professional life. The second was a sexual freedom and frankness rare in those days, even for a woman artist. She soon dumped Disher, moving on to make a new identity for herself in the years of hectic gaiety that followed the war. Something of their frivolity and zest stayed with her, surfacing in her seventies when she saw a photo of Tony's father as a subaltern in the Boer war: "Eve . . . felt really devastated that she never had the chance of meeting the fascinating young Philip Powell." She had innumerable friends and indomitable courage. Her conversation was an eye-opener for someone like Violet, who had had little time or opportunity before her marriage for much experimentation of her own.

Eve was currently living with an exceptionally handsome and much younger lover, Arthur Elton, who had been happily homosexual until he took up with her. Elton was a scriptwriter already beginning to make his mark as a pioneer in documentary films. They made a striking couple, Arthur towering over Eve, who looked like a pretty little doll beside him. She painted him reading with his head propped on one hand, a big blond giant with floppy hair and a powerful sexual presence, rendered in a restricted range of rich warm browns with the odd shade of grey on a small canvas that seems barely big enough to contain the energy radiating from its subject. Eve never showed the portraits she painted with such assurance and directness: intimate, affectionate, low-key paintings conveying her relationship with her friends as much as their external likeness. In two of Eve's deceptively simple portraits, the young Violet looks as relaxed and casual as if the painter had caught her when she wasn't looking.

Reitlinger was an old friend of Eve, and so was another entertaining art-world friend of Tony's, Brocas Harris. Eve painted both of them: Reitlinger with a trio of Iznik plates from his collection, Bro with his equally beloved Siamese cat. For the next two or three years the Powells spent successive Christmases with Eve and a small group of friends at pubs on the south coast, convivial gatherings (one year the painter David Jones came for lunch, and stayed all day) organized by Brocas. He was a gregarious Australian who had left a thoroughly conventional family behind him to make his way in the less repressive atmosphere of London, where he was taken up initially by Cedric Morris and Duncan Grant, later by an irrepressible adman, another of Morris's ex-boyfriends called Bobbie Bevan. Violet had a soft spot for Brocas, who had a country cottage in the grounds of his English family's place at Boxted, and shared a flat with Bobbie in Russell Square, collecting contemporary painting and cultivating a talent for fine embroidery.

Tony's film career had stalled that spring. By the time he finally got the hang of quota-quickies, his contract with Warner Brothers at Teddington was almost up. The last treatment he worked on—"like the final labour imposed by an enchanter into whose power one has fallen through imprudent search for hidden treasure"—was a biopic about the nineteenth-century philanthropist Dr. Thomas Barnardo, who founded a chain of homes for destitute and abandoned children. Tony wrote it alone at home (presumably the first script of any kind to emerge from his new study) to the satisfaction of his studio bosses, who unwisely dispatched him to clear permission from Barnardo's only child, Somerset Maugham's notoriously tough ex-wife Syrie. Tony's half-hearted salesmanship got him nowhere, and *The Boy from Barnardo's*—a taut, gripping, eminently professional treatment in the view of MGM's London reader, Walter Allen—was shelved along with all his other scripts. In late April 1937 Tony left the studio. On 3 May he sailed with Violet from the docks at Tilbury for Los Angeles. Although he claimed in retrospect to loathe the work, despise the system and deplore its products, he spent most, if not all his Teddington takings on this trip to California, where his agent assured him MGM was hiring hands, and needed British input for the film *A Yank at Oxford*.

At the end of a four-week sea voyage via the Panama Canal, Tony's first view of America was not a pleasant shock: "melancholy miles of motor dumps, drug stores, real-estate offices, cinemas, barbecues, near-Spanish bungalows and apartment houses." Far from a glossy, streamlined vision of the future, the coastal settlements around Los Angeles had already merged into a vast, messy, unplanned suburban sprawl. Too much ice-cream and too little exercise meant Californian women could not compare with the girls of Berlin's film world. Hollywood itself reminded Tony of nothing so much as military training at Aldershot: a "terrible place" with drab, featureless vistas on all sides of long straight avenues designed to eliminate any form of normal human contact.

The Powells found a cheap apartment in Beverly Hills at 357, North Palm Drive, the epicentre of this wasteland, and hired a car so Tony could set out to seek his fortune at Metro-Goldwyn-Mayer. Louis B. Mayer himself was handling recruitment for *A Yank at Oxford* (intended as a booster for his corporation's rising star, Robert Taylor), but it was an underling called Warner Groat who saw Tony on 4 June. His interview the day before with one of Paramount's producers, Manny Wolfe, had gone badly. Groat told him to ring back in ten days' time. When he duly telephoned on 14 June, he was told to drop in next day in case anything turned up, and that was the last he heard from any of the movie moguls he had come to see. Tony remembered them all too vividly, huddled round the central table of the MGM canteen, "a picture by some Netherlands master of the money changers about to be expelled from the Temple, or a group of appreciative onlookers at a martyrdom."

Violet, whose relatives spanned the globe, produced a Great-aunt Mabel who knew Douglas Fairbanks's third wife's sister, and gave a party for the Powells to meet him. Tony glimpsed Marlene Dietrich in a bar. She was the one star he had hoped to set eyes on in Hollywood, and what impressed him most about both her and Fairbanks was how startlingly small they were off screen. Apart from a handful of brief encounters arranged by the obliging Great-aunt Mabel, this was the sum total of his contact with the stars. He and Violet stayed on a further month, exchanging cocktails with the expat community and taking in the scene. On 14 July they watched a vigorous all-black production of *Macbeth*, performed by a cast of over a hundred, put on for the unemployed and punctuated by shoot-outs, with an African mud fort as the Scottish royal palace and a rousing "shake-those-feet hot number" at the banquet in Act III. Tony reviewed the play as the American correspondent of *Night and Day*, a short-lived London weekly edited by Graham Greene ("All God's Chillun Got Kilts" was his title for Tony's piece). A second dispatch covered a preview of *The Spanish Earth*, Hemingway's anti-Franco film scrappily constructed from documentary footage of the fighting in Spain.

At some point the Powells moved south to 9460, Wilshire Boulevard, just under halfway along one of the dismal avenues running for sixteen miles westwards from downtown Los Angeles to the ocean at Santa Monica. From here they made excursions in their elderly car up into the scrubby hills inland, attracting incredulous attention from local armed police by picnicking on the dusty ground among cactus, palm and yucca. Tony's one undiluted pleasure was Californian wine at four shillings a bottle ("Without wine the place would have been a wilderness indeed"). The local gin was cheaper still, and the hangovers correspondingly brutal. Forty years later Tony quoted bitterly in his memoirs a compatriot's remark about the lights of Santa Monica: "It would be Hans Christian Andersen if it wasn't so terribly Grimm."

The only real friend the Powells made was Rex Evans, a nostalgic Londoner who worked in MGM's research department, and was already getting small parts in big movies. Portly, hospitable, unfailingly good-humoured, Rex supplied their one link with the film community, dispensing tips and gossip, telling them where to go, and often taking them there himself. At a farewell lunch with Rex three days before they left town, he and his friend Elliot Morgan spotted Scott Fitzgerald in the MGM canteen. The two novelists took to one another at sight, settling down to a long companionable talk about British and American approaches to books, life and art. It was an unexpectedly satisfactory ending to a stay that had otherwise proved as futile for Tony as for other English novelists before and after him in Hollywood—Waugh, Greene, Huxley, Malcolm Lowry—all of them dismayed by a febrile alien culture and its scary ethos.

On 23 July they cut their losses and drove south to Mexico, spending their first night in a vast empty barrack-like hotel where the manager introduced them to the locals as King Edward VIII and Mrs. Simpson, currently the world's best-known English couple (Edward had renounced the throne six months before to marry the divorced Wallis Simpson). Three days later they flew to New York, which seemed, after nearly two months of Hollywood hysteria, infinitely restful, even sleepy, a comforting impression Tony retained ever after. "I have almost come to think of it as a quaint old seaside town," he wrote a decade later, "with pleasant bars in crimson velvet & gold on (I think) 2nd & 3rd Avenue that have scarcely altered since the 'nineties."

When they finally reached home on 14 August, landing this time from a French merchant ship in Plymouth, Tony saw with clarity something most people still desperately avoided seeing, the inevitability of another war with Germany. The next two years were shadowed—"as possibility became probability, probability turned into the real thing"—by the same threat as had hung over his boyhood. He had very little money left, no car, no job, no prospects and, worst of all, he had returned to London "without even the germ of a book in my head." Getting on for two years had passed since the publication of *Agents and Patients*. He had never gone so long between books before. The first three had followed one another without pause, the fourth had been unavoidably held up by meeting and marrying Violet. This was altogether different. Tony defined the state of mind that now engulfed him as sloth or *accidie*, "the feeling that nothing's worth doing. I'm absolutely overcome by that most of the time."

He said that, of the Seven Deadly Sins, this was the one that tempted him the most. Writing books kept sloth at bay but inspiration had now dried up, perhaps for ever. The black depression of August 1937—held off by the incessant activity of the past three months, brought on by a spiralling overdraft and approaching war—was, if not the first, the deepest and most disturbing Violet had seen. These moods disabled Tony, dragging him down out of reach into black gulfs where it was impossible to shift what he called "my awful bag of gloom" on to anyone else's shoulders. Violet would evolve coping strategies with time, watching, waiting, learning to keep her distance so as to avoid being sucked into the same abyss herself. The pattern was always the same. The darkest period could last days or weeks, sometimes more, followed by the slow return of energy and purpose. This time it seems to have taken longer than usual before, as Tony put it in his self-deflationary way, "some sort of a recovery took place." It was late autumn or early winter when he started work on a novel about an elusive oriental traveller, spurred on perhaps by an unsigned postcard from Bangkok of the pagoda at Wat Arun, a riot of proliferating pillars and porticos, banners and balustrades, spires and ziggurats in glittering inlaid tiers of gaudy green, blue, pink and orange. "Architectural purity is all the rage here," Reitlinger wrote on the back: "This is probably an early work of Gropius."

The death of Gerald Duckworth on 28 September gave Tony the push he needed. "Now what about *that* novel?" wrote Miranda, who had urged him to put what went on at Duckworths into his next book: "I suppose you will have to let the Managing Director's corpse get decently cold . . . it's too early yet to play hell in Henrietta Street." But even before he heard from her, Tony had begun the novel Miranda had in mind, taking his title, *What's Become of Waring*, from Robert Browning's poem about a lost friend of his youth. The book kicks off innocently enough with one of Tony's private jokes, a chance encounter with a disruptive character called Eustace Bromwich, "dark red in the face with gleaming white eyeballs," based on a friend of Reitlinger's who recognized himself at once with considerable satisfaction. Basil Hambrough was an ex-guardsman said to have served at some point with a Cossack unit, later forced to leave his regiment under a cloud of gambling debts, part Russian, immensely funny, always immaculately turned out, and widely travelled in Asiatic countries. He was the young subaltern who remembered Tony's father gibbering with fury in 1915. His letters were comic masterpieces, so ludicrously daft that Violet and Tony saved them up to share with one another whenever they were apart. Hambrough turned out to be too well realized in life to go far in fiction but, though Bromwich plays only a minor part in a tight plot—probably the tightest in any of Powell's novels—he hits the jackpot at the end with his engagement to pretty, witty Roberta Payne, another stylish chancer half his age.

Hard up, sexy and resourceful, Roberta persuades an infatuated publisher to commission her memoirs. Hugh Judkins is a plodder, running the firm of Judkins Judkins with cautious efficiency in face of perpetual obstruction from his elder brother Bernard, who loathes books ("he had only entered the trade to take his revenge on them. His life . . . became one long crusade against the printed word"). The Judkins brothers, as the novelist L. P. Hartley promptly pointed out, are faithful portraits of the author's ex-employers, Tom Balston and George Duckworth. Tony had enjoyed himself with both, transposing Bernard's inertia and resistance into a comic key, inventing ingenious torments for Hugh. Wracked by nervous tension, alternately vibrating from head to foot or laughing with "a noise like water hissing from a siphon," growing steadily more unhinged by Roberta's treatment, Hugh ends up so badly knocked off balance—"mad but with the madness of pathology, not satire," said the admiring

Hartley—that in a moment of reckless clarity he achieves an ambition most publishers can only dream of, and rejects, returns or cancels virtually every title on the autumn list.

Judkins Judkins's list of authors is admittedly no more inspiring than Duckworths', indeed many of the names on it might have fitted in well at Henrietta Street, starting with Waring himself, the popular travel-writer nobody has ever actually met. Other prime candidates for Duckworths include Hugh's pride and joy, the money-spinner Shirley Handsworth who is clearly based on Godfrey Winn, Bernard's dour favourite Minhinnick ("he looked every inch an unsuccessful literary man"), and the artless Captain Hudson, a Territorial adjutant and first-time writer whose "real life was lived among the shimmering domes and minarets of T. T. Waring's Orient where all the men were brave and all the women, with the possible exception of Roberta, chaste." *Waring* is classic English comedy undercut by a sense of peril and dislocation more pronounced than in any of Powell's previous novels. Uneasiness pervades the book, implicit in Hudson's gullibility, Hugh's nervous tics and sexual repression, above all the entire family of Pimleys, Hudson's putative in-laws, social dimwits epitomizing the profoundly inarticulate, outwardly conventional and inwardly volcanic people who fascinated Powell. He treats the suburban Pimleys—easily satirized by any competent novelist of the period—with an interest and sympathy that in no way minimize their social awkwardness, emotional inhibition and retarded intellectual development.

Roberta Payne, whose book was discreetly dropped by Judkins Judkins, owes something to Inez Holden but even more to Miranda Hayward, who never got her novel published either. *Girl Gone Wrong* had been unanimously rejected as too slight, perhaps a euphemism for racy, given Miranda's unromantic bluntness ("I now know what the woman meant who informed G. B. Shaw she didn't like a finger poked in her eye either," she wrote, describing how she lost her virginity to an unprepossessing boyfriend on a groundsheet in a wood full of biting midges). Miranda embarked instead on the second stage of her career as an adventuress. She left Duckworths as soon as she had saved up enough to sail for India, preceded by a glowing reference from Tony that secured her a new job with the Oxford University Press in Bombay. Violet and Eve went through their wardrobes again, providing frocks and floaty evening dresses, while Tony produced a £5 note (more like £200 in today's money). Throughout the next twelve months, while he wrote and published *Waring*, Miranda sent him long letters from Bombay, where she and the British memsahibs confronted one another with horrified dismay. Exacerbating the situation as best she could by picking up a German boyfriend and becoming pregnant with his child, Miranda found herself reluctantly obliged to marry him, and even more reluctantly forced by ominous news from Europe to contemplate coming home, "with or without the chip off the old Reich." Tony must have felt at times as if he was getting real letters from a fictional character.

In the New Year of 1938, Reitlinger introduced the Powells to another friend, a fellow novelist who had recently resigned his London job and moved to the country to become a full-time writer. This was Malcolm Muggeridge, who had built up sufficient reputation as an able and enterprising journalist to try supporting his family for the first time on a freelance basis. Muggeridge's wife was Kitty Dobbs, a niece of Beatrice and Sidney Webb, the nearest equivalent to royalty acknowledged by the British Left, which had angrily disowned Muggeridge when he described in print what he had seen as a correspondent in Russia. He was currently working on his third novel, and reviewing fiction at £5 a week for the *Daily Telegraph*. Tony whose only earnings now came from intermittent reviewing, mostly for Graham Greene on the *Spectator*, also faced a future without salary or safety net. Both knew that they were marking time.

In March German armies entered Austria. Britain began slowly to rearm. Gerald Reitlinger, whose father had been a banker in Vienna, was included on the SS death-list, compiled as part of Hitler's plan to invade Britain. His characteristic response was to get hold of a record of the Nazi anthem, the "Horst Wessel Song," and sing along as he played it on his gramophone. Muggeridge summed up the jumpiness of this waiting period in a story about a neighbour, a testy English colonel who found his drive blocked by Reitlinger's car. "It was a pitch-black night, and the Squire as he went out saw no one, only heard a voice roaring at him. I think he thought the pogroms had begun."

Profound, ingrained, ancestral resignation informed Reitlinger's attitude to the Nazis' persecution of the Jews, accelerating in 1938 with terrible speed and painstaking thoroughness. He faced it with a combination of grim acceptance and absurd English irony, playing games of make-believe in face of a reality without comfort. That spring Woodgate's long theatrical tradition reached its grand finale with an ambitious staging of the Tranby Croft scandal, a ludicrous affair that mesmerized Victorian society in the 1890s. Violet played Mrs. Arthur Wilson, the Hull shipping magnate's lovely wife whose house party—including the heir to the English throne (impersonated by John Lloyd in a mighty beard)—was wrecked when one of the illegal gamblers at her baccarat table accused another of cheating. Tony played Sir William Gordon-Cumming, the wicked baronet at the centre of the fuss. A double-page photo spread in his album shows him as the outcast Cumming, slinking off with bowed head towards his ruined future in an impressive final sequence: "The Open Road," "The Weary Miles," "Would God I Had Never Cut a Pack," and a last accusing snap, "The Finger of Scorn in Old Age."

Muggeridge was too literal-minded to see much point in what looked to him like childish play-acting. Tony's first encounter with him marked the start of forty years of friendship, but what struck him most at the time was the Muggeridges' obstreperous home life. The Mill House at Whatlington looked like "the home of the Old Woman Who Lived in a Shoe, children swarming all over the steps, children's faces looking out of every window, yet more children, one felt, concealed in the garden at the back" (in fact there were four young Muggeridges, apparently backed up by reinforcements from the village). Muggeridge was the first contemporary with a young family Tony knew well. Of his three closest friends, Reitlinger's marriage had begun dissolving in its first few weeks, Heygate's had ended in violence and divorce, and Lambert's was currently heading the same way.

For the past twelve months the newly married Powells had watched the Lamberts tear each other apart in a three-sided scrimmage acted out on and off stage at Sadler's Wells. Flo told Violet she first realized something was up when she came across her husband's note to Margot Fonteyn, starring on the first night of Ashton's *Nocturne* with Constant conducting in the pit. If Violet became Flo's confidante, Tony was Constant's: "he was, early on, the shyest man with women that you can imagine . . . tremendously awkward, and not in the least experienced." Rows with Flo deteriorated into punch-ups (once he hit her so hard the police arrived to break things up), while Constant struggled to detach Margot from her first lover, the young dancer Michael Somes, with whom Ashton, too, was madly in love. "You know the ballet world," Billie Chappell wrote to Tony: ". . . it's not really plausible being alternately deadly dull and then violently over-dramatic."

Violet started a second pregnancy that summer, leaving London in early August to stay at Dynevor Castle in Carmarthenshire, where her Aunt Markie had offered to look after her in the risky first few months. Her doctor was confident all would go well this time so long as she followed orders, resting for hours each day, drinking milk and taking short strolls under the strict supervision of Aunt Markie. Lady Longford's elder sister, the brightest and most outgoing of her siblings, courted by innumerable suitors, Markie had married Walter Rhys of Dynevor, a brilliant young politician expected to go far until loss of hearing in his middle years forced him to abandon a career in active politics. The couple retired to Wales, where he became in turn high sheriff and lord lieutenant of the county. By the late 1930s their four children had left home and Walter, now stone deaf, had settled for a regime of unrelieved tranquillity at Dynevor, which became a byword among the young Pakenhams for unutterable boredom.

Violet and Tony badly wanted a baby (they referred to this one as "Waring," presumably because it remained unseen, like the book's elusive hero), and both accepted her aunt's proposal as the only practical solution, but separation at this point was hard to bear. Violet was lonely and fearful. Tony warned her he was growing "very wild and savage" with no one for company but a pair of cats (Bosola had acquired a Siamese companion, a boisterous young extrovert called Paris). His anxiety was exacerbated by worry about his book, and in particular by "a very ominous letter" from Balston, who was currently reading the manuscript. Paralysed by nerves, weighed down by depression, sometimes too despondent to get out of bed, Tony waited until a second letter arrived from Balston, withdrawing any possible objection on the grounds that no reader could conceivably identify him with Hugh. "So this afternoon, skipping & carolling, I shall scamper off to Heath's . . . ," he wrote, light-headed with relief: "I feel a load of about five hundredweight off my mind." Violet was as jubilant as he was. "I could walk on my hands & I probably will," she wrote from Dynevor. The next step was to find a publisher. When Duckworths not surprisingly declined to offer even the smallest increase on its standard advance, Tony consulted Graham Greene, who spread the word, triggering immediate interest from Macmillan, Harrap and Hamish Hamilton. Cassell weighed in too, offering £100 advance on royalties, presumably more than any of the others since theirs was in the end the winning bid.

Negotiations were still dragging on when, on 17 August, just under two weeks after Violet reached Dynevor, she lost her baby. "Darling don't be sad or worried please," she wrote, describing what had happened with heroically controlled detachment: "I can't imagine you will want to spend the time or money to come down here . . ." The only distress signal she allowed herself was at the top of her letter, where, instead of a date, she wrote "Dies Irae," remembering the wild lament at the end of Constant's setting of *Summer's Last Will and Testament*. Preoccupied by publishers, and unwisely reassured by her apparent calm, Tony took her at her word and stayed in London, to the dismay of his parents, who were appalled by what seemed callous indifference to Violet's calamity. Colonel Powell's rage was almost incoherent. "There was a fearful to-do . . . ," Tony wrote forlornly, describing his mother's disquiet and his father's recriminations when he failed to drop everything and leave for Wales. "I now feel absolutely *frightful* about not having done so . . . really I suppose from their point of view they are quite right but one's life is really so different from theirs that I can't explain. Or isn't it—and am I quite wrong. I really don't know by this time. Perhaps I am more loathsome than is possible to express in less than 7,500 words . . ."

Violet's response was a vehement five-point tirade, insisting that his presence was the last thing she wanted, and threatening to go into a relapse if his parents continued interfering: "I've been ill often enough in the last four years to know my own mind & mean what I say & that you can grasp even if they're too boneheaded to do so." She and Tony were both beside themselves by this time with mutual disappointment, frustration and unhappiness. They had evolved a private code to deal with Tony's depressive furies, a kind of insurance or protective armour against the environment he first encountered at Pakenham Hall in August 1934, when Elizabeth Pakenham described him as a dwarf. From then on Tony's dwarfishness became a symbol of everything that made him eccentric, singular and seductive to Violet. His letters were often illustrated by tiny strip-cartoon images of himself in beard, boots and bobble-hat, plodding grimly through the rain under a dwarf umbrella, or responding excitedly to a loud bang in the street ("I rushed upstairs for my green pointed hat and red boots and went out to see what had happened"). Now his jokey scribbles helped to distract them both. "Nothing is sadder than an angry dwarf," Violet wrote in French, comforted by Tony's solidarity in the miserable summer of 1938.

When she got back from Wales at the end of August, he made her laugh by reviewing the memoirs of an Italian bookseller called Orioli, an ex-barber who had numbered among his clients the celebrated dwarf Mingulé, promptly adopted by Tony as his alter ego. Much of his current *Spectator* column was taken up by a long quote from Orioli, describing Mingulé's fastidious elegance, stylish turn-out and beautifully parted hair ("I had to curl the front of it every week with a hot iron, and the ends of his moustache as well"). By the time the piece appeared in print, the Powells were on their way to France with Wyndham Lloyd, always a kind and consoling friend in time of trouble. They got their balance back, recovering physically and emotionally in the course of a leisurely wine-sampling September holiday, driving through the rolling vineyards of Bordeaux.

The only drawback was the "horrible shrill screech" of Adolf Hitler's voice, emerging from the radio at hotels, restaurants and cafés along the way. They returned to London on 29 September, the day the prime minister, Neville Chamberlain, spent in Munich trying to avert all-out war by bargaining with Hitler over Czechoslovakia. Tony's name was on the Army Officers Emergency Reserve, and both he and Violet now enrolled as air-raid wardens, attending lectures on the effects of poison-gas attacks: "Neuralgia Pain in Jaw," "Aching of Frontal Bone," "Sneezing and Sometimes Vomiting," "Acute Depression": in short "an image of life," said Tony, who was knocking on doors and drawing up lists of residents needing gas masks. The house at Chester Gate had been painted earlier in the year, and the basement sitting room was made gas-proof that autumn. In December Tony got a postcard from Miranda, now forcibly repatriated with her husband Hans Christen to Germany, where for the first time she saw

Nazis saluting a gigantic image of Hitler on Frankfurt station as she waited for a connection with her baby: "Its mother shivered uncontrollably," wrote Miranda. Christmas 1938 was the coldest within living memory. With snow lying five or six inches deep even in central London, the Powells escaped to stay with Brocas and build "abominable snow women" in his garden at Boxted.

As part of his preparations, Tony needed a project to keep him sane through the coming months or years of war when it would be impossible to concentrate on anything so demanding as a novel. Wanting something scrappier and more prosaic, requiring no creative input, he picked biography instead, and was briefly tempted to write a life of Edward Lear. "His genius is rooted in a gentle melancholy," he wrote, defining what he liked about Lear, "which the horrible fate of the heroes and heroines of his limericks illustrates graphically." But in the end he chose an even more congenial subject, the almost entirely forgotten seventeenth-century antiquarian John Aubrey, whose *Brief Lives* of his contemporaries pioneered, as Tony said, a wholly new and strangely modern way of confronting "the oddness of the individual human being." Born and bred in Wiltshire, Aubrey too had lived in times of violence and conflict when England faced a dangerously uncertain future. In February 1939 the Powells left London to spend a few days visiting Aubrey's birthplace at Easton Piers near Malmesbury in Wiltshire, moving on to Broad Chalke in the south of the county where he first became a writer, and inspecting on the way the prehistoric stone circle at Avebury which he discovered.

What's Become of Waring came out from Cassell in March. "Mr. Waugh carries the heavier guns," said Hartley in his novel round-up, "but Mr. Powell hits the target quite as often, and drills a neater hole." Lady Jersey, in her ninetieth year, wrote to say that, much as she liked the book, she doubted Browning would have approved of Waring's exposure as a total fraud ("She spoke as someone who had known Browning," said Violet). Edith Sitwell was enraptured, especially by Hugh Judkins, whose prototype had been her editor at Duckworths: "I must not be misunderstood, of course, when I say I have known him well, have often visited him at his office, and clattered down the chessboard to his dinner parties. Also I feel I know those sudden bursts of temper and argumentativeness, the laugh, and the feeling of a blackboard as spiritual background." Miranda sent an enthusiastic fan letter with an ominous postscript to say Hans was with the army in the Rhineland. Tony himself said that what struck him most, on re-reading *Waring* four decades later, was its pervasive tension, "the racking international atmosphere of the epoch" that broods over the novel's apparent buoyancy and light-heartedness.

Publication coincided with Hitler's annexation of the free port of Memel in Lithuania on 23 March, an invasion widely expected to spark more general hostilities. A week earlier German armies had violated the agreement signed at Munich by occupying Czechoslovakia. When neither Britain nor France offered any armed response, the outbreak of war was once more postponed but it was clear that normal life could not resume. The standard publishing process of distribution, marketing and sales had been so effectively disrupted that most of Cassell's copies of *Waring* remained in store (where they were destroyed a year later when a German bomb set fire to the warehouse).

All through the spring and summer of 1939, Tony plugged away at his biography of Aubrey. Violet found an 1813 edition of the *Lives* in the library on a quick visit to Pakenham Hall in July. "You can hardly hear yourself speak for the noise of banshees keening and you can't see the hills beyond the lake for rain," she wrote, confirming Tony's dim view of Ireland: "the leprechauns who've taken shelter in the house keep on getting between my ankles." Violet had applied before she left to join the Port of London's civil defence force, the River Emergency Service, as a volunteer nurse. In August she and Tony took a last holiday in France, visiting Dijon, Macon and Beaune, sampling the delectable local food and wines of Burgundy, lingering in the church at Bourg-en-Bresse to admire the sculpted figures on the tomb of a fifteenth-century Duke of Savoy, *Les Pleureuses*, a band of weeping women "only too appropriate at that moment in European history," said Tony.

On 23 August Germany signed a pact with Russia. War was now inevitable, and parliament was recalled in Britain. Abandoning the last week of their holiday, the Powells returned next day, assuming that Tony would be mobilized immediately by the army, while Violet would be swept up as a nurse in the mass evacuation of London's civilian population. On 1 September Hitler invaded Poland. England declared war two days later. The Powells had spent the previous ten days tying off the loose ends of their old life, packing things away at Chester Gate and evacuating the cats. A phone call from Violet's doctor just before midnight on 3 September confirmed that she was starting another baby.

She broke down next morning on the station platform at Paddington as Tony saw her off again to Dynevor, where she was to spend the next eight months in bed. Uncertainty about when or where they would meet again exacerbated her fear and dread. "I *know* I'm glad about this baby," she wrote sombrely next day, "& I expect in time I shall get around to feeling glad too."

Tony, awaiting his call-up papers in a fever of impatience at Chester Gate, found that the emergency reserve meant nothing of the sort. He sent Violet a picture of a civilian dwarf saluting in bobble-hat with gas mask, and settled down to wait. Wyndham Lloyd moved in with him, bringing a stirrup pump in case of incendiary bombs. Lambert was filling sandbags in Hyde Park. Hambrough had turned up the day after England declared war, already impeccably kitted out: "He really might never have worn uniform before, for all the fun he was getting out of it," said Tony. He himself started negotiations to take over his father's elderly service dress, a transfer that for Colonel Powell meant finally acknowledging the bitter fact that so far as the army was concerned he was now unemployable. Malcolm Muggeridge, who had returned to London leaving his family in the country, dropped in to find Tony "mournfully polishing his father's Sam Browne belt."

On 10 October he received a phone call from a Captain Perkins at the War Office, explaining that his wife ran the cattery where the Powells had boarded out their cats, and asking if he would like his army summons speeded up. "Like hell I should," said Tony. The mixed emotions he had forcibly suppressed till now made him break off his report to Violet "for another letter when I feel calmer." The prospect of an army career had once filled him with an almost visceral horror—"I don't think it's going too far to say that I would *rather* starve"—but war itself seemed to close off other options. In a second letter two days later ("so underlined it looked as if it was written by Queen Victoria," said Violet), Tony was sufficiently recovered to sign himself off as a military dwarf brandishing a sword. He bought an army greatcoat from Moss Bros., and a pair of "real dwarfs' boots without toecaps." In these first uneasy months, Tony's dwarfs worked overtime, as a means of both distancing and confronting the ambiguous realities of public disturbance and confusion that now overshadowed private grief and loss, and the shock of a separation with no end in sight.

Tony and Muggeridge filled in time with long talks and walks round Regent's Park. They and their friends were all in similar states of suspended animation that autumn, wangling jobs, waiting for papers, inserting themselves on to waiting lists, swapping news and rumours of one another's postings. Reitlinger had embarked on a hopeless attempt to join the Marines. Varda (finally married to Dennis Proctor, to the astonishment of her friends) was driving an ambulance in Stoke Newington. Lambert, rejected by the army because of lameness and defective hearing, had set about boosting civilian morale by touring the north with the Sadler's Wells Ballet. Tony's own prospective posting roused considerable envy ("the Squire is liable to have several Knipchen fits of rage and jealousy about you," said Hambrough), but produced no practical result.

In November he returned reluctantly to Aubrey, sending Violet a self-portrait of a bearded bespectacled dwarf hunched over a typewriter. The two wrote constantly, and Tony sent regular consignments of books to Wales from the London Library. Painting was out of the question now that she could no longer leave her bed so Violet read omnivorously, covering the field from Thomas Browne to Balzac and Robert Burton, gulping down poetry, biography and memoirs, devouring nineteenth-century historians and novelists, anything but Walter Scott, whom she and Tony both found unreadable. Tony tried Swift for the first time ("Do you want Gulliver when I've finished with him?"), and both immersed themselves in Pushkin. Exchanging notes about the books they read, swapping, shifting and shaping one another's opinions, had been a key element from the start in the Powells' marital conversation, and now in these months of enforced separation they continued it energetically by post. "My darling, I miss you too," wrote Violet, when Tony complained about being unable to consult her, "particularly when I disagree with something I'm reading, and want to argue about it." She entered one of her clerihews for a *Spectator* competition and won it, whereupon the editor invited her to set the next one. Tony himself had once come

The army makes a man of Reitlinger, pictured here with Tony
and their friend Francis Watson.

second in a *New Statesman* competition devised by Cyril Connolly
to see who could describe the most truly terrible dinner in an English
hotel (the wine Tony drank was a Château Malfoutueux, heated up
for him in a bucket of scalding-hot water in a fake-Tudor inn where
the proprietor wore an Old Dotheboys tie).

Reitlinger meanwhile managed to sign on that autumn with an
anti-aircraft battery at Sevenoaks, wearing a private's uniform tailor-
made in Savile Row. "He looks an absolutely new man, clean, shaved,
cheerful," said Tony: "I've often heard of the army being the making of a man but I've never seen it happen before." He invited Muggeridge to dinner with the Proctors ("If I was a woman I'd rather be
married to Gerald than to that man," Muggeridge said afterwards),
and an entertaining friend called Francis Watson, one of John Lloyd's
knockabout ex-boyfriends, a museum curator currently employed by
the Admiralty (he ended up after the war head of the Wallace Collection in London). Watson arrived with a young and thoroughly
conventional girlfriend, who was appalled when her host began a

ferocious argument with Muggeridge as to which of the nation's two populist gurus—the writer J. B. Priestley and the scientist J. B. S. Haldane—was the more to be despised. "I think we shook her to the depths of her being," Tony reported with satisfaction, "and Mugrom agrees." Muggeridge himself (always known for some reason as Mugrom by the Powells) was marking time at the Ministry of Information while angling for the RAF. He and Reitlinger were both eventually posted to Field Security to learn to ride a motor bike and fire a revolver: "the Squire may make the fields secure," Tony wrote to Violet, "but I certainly don't think the roads will be."

A second phone call from the cat-minder's husband at the end of November was followed on 6 December by Tony's official summons to join the 5th Battalion of the Welsh Regiment at Haverfordwest in Pembrokeshire in five days' time. "*Je te couvre de baisers*," he wrote to Violet, signing off, almost giddy with relief, as an elegant French dwarf with spade beard, frogging and high-heeled boots, gallantly doffing his bobble-cap. For Violet at Dynevor, boredom had begun to take over from despair now that the dangerous early months of pregnancy were nearly over. "Darling I can't tell you how much I'm longing to see you," she wrote, making wild plans to borrow a cottage and set up house with Tony on the edge of camp. He said he felt further from her in Wales than he ever had at Chester Gate ("when I sometimes pretended that you were really only next door"). Both of them were conscious of what Violet called "the curious, dreamlike, unreal quality of life" in these first months of war, when the opposing forces on each side seemed momentarily stunned by the enormity of what was about to happen. "I had originally assumed it was just my inactive life," wrote Violet, "but maybe Hitler, Stalin, the Pope & Gort are all feeling the same sort of thing."

7

1940–45

Tony was caught up in a tidal swell of feeling that overtook even professional sceptics like Muggeridge who, as George Orwell said, found they were patriots after all at this point. Friends determined to carry on as if nothing had happened made Tony so cross he lost his temper in "an absolutely hammer-and-tongs argument about the war" with Bobbie Bevan and the Widow Lloyd ("I wondered whether I really hadn't gone a bit too far in telling Bobbie & the Widow what I thought of people like them," he wrote afterwards, clearly relieved when both agreed "they hadn't enjoyed themselves so much for ages"). He dashed off a rude rhyme about two celebrities of the British Left, W. H. Auden and Christopher Isherwood, who moved to the US in 1939 for the duration of the war:

> *The literary (or left-wing) erstwhile well-wisher would*
> *Seek vainly now for Auden or for Isherwood;*
> *The Dog-beneath-the-skin has had the brains*
> *To save it, Norris-like, by changing trains.*

The squib stung precisely because it was so clever, as Isherwood noted in his diary. Before leaving London, Tony posted it off on an anonymous postcard to Tom Driberg, founder of the most celebrated of all gossip columns, William Hickey on the *Daily Express*. Driberg refrained (or more likely was restrained by his proprietor, Lord Beaverbrook) from publishing it himself but circulated it widely by word of mouth until it eventually appeared over the signature "Viper" in the *New Statesman* in February 1940.

By this time Tony was in Northern Ireland with his regiment and the rest of the 53rd Welsh Division, which had left Wales on 18 December 1939, posted to Portadown in northern Armagh to repel the German invasion expected at any minute. A drab manufacturing town "on the boggy shores of Lough Neagh," Portadown was a Unionist stronghold. The soldiers of the 5th Welsh took over a disused flax factory ("looks like the sort of barracks the Foreign Legion are usually represented as inhabiting") with their officers billeted nearby in the Imperial Hotel ("exactly like the one in the film of the same name"). Tony found the architecture as grim as the implicit menace hanging over British soldiers, always prime targets for snipers from the banned Irish Republican Army (itself actively in favour of Nazi landings). He asked Violet for a blue-nosed Browning automatic as well as the dwarf jersey she had knitted him for Christmas. Dour, tight-lipped, Protestant Portadown confirmed both his long-standing mistrust of the Irish, and his instinctive liking for the friendly young Welsh miners of his own company, "talkative, good-natured, witty, given to sudden bursts of rage, unambitious, delighted by ironic situations . . ."

Officers and men came from local families in the coal fields behind Cardiff, all closely related, intermarried and intimately familiar with one another's ways, all speaking or more often singing with the soft musical lilt of the Welsh valleys. Second Lieutenant Powell looked and sounded like an outsider ("I don't expect you will be able to understand much of what I say when we next meet," he warned Violet). Ten or fifteen years older than any of the other subalterns, he belonged to an antiquated generation—"elderly to the point of senility" in their eyes—that made it natural enough for him to be on familiar terms with successive commanding officers. A slightly younger contemporary of Tony's father, Lieutenant Colonel W. G. Hewitt, had disquieting memories of that splenetic temperament, and made it clear with considerable tact that his sympathies lay with the son. "I hope to live to see the day your father salutes you," wrote Heygate, "that ought to rattle him." Even Tom Balston had now been called up again as a staff captain at Southern Command on Salisbury Plain. "Sooner or later I shall have to go and work for him again," Tony wrote without enthusiasm: "This will be another nail in my father's coffin."

Becoming a platoon commander on £1 a week with allowances meant he could pay off his overdraft for the first time in three years. His job was to turn the twenty or so men under his command into soldiers as part of the slow, laborious, often maddening but systematic and wholesale makeover of the UK's civilian population into a serviceable army. Taking his turn as acting company commander on New Year's Eve 1939, Tony marched down the main street of Portadown at the head of a hundred men, all singing the plaintive refrains of "The Quartermaster's Store" ("There's rats, rats/As big as bloody cats/In the quartermaster's store . . ."), a song of ancient scurrility that startled him by suddenly evolving new words: "There's Powell, Powell/Looking for a towel/In the quartermaster's store . . ." Tony described his consternation in a letter the same day to Violet, sending her a sketch of massed dwarves saluting smartly on church parade. "I think it must have been rather lovely," she wrote back soothingly, "to have your company singing to you by name."

Tony taught his platoon routines familiar to him from earliest years: drill, inspection, guard-duty, trench-digging, route marches and rifle practice, picturing himself as a booted dwarf with gritted teeth and savage grin brandishing an outsize revolver. The men needed perpetual attention like children, at once exasperating and forgiving, easily pacified with sweets and comics, endlessly having to be looked after, told what to do, taken to the dentist or marched off to church. He got on well with his batman, Private Ellis, who had read the same boys' stories as he had about trench warfare ("when we meet I see in his eye that he too is thinking: which of us is going to get the VC, and which be carried on the other's back?"). He lost a stone in weight, had his hair brutally cropped by the regimental barber— "in spite of the sermons in skulls all round me"—and learned to think nothing of marching ten or fifteen miles in a day. He told Violet that if he had a complaint to make, it would be that his regiment didn't talk about women nearly enough for his taste.

At first the army's absurdity amused him: "playing Red Indians with some soldiers in a field," dressing up for reconnaissance "like the White Rabbit in *Alice in Wonderland*, including tin hats & loaded rifles," or spending whole days on end "inspecting lavatories and tasting mugs of tea the men don't like." But cumulatively its tedium and inanity drove him to the kind of explosion he had witnessed as

Tony's experience with the Welsh regiment bore fictional fruit almost quarter of a century later.

a child from his father. When his leave was postponed at the end of January, he drew himself for Violet as a booted dwarf casting his bobble-cap to the floor and tearing his hair out. Rage and frustration overcame him regularly at the end of the week when he had to dole out pay-packets, a weary ritual that made him want to "go off into fits of wild laughter like Cecil Gray, and be carried out and treated for *canopis indica* [cannabis] poisoning." Once he silenced an entire room of soldiers by his ferocious response to a sergeant who came into the room without saluting ("You should have seen his salute when he came up for his pay. I thought his foot would go through the stone floor he stamped so hard"). Nobody held these outbursts against him, and Tony himself found that nothing restored his sense of proportion quicker than listening to off-duty sergeants keeping up "a running commentary of filth that warmed my heart." He particularly liked his own platoon sergeant, who made him laugh, and steadied him when things threatened to get out of hand. "It will pass, sir," said Sergeant Ashman, "like other days in the army."

Fellow officers were generally less easy to deal with. Tony served under a succession of company commanders who were still basically bank clerks or Cardiff branch managers, like Captain Horace Probert, testy and truculent, for ever fussing over minor points of army procedure like Shakespeare's Fluellen, the sententious, leek-eating Welshman in *Henry V*. Altogether more problematic was Captain Penn-Jones. An elderly ex-Territorial like Tony, fat, bald, chinless, gap-toothed with disgusting personal habits and unfailingly defective judgement, he inspired foreboding from the day they met: "long experience of figures of this sort tells me that one of these days he will do something that no one in the battalion dreams of now, even though they think him pretty funny." Shiftless and sloppily dressed, sometimes blind drunk, fond of issuing wild threats and making advances in his dressing-gown to other ranks, at one point formally under arrest, Penn-Jones somehow managed to survive for just over four months.

Serial reports on his career in Tony's letters kept Violet awake at night: "As I lay in the darkness Penn-Jones's face seemed to leer at me from the four corners of the room." Tony saw him initially as a character out of a novel by Evelyn Waugh ("He is in some ways tremendously like Captain Grimes"), but the character Penn-Jones directly inspired nearly thirty years later was Lieutenant Bithel in the *Dance*, a pairing that pinpoints the difference between Waugh's harsh, brilliant, satirical eye, and Powell's less clear-cut and more searching focus. Bithel's shambolic military career, and summary ejection from the army, supply a grotesquely comic parallel to the wretched, even tragic sequence of muddle and miscalculation that brings disgrace on Captain Gwatkin in *The Valley of Bones*, and shatters his personal romance of military glory. Tony never found out what finally put paid to Penn-Jones—"The poor old boy was apparently very upset & had seen nothing eccentric about his own behaviour at all"—but his trajectory followed the kind of pattern that shapes the *Dance*.

At that stage Tony was more worried about his last novel than about what he might write next. He was starting to dread encounters with John Stack, a fellow subaltern with an uncanny resemblance to Captain Hudson in *What's Become of Waring*: "the most ghastly feature of the whole business," said Tony, "is the knowledge (but I can't really admit it to myself) that I invented him." It was a queasy feeling that went with the job. "Any groundwork on the military novel yet?" John Heygate asked breezily, as if the war had been laid on as a bonus for novelists. But although the army claimed his exclusive attention, deep down Tony too was always aware of a jostling pool of fictional identities waiting for a chance to take shape. Even his delight in Sergeant Ashman's stories about his girlfriends could be justified on professional grounds: "I know it's prejudicial to discipline to listen to him, but they are so funny I feel that as a writer I should."

Tony was one of a group posted for training in January to Ballykinler Barracks, a former concentration camp for suspected IRA prisoners near the Republican border in County Down. No one apparently knew why they had been sent, or what to do with them when they got there. The salt marshes stretching to the coast seemed as unreal as everything else, "like the *second* scene in Foreign Legion films, where they have left Sidi-ben-Abbes & are living in a cardboard fort surrounded by limitless sands." Tony spent a weekend with the Herdmans at nearby Strabane and visited Mary's younger sister Pam, who had flirted with him as a schoolgirl, and since made a bickering marriage to an ex-racing driver called Trevor Macallan: "an awful little tick with a fully justified social inferiority complex," Tony wrote smugly to Violet, "made worse by the fact that he hasn't quite managed to get into the RNVR yet so he feels bad in the presence of uniform." Pam's husband would reappear eventually, threading his way through successive volumes of the *Dance* as Jimmy Stripling, a minor character hideously associated with pangs of retrospective jealousy.

Depression, held off for two months by ceaseless physical activity, returned sporadically after a week's leave at Dynevor with Violet in early February. Now almost seven months pregnant, she had been allowed up by her doctor for the first time the month before, and her infectious energy and appetite for life made Tony's return to Portadown almost more than he could bear. He still liked his Welsh regiment, especially after sharing barracks at Ballykinler with the Royal Irish Fusiliers: "this regiment gives one a very Waterloo feeling as opposed to my Welshmen who are purely mediaeval & make one think of Crécy & Agincourt & all that sort of thing." But his company was now stationed at Newry, a garrison town twenty miles nearer the Republican border than Portadown, with an ingrained tradition of IRA sympathies and murderous hostility to British soldiers. Tony's original impatience to get into the army was already mutating into an equally feverish eagerness to get out, or at least to find some sort of job better suited to his age and aptitude. He applied to anyone he could think of from the CO downwards, contacting friends in the army and trawling through acquaintances he hadn't seen for years. One or two held out faint hopes but, after two or three months without apparent result, he sank back into depression. "My life has been so like the *Morte d'Arthur* lately ('go to the 7th tree and there you will find an old woman who will hand you a ring. Take the ring to the lake & throw it in, when, etc etc . . .') that I really feel more or less completely powerless to affect the wheels of the juggernaut . . ."

An OCTU (Officer Cadet Training Unit) refresher course at Aldershot in late February turned out to mean in practice handling more barbed wire and digging yet more useless holes in bare rock. "I thought we were going to be shot at the end of the morning, and buried in the holes, but such was not the case," he wrote glumly to Violet, herself planning to move for the birth of her baby to Oxford, where her gynaecologist, Mr. Flew, was a consultant at the Radcliffe Infirmary. On 2 March Tony came over to Oxford from Aldershot to help her settle into a boarding house called Park Grange, a reunion that turned "the awful boredom of living among men only" into an ordeal beyond endurance. "My darling, I hope you didn't have a lousy journey to spoil our lovely weekend, & that your room-mate turns out to have only bubonic plague & not impetigo," Violet wrote cheerfully afterwards.

Starved of company for the last six months, she meant to make up for it now. Relays of visitors, relatives and friends headed down South Parks Road to her room. Her brother Frank, newly installed in North Oxford with Elizabeth and their three small children, was lecturing that summer on an extension course. Violet had always liked the indomitable Elizabeth, herself currently teaching Latin at a boarding school in Islip ("Does she know any?" asked Violet, "but a little thing like that wouldn't stop her"). She and Frank were both passionate socialists, prospective Labour candidates for parliament, and activists in workers' education with a highly developed taste for parties, high tables and university gossip. Oxford was full of young soldiers and airmen on leave, only too happy to take a pretty young woman out to dinner at the Randolph Hotel or lunch at the Golden Cross. At Park Grange fellow lodgers included at least one brigadier and an RAF pilot who said, when asked by a small boy how he got his VC, "Bit of bombing, y'know, bit of bombing." Violet visited her grandmother, who had finally taken to her bed, attended by descendants and cracking gallows jokes at Middleton Park.

Well before the baby was due in early April, the room at Park Grange was so crammed with cradles, baskets, bassinets, baby clothes and shawls that Violet barely had space for her bed. She ordered nappies, chose a pram as a present from Tony's parents, and arranged for her mother's former maid, Annie Reason, to move into a room on the top floor at Park Grange. Reason, who had given the Pakenham children what little mothering they had, was still indispensable on family occasions, moving round the sisters to look after their babies in turn. Bemused, disengaged, even faintly incredulous, Tony in Ireland could offer little help or guidance beyond warning Violet to avoid at all costs giving birth on his father's birthday, 21 April.

She had had more than enough recent experience of her father-in-law's attempts to commandeer her life, rejig her travel arrangements and brief her at length on his views about the dire mismanagement of the British army. "He throws red tape about like carnival streamers," said Violet after one of his visits. The spectacle of his contemporaries from staff college moving swiftly up the military ladder, as he had once reckoned on doing himself, threw Colonel Powell into paroxysms of self-pity. "I do feel rather sorry for him, he gets in such a state whenever he sees anyone in uniform, including the hall porter," wrote Violet, describing for Tony a lunch at the Randolph when her mother-in-law finally confessed afterwards in private "that she got to dread your father coming home in the evening."

As April drew on with no sign of the baby, even Violet found her nerves stretched by one false alarm after another. "The awful thing that Reason has just pointed out is that April 20th is Hitler's birthday, so I shall have to be careful," she wrote to Tony on 17 April: "I said I thought you would prefer the 20th to the 21st even then." In the event her son sidestepped both his grandfather's birthday and Hitler's by arriving on 25 April. Tony took the night boat back across the turbulent Irish Sea for the fifth time that year to spend a week's compassionate leave with his wife and new baby. He had sometimes wondered in Ireland if the whole thing wasn't an elaborate hoax, but now reality transfixed him. He said that becoming a father changed profoundly the way he looked at the world. Violet was radiant. They called their son Tristram Roger Dymoke Powell, and chose as god-parents the Widow Lloyd (who argued strongly in favour of Tris-megistus), Wyndham Ketton-Cremer and Elizabeth Pakenham (the christening in Christ Church Cathedral was tactfully arranged by Violet to take place in late May without Tony, who had no faith in any life but this one).

For both of them, their baby took a while to get used to. Back in Ireland, Tony found it "difficult to believe that he will still be there when we next meet." Violet, who was breastfeeding, said it was a week before she got over being surprised when Tristram reappeared every morning. Reason was claimed almost at once by Violet's sister Mary (newly married to a colonel in the Grenadier Guards, Meysey Clive, and in the early stages of pregnancy herself). A broken-down Dickensian crone called Sister Flood, with a face that looked as if it had been trodden on or bitten, took over for the next few weeks and turned out to be highly efficient. Violet made the most of this brief tranquil interlude in an Oxford smothered in spring blossom, cocooned from danger abroad, and still largely absorbed in its own concerns. She knew several other young mothers, including her school contemporaries Ty MacRae, Rachel Cecil and Billa Harrod as well as a circle of lively ambitious young dons: Rachel's husband David (just ahead of Tony at school and university), the economist Roy Harrod, who had married Billa, his friend Freddy Ayer and another brilliant, gregarious philosopher called Isaiah Berlin.

Violet knew perfectly well that the illusion of normality was non-sensical. British troops had been fighting in Norway ever since the German invasion of Scandinavia a fortnight before Tristram was born. Tony told her that Hitler's armies would soon be on the move across Europe but no plans had been made for herself and the baby by the time he left to rejoin his regiment. He and his platoon were cur-rently defending the 53rd Division's tactical school at Gosford Castle, a gigantic pale granite folly erected a century earlier in the shape of a Norman stronghold in County Armagh. Tony amused himself by pretending to be "like Edward, an Irish peer who has been forced to have a lot of people he doesn't like to stay with him." From his point of view Gosford was the culmination of all the absurd, ignominious Foreign Legion fantasies inflicted on him by the army. He loathed the place and the inefficient military bureaucrats who ran it. "There are

Lieutenant Powell defending Gosford Castle

no newspapers here and the wireless is broken," he wrote to Violet the day he arrived, 6 May: "so I expect we shall go on living here long after the war is over, a curious little colony with our own laws and customs. I sometimes wonder whether perhaps the clash has already come, and I am in fact in an asylum."

Four days later German armies crossed the border into the Netherlands, which surrendered on 15 May. Belgium was defeated by the end of the month. The Germans pushed on across France, reaching the Channel ports, forcing the British army into the sea at Dunkirk, and entering Paris on 14 June, after which France collapsed. Henry Lamb wrote to say he had seen the same armies fighting over the same ground as a young army doctor in the first war ("all the ghastly memories . . . which I had succeeded in keeping sealed up in forgetfulness have come pouring out in an overwhelming flood"). Constant Lambert and the Sadler's Wells Ballet, dispatched on a goodwill tour of the Netherlands by the British Foreign Office in May, joined the tens of thousands fleeing for the Channel coast before Hitler's racing tanks. "I had to stop in the middle of writing to Freddie Ashton as it suddenly struck me that the poor old ballet must be in the thick of things," wrote Violet. Miranda Christen had sailed with her own new baby at the beginning of the year to join her husband in Java, where he assured her they would be perfectly safe so long as the Dutch avoided defeat by Germany. "Poor old Miranda, I'm afraid she really has bought it this time," wrote Violet.

She herself had nothing in prospect and nowhere to go. Her boarding house was threatened with requisition, and in any case the Morris motorworks made Oxford an obvious target for German bombs. London was too dangerous, Dynevor too remote. She had been invited to stay by her sister Julia, who had married a dashing if unreliable and impoverished husband called Robin Mount, and was currently bringing up her own first baby in a cramped cottage at Chitterne in Somerset, too close for comfort to the military installations on Salisbury Plain. Violet's only other option was to share with John Heygate's wife Gwyneth, who had rented a house for the summer at Boxted in Sussex near Tunbridge Wells, directly under the flight path of bombers heading for London. On 24 May Tony summed up her dilemma in an impersonal situation report, making it clear that Violet, on her own with a four-week-old baby, faced alternatives that were all unsafe or unsatisfactory or both. "My childhood had been blighted by the First World War," she wrote sombrely, "and the Second World War . . . cast a black cloud over my first days of motherhood."

On 4 June she moved in with Gwyneth, who had a small son called George and a baby, Richard, three months older than Tristram. Two bombs fell the same day on Ashdown Forest, near enough for Gwyneth to hear them explode. She was a small cool blonde, always known as Gwyfkin, with film-star looks (she had abandoned a promising career after her first film to marry John), and a conventional outlook that grated on Violet, but she had a nursemaid to look after the children, a housemaid to cook, clean and wash nappies, and the formidable management skills of a good general. "I've just remembered that Gwyfkin's a crack shot, which may be useful," added Violet. John had inherited an Irish estate together with the family baronetcy from an uncle earlier that year, when he simultaneously published the third and last of his books about himself and Tony on the same motoring trip to Berlin. *These Germans* drove Violet wild—"I have a lot to say about Heygate's book, & then some"—but her furies though fierce were short-lived, and in any case John was away training as a gunner at Clacton-on-Sea. "I would give the world to visit Clacton & collect a few salutes," said Tony, when he heard.

He had spent no more than a few days' leave with Violet for nearly a year, and was missing her badly. "I shot Mussolini with my Browning," he wrote to cheer them both up, "and afterwards went to bed with you, a happy combination of business and pleasure." Italy joined forces with Germany as soon as it was clear that the rest of Europe had been overrun. Tony felt he was playing soldiers at Gosford, sleeping on the floor in a toy fort with a gun at his side as duty officer, and rising at dawn to inspect the guard. Once he fell into a canal fully dressed on a night exercise, and had to swim ashore, which impressed everyone, including the CO ("Though he himself appointed me, Bill Hewitt's manner changed completely when I had to deal with him 'in the field'"). Tony was being tried out for a job in liaison: "the great qualification seems to be possessing a lot of coloured pencils," he said, sketching himself as "the Liaison Dwarf" in tin hat with pistol playing blasts on his bicycle bell.

It was Violet who came under fire that summer as RAF pilots fought the Luftwaffe for control of the skies over southern Britain. The first sporadic coastal raids gave way in July to a sustained and concentrated attack intended to force Britain into alliance with Germany, or alternatively smash British air power for ever. The house outside Boxted, called Dolloways, commanded an uninterrupted view of rolling fields and woods stretching twenty miles to the Channel coast as German bombers streamed overhead, heading inland for London from captured airfields in Normandy and Belgium. Violet, still breastfeeding her baby every few hours, watched the night sky lit up by explosions. Next morning there were bomb craters, and sometimes wreckage strewn over the fields. She barely mentioned the raids in her letters, save to say once that they were waiting "to see if the All Clear will go in time for us to have tea in the garden." The sun shone for weeks on end from a clear sky. "The weather is like stale treacle with flies stuck in it," said Violet at the height of a battle that lasted all through that hot dry summer and well into the autumn, reaching a peak of intensity in August and early September.

Violet was further dismayed by the internal set-up at Dolloways, where the Heygates' marriage looked increasingly shaky. Gwyneth kept her options open by flirting with fighter pilots in Brighton, and filling the house with London friends at weekends. "By the way has Peter Quennell been told about the war yet?" asked Tony, intrigued by Violet's gossipy bulletins from a literary world still apparently oblivious to external threat. "Peter Quennell . . . now *has* been told about the war," Violet replied, "& is rather worried about it." In the intervals of manning a gun at Clacton, John had started a new novel, and was showing signs of strain. He came home whenever he could to renew hostilities in what Violet called "the Great Nurse War," a running battle between himself and his children's nanny, who did her best to keep him away from his new baby. Even more worrying was the effect on his elder son George, a deeply disturbed four-year-old who vented his feelings on a female doll called Horrified. "He not only beats her, kicks her, jumps on her and throws her under the wheels of the pram . . . he also shuts her up in a prison made of the fireguard," Violet reported to Tony, who said it sounded only too like the regime of battery and assault he had witnessed ten years earlier "in the case of his father, and the father's first wife." Evelyn Gardner herself, now married for the third time to a fighter pilot called Ronald Nightingale, was living not far away in Kent with a baby son of her own. The bombing made it impossible to meet but Violet forwarded her sharp, vivid, vigorous letters to Tony, who said they backed up "the theory that she writes all her husbands' books."

After four sleepless months with a baby still waking at night to be fed, under a bombardment steadily increasing in scale and ferocity, Violet decided to join Tony in the comparative safety of Ireland. He did all he could to discourage her—"you realise of course that I should be working all day & have my meals in the mess & sleep in the mess"—before reluctantly agreeing to apply for the necessary permit at his end. She negotiated the complex practicalities of wartime travel with impressive speed, clearing her application with the Passport Office in London, obtaining a respirator for Tristram (a large clumsy contraption like a heavy metal holdall big enough to put a baby inside), and embarking on the tortuous journey by train and ferry via Stranraer in Scotland, only to find when she reached Belfast on 10 September that Tony had arranged nowhere for them to stay.

He himself was also in Belfast by now, having managed at last to leave the Welsh battalion for a desk job as assistant camp commander at the 53rd Division's headquarters, "one of the least distinguished jobs in the army," as he said himself. He functioned as a kind of low-level military housekeeper in charge of everyday requirements—from vehicle distribution to rations and rubbish disposal—of the clerks, drivers, batmen and cooks needed to service the unit. The work was unremitting, painstaking and dull but Tony consoled himself by thinking of Stendhal: "I am now doing the sort of job that most of his life was spent at during the Napoleonic campaigns. I am no doubt getting more and more like him." Violet found another boarding house for herself and the baby, rescued Tony from the "nightmare of cheerlessness and squalor" that always threatened to engulf him in an all-male society, and set about organizing a social life, activating the network of contacts that enabled her to find local connections wherever she went from Stranraer to Santa Monica. Peacetime conditions still in place in Belfast (which had seen no enemy action at that point, and more or less given up expecting to see any) made everyone feel more relaxed, including the army. Tony was given permission to live at any rate part time for the next four months with his wife and child.

His job put him in daily contact with the officer in charge of the mess at Divisional HQ, a humorous, efficient and obliging young barrister with political inclinations called Jo Grimond. Tony and his superior officer, Captain Thomas, exchanged highly competitive dispatches with Captain Grimond on questions such as why the HQ milk supply had gone sour. "Either Dennis Thomas or Tony Powell sent back a note that it was fresh when it left their premises," Grimond wrote, quoting the pert postscript word for word nearly forty years later: "You must have a witch in the Mess, suspect A/Q" (assistant adjutant and quartermaster general, in other words Jo's CO). Exceedingly funny himself, irreverent, maladroit, irredeemably unmilitary, Jo was the antidote Tony needed to army bureaucracy. Soon the Powells were sharing a rented house at 19, Wellington Park Terrace with the Grimonds: Jo, Laura and their son Andrew, just twelve months older than Tristram. The two husbands set off for work together every morning on motorbikes, and the infants shared a pram ("The Club-men" was Tony's caption in the family photo album under a snap of Tristram and Andrew seated solemnly side by side on their pillows).

Any illusion of comparative normality ended in the New Year when Tony was ordered for reasons he never fully understood to leave Ireland at a week's notice. His instructions were to report to St. John's College in Cambridge on 13 January 1941 for a politico-military crash course staffed by academics and set up by Military Intelligence. It aimed to prepare junior serving officers—twenty or so subalterns, captains and majors—for the political, social, economic and cultural problems bound to arise once the Allies had defeated Germany, a highly implausible scenario at a point when Hitler had just seized most of Europe and was drawing up plans to conquer Russia as well. The idea of spending the next eight weeks listening to Cambridge dons lecturing on the racial origins of conflict struck Tony as frankly preposterous. "The syllabus, apart from being Everything . . . is mostly the sort of thing one argues about at Woodgate," he wrote to Violet, adding that the recommended reading list included a book by Reitlinger that he had himself published at Duckworths. A sense of unreality crept over him again: "all the dons and scouts look so stagey that I simply can't believe I am not in a film."

The grounding on offer was intensive, wide-ranging and so thorough that Tony had trouble at times assimilating his notes on the Visigoths while simultaneously sorting out "bracicephalous populations & synthetic-steel cartels & what on earth I'm going to do with the Sanjak of Novi Pazar." He drew himself as a bespectacled, bearded and booted dwarf in a bobble-cap, scribbling earnestly beside a pile of leather-bound books in the Wren Library. Writing essays made a pleasant change from army dispatches, but his overwhelming sensation was of relief at finding himself however briefly back on home ground in relatively familiar surroundings among his own kind of people. One of his fellow students was Goronwy Rees, then a Communist undercover agent beginning to make a name for himself as a journalist in London. Another was the father of a very pretty "ex-Sadler's-Wells ballet girl," known to Tony and Violet by her stage name, Rowena Fayre. A third was a fellow novelist called Geoffrey Dennis, rather older than the rest, a League of Nations bureaucrat who effortlessly outflanked the other students' scheme to rag him as a misfit (a piece of horseplay reproduced with its sequel and Lieutenant Bithel as its object more than twenty years later in *The Valley of Bones*).

Tony renewed relations with Bowra, met Freddy Ayer (whose response was distinctly cool), and was taken aback to find that any mention of Frank Pakenham over dinner at high tables "always causes everyone to go off into fits of uncontrollable laughter, which is rather embarrassing." The Fellows of Trinity, where he had rooms, turned out to include his first Greek teacher at Eton, Andrew Gow, whom he remembered as a tedious pedant with disorderly eyebrows and side-whiskers nicknamed Granny by his pupils. But Gow proved as hospitable now as he had once been curtly dismissive, taking Tony for walks and entertaining him in his rooms with unexpectedly fine wines, and an equally impressive collection of French Impressionist drawings.

At weekends he caught the train up to London, where Muggeridge met him at King's Cross Station, and took him back to his lodgings in Hammersmith for what Tony called "a colossal dish-up of gossip." Malcolm was following in Tony's footsteps by having an affair with Juliet O'Rorke. Tony was hoping to follow in Malcolm's by transferring to the Intelligence Corps (a grander name for what used to be Field Security). They dined at the Café Royal, always one of the best places in London to catch up with friends, and Tony bumped into the Lamberts on Piccadilly. This was his first real sight of the devastation caused by the Blitz, and he made his way north to check on the house at Chester Gate, boarded up but so far untouched by bombs, looking like something left over from a far-distant fairy tale, "one of those houses where the bride did not turn up on the day of the wedding that have remained as left for twenty years . . ."

By the second week in March Tony was back at his desk in Belfast, where Violet had rapidly assembled a circle of old and new friends ("You manage to make Belfast sound pretty gay," said Tony, who had not done too badly in that line at Cambridge himself). The city was almost wholly unprepared for the first exploratory air raids that came with the full moon in early April. Belfast had few bomb shelters, no searchlights, smoke-screens or gas-masks, and no RAF fighter planes to deter the two hundred Luftwaffe bombers that returned a week later to smash the factories and the great dockyards lining the lough. Fifty-five thousand houses were damaged on 15 April when nine hundred people died, the greatest loss of life so far in any single night of the Blitz outside London. Violet retreated to Pakenham Hall with Tristram, who was just short of his first birthday. Under a bombardment that lasted nearly a month, Divisional HQ also moved out to another Anglo-Irish fake-Gothic bastion, Castlewellan in County Down, where Violet rejoined the camp, finding rooms in the village for herself and the baby.

Tony was promoted to full lieutenant in early summer, and simultaneously transferred to the Intelligence Corps, news that upset his father, who could never "make up his mind whether success or failure in a son was the more inimical." The older Powells had been on the move again since the start of the war, flitting from one temporary lodging to another, even touching down briefly at Chester Gate before settling on Violet's boarding house, Park Grange in Oxford, where Colonel Powell watched with misgiving as Tony showed signs of finding his feet in the army. Renewed threats to reduce his allowance, or withdraw funding for the Chester Gate house, culminated in what looks like an attempt by Philip Powell to compensate for the total failure of his own military career by sabotaging his son's. But Tony had learned how to deal with this sort of ploy: "I don't think it matters in the least what he says and does," he told Violet, explaining that at last he felt sufficiently sure of himself to be able to neutralize any intervention his father might make.

At the beginning of August Violet and Tristram saw Tony off from Belfast for the final stage of his training at Matlock in Derbyshire. He spent the next six weeks attending a War Intelligence course at Smedley's Hydro, a vast, blackened, pillared and crenellated Victorian spa building that dominated the town like a great liner moored alongside the rushing waters of the River Derwent. "Bedlam in a *Morte d'Arthur* setting," said Patrick Leigh Fermor (who trained as an underground resistance agent at Matlock). For Tony the course seemed to start well, when he was singled out in the bar on his second day by the commandant of the Military Intelligence Training Centre, Colonel K. V. Barker-Benfield, always known as Bumblefumble in letters to Violet. The colonel bought him a drink, and asked him to write a report on the Cambridge course (devised by himself as a way of spotting suitable candidates for offbeat, undercover or more general intelligence assignments). "He isn't much to look at," Bumblefumble apparently said of Tony, "but as soon as he opens his mouth you can see what an astonishingly intelligent person he is."

After that things went downhill. Tony felt ill most of the time, suffering from bad dreams, insomnia and indigestion. It took him a fortnight to get used to either the food or the climate, and even then his liver gave constant trouble ("I can't decide whether I will send mine to the Imperial War Museum, or use it for sabotage in enemy factories in occupied territory"). The work was uncongenial, the schedule so gruelling that he got up every morning already feeling exhausted. "I wish you were somewhere near," he wrote to Violet, "but I think it would be quite hopeless for me to attempt to cope with the work if you were." His room-mate was an officer from the Queen's Victoria Rifles called Adrian McLaughlin, who rated comfort above army regulations and had brought his manservant with him. McLaughlin had a car as well, and at the end of the first week Tony escaped in it to Renishaw for lunch with Osbert and Edith Sitwell. Older, stiffer, still writing hard, brother and sister were pleased to see him but mystified by his chauffeur. "Osbert has already worked himself up into a state about McLaughlin (whom he will call MacCochrane), saying he is sure he is just a character out of one of my books, a suspicion in which there is an element of truth."

The visit proved a success, which was more than could be said for the rest of the course. Evelyn Waugh was said to have flunked it, and Malcolm Muggeridge, who followed Tony to Matlock that autumn, found it "infinitely more detestable than everyone had led me to understand. After Smedley's anywhere seems bearable." Malcolm at least had a natural aptitude for subversion and covert operations (he spent much of the next year running an East African espionage network from Lourenço Marques, with Graham Greene as his opposite number running the spies on the west coast). Tony could never take cloak-and-dagger games seriously. He was beginning to feel more like one of the prisoners in a painting he'd seen in Moscow with Violet: "I look like the picture in the Tretyakov called *Back from Siberia*."

Violet packed up and returned to Oxford, planning to park Tristram and spend the two weeks of Tony's leave in September with him in London: "You speak of summoning temporary nannies from the vasty deep," said Tony, echoing Glendower in *Henry IV*, "but will they come?" Finding a child-minder posed no problem for Violet, and the couple made the most of their first time alone together since their son was born. They borrowed Gwyneth Heygate's London flat, gave riotous parties for friends, including the Lloyd brothers, and fitted in a quick trip to see Julia at Chitterne before Tony had to return to the IT depot at Pembroke College to await posting. Back at the boarding house, Violet investigated the possibility of moving in with Eve Disher in Hampstead, now that the war had swept Arthur up too ("I don't mind Arthur Evans sleeping in my bed," said Tony, "so long as I'm not in it"). But the one good thing to come out of Matlock was a more inviting proposition from a fellow student, Captain Andrewes, a young classical historian from Pembroke College: "seems nice as stage dons go," said Tony, "& doesn't like Forster." Andrewes had a wife called Alison living with their new baby daughter in a basement flat on Wellington Square, conveniently close to the hub of wartime Oxford, where Violet now joined her with Tristram.

The two girls were both in their late twenties: energetic, sociable, under-employed and determined not to give in to the contemporary Blitz spirit of austerity and puritanical drabness. Alison looked like the seductive blonde barmaid painted by Edouard Manet at the Folies Bergères. Violet, who was the older by a year, was beginning to remind people of Manet's sleek, plump Mlle Victorine, dressed up as an irresistibly implausible matador with sword and pink cape in close-fitting black silk knee breeches. Of the two, Alison had had the more eventful career. She had gone down from Somerville College with a degree in English at twenty-two to marry a don fifteen years older than herself, the classical archaeologist Alan Blakeway, director of the British School at Athens, a charismatic character whose scintillating wit and mesmeric personality electrified a whole generation of undergraduates, including Isaiah Berlin and his close friend, Tony Andrewes. When Blakeway died suddenly of blood-poisoning barely a year after the marriage, Oxford was devastated. The young widow returned from Greece, rebuilding her life as a reviewer for the *Sunday Times* and marrying her husband's pupil Tony Andrewes two years later.

She and Violet formed a lively ménage at Wellington Square. The two shared a great many friends, ranging from Berlin and Bowra to the young Cecils, but Oxford was too likely to attract bombs to be ideal for bringing up babies. Tristram was nearly two, and Holly Andrewes (always known as Jig) not yet one when the four of them moved at the beginning of 1942 to a small semi-detached suburban house at Petersham in the Thames Valley, near enough to Richmond Station for Violet to catch the train up to London, where Bumble-fumble had finally fixed Tony up with a job in Military Intelligence.

He had been posted at the end of September 1941 to a small section of the War Office responsible for keeping in touch with the various Allied governments that had fled at the start of the war to Paris, regrouping in exile in London after the fall of France. Tony worked in the old War Office building at the top of Whitehall as a general dogsbody, being promoted to captain after a few weeks and assigned as assistant to Major Alexander Dru, dealing initially with Poland. Alick Dru himself was a small, neat, polite person in wire-framed spectacles with slicked-back hair and a non-committal manner, unassertive, inconspicuous and superlatively self-contained. "I really can't quite make out what his line is," said Tony, who was baffled by how well the two got on from the start. Dru's prodigious and promiscuous reading, especially in French, was an immediate attraction. So was his unfailing ability to produce information, sometimes startling, often arcane but always sharply relevant to whatever the business in hand.

Absolute detachment co-existed in Dru with an unexpectedly practical grasp of the essentials of any given situation, and their implications. Tony said Constant Lambert was the only other person he knew with anything like Dru's "lethal quickness" of mind. He could divine and defuse tension almost before it gave trouble. He was prepared to take infinite pains to resolve the trickiest, most time-consuming or trivial problem but had no patience whatsoever with standard solutions and routine procedure. "I really cannot endure boredom," he once told Tony, "the boredom of setting out plainly all that ought to be set out plainly." His approach was immensely congenial. After just over a month in the job, Tony invited Dru to dine at the Travellers, where they shared one of the best bottles of Burgundy either had ever tasted ("The violets burst out all over when you drank it"). It marked the start of a friendship that lasted the rest of their lives. Tony was already beginning to dread the possibility that the army might exercise its right to shunt him off elsewhere without warning or explanation. "I feel rather as Laval must," he told Violet (Pierre Laval was the pro-German, fascist head of the Foreign Office in the French collaborationist government at Vichy), "that there is always someone round the corner waiting for him with a brick."

He and Dru settled quickly into a relationship that suited them both. Dru had read Tony's book reviews, Tony was impressed and intrigued by the range and scope of Dru's religious and philosophical reading in English, French and German. He had a knack of abstracting himself from human affairs—what Tony called "an armourplated withdrawnness"—that added to the sense he gave of being indefinably alien, perhaps because he was only half English. An only child, brought up by a French father (his mother had died when he was young) who sent him to school at Downside Abbey, he grew up "a Frenchman translated into an Englishman." The transition though smooth was never quite complete. Part of Dru always remained a quintessentially French intellectual. He was learning Italian in the office he shared with Tony because he wanted to read Petrarch in the original. He had taught himself Danish as an undergraduate at Cambridge in order to translate Søren Kierkegaard, whose *Journals* remained so far his only published book.

His first and only job on leaving university had been a brief stint with an oil company that bored him so much he resigned and returned to Kierkegaard until he was recruited, a few months before the start of the war, by the director of Military Intelligence, Major General Beaumont-Nesbitt, who needed an assistant military attaché for the British embassy in Paris. Dru, gazetted as an emergency commission, was an inspired choice for a job requiring extreme tact and delicacy in time of chaotic turmoil. "I particularly admired the earthiness of his logic in military matters (perhaps the only thing about him that was entirely French)," wrote Peter Wilkinson, the officer representing the Polish Mission in Paris, later one of the founders of the Special Operations Executive: "I had the impression that he felt unusually intensely . . . about the war, and took considerable pride in being an outstandingly efficient officer."

In the autumn of 1941, when Tony joined him, Dru needed all his diplomatic agility in dealings with the Polish government-in-exile. Britain had declared war when Hitler's forces marched into Poland in 1939, an invasion from the west shortly followed by Stalin's Red Army pouring in from the east. Well over a million Poles—intellectuals, aristocrats, churchmen and army officers—were killed, imprisoned or deported to slave labour camps. The country itself faced extinction in these years when large parts of its territory were carved off for incorporation into East Prussia and Silesia. Ethnic Poles were expelled in favour of German settlers. Schools and universities were closed, artworks and libraries plundered, industrial and economic resources appropriated wholesale by both Germany and Russia.

Twenty or thirty thousand young soldiers eventually escaped to England to join the Polish Independent Parachute Brigade, newly formed and currently training near Fife in Scotland for the sole purpose of liberating Poland. This army in exile was by far the largest, toughest and most highly skilled of any force mustered by the defeated European countries just as Poland's underground resistance at home was the best organized and most ruthlessly efficient. The London Poles seemed indomitable to Tony: fierce, confident, highly entertaining, already profoundly uneasy about what had happened to some two thousand Polish officers who had vanished without trace in Russia, presumably dispatched to Siberian labour camps. In July 1942 he travelled up to Scotland to spend a week making contact with the Polish Corps and their British liaison officers. In September he asked all his friends to a Polish party in London.

Now that he was back on home ground, Tony missed his wife more acutely than ever ("I hardly exist without you," he wrote), so much so that he continually caught sight of her on the street, a delusion that left him as soon as they worked out ways of seeing and speaking to one another on a regular basis. He saved up his one free day a week to spend alternate weekends with Violet and Tristram in Petersham, and she joined him whenever possible for a night in London, leaving Alison to look after both babies. On days when they were apart they exchanged long midnight phone calls. Violet had initially arranged for Tony to stay in the Yorkes' comfortable, well-heated house with cook and housemaid at Rutland Gate in South Kensington, an experiment he reluctantly accepted on the understanding that Henry would be out most of the time dealing with bomb damage as a fireman in the Auxiliary Fire Service. Henry's reception turned out to be as surly as Tony anticipated. For the past decade and more the two had inhabited different worlds, the Yorkes rarely missing a smart party, arty or otherwise, the Powells operating for preference on a scruffier literary scene. "I think he now realises I'm not going to dance round him singing: 'Who isn't in the army? who's rich? who likes James Hanley's books?' etc etc," Tony wrote at the end of his first week, but their friendship was irretrievably over. After a fortnight he moved with relief into a one-room flat belonging to the Lloyds, Gwyneth Heygate's family, in a block on the King's Road.

He had returned to the blacked-out capital in time for the great air raids that followed German defeat on the Channel coast, continuing on and off for the next three years and reaching another peak towards the end of the war with flying bombs over London: "an empty, dark city, torn with great explosions," wrote Muggeridge, whose apocalyptic inclinations were well served by the Blitz, "racked with ack-ack fire, lit with lurid flames, acrid smoke, its air full of the dust of fallen buildings. I remember particularly Regent's Park on a moonlit night, full of the fragrance of the rose gardens; the Nash terraces perfectly blacked out . . . white stately shapes waiting to be toppled over—as they duly were, crumbling into rubble like melting snow." The house next door to the Powells' in Chester Gate received a direct hit that left number one still standing, but Tony preferred his anonymous bachelor pad with a pub round the corner serving inadequate meals on skimpy wartime rations, after which he generally retired to spend the rest of the evening in bed for warmth, working his way steadily through a heavy pile of Aubrey's more laborious contemporaries, "calming to the spirit when the blitz was reverberating through the night air."

From time to time he found himself caught up in the arbitrary encounters characteristic of wartime when migrants without homes to go to roamed restlessly in the black-out: random combinations of strangers, intimates, people he hadn't seen for years washed up in the same club or café or Chelsea speakeasy. Old and new friends appeared suddenly on leave or in transit, disappearing again just as abruptly: Jo and Laura Grimond catching a train for Scotland, the Widow Lloyd rejuvenated as an RAF flight officer, a despondent Reitlinger evicted from the army supposedly on health grounds, Waugh back in England with the Commandos after the disastrous battle for Crete, Cyril Connolly in a reserved occupation as editor of *Horizon*: "all quite enjoyable," Tony reported to Violet, "though a *very* poor substitute for having you in tow, my darling." Letters from pre-war personalities like the Sitwells now seemed "quite inconceivably boring, while Adrian and Constant make one shake with laughter after fifteen years or so." Adrian had been dispatched as a war artist to paint generals in

Cairo. Constant, still boosting morale on tour with the ballet all over the British Isles, sent Tony a "Ballad of LMS Hotels," a rousing gastronomic guide covering every station hotel on the London, Midland and Scottish line to be sung to the tune of "There Are Fairies at the Bottom of the Garden":

> *There are LMS hotels at Ayr & Dornoch,*
> *There are LMS hotels at Leeds & Crewe;*
> > *At Stratford-upon-Avon*
> > *The salami's made of raven*
> *And they charge you 10s 6d for Irish Stew.*

> *At Holyhead & Liverpool & Euston*
> *The halibut supreme is cooked in glue;*
> > *At Edinburgh & Glesgie*
> > *The supper's one kromeski*
> *And they charge you 10s 6d for Irish Stew . . .*

> *At Manchester and Morecombe, at Birmingham & Bradford*
> *The food and drink would make an ostrich spew;*
> > *But old Sir Arthur Towle*
> > *Has a gizzard like an owl*
> *And he actually enjoys the Irish Stew.*
> *Chorus: Aye mon! and he actually enjoys the Irish Stew!*

Constant remained a firm friend although marriage had interrupted their dialogue, and the exigencies of war completed the process. But Tony's closest companions at this point were Dru and another new friend, George Orwell, first encountered round about the same time at the Café Royal through an ex-Duckworths author, Inez Holden. Tony had been sufficiently impressed by the ferocious desperation of Orwell's *Keep the Aspidistra Flying* to send him a copy of *Caledonia* together with a fan letter that was received with scant enthusiasm. Orwell's sole comment was that he was glad to find someone "hitting back at the Scotch cult" by calling its practitioners Scotchmen instead of Scotsmen: "I find this a good easy way of annoying them," he said. Orwell's prickliness, and his well-known disapproval of any but the plainest working-class usage, made Tony expect the worst, especially since he was celebrating a visit from Violet by dressing up to take her out to dinner in his father's ancient patrol uniform, a dandified outfit in navy blue with brass buttons and red stripes down the trousers, secured by a strap under the instep. It was characteristic of both men that, far from driving them apart, Tony's atypical ostentatious impulse drew them together. A knowledgeable exchange about military tailoring initiated what rapidly became for both a key friendship.

George liked Tony's dry wit, ironic humour and sharp, unsparing, speculative eye. Tony was initially fascinated by George as the antithesis of Cyril Connolly, each publicly exemplifying for their contemporaries opposite brands of romanticism: "one lean and ugly, the other fat and ugly, one phonily abstemious, the other phonily self-indulgent," said Tony. All three had been indelibly marked by schooldays at Eton. Tony, who had been well aware of Connolly but never came across Orwell at school, knew him from his writings as a brilliant left-wing polemicist with powerful convictions informed partly by an entirely rational response to inequality and injustice, partly by an idiosyncratic inner vision of "working-class life as it was about eighty years before his own day (anyway how he imagined it)." But each instinctively responded on a much deeper level to something humane and generous in the other, and over the next few years Tony came to recognize behind the hard-hitting facade an innate sweetness in George, "a friend for whom it was impossible not to feel a very deep affection."

Tony read George's latest book, *The Lion and the Unicorn*, a wartime manifesto that starts with a characteristically reassuring analysis of England and its people, going on to predict imminent revolution and to outline with approval the kind of British socialist state ("We cannot win the war without introducing Socialism") that would follow the overthrow of capitalism: a planned economy with industry and banks nationalized, incomes forcibly curtailed, private ownership of land abolished along with the class system, all opposition suppressed by the state ("It will crush any open revolt promptly and cruelly"), and the empire remodelled as a version of the USSR. "It seems to me to be purest fascism," said Tony, "but I suppose he knows best."

George had been able to carry on writing because his damaged lungs made it impossible for him to join the army, or even to find

George Orwell, "a friend for whom it was impossible
not to feel a very deep affection"

war work. His long bony face and the lines etched on it by pain and
hardship, something obdurate and angular in both mind and body,
reminded Tony of Cézanne's portrait of Victor Chocquet. Like Dru,
Orwell had elements of a French intellectual in his make-up, "one of
those fiercely melancholy French workmen in blue smocks pondering the meaning of life at the zinc counters of a thousand estaminets."
He had the same almost ideological horror as Dru of anything that
could be construed as servile or ingratiating. A naturally philosophical temperament co-existed in each of them with a surprisingly matter-of-fact grip on practicalities, and both took satisfaction in making
themselves disagreeable where necessary. "Always put them to trouble in return," George advised Tony, discussing editors rash enough
to criticize or correct his work: "It discourages them from making
themselves awkward in future." It might have been Dru talking about
War Office superiors, but Tony's attempt to introduce his two friends
over lunch proved a dismal failure. Neither could find anything to say
to the other so that after a while the meal proceeded in silence.

Alick Dru and Tony had evolved their own methods of staying sane in face of the tensions generated by daily contact with the
impotent representatives of beaten and occupied countries (Tony
calculated that one particular attaché had written him more than ten
thousand letters by the end of the war). They invented running jokes
that reduced both to helpless laughter, and made up joint serial stories

sprouting from the manifest weirdness of current reality. Dru had a natural gift for mythologizing anyone he met, seizing on perfectly normal behaviour or mannerisms and building them up with fantastic distortions and exaggerations into preposterous fictional versions of themselves. The officer in charge of military liaison, Lieutenant Colonel J. C. D. Carlisle (Dru called him Honest Jack), was a forceful character of considerable charm and distinction whose efficiency, manipulative powers and love of intrigue largely shaped his section. "He became a kind of cult to Dru and myself . . . ," said Tony, "a near-Shakespearian figure, who would have been superb proclaiming in blank verse, like Polonius, his personal rules of conduct in life."

Another of Dru's favourite subjects was Major E. C. Bradfield, known as Bradders, who spoke fluent Danish and was responsible for the Norwegians. Fussy, good-natured, self-absorbed, "an altogether phenomenal egoist," he looked in some lights like the Emperor Vespasian, in others "like an immensely genial troll" come down from the Scandinavian fjords to bombard his colleagues with inordinately long, muddled and peremptory minutes. Adopted as a boy by a childless Dane (possibly his natural father), he had lived alone before the war in his inherited castle in Jutland, farming the land and playing the piano in his spare time. Passed through the filter of Dru's imagination, Bradders re-emerged as a tragic hero. When Donald Wolfit played King Lear in London, Dru insisted Bradders must be prevented from going "as really it was too like him," and Tony (who had enjoyed the production so much he claimed to have got up and joined in the last few scenes) fully agreed. Long after the end of the war Dru was still toying with plans for collaborating with Tony on a memoir of Bradders: "What a work! . . . A whole chapter on artificial insemination & piano technique! I could easily sketch out the chapters if only you would do the writing."

This is precisely what seems to have happened in the case of the most elaborate of all Dru's imaginative creations, and the one with the most far-reaching repercussions. Denis Capel-Dunn had been his contemporary at Trinity College, Cambridge, and later his flatmate in London, pursuing an undistinguished career at the bar in civil life. Dru nicknamed him the Papal Bun on account of his grandiose view of his own importance, claiming he had been such a nonentity as an undergraduate that "people used actually to *worry* that he would

Colonel Denis Capel-Dunn, who gave Tony, as his assistant, direct access to the underground bunker in Whitehall where Churchill and his chiefs of staff ran the war.

not be able to earn a living." Tony found him dull and pompous, remaining baffled as to what it was Alick found so fascinating, and so extremely funny, about this Cambridge friend. In wartime Capel-Dunn moved smoothly into a key position at the Cabinet Office in Whitehall, operating as secretary to the Joint Intelligence Committee with an office in the reinforced steel bunker two floors below ground level where Winston Churchill and his defence chiefs came together to conduct the war. Tony said it was one of the greatest shocks of his life when Capel-Dunn picked him in 1943 to be his sole assistant. Carlisle's objections were overruled on the direct intervention of the prime minister, and at the end of February, Tony reported for work.

The Joint Intelligence Committee, consisting of the heads of the army, navy and airforce, the War Cabinet and the prime minister, met daily to receive briefings, review developments and formulate plans. One of the responsibilities of its secretary—and now of his new sidekick—was to summarize each day's deliberations concisely and clearly in a document to be laid before the committee next morning. The job entailed working fourteen hours a day, sometimes longer, and carried with it in Tony's case promotion to acting major, and every likelihood of becoming in the near future a lieutenant colonel like his father. Capel-Dunn had been running the JIC for the past three years, acquiring in the process an "unrivalled knowledge of the machinery of the higher direction of war," frequent opportunities for influencing policy, and a formidable network of contacts that fuelled almost boundless personal ambition.

Tony, better placed than ever to observe at first hand the workings of power, laid down the foundations of what became a lifelong speciality. Quarter of a century later memories of this period resurfaced to form the basis of *The Military Philosophers*, where Jenkins witnesses the arrival, in the palatial entrance hall of the War Office, of the commander of the Imperial General Staff, General Alan Brooke:

"My [attention] . . . was at that moment unequivocally demanded by the hurricane-like imminence of a thickset general, obviously of high rank, wearing enormous horn-rimmed spectacles. He had just burst from a flagged staff-car almost before it had drawn up by the kerb. Now he tore up the steps of the building at the charge, exploding through the inner door into the hall. An extraordinary current of physical energy, almost of electricity, suddenly pervaded the place. I could feel it stabbing through me. This was the CIGS."

An encounter with Field Marshal Montgomery twelve months later enables Jenkins to contrast Brooke's magnetic impact—immediate, irresistible and undeniably reassuring—with the icy willpower brought to bear by the field marshal, "an immense, wiry, calculated insistent hardness, rather than a force like champagne bursting from the bottle . . . One felt that a great deal of time and trouble, even intellectual effort of its own sort, had gone into producing this final result."

The origins of Tony's expertise in the field of power and the will undoubtedly lay with Capel-Dunn. He turned out to be a workaholic, hectically determined "to get through ten times as much work as everyone else," unwilling to offer his new subordinate even the smallest advice or guidance, and more purely materialistic than anyone else he had ever met. Capel-Dunn was short, stout, graceless, totally lacking in humour and superlatively good at his job, "a squat

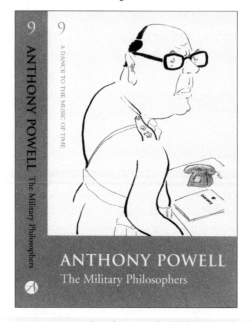

Lieutenant Colonel Kenneth Widmerpool,
drawn by Mark Boxer, at the height of his
wartime power and influence in Whitehall

figure in a sodden British Warm . . . famed for his forcefulness with
subordinates . . . manipulation of equals and ingratiation of superiors, particularly those of ministerial rank." Perhaps he singled Tony
out for the same reason Kenneth Widmerpool picked the narrator in
the *Dance* to work as his underling, because he was the best of a bad
bunch of candidates. Capel-Dunn was known by colleagues as the
Frog Footman, and as Young Bloody by fellow members of Brooks's
in Piccadilly. Jenkins's account of Widmerpool's subterranean workplace in Whitehall re-creates the vast underground labyrinth where
Tony worked under the pavements of Great George Street: "it was
impossible to remain unaware of an atmosphere of exceedingly high
pressure in this place . . . the power principle could almost be felt
here, humming and vibrating like the churrings of the teleprinter."

Widmerpool has passed into contemporary folklore as the lumbering, initially comical but in later volumes steadily more sinister
embodiment of the quest for power that is one of the hinges on which
the *Dance* turns. Long afterwards Powell himself conceded that

Capel-Dunn had been a model for Widmerpool "in so far as you can say that characters in novels are modelled on anyone." But, as he also pointed out, Widmerpool's career runs right through the sequence, spanning the fifty years that elapse between the first and last volumes, which suggests that traces of a good many other real people fed at one point or another into the *Dance*'s fictional archetype. Tony's stint as Capel-Dunn's aide lasted nine weeks, starting in terms of the fictional calendar towards the end of Chapter 2 of *The Military Philosophers*, and ending at some point between chapters 4 and 5.

He had been seconded to the Cabinet Office at a time when popular approval of Russia as an ally, comparable in importance only to the US, was at its height. Any hope of defeating Hitler depended heavily on Russia's continued success on the Eastern Front, but support for the USSR was potentially compromised in April 1943 by the discovery in Katyn Forest near Smolensk of mass graves containing the bodies of the missing Polish officers, evidently massacred by their Russian captors. At the end of April, when the Polish government in London demanded an explanation via the International Red Cross, the USSR broke off diplomatic relations with Poland. General Sikorski, the exiled prime minister, discussed the situation with Churchill, who was obliged to point out that sympathy with the Poles could not be allowed to jeopardize future Anglo-Soviet relations. He had no choice but to accept Russian assurances that blame for the massacre lay with the Germans. Tony had been for too long too closely identified with Polish interests to underestimate the shameful side of the pragmatic British response, accurately exemplified in *The Military Philosophers* by Widmerpool's contemptuous dismissal of Polish protest: "They are rocking the boat in the most deplorable manner . . . How, as I say, can we approach our second most powerful Ally about something which, if a fact, cannot be put right, and is almost certainly, from what one knows of them, the consequence of administrative inadequacy, rather than wilful indifference to human life and the dictates of compassion?"

Capel-Dunn's patience finally ran out at this point. He sacked Tony, who pleaded to be allowed to stay on for another two or three weeks, just long enough to confirm his right to the rank and pay of major. The request was refused because, according to Capel-Dunn, "my nerves wouldn't stand it." Tony's summary dismissal left him with a humiliating sense of failure, rubbed in if anything by a handwritten note from Capel-Dunn, dated 12 May 1943:

Dear Tony . . . although I am very sorry that our experiment was unsuccessful, I much enjoyed it while it lasted. Nobody could have been a nicer colleague. I only regret that my impetuousness in dragging you into a job for which you were not suited must have exposed you to some distress. I hope we may soon meet again. Yours ever, Denis

Almost exactly two months later Sikorski (who was head of the Polish army in exile as well as prime minister) died in a plane crash over Gibraltar. His loss was a blow from which his country never recovered. The exiled London government, having rejected the Russian account of Katyn, also dismissed the findings of a British court of enquiry that ruled out sabotage in Gibraltar. But over the coming months, as the Allies strengthened their commitment to Russia, the Poles were forced slowly to face the fact that their reconstituted army, initially welcomed by its hosts, had become a liability. The 1st Polish Armoured Division would never now attempt the liberation of Poland. Extreme pressure ensured that, in the summer of 1944, it took part instead in the invasion of Normandy, fighting fiercely alongside British forces in Operation Overlord, the campaign to retake western Europe. With their government-in-exile marginalized, their army commandeered by the West and Russian forces advancing steadily further into Poland, the London Poles were well aware that their country risked exchanging German occupation for rule by the USSR. The future was made plain in August when the Red Army stood by at close quarters without intervening in the Warsaw Uprising that left Polish resistance crushed, two hundred thousand or more dead, and the capital in ruins.

After his fiasco in Great George Street, Tony had reverted to captain and returned with relief to his old job in military liaison at the War Office with Dru. From now on he handled relations with the exiled military attachés of Czechoslovakia, Belgium and the Duchy of Luxembourg. The Czechs, like the Poles, faced national extinction but,

Alick Dru on a weekend visit to Dunstall
Priory

having been betrayed by the West after Munich, they were the only
Slav nation to welcome the arrival of the Red Army, discovering too
late the extreme brutality of their liberators. Belgium remained relatively unproblematic, and the tiny Luxembourg government-in-exile
conducted its affairs with a wit and gaiety that delighted Tony (who
became London correspondent of the German-language *Luxemburger Wort* for a year or more after the war).

Dru himself, a sexual enigma so far as the Powells were concerned,
had surprised them in March 1943 by marrying Gabriel Herbert, the
eldest of four young Herberts of Pixton Park in Somerset. A sturdy,
wholesome, thickset young woman who loved horses and had no
intellectual leanings whatsoever, Gabriel bore Alick a daughter nine
months later, followed in quick succession by two more. Evelyn
Waugh, married to Gabriel's younger sister Laura, took an instant
dislike to the "small but dapper Downside man of French extraction"
who was his new brother-in-law. The Waugh children were taught to

refer to their Uncle Alick as the Pig-Walloper (from Dru's supposed habit of beating his pigs to tenderize their meat after the war, when he became a farmer).

Tony and Violet took a peppercorn lease on a house belonging to her Uncle Dunsany, Dunstall Priory near Shoreham in Kent, where Samuel Palmer had painted his paradise just over a century earlier. "This Regency villa sails like a ship over the Darenth valley," said Violet, who had stayed as a child at the Priory, sheltered by beech-woods rising steeply behind and looking out over water-meadows below. It was near enough to London for Tony to come down most weekends, often bringing an attaché or two with him. Major General Regulski from Poland, the Czech Colonel Kalla ("I think we are the only nice people he has ever met," said Tony), the Free French liaison officer Captain Jean Kéraudren, and the Belgian Commandant Kronacker were all regular visitors at Dunstall. "The landscape reminded them of France, Poland, Belgium," said Violet, "wherever, in fact their homes had been on the continent."

Tristram was four in April 1944, and his father's letters filled up with dwarfs boating and playing with bucket and spade, or alternatively fighting and firing off shells. In June, as Operation Overlord got under way, RAF bombers from Biggin Hill roared overhead on their way to the fighting in Normandy. The first of the flaming flying bombs, German V1s, headed the other way in continuous raids that lasted anything up to three days and nights without stopping. "We went for a walk in the afternoon through fields which seemed to have been sewn with dragons' teeth," Tony wrote, describing a visit from Kronacker, "incendiary bombs, exploded and unexploded, lying every few yards, including a whole basketful which had failed to ignite." When a bomb fell on the farm just up the hill from the Priory, killing two small children and their mother, the sister of the girl who helped look after Tristram, Violet left at once, taking her son with her on another round of visits to relatives and friends in the country as far away as possible from London and the Channel coast.

Unable to leave the capital, Tony tried initially to use the Priory as a weekend writing retreat, making a desultory start on the introduction to his life of Aubrey in July. His aim was to shift Aubrey from "an agreeable, fairly intelligent, muddleheaded spendthrift" at the margins of history to a central position as a chronicler of contemporary life in the seventeenth century. But patchy concentration and constant night raids made progress painfully slow. "I think you need not re-write your book on Aubrey," wrote John Heygate, stunned by a letter so full of London gossip it made him gasp for breath: "*you have become Aubrey.*" Heygate was right in the sense that Tony's two realities were starting to coalesce: the Whitehall of Aubrey's day seemed to merge with the V1s overhead on nights when it was his turn for fire-watching duty from the roof of the War Office. "I saw some stuff coming over from the vantage of one of the pepper castors," Tony told Violet, "a thing I never expected to see when I used to walk up Whitehall in Charles II's time."

Some miracle had stopped the Powells' house on Chester Gate from going the same way as the burnt-out ruin next door, although all its windows had been smashed at least twice, broken water pipes had flooded the kitchen, and much of the furniture was still in store. Tony was starting to make it habitable again when the V1 bombs were succeeded in September by V2s, supersonic rocket-propelled missiles, so fast and silent they were almost impossible to detect until they exploded. Fatalism was the only feasible response. Tony had got the pipes mended and electricity restored by the time Violet returned to move back with him and Tristram into their house in late November. Muggeridge, currently working for MI6, slept on week nights in one of the rooms on the top floor, and the Drus set up camp in the other. "One morning . . . from my bed in Chester Gate I saw a glowing red worm wriggling down the grey sky of dawn," wrote Violet. "Then a shaking of the ground was followed by an explosion. I suddenly realised that I had seen the track of a V2 rocket, rather as an ornithologist might glimpse a rare bird."

The liberation of Paris in August 1944, followed by Belgium and most of the Netherlands that autumn, was celebrated by Military Liaison with guided tours of the Normandy battlefields. Colonel Carlisle and Tony escorted a party of fourteen Allied attachés, including Colonel Kalla and General Regulski (Ypres and Passchendaele had been freed by the Polish 1st Armoured Division). Devastation, wreckage and more sinister future developments awaited many of them on a return to their own countries that could not be indefinitely postponed. Confrontation with the ravaged countryside of northern France roused mixed emotions. Even Tony was reduced briefly to tears (although it was not until he got home that he recognized the seaside town of Cabourg, where they spent a night, as the model for Proust's Balbec). At 21st Army Group headquarters a few miles behind the front line, the attachés received a tactical briefing from Montgomery himself ("Already a stylised figure . . . he had not yet hardened into an exhibit"). Afterwards Tony identified units from his old Welsh regiment among the soldiers they passed on the road.

Back in London, he arranged for several attachés to have their portraits painted by Henry Lamb, who succumbed to a feverish cold that turned the commission into a nightmare as he wrestled in agitated dreams with every wrinkle, fold and highlight of tunics, belts, gongs and pips. "Each cough was an uninspired brush stroke to be corrected & boshed by the next. After another such night I awoke imagining that my nose actually was nothing more . . . than the peak of Gen Regulski's Polish cap . . ." Henry seems to have picked up something of Tony's own foreboding as the war drew to a close.

Victory in Europe in May 1945 produced immediate problems. Revolution threatened to destabilize the new democratic regime in Belgium, where communism still held a powerful appeal for a generation of young Resistance fighters who had grown up under German occupation. Tony defused the situation by bypassing official channels, using highly unorthodox strategies picked up from Capel-Dunn to organize the immediate dispatch of thirty thousand young Belgians for training in Northern Ireland. Dunn himself had been one of the panel of jurists who drew up the United Nations Charter, designed to ensure world peace and signed by fifty countries in the US on 26 June. Returning from the ceremony, he died when his plane crashed into the Atlantic with no survivors. "The Bun seems to have slipped into the arms of Jesus on his (the Bun's) way back from San Francisco," wrote Tony, noting philosophically that he would almost certainly have been on the same plane if fate had not intervened on his behalf.

Violet had left by this time for a seaside holiday with Tristram, staying in a furnished bungalow on the north coast at Lee, near Ilfracombe in Devon, where Tony was to join her as soon as the army released him. She was expecting another baby in the New Year, and he begged her to consider staying on in Lee for the birth. Over the rest of the summer, alone at Chester Gate with his two lodgers (Gabriel Dru had reluctantly gone back to Pixton in January to give birth to her own second baby), he embarked on a programme of furious clearance and cleansing, shifting furniture, rehanging curtains, unpacking crates of books from the depository and throwing out unwanted items, including all Violet's golf clubs and polo sticks. "'Overlord' will be child's play by comparison," he told her, summoning plumbers, a chimney-sweep and a window-cleaner. He triumphantly mastered the rationing system ("I got syrup & spam & sardines on points, also some sugar & some Tiptree jam"), taught himself to cook ("It gives one a great sense of power"), and deluged Violet with house-keeping queries: "How many latch-keys have we, and where are they?" "What do you do with the pile of newspapers under the table when you can't reach the table because the pile of newspapers is too high?"

Every morning Tony and Alick caught the bus into work with Malcolm, who transfixed their fellow passengers by "calling down . . . anathema on all mankind at the top of his voice" (he had just started work as a leader writer on the *Daily Telegraph*). The other two headed for the War Office, and a highly competitive round of diplomatic farewell lunch, dinner and drinks parties. The French outdid all the rest with an interminable reception at the embassy, followed by a film of stupendous banality about the Champs-Elysées ("It was like lying on the rack with someone reading Priestley aloud beside me," said Tony).

The outlook for democracy in Eastern Europe looked dismal. Even before the end of the war, Yugoslavia had been handed over to Marshal Tito's communist Partisans by the British government in a dramatic switch of allegiance. Tito's opponent was Britain's former ally, General Draža Mihailović, a patriotic nationalist of the old school whose Chetnik forces had fiercely opposed the Nazis, and who now found himself outmanoeuvred by Tito's instinctively clandestine mentality, CP training and superior communication skills. Tito was portrayed as the true hero of Yugoslav nationalism in a series of heavily biased reports from under-informed British agents in the Balkans, written in a style "more suitable to an adventure story in the *Boys' Own Paper* than a sober appreciation of what was happening," said Tony, reading them with dismay in the office although he was not personally involved with Yugoslavia. Support was officially withdrawn from Mihailović in February 1945, clearing the way for Tito to make himself dictator. His discredited rival was hunted down, captured and executed: "one of the tragedies witnessed in slow motion by MIL," Tony wrote bleakly more than three decades later.

Poland had been top of the agenda at the meeting in Yalta that February between Churchill, Roosevelt and Stalin, who made it clear that territory already seized would remain in Russian hands, and that there could be no question of the Polish government-in-exile returning to Warsaw. At the end of the month, the head of the Polish resistance, General Okulicki, was tricked into giving himself up to the Russians, and jailed in the Lubyanka prison in Moscow to await a show trial (he was convicted and murdered, like Mihailović, in 1946). Stalin's promises of free elections, free speech and the restoration of democracy at Yalta were clearly as worthless as the provisions of the Munich Agreement seven years earlier. Tony noted Okulicki's arrest long afterwards as a key event in the closing stages of the war. Diplomatic relations with Britain's Polish allies in London were officially broken off in July in favour of the new Moscow-based, communist regime in Warsaw.

Tony let his house to the Regulskis, who could no longer return safely to Poland. Initially Colonel Kalla and his London staff took a more sanguine view of Czechoslovakia's relations with Russia ("Big Brother" was their optimistic term for the USSR). Josef Kalla urged Tony to bring Violet to see him in Prague as soon as possible after the baby was born. But in July one of Kalla's colleagues returned from a home visit, bringing news that his entire family had been murdered except for his wife, who had spent three years in a concentration camp ("He has brought her back but I gather in a pretty bad state," Tony wrote sombrely). "We can only hope for the best," said Kalla, coming to say goodbye before he, too, left for Prague. He was promoted to brigadier general on arrival, posting off a polite but evasive reply to a letter from Tony, who heard much later that Kalla had been placed under house arrest, and died soon afterwards of "a heart attack." In Czechoslovakia, as in Poland, programmes of mass deportation, torture, imprisonment and the elimination of the intelligentsia were about to get under way.

Depression threatened to overwhelm both Tony and Dru. "I think Alick's despair is getting pretty bad," Tony told Violet at the beginning of August. By the middle of the month, he was on his own in the office as one by one his colleagues—Carlisle, Bradfield, Dru himself—received their demobilization papers and left. Representing MIL at the Victory service in St. Paul's Cathedral on 19 August, Tony sat next to "the little pimp who has come over as Tito's representative," reporting that he combed his hair throughout the proceedings. The Russians did not attend, although Tony reckoned he was probably the only person present to note their absence. On Dru's recommendation he read the *Journal intime* of the Swiss nineteenth-century philosopher Henri-Frédéric Amiel, and in his final weeks in the army he relieved his feelings by writing two long articles about Amiel for the *Cornhill* magazine, quoting his grim estimate of what rule by the Russians might be like for countries in their power:

They would bring us a Polar despotism—tyranny such as the world has never known, silent as darkness, rigid as ice, insensible as bronze, decked with an outer amiability and glittering with the cold brilliance of snow, slavery without compensation or relief . . .

On 1 September Regulski and his wife moved into the house at Chester Gate, bringing with them an aide-de-camp and "line upon line of relations and dependants." Polish pictures appeared on the walls. Strings of onions festooned the kitchen with jars of gherkins and rows of tomatoes lining the windowsill ("looks exactly like Mr. Badger's house," said Tony). In the Horrors Room, where the Powells kept their junk, a Polish soldier sat cleaning the silver. "Whether you will ever get back into the house again is, to me, very doubtful, though they would always be delighted if you were to come & stay," wrote Dru, who had negotiated the deal: "That is roughly how I see the position; & no doubt how they do." Tony retreated to the Drus' old room on the top floor in what was now for all practical purposes a Slav household. When the army finally let him go in the first week of September, he left for the seaside to spend his three months of paid demobilization leave reassessing his priorities and re-knitting the fabric of his marriage, reunited with his family for the first time in peace and quiet at Lee.

But he was overtaken that autumn by the chronic, cumulative, physical and emotional exhaustion of long exposure to dereliction and death: sleepless nights punctuated by thuds and crashes, broken glass littering the pavements next day, piles of fallen masonry, clouds of thick dark acrid smoke, houses gutted and bombed sites pitting the streets. The depression that engulfed Tony at Lee was one of the blackest of his life. He had been thirty-three years old when the war started. Now he was approaching his fortieth birthday, and had lost what should have been the most productive years of his life. Insomnia swallowed his nights. Every morning he wished he were dead. A week's visit from the Muggeridges in mid-October reinforced his debility. He already knew what Muggeridge called "the agonising, futile longing to write again," and he admitted to Muggeridge much later that for many months this almost physical longing—"like jealousy, really tearing at one's flesh"—co-existed with an equally agonizing certainty that he would never write anything worth reading again.

8

1946–52

It took ten years to work out how to confront what Tony defined as his central subject—"human beings behaving"—in successive instalments of a single long novel, instead of having to begin all over again with a fresh cast of characters in a new set-up every couple of years. He found the answer in repeated encounters at the Wallace Collection in London with Nicolas Poussin's *A Dance to the Music of Time*: a painting that produced an impact as powerful and disturbing as his first sight of Bruegel's *Hunters in the Snow* twenty years earlier. "I knew all at once that Poussin had expressed at least one important aspect of what the novel must be."

Poussin's *Dance* shows three young women and a man, plump, pale-skinned, barefoot, loosely draped in blue, green or soft warm brick pinks and yellows, dancing hand in hand in a burst of brilliant sunlight. Their music comes from some sort of classical banjo strummed by a bald, bony, bearded old man with nothing on and a large pair of wings implausibly attached to his shoulder blades. In the bottom corners of the canvas two baby boys play with grown-up toys (Time's hour-glass, and an equally symbolic clay pipe for blowing bubbles). Two even tinier figures at the top represent a couple of Greek gods—Dawn leading the Sun in his chariot—both decidedly insignificant against the magnificent skyscape of dark tumbling rainclouds that infuses the whole canvas with threat and drama. Poussin's non-committal approach to classical allegory remains now as then essentially modern. "The one thing certain is that the four main figures depicted are dancing to Time's tune," said Tony.

What hypnotized him was the way the painter captures the fluidity

and perpetual movement of life itself, while at the same time empha-
sizing its rhythmic overall pattern with masterly lack of fuss in a
canvas "somehow serene and clear." Poussin's masterpiece, as Tony
explained it to Muggeridge (who had never seen a classical painting
before), combines extreme pictorial lucidity with richly ambivalent
layers of meaning, something no contemporary painter could hope
to achieve at a time when the arts in Britain were still not entirely free
from the banal aftermath of nineteenth-century romanticism. Poussin was forty when he started painting his dancers in the late 1630s,
the same age as Tony at the end of 1945. The first steps of his own
fictional *Dance* were coming closer but for the moment any sustained
imaginative effort was beyond him.

He fell back on Aubrey, having sorted his notes into some sort of
order that autumn at Lee in a cottage at the head of a deserted inland
valley facing out over the sea, surrounded on all sides by an emptiness that suited his mood. Lee had been colonized by a small complex community of high-powered, intellectual women congregating
round T. S. Eliot, who got on well with Tony when he came for a
fortnight's sea air. No longer the remote bardic oracle of an awestruck younger generation, Eliot was still a faintly forbidding figure,
setting an example of stern self-containment, long solitary cliff-top
walks and studiously trivial small talk. "This amalgam of tea-party
cosiness with a cold intellectuality . . . gave Tom Eliot's personality that very peculiar flavour," said Tony, struggling with his usual
demons of lassitude, apathy and doubt. His typewriter stopped functioning, and some days he felt so weak he could scarcely get up a hill.
Back in London in the New Year, he agreed with Muggeridge that all
either of them wanted was for their lives to come to an end.

The death wish was tonic for both of them. Muggeridge left for
New York as the *Telegraph*'s US correspondent that spring, and Tony
finally put a stop to months spent picking through manuscripts in
the Bodleian Library in Oxford, the kind of "genealogical potterings" that became over the next thirty years his standard routine for
kick-starting "the novel-writing machine within." Aubrey's papers,
many of them bundled up virtually untouched for centuries in Duke
Humphrey's Library, suggested at first glance an image of muddle
and confusion that corresponded to the workings of their owner's
mind. But if Aubrey's multiple projects often ended up scrappy or

unfinished, enough survives to give a clear sense of his subtle ironic humour, his genius for friendship, his inexhaustible curiosity and keen grasp of the ways of the world, the sensitivity that set him apart from his contemporaries, above all the sheer originality of "his presentation of life as a picture crowded with odd figures, occupying themselves in unexpected and sometimes inexplicable pursuits" in the *Brief Lives*. It is not hard to understand his appeal for a biographer contemplating something similar in fiction. There is a strong affinity in Tony's account of Aubrey at forty, wary and watchful with the uneasy expression of an observer for once under observation himself, captured in a contemporary pen-and-ink drawing with a casual informality missing from most portraits of seventeenth-century celebrities in business, science or the army:

> Here is the face of a man who has half explained to himself the follies of the world: who has failed; and yet achieved something— while so many of these men of action and affairs have sunk into oblivion, with the causes for which they lived and died, by some vitality less unreal than theirs, he has remained alive.

A book that began as an undemanding exercise for keeping its author on track during the war seems in some ways to have become a blueprint for the long novel incubating at the back of his mind. Aubrey's relationship with his contemporaries began to sound more like a projection of the role played by the narrator in Powell's *Dance*, and by the author who stands behind him: "He contemplated the life round him as in a mirror . . . scarcely counting himself as one of the actors on the stage . . . He was there to watch and to record, and the present must become the past, even though only the immediate past, before it could wholly command his attention. For him the world of action represented unreality." Powell's biography of Aubrey stands as the first serious attempt in three centuries to do justice to its subject's achievements, in particular the *Lives*: four or five hundred compressed biographies that pin down each individual with a penetration, vitality and frankness rarely surpassed since in British biography. Together they make up a gallery of miniatures without parallel or precedent covering, as Tony said, every aspect of the national character: "the good and evil; the ingenuity and the folly; the integrity and the hypocrisy; the eccentricity, the melancholy and the greatness of the English race."

But, biographically speaking, there is a key element missing from *John Aubrey and His Friends*. Meticulously researched and conscientiously put together along dry, mechanical, academic lines, the text remains little more than an assembly job and, for all the author's evident respect and affection, its subject never comes to life as Aubrey makes his own subjects do. Mental and physical obstacles blocked the way of both author and subject. Wartime conditions, constant disruption, cramped spaces and snatched parcels of time handicapped Powell just as Aubrey's sociable temperament, shortage of money, irregular habits and eventual homelessness made it impossible for him to concentrate for any length of time. Possibly the biographical format inhibited Powell's imagination, perhaps the deep depression that gripped him as he wrote sapped his energy. Or maybe the book simply reflects the London in which it was written—"bomb-defaced weary squalid"—from notes jotted down in an Oxford shabbier and more self-absorbed than ever after the war.

"How absolutely awful Oxford is," Tony wrote at the end of December 1945 to Gerald Reitlinger, who had caused general astonishment nine months earlier by marrying Anne Graham Bell, a second wife as unexpected and almost as striking as the first. An energetic South African blonde with Bloomsbury affiliations and a background in art and design, Anne Reitlinger already had a small daughter from an earlier marriage, and now she confounded her new husband's old friends by bearing him a daughter too. Venetia Reitlinger was named for the seventeenth-century beauty Venetia Digby, greatly admired by Aubrey for her "most lovely and sweet-turn'd face," her shapely figure, delicate dark-brown hair and the colouring of a damask rose.

A month later Violet gave birth to a second son, John Marmion Anthony Powell, born in the small hours of 11 January 1946. Tony came back from Oxford at once but Lady Jersey, captivated at sight by the newborn Tristram five years earlier, had died just too soon to meet John. "I felt her loss almost like that of a mother," said Violet, whose siblings were all too preoccupied with young families of their own to make much of this new arrival. Muggeridge agreed to stand godfather to the baby—"strange, red little creature straining and agonising to get into the world which Tony and I are so anxious to leave"—whose arrival raised in acute form the problem of earning a living. Dispatching Aubrey was the first priority, and Tony promptly completed the manuscript in three months flat. In February he got word of an opening on the *Strand* magazine, and hired a new agent to negotiate terms. David Higham of Pearn, Pollinger & Higham was far from encouraging, explaining that the only authors who interested him were either solidly established commercial propositions or promising newcomers, and infuriating Tony by citing Michael Meyer—not yet thirty and already pushing hard at his elders' heels—as the type of client he had in mind. The *Strand* job fell through but by the end of April Higham had extracted Tony from any obligation to Cassell, and secured offers for *John Aubrey* from Oxford University Press, proposing to stump up £50 advance on royalties, and from Eyre & Spottiswoode with a bid of four times as much.

The firm had just let Graham Greene loose on its fiction list with instructions to ginger it up, a potentially risky move for an outfit as doggedly unadventurous as Eyre & Spottiswoode: "by no means so broken down an equipage as Duckworth's . . . ," according to Tony, "nevertheless a chassis set rattling ominously under the force of the new dynamo." Greene promised £200 down payment on Aubrey as bait for a three-book contract, guaranteeing £300 on delivery of each of Powell's next three novels as well as volunteering to reprint at least one of his pre-war titles. As an editor he had been pursuing Tony for years, publishing his travel pieces in *Night and Day*, and later his book reviews ("I wish to God you would do some for me") in the *Spectator*. He was a professional cynic, like Muggeridge, who tended to agree with Greene's view that the only way out of the world's troubles was the atom bomb. "Of course, his prayer will never be answered," Malcolm said, sending Tony a shrewd analysis of Graham's peculiar brand of austerity: "I asked for a bomb, & they gave me dollars. If he joined the strictest & remotest religious order in the world, cheques would continue to be paid in."

Tony said he doubted Grumble had ever had a day's pleasure in his life—"except possibly the other evening when he saw a sailor robbed in a haunt called Ward's Irish House under Piccadilly"—but this latest publishing coup raised a wintry smile. Powell represented a considerable catch, "one of the really important additions to our list," according to Greene's fellow director, Douglas Jerrold, whose stiff collar, black coat and striped trousers made him look like an escapee from *The Forsyte Saga*. "I have seldom signed contracts with as much satisfaction," wrote Graham. Tony took him along to replace Muggeridge at lunch on Fridays in the small, scruffy Authors' Club on the Embankment. He and Malcolm had got into the habit of lunching there at the end of the war with George Orwell, then still an obscure, ill-paid journalist having trouble finding a publisher for *Animal Farm*. Others joined them from time to time, chiefly Muggeridge's congenial old friend and mentor Hugh Kingsmill, but these gatherings remained strictly all-male. Violet had never much warmed to Graham. She didn't like having to put on an evening dress and catch a bus all the way out to his house in Clapham for dinner and, when he abandoned his wife and children, she grew tired of him talking obsessively about his sexual hang-ups ("I will cheerfully give him 2s 6d if he doesn't mention tight breeches for a fortnight").

But she got on easily and well from the start with George and his wife Eileen. The two couples often ate supper at one another's houses, grumbling about problems with publishers, and getting to know each other's children. When Eileen died suddenly in the course of a minor operation in March 1945, leaving George to bring up their newly adopted baby son on his own, the Powells provided back-up and babysitting. If George had to give a talk in the evening, or attend a political meeting, he dropped Richard off first in his carry-cot at Chester Gate, and collected him afterwards. Violet liked the way he hoisted the baby on to his shoulders, "looking like St. Christopher with the Christ child," even on buses where George was so tall that the child's head scraped the roof. Tony noted with amusement that, by the time Richard was old enough to be asked to a children's party, his father had somehow "managed to dress him like an inmate of a reformatory for infants." Orwell combined a rare grasp of reality, at once prescient and practical, with an absurd, inverted romanticism that always disarmed both Powells. Once, when Tony left him alone for a moment in the nursery at the top of their house, George slipped what looked like a fur-trapper's massive clasp-knife into the new baby's cot, explaining rather shiftily when questioned that he meant it as a plaything for John.

In the spring of 1946 he disappeared, heading for the Hebrides to set up house with Richard (along with the girl hired to look after him) on the bare rocky island of Jura off the west coast of Scotland. Before he left, he arranged for copies of the socialist *Tribune* to be delivered to Chester Gate for six months so as to do Tony good. "I can't say it has had a very strong effect yet," Tony reported after the first few issues, "except to confirm my impression that the greater part of the present House of Commons are totally unfitted to govern." Already beginning to miss Malcolm's company more than he had thought possible, Tony was surprised to find how much he missed George too, in spite of the long rambling monologues on burning issues— bumping up voter turn-out at local elections, or the shortcomings of jury service—that drove his friends to distraction. His willpower was so strong that it overrode all attempts to interrupt him, probably without his even noticing anyone had attempted anything so frivolous: "rather like Christian in the *Pilgrim's Progress* might have felt, if asked for cigarette cards," said Tony.

He sent off a lewd postcard to cheer George up on his barren boggy rock in an isolated farmhouse two or three hours' walk from the nearest shop with no electricity or running water. Tony had an endless supply of cards like this one by Donald McGill, showing a sexy girl in a newsagent's:

MALE CUSTOMER: "Do you keep stationery, miss?"
YOUNG LADY ASSISTANT: "Sometimes I wriggle a little."

"I think the crofter who brings the post the last 7 miles might have suppressed it if he had seen it," George answered cheerfully, explaining the real reason why he was there: "I know that if I return to London & get caught up in weekly articles I shall never get on with anything any longer." He had just published *Animal Farm*, and was beginning to move towards *Nineteen Eighty-Four*. Tony, nowhere near a new novel himself, could already feel closing round him the trap that George had escaped. Muggeridge, the third in their post-war trio of novelists, was reluctantly beginning to admit that he was better suited to newspapers and the political scrum: "They draw me as alcohol draws a drunkard." Even John Heygate had more or less ceased to think of himself as a writer. Muggeridge described a visit to him six months after the war: he had given up alcohol (which didn't stop him knocking back lighter fuel instead), and was being treated

Miranda Christen in mid-career
as an adventuress

for syphilis while waiting for his divorce decree to come through, eyeing up girls again and making plans to get back into the army. "Actually I think he's quite enjoying himself, especially his syph, which makes him feel like Gauguin."

At this point Miranda Christen reappeared, having also in practice shelved her ambition to write. Last heard of in occupied Java as Japanese forces closed in on the Dutch, she had been saved by her swastika passport since Japan at that point was Germany's ally. Five years in the East had transformed her into a slender, slant-eyed beauty with a glamorous war record, a stamp collection worth a small fortune, and considerable experience of business management. Tony urged her to write her memoirs, installing her with her little daughter in George's empty flat in Islington, where she fell on his old copies of *Horizon*: "years of book deprivation made me feel like Rip van Winkle set down in a gingerbread house."

She had come back to England to apply for a divorce and re-establish her claim to a British passport, taking a secretarial job in the City to tide her over until she could sail east again to pick up where she left off as an adventuress. Miranda's plans involved unspecified business enterprises: "she wants agents who will stop at nothing," said Tony, introducing her to Bobby Roberts, himself just back from the Indian subcontinent, where he had done unexpectedly well in RAF publicity from a base in wartime Calcutta. "We peacetime deadbeats do get a break when there's a war on," said Squadron Leader Roberts, who impressed even Miranda with his favourite party trick of stepping out of a fast-moving taxi bowling along Oxford Street in the early hours of the morning. Bobby was still a sturdy drinker, sipping surgical spirit if all else failed now that alcohol was in short supply. Miranda liked his recklessness, absurdity, insubordination, while remaining always too hard-headed to succumb to his sexual advances. "Bobby was sheer bliss," she said fondly, when Tony wrote to tell her of his death more than thirty years later.

Tony himself, in spite of Orwell's dire warning, plunged deeper than ever before into book reviewing. He still contributed on a regular basis to the *Spectator* as well as to the literary pages of an ambitious publication, the *New English Review*, brought out by his new publisher and overseen in theory by Jerrold, but edited in practice by Kingsmill from the smoking room of the Authors' Club. Kingsmill relied on Tony for the *Review*'s "Books of the Month" feature, a knowledgeable appraisal of current publications signed Thersites, after the bloody-minded bastard in the *Iliad* and Shakespeare's *Troilus and Cressida*. In the autumn of 1946 he also took over Malcolm's old fiction column on the *Daily Telegraph*, covering four or five new titles a week. Occasionally he came across a gem: "the author can describe a squabble about a smoking chimney for a dozen or more pages until the reader is weak with laughter," he said of Ivy Compton-Burnett's *Manservant and Maidservant*. Mostly his response was restrained and stoical with rare flashes of exasperation: "Mr. Nevil Shute clearly intends that his novel should teach a moral lesson, but for the life of me I could not tell what that moral lesson was." Like many others in the same line, he found enemies easier to deal with than friends. "His striking dialogue suggests the conversation of a group of visionaries in a fish queue," he wrote enigmatically of Henry Green's seventh novel, *Back*.

Bulk novel reviewing, then as now, is the pits of the trade. It pays basic bills but, as treadmills go, this one seemed to Tony more punitive even than quota-quickies. For the next twelve months he read and reviewed twenty or more books a month, double that if you count his succinct and pithy notices in the "Books of the Month" column. They ranged from a reissue of Sir Thomas Browne's seventeenth-century *Urn Burial* to latest excavations in the *Sutton Hoo Ship Burial*, from André Simon's *Concise Encyclopaedia of Wine* to *Plato for Pleasure* and Hugh Trevor-Roper's *The Last Days of Hitler*. Thersites rapidly developed a personality the opposite of his namesake's: generous, fair-minded, funny and almost heroically inclusive. Not content with covering biography and autobiography, history, politics, economics, science, sport and the arts, he included judicial round-ups of the little magazines that proliferated in Paris and London after the war from *Synthèses* and *Poésie* to *Polemic*, *New Writing* and *The New Road*, warmly welcoming even fugitive undergraduate flysheets like Cambridge university's *The Bridge* as a sign of returning normality ("Let them—like the *Bridge*—be as undergraduatish as possible. We can take it").

In his spare time he compiled an anthology, *Novels of High Society from the Victorian Age*. He also dispatched once a fortnight a topical bulletin to the *Luxemburger Wort* covering local and national issues from London's Victory celebrations and the royal family's schedule to the partition of India, the opening shots of the Cold War, an absurd proposal for a Channel Tunnel, and the Labour government's struggles with coal production, the steel industry and the national transport strike. Personal experience lay behind his account of manoeuvres by the British Communist Party to strengthen its position in UK trade unions after the war. Routine meetings of the National Union of Journalists were very nearly commandeered, even at the *Daily Telegraph*, by a determined communist faction narrowly defeated by Muggeridge and others, including Tony, participating for probably the first and last time in his adult life in direct political action.

All of his articles were written on the dining-room table in a house ill adapted to the conflicting needs of a newborn baby, a six-year-old schoolboy and a writer chronically short of both time and space. He learned to work to a rumbling continuo of the front door opening and shutting, the telephone ringing in the hall and feet running up and down stairs all day between the basement kitchen and the nursery on the top floor. Violet did much of the running. In an age of transition, when domestic service was already a thing of the past but the electrical appliances that replaced it had not yet fully materialized, women like her had to learn on the job. The house that had once seemed a dream of space and convenience was turning into the opposite. It ate money, and was impossible to clean. The Powells had a daily charwoman, and generally a transitory untrained girl acting as cook, skivvy, mother's help or nurse when the children were small. Food was still rationed, and wine for all practical purposes impossible to come by. Parts of the house seemed to be falling to pieces. Damp made patches on the kitchen wall, and at one point dry rot festooned the hall, with workmen blocking the entrance so that the only way anyone could get in or out was through the basement.

Violet kept house efficiently and without agitation, but at times even she longed to get away from Chester Gate and its problems. What always changed her mind was Regent's Park itself: "the wave of scent from flowering trees and shrubs that rolled over one . . . on a spring evening made the idea of living anywhere else unbearable." The neighbourhood, like many others in London, had not yet entirely lost the character of a village community. People met and gossiped in the butcher's or the baker's on Albany Street, and their children played in the sandpit on Park Square. One was a striking red-haired infant the same age as John called Jane Asher, the granddaughter of Mrs. Meyrick, who had kept the most notorious of all 1920s nightclubs at number 43, Jermyn Street. "That little girl will get off with man, woman or child," Violet said of an older, even more eye-catching nymphet, who left for Hollywood ten years later to make her name as Joan Collins. Everyone knew everyone else. A bust of John Nash stood outside a small house on Chester Terrace belonging to the new Duke of Wellington, who had been Tony's fellow student Gerry Wellesley on the Cambridge Intelligence course. Christopher and Elizabeth Glenconner, living a few doors along, became lifelong friends.

Even the policeman who came to tell the Powells that their kitten had been run over was neighbourly enough to find them a replacement (the two previous cats had settled into their second home too well to leave it: "It sounds as if Mrs. Perkins is reading Proust aloud to them," Violet said drily). A small tabby tom with a white bib, eight months old and more than a match for Tony, duly arrived when Violet was away with the boys in April. He was given the name of Albert after a visit from Commandant Albert Lechat, a tall lanky young assistant to the Belgian military attaché who had made Tony laugh in the war. This new Albert stamped his personality on a role that would be played with strong individual variations over the next half-century and more by successive cats attached to the Powell household. He amused and distracted Tony, providing warmth, entertainment, undeviating attachment and a much-needed infusion of energy when long strenuous hours at the desk left him drained and depleted. Albert was ingenious, resourceful and tough with an expressive repertoire of ploys for registering displeasure whenever his owners failed to give satisfaction. Battles of will between him and Tony were generally resolved in Albert's favour. "He hardly ate anything for twenty-four hours as a protest," Tony reported after an early dispute over left-overs, "but has done a lot of running up the curtain to take it out of me."

Violet's simple solution to having no room for a separate study was to remove the children bodily at frequent intervals. Her sisters Pansy and Julia both struggled to contain growing families in small West Country cottages, and Frank's house was crammed to bursting, but Edward always had room at Pakenham Hall. A less daunting prospect was Mary, whose husband had been killed in action in North Africa after barely three years of marriage, and who was now bringing up a young son and daughter at Whitfield, the Clives' run-down family estate on the edge of the Black Mountains in Herefordshire. Violet set what became over the next few years a standard pattern, taking the boys to stay with their Clive cousins at Easter and in the summer, sometimes for John's birthday in January as well. Tony stayed behind alone to work. He sent a birthday present for Tristram ("the gnome I caught in his bedroom") and, as always when writing threatened to overwhelm him, embarked on a massive programme of shifting the furniture. "When my obituary appears they will see that few removal men read of my death without a tear in their eye," he told Violet, "as I seem to know most of the ones in London personally by now."

Books for review continued to arrive by every post. They piled up all over the house in tottering stacks for removal and recycling (all freelance authors traditionally boosted their meagre incomes by selling surplus review copies to the second-hand bookseller Thomas

Gaston in Chancery Lane). Tony even brought parcels of books for review with him on family holidays, generally visits to relations or summer house-swaps. In August 1946, they borrowed a house belonging to Tony's Aunt Katherine, or Kitten, at Plas Canol near Barmouth, overlooking Cardigan Bay in South Wales. "Having a real Aberbananer time here with Evans the Horse etc," he wrote on a ribald postcard to Basil Hambrough: "The weather here is filthy and there is nothing to drink."

Overwork and exhaustion compounded Tony's long-standing depression. He had received a horrifying letter from John Heygate in Ireland, struggling to drag himself back from the suicidal depression that had taken him to the verge of madness ("I just wanted you to know that Maltravers the extrovert and exhibitionist has come up against it, and himself needs a Chipchase"). Tony described his own condition to Dru, who, as a good Frenchman, diagnosed a liver complaint and prescribed a strict detox diet with no alcohol. Frank Pakenham put the problem down to lack of religious feeling, and also appealed to Dru ("I am very worried about my brother-in-law"), urging him as a fellow Roman Catholic to rope in the Church since nothing else seemed to have done any good. In the end the patient himself consulted a doctor, who assured him that despair was a perfectly normal response to demobilization. "I don't know when I have felt so gloomy with less reason than during 1946," Tony wrote dismally to Muggeridge at the end of the year.

The winter of 1946/7 was the harshest Britain had known for three centuries. The grimy London fog was so dense that one of the guests at the Powells' Christmas party took fifty minutes to come by taxi from a house seven minutes' walk away. Snow lay thick on the ground until the middle of March. The gas pressure at Chester Gate fell so low as to be virtually useless, and shortage of coal shut down the power stations causing frequent electricity cuts. Tony explained to his continental readers in Luxemburg that cold weather had never been taken seriously in England, where almost nobody had central heating, still less double glazing, and water pipes traditionally ran up the outside of house walls so that they froze and burst in sub-zero temperatures. The Powells' pipes were no exception. Buckets of water had to be fetched from the pub opposite, and the Glenconners up the road provided hot baths. Tony spent hours every morning laying, lighting and tending coal fires. Tristram caught chickenpox, followed by German measles. Violet caught them from him and was seriously ill, having already been prostrated for two weeks with flu. The cleaner went down with flu too. Malcolm sent a ham from America for Christmas, sending another when Tony ate his way through the first for supper night after night.

George was back in London that winter, looking more haggard than ever as tuberculosis tightened its grip. *Animal Farm* had made no great impression as yet on the general public, still inclined to accept at face value the official view of Stalin as Britain's friendly, helpful Uncle Joe. Tony watched grimly as the USSR systematically extinguished any hope still entertained by exiled East European governments of the democratic freedom guaranteed by the Allies. Appalled by Poland's rigged general election in January 1947, he confidently predicted in the *Luxemburger Wort* that the British government would never recognize the fraudulent new communist regime. When he was proved wrong, he let rip in the *New English Review* against the terror tactics employed by Poland's rulers, "a gang of Russian-nominated and controlled politicians backed by their murderous secret police." He thought of old friends like Josef Kalla, and his colleague Miroslav who had been among the most active anti-communists in the Czech embassy ("poor old Miroslav . . . probably hanging by his thumbs at the moment"). Tony understood better than most the political passion behind the furious imaginative energy of *Animal Farm*, and he knew what courage it had taken to write. It made "a permanent dent in the whole Marxist structure," he wrote looking back thirty years later: "especially courageous on the part of a writer, himself of the Left, laying his professional reputation open to smear and boycott, which those he so devastatingly exposed hastened to set about."

Tony was the only other novelist George knew well and they talked about books, their own and other people's, continuing the conversation by post when he left again for Jura in spring. Soon afterwards he wrote to Miranda (who had moved back into his Islington flat the day after he left), asking her to recommend a professional typist for his new book, and accepting with alacrity when she proposed doing it herself. She took £2 off her rent of £3 a week, and worked in the evenings after she got back from the office on the typewriter George had left behind in the flat. All through that stifling hot summer she typed the manuscript of *Nineteen Eighty-Four* as he wrote it. "I was riveted from the start," she said, looking forward to the arrival of a fresh instalment through the post every two weeks or so. Miranda retailed the plot bit by bit as it came to Tony and Violet, who were mesmerized as she was. George was due back in the autumn so she booked a cheap passage on a ship sailing for Singapore in November, but by that time he had collapsed, lying flat on his back, overcome by weakness, cut off on the island by high winds and rough seas that prevented his making the journey to see a consultant on the mainland. He told Tony that he had had to abandon his book halfway through, and didn't know when he'd get back to it.

Tony himself, impressed perhaps by George's writing retreat, tried out a new scheme that summer, staying behind alone to work while his family moved out of London to a cottage called Firstead Bank at High Hurstwood, near Buxted on the Sussex Weald. The plan was for Tony to visit at weekends, Violet to rest and keep hens, the boys to grow healthy and strong in clean country air, but the experiment ended in disaster. Violet, who was expecting a third child in December, had to return precipitately to London to see her doctor, who put her to bed, where once again she embarked on the slow, wretched, all too familiar routine of trying to save her baby. Sister Flood came to look after her while Tony shuttled between London and the boys, left behind with their nurse at Hurstwood. "My darling, I'm terribly sorry things are going to go wrong again," he wrote on 8 August, trying to console her: "I do hope you have not had too bad a time. Anyway, we have two very nice children to be going on with. Do look after yourself and don't hurry back . . . Tristram and John send their love."

Unexpected sympathy and distraction came from Alick Dru, whose wife Gabriel had also suffered a miscarriage a few weeks before Violet. The Drus, who already had three little daughters under four, were living on a tumbledown farm at Launcells Barton near Bude in north Cornwall, where Gabriel had taken to farming with vigour and relish. By preference she was never off a tractor but rats stole Alick's papers, fire broke out in his library and the dog selected books to eat from his bookcases, slightly mollifying its owner by picking on Muggeridge first. "I have put your works on the top shelf," he reassured Tony, who had arrived on a visit with Violet the year before to

Tristram and John at Firstead Bank

find Alick strolling about in plus-fours, conferring in French with the
Basque cook in the kitchen, and in faultless German with the three
prisoners-of-war who worked as farm labourers. He was currently
reading the whole of Chateaubriand in French as a prelude to working his way through Boulanger, Sainte-Beuve and Charles Péguy.
"Everything at the moment is depressing in the extreme, and nothing
seems to go right, and the work to be done heaps up unrelentingly,"
he wrote plaintively: "Yesterday I began reading Swedenborg."

He had urged the Powells to find somewhere near Launcells for the
summer instead of what he called "stockbrokers' heaven" at Hurstwood, and now he invited them back for another visit. "Like Kierkegaard, I write for one reader only," he told Tony, "in this case for
you." His car had a broken back axle but he hoped to get it mended
in time to meet the London train. "Violet, I presume, will arrive
by parachute, elegant, unruffled," he wrote, fitting her smoothly
into his lugubrious but highly enjoyable picture of country life as
a litany of hardship and calamity, hurricanes and floods, sick cows,
dead sheep and defective tractors ("I went out earlier this morning
& the only remaining tractor fell to pieces in front of my eyes: nuts
& ball bearings fell *through* the steel plates. Yesterday it had been
working perfectly"). The opening chapters of Dru's projected life's
work on Kierkegaard were turned down by Oxford University Press
in November, and he blamed Tony ever afterwards for persuading

him to carry on with it. "The whole thing is being re-cast, re-written etc . . . ," he wrote pessimistically: "I feel like the author of the gloomiest psalms, who no doubt kept sheep (which always died) and wrote to make something on the side."

That autumn Tony himself managed at last to escape from the maelstrom of freelance reviewing, slipping the clutches of the *Spectator*, the *New English Review*, the *Luxemburger Wort* and even the *Telegraph*'s gruelling fiction column to resurface in the quiet, tranquil, slow-moving waters of the *Times Literary Supplement*. Its prospective editor, Alan Pryce-Jones, had offered him the job of chief novel reviewer and fiction editor, which meant in practice looking in at the office once or twice a week to sift through the new books and pick out those worth reviewing, taking one for himself and assigning the rest to his various reviewers. Apparently undisturbed since its Edwardian inception in a corner of the mighty mansion housing *The Times*, the *TLS* was undergoing a brisk overhaul at the hands of Pryce-Jones, a debonair, dashing, cosmopolitan character under whom Tony detected "a faint but perceptible odour of chic sometimes drifting through the dusty caverns of Printing House Square."

Alick Dru had been urging Tony for months to join him as a reviewer on the *TLS*. Scholarly, eclectic, undisciplined, he approved of the paper on account of its venerable pedigree, the anonymity of its contributors, its lofty disdain for topicality and the universal scope of its coverage (its writ ran, according to Pryce-Jones, from the Albanian epic and the work of the Uruguayan symbolist Herrera y Reissig to the whole spectrum of contemporary writing). Alick took a high line with money, living off a small inheritance from his father and seeing no call whatever to earn a living, but for Tony the chief attraction was a regular salary, however meagre (the *TLS* paid him £350 a year together with a fee of three guineas per article).

He kicked off with what looks like a manifesto, a comprehensive enquiry into the development of the kind of novel written by his own generation between the wars. He defined the peculiar flavour of these interwar novels as melancholy and satirical, noted their "lively dialogue and bare descriptions" as well as a particular affinity with Chekhov, and identified "the convergence of an English and a Russian tradition" as the key factor that made them so different from nineteenth-century fiction. He saw his generation's immediate predecessors as Norman Douglas, Saki, Ronald Firbank and Wyndham Lewis, dismissing James Joyce's *Ulysses* as a blind alley, and Virginia Woolf's *Mrs. Dalloway* as a fashionable experiment with "a distinctly Edwardian bouquet." His pretext was a reissue of three early novels by William Gerhardie, but his main aim was clearly a personal one: to work out where the novel had got to, and what it might do next. "Where do these paths lead? Cosmic despair, English or Russian, needs delicate handling after a hero is thirty."

Tony was forty-one when this piece was published, and the best that could be said for his new job was that it gave him his pick of a more high-powered bunch of novelists than he ever had on the *Telegraph*. He reviewed John Steinbeck's *Wayward Bus* (not up to the author's usual authoritative accounts of "the lives and the preoccupations of the half-baked"), and C. P. Snow's *The Masters*, the fifth of eleven episodes in a wildly successful saga of donnish intrigue and high-table gossip set in a thinly fictionalized Cambridge ("it would give a foreigner a fair idea of the types he might meet . . . in such circles" was Tony's unenthusiastic verdict). He ended the year with *Scott-King's Modern Europe*—"concise, witty, makes its points with hammer blows"—by Evelyn Waugh, who had scored a colossal hit two years earlier with *Brideshead Revisited*. Tony passed on to Muggeridge a nice story about Waugh told him by Violet's brother Frank, now ennobled as Baron Pakenham with a post in the new Labour Cabinet. On a tour of the House of Lords with Frank soon after US sales of *Brideshead* reached half a million copies, Waugh made the mistake of mentioning this fact to a "little old peer" who'd never heard of him, but did his best to be reassuring: "'Oh I don't call that bad as I don't expect you've been at it very long. I know sales do improve if you stick at writing. For example my brother . . . sold two and a half million of his last book in America.' Collapse of Evelyn who recovers after a bit & says: 'I'm afraid I didn't catch your name.' Little Old Peer: 'Maugham.'"

Virtually the entire run of Tony's last book had been destroyed by enemy action while still in the publisher's warehouse. Contemporaries like Waugh, Greene, and even Orwell were beginning to think about collected editions but he had published nothing for eight years, and was nowhere near starting a new novel. The closest he had got was to spend the last year re-reading Proust's *Remembrance of Things*

Past, finding it "all much funnier and more poetic" than it had seemed to him as an undergraduate stunned by its psychological realism. "It is, in fact, more like a huge poem than a novel," he told Malcolm, asking him to send a compact American omnibus edition in two or three volumes, easier for reading and reference than the English publisher's twelve separate books. Tony could never see Proust as a tailpiece to the Victorians: he always seemed to belong to the future, not so much "a last gasp of the past, rather . . . a broad hint of what was to come." In February 1947, at the frenzied height of his reviewing with a turn-over of roughly a book a day, Tony somehow cleared space and made time to read and think about Proust. "I have begun it at the beginning again," he told Muggeridge, "and hope to work all the way through."

It was a first practical move towards the new kind of novel that still lay just outside his conscious grasp. Malcolm himself returned from Washington in late summer, moving with Kitty and their four children into a house almost directly behind the Powells' on Cambridge Gate, the next street along heading south from Chester Gate. That autumn he and Tony started walking round Regent's Park again as they had first done nearly ten years before. "I can't say how much I've missed your company and talk," said Tony, perhaps disorientated by the amount of Violet's time and attention claimed by two small children. Malcolm's stint in the US had made him an even more enthusiastic post-war pessimist, confidently anticipating on the one hand the fall of the Labour government, on the other the collapse of the capitalist system followed by a communist power-grab and control of the West by Soviet Russia. Tony remained invincibly apolitical but Malcolm's cataclysmic vision spoke to his own periodic mortal gloom. Both of them dreaded waking at dawn to confront vistas of nothingness, both still thought fondly of death. Their instinctive rapport went back to the earliest days of their friendship, and made them seem somehow connected. A fellow reporter in the *Telegraph* office assumed they were brothers.

What drew them together was the urge to make sense of human behaviour, a mutual compulsion not yet affected by the disparity between Malcolm's tendency to moralize and Tony's even stronger need to understand. "It will be wonderful to get back & talk & talk & talk," Malcolm wrote from New York. On his liner crossing the Atlantic he imagined himself and Tony, if only he'd been there,

Malcolm Muggeridge and Tony making sense
of human behaviour in the period after the war,
when they grew so close that people took them
for brothers

inventing imaginary backgrounds for their fellow passengers, and bringing them to life as if they were characters in a story: "Alone I cannot do it." On his return in late summer 1947, they started dropping in and out of one another's houses to play chess, and talking again for hours in the park or on the phone. They bounced ideas off one another as Tony had once done with Lambert, swapping gossip about people they knew and making up scenarios about people they didn't. "I wish you were here to formulate it all with me," Malcolm wrote when they were apart, describing a process of sorting out what they saw that seems to have been as important for him as for Tony, whose next novel now began to fall into place.

It starts with an extraordinary warm-up, moving out in a great wheeling circular movement through time and space from a coke bucket in falling snow, with workmen crouched over it beside a hole in the road opening on to the sewers below. A spurt of flame from the burning coke leads on via fragmentary images of ancient Rome and Poussin's *Dance to the Music of Time* to an invocation of schooldays, and the brooding forces—"memory . . . enigmatic and inconsolable"—needed to bring them to life, before looping back again from the present to another bleak wintry scene, quarter of a century earlier, where a solitary schoolboy in an ill-fitting cap plods along an empty road to his boarding house through the grey drizzle of late afternoon. This turns out to be Kenneth Widmerpool, more ludicrous than menacing at this stage, an ungainly unpopular nonentity with something odd and invincibly obdurate about him. On the next page a first glimpse of Charles Stringham frying sausages for tea establishes him at the opposite extreme of the axis of power and imagination on which the whole novel will turn.

Tony read this opening section to Malcolm one late afternoon in March 1948, reading him a further instalment ten days later. "Quite excellent, humorous, characteristic," Malcolm wrote that night in his diary. Long afterwards he recalled those distant days when he lived in Cambridge Gate:

> I used to walk round Regent's Park most afternoons with Tony Powell at the time he was writing the first volume of his *Music of Time*, and we would discuss, as we went along, the forthcoming adventures of his characters. Had the time come for A to seduce B? And if C got to know, how would he react? And D—what if anything would she feel if C, as he was bound to, told her about it? By the time our walk was over, I had to jerk myself back into my own identity, so absorbed had I become in these fictional beings.

On the face of it, this is nonsensical. The characters in Tony's opening volume move from one all-male environment to another first as schoolboys, then undergraduates. Malcolm's account makes *A Question of Upbringing* sound as banal and conventional as the novel he published himself at this point, and wisely did not follow up. What rings true is his account of the intensity and intimacy of these exchanges. The two friends had reached a point where their roads sharply diverged. Malcolm had just been made deputy editor of the *Telegraph* in a vain attempt to tie down the restless energies that finally found their outlet a few years later, when he began turn-

ing himself into one of the first and greatest TV celebrities Britain
has ever produced. Tony had also embarked on an enterprise hard at
that stage to define or pin down that would occupy him at full stretch
for the next quarter of a century. But for two or three years after the
war, when with intense effort Tony assembled and put into place the
machinery that would drive the *Dance* forward, Malcolm served in
some sense as a collaborator, a resourceful and responsive alter ego
providing feedback, making suggestions and asking pertinent questions. In July Tony even took him to Eton to sit in the sun on the edge
of the playing fields, and wander round the ancient college buildings
that had stirred him into action at the start of the *Dance:* "the sombre
demands of the past becoming at times almost suffocating in their
insistence . . ."

As Tony worked on *A Question of Upbringing* all through that
spring and summer, he sent bulletins to Jura, and received in return
wry, dry, sometimes harrowing letters from Orwell, struggling to finish his own novel. George had been finally diagnosed with TB and
spent the first half of the year in hospital in Glasgow, unable to see his
son Richard for fear of infecting him, sending news of the boy's rude
health and boisterous energy as his own strength drained away. In
March he thought his lungs were beginning to clear, and by June he
was looking forward to a visit from Richard ("I suppose I shall hardly
know him after six months"). They compared notes about Graham
Greene's latest novel, *The Heart of the Matter*, earmarked even before
publication as a bestseller. Both of them reviewed it, George pointing out bluntly in the *New Yorker* that "a perception of the vanity
of earthly things, though it may be enough to get one into Heaven,
is not sufficient equipment for the writing of a novel." Tony, whose
contributions to the *TLS* included from time to time long detailed
assessments of major figures like Conrad, Proust, Joyce, even Somerset Maugham, devoted one of them to Greene's work in May, exploring his own ambivalent feelings about it by tackling them head on in
a subtle and elegant analysis that delighted the publishers. "They all
thought Tony's notice in the *TLS* excellent," Malcolm noted in his
diary, "except Graham himself, who . . . detected that it was much
more critical than appearances might suggest."

Graham's misgivings had disruptive consequences four months
later over a lunch at the Authors' Club with Malcolm and Tony, who

raised the question of what had happened to his life of Aubrey. He had handed over the manuscript two and a half years earlier, and promptly returned corrected proofs, but interminable delays and postponements meant that publication was only now set for September. When Graham remarked casually that he was going to have to put it off yet again, Tony lost control. He was not for nothing his father's son, and the ensuing row left Graham white with rage. "It's a bloody boring book anyhow," he said tersely, an insult all the more wounding because it wasn't entirely untrue. Tony demanded, and got, an immediate release from his contract. Matters were not helped by frantic protestations from Douglas Jerrold that Graham had overstepped his authority, and that the firm had every intention of holding Tony to his legally binding agreement. "Jerrold . . . could bring instantaneous and inextricable confusion to the simplest transaction," Tony wrote in retrospect, adding coldly that "Jerrold's capacity for making heavy weather was, in its own field, unsurpassed."

The upshot was that after prolonged altercation within the firm Graham resigned and left the country, cheerfully inviting Tony round for a drink as if nothing had happened when he got back. But Tony's decision to leave had hardened by this time in spite of strong resistance from Higham, who saw no reason to throw over an excellent contract, and prompt action by Eyre & Spottiswoode, who brought out *John Aubrey and His Friends* in a handsome jacket on 10 December. Tony dedicated the book to Malcolm (who wrote the blurb) but it was another twelve years before he spoke to Graham again, and he never forgave Douglas Jerrold.

Colonel Powell made a bad situation worse at this point by writing to emphasize the extreme precariousness of his son's financial situation: "I BEG YOU TO TREAT THIS LETTER AS ONLY PUTTING YOU INTO THE PICTURE. NOTHING MORE." The older Powells had resumed their transient lifestyle after the war, shuttling between residential hotels in the Home Counties, but falling dividends and the rising expense of board and lodging for two (up from ten to a ruinous fourteen guineas a week) put Tony's allowance at risk. It came to £30 a month, just enough to cover school fees for Tristram, who was due to start as a boarder at prep school that autumn. The colonel was threatening in direst secrecy—"your mother doesn't know & *must never know*"—to break the ultimate taboo of his generation by drawing on capital. "<u>THIS</u> <u>IS</u> <u>NOT</u> <u>ASK-</u><u>ING</u> <u>YOU</u> <u>TO</u> <u>CUT</u> <u>YOUR</u> <u>ALLOWANCE</u> <u>BUT</u> <u>ONLY</u> <u>TO</u> <u>GIVE</u> <u>YOU</u> the situation." Emotional blackmail from his father was familiar enough, but the fact that he was used to it can't have been much comfort to Tony with two sons to educate, relations with his publisher at breaking point, and nothing coming in except his pay from the *TLS* for a job that could be terminated at any moment. He wrote back by return to suggest selling off the family furniture, a proposal eagerly accepted by his father, who had calmed down sufficiently to send only a small, unkind, parting stab: "Things may buck up a bit, & you may make a fortune out of your next book!"

Tony's next novel was giving trouble, and so was the slim volume he'd slipped in before it. He had agreed for Aubrey's sake to edit a selection of the *Brief Lives* for the Cresset Press, although he got no royalty and grudged the time taken from his novel, itself still causing problems with his agent as well as his publishers. Tony had rejected Jerrold's overtures and overruled Higham on the unconvincing grounds that he preferred not to be pinned down at this stage over a book still very far from completion. The agitation he always felt at the prospect of handing over a manuscript was now worse than ever because of the enormity of this particular project, and his own uncertainty about it. He cheered himself up by putting together a parcel of books by Barry Pain, a turn-of-the-century humorist with the dark streak that appealed to Tony in the Edwardians ("a more morbid collection of men could not be named," he said of the light versifiers he read aloud to Tristram at bedtime). The book package was for Orwell, currently struggling to type out his own newly finished manuscript in time to meet a publisher's deadline on Jura. "I love anything like that," he wrote happily when he got it, explaining that he was still too weak to sit up at a table for long, or spend more than a few hours out of bed even though he'd left hospital in July. *Nineteen Eighty-Four* had taken almost more than he had to give: "it's a ghastly mess now, a good idea ruined, but of course I was seriously ill for 7 or 8 months of the time."

In the New Year George wrote again from a sanatorium near Stroud in Gloucestershire, where he hoped that nursing and rest might lessen his exhaustion: "How about you? It's a god awful job trying to get back to writing books again after years of time-wasting."

When Tony asked by return if he could visit, George arranged for a car to meet him at the station, and laid on lunch and tea. In late February Tony came again with Muggeridge, this time walking the seven miles mostly uphill from the station. They found George dreadfully decayed but otherwise entirely himself, still smoking and coughing, with a bottle of rum secreted under the bed which the three of them finished off between them. He said he hoped to live another ten years, long enough to see Richard into his mid-teens and write at least two more books. "I am not sure he will pull this off," Muggeridge wrote in his diary.

In May George told Tony he was likely to spend the rest of his life bedridden—"or if not in bed, at any rate at the bath-chair level"— and that the consultant reckoned that his only chance of surviving for even a few more years was to write nothing for the next twelve months, perhaps longer. *Nineteen Eighty-Four* was due out in June. Terrified by its dystopian reality, his publisher told Muggeridge that booksellers who read it claimed to be too scared to sleep at night ("When I told this to Tony Powell, he laughed long. The idea of anything keeping booksellers awake was, to him, irresistibly funny"). It was typical of George that, in the month of his own book launch, he managed to get hold of Tony's biography and his collection of Aubrey's *Brief Lives*, and to read both of them. In August he moved back to London, where he could receive old friends and new admirers from his bed in University College Hospital, half a mile away from Chester Gate.

It was clear by now that George was dying, and many were appalled that autumn when he married Sonia Brownell. Sonia had been one of the smartest and most eye-catching, probably also the ablest of all the girls in Cyril Connolly's legendary entourage, going on to become in all but name his assistant editor on *Horizon*, currently its acting editor in Cyril's absence abroad. George told her that he would get better if she married him. Most of his male friends bitterly resented her as an intruder but Tony, who dropped in to see George almost every day, watched him revive and become himself again in her presence. Violet liked Sonia too, admiring her generosity and courage. Tony found George a red-velvet jacket (virtually unobtainable in the postwar era of austerity and clothes rationing) to wear for the ceremony, which took place at his hospital bedside on 21 October. From then on Sonia arrived every day with books, wine, gossip and plans for the future, bringing warmth, gaiety and comfort to the last months of George's life. Tony said his "old Wodehousian side" returned so that he seemed in some ways livelier and more relaxed than ever before.

Tony and Malcolm walked over to the hospital after lunch on Christmas Day, 1949, and found George alone: "all the time there was the stench of death in the air, like autumn in a garden," Muggeridge wrote in his diary that night. George died a month later on 21 January 1950. He had stipulated a Church of England funeral, which Tony organized for him with Malcolm's help, dealing with undertakers and persuading the vicar of Christ Church in Albany Street (the Powells' parish church, although neither had ever attended) to conduct the service. *Nineteen Eighty-Four* had made a powerful impact, and *Animal Farm* was beginning to be widely known, but George had as yet nothing like the reputation that eventually made him a key figure of the twentieth century. Fifty or sixty people attended the funeral, moving on afterwards to a gathering at 1, Chester Gate. Tony chose the hymns, and a reading from the bible:

> The Lesson was from Ecclesiastes, the grinders in the streets, the grasshopper a burden, the silver cord loosed, the wheel broken at the cistern. For some reason George Orwell's funeral service was one of the most harrowing I have ever attended.

Tony had finally finished his own, much interrupted novel two months earlier, and delivered it to Eyre & Spottiswoode as his contract obliged him to do. "We . . . are more than optimistic, we are enthusiastic," wrote Jerrold when he read it, with no apparent suspicion that he was about to be double-crossed. Higham remained dubious about Tony's chances of finding another publisher, but he reckoned without Malcolm's infinite capacity for intrigue. At his suggestion Tony had already produced a second, clandestine copy of the manuscript to be handed over to the chairman of Messrs. William Heinemann by Malcolm, who as Heinemann's official literary adviser urged him to accept it, which he did. Tony meanwhile asked for, and got, Greene's confirmation in writing that he had indeed offered to annul the existing contract. Confronted with what was in effect a done deal, Jerrold fought back angrily, knowing defeat was inevitable. At the end of February Tony signed a new contract with Heinemann, reluctantly negotiated by Higham (who had had to extricate him formally from the clutches of Eyre & Spottiswoode before selling the new book to its next publishers on almost identical terms, except for a small reduction in royalties).

Heinemann's chairman was A. S. Frere, a dashing First World War pilot, clubman and party-goer, "the world's . . . amateur champion in tap-dancing on café tables," who had steadily built up the business in a fruitful but ill-tempered partnership with his managing director, Charles Evans. "He didn't like what he thought was my 'highbrow nonsense' just as I didn't like his trash!" said Frere: "it made for a balanced list." Financial solvency came from the kind of dependable, middle-of-the-road names—Galsworthy, Priestley, Maugham himself—that Tony had been making hay of for years. Evans had recently died, leaving a useful legacy of bestsellers like Neville Shute and Georgette Heyer to his son Dwye, who succeeded him. Conrad added a touch of class and Greene, who commanded both prestige and sales, was "the firm's ideal author." A rich backlist made it possible to take on a risky proposition like Powell, who was already causing friction with a rival publisher, and whose own agent had little faith in his current market value ("it is ten years since a novel of yours was published," Higham wrote frankly to Tony, "and *What's Become of Waring* didn't have any sales to speak of ").

Tony, who liked Frere for his sardonic jokes, his genuinely literary instincts and even his testiness, plunged immediately into a dispute about whether or not the firm should openly acknowledge his novel as the first instalment of what was at this stage designed to be "at least a trilogy." This kind of admission with its stigma of something incomplete and ongoing was traditionally abominated by the publishing trade but Frere agreed to it, provided he could "soft-pedal the series title, *Music of Time*, by putting it on the half page," in other words tucking it away so unobtrusively that in the end the printer forgot to include it. Even this did not greatly upset Tony, whose relationship with Heinemann ran smoothly from the start. Possibly his early years as a publisher himself made him more accommodating than most, or perhaps he had already earmarked a very unusual young man newly arrived in the Heinemann office.

Roland Gant joined the staff in 1950 after four years' experience as publicity manager for the Falcon and Grey Walls Press, a rickety

Roland Gant: "a publisher in a million"

outfit about to go bankrupt belonging to the Tory MP Peter Baker (who was shortly afterwards jailed for seven years as a fraudster). Slight, inconspicuous, the reverse of flamboyant, Gant had survived hair-raising wartime experiences in a bomb disposal squad, and later with the Resistance in occupied France, ending up in a Nazi death camp. Tony said he was the only person he knew who'd been forced to dig his own grave. He had studied medicine in Paris before the war, becoming a close friend of Stéphane Grappelli at the Hot Club de France, singing himself as a student in Parisian cabaret, and later whenever he could in New York jazz clubs. When in England he played alternate parts as "either a professional Scot or a professional Frenchman." Although his books were officially handled by Frere, Tony became lifelong friends with Roland.

Frere promoted Gant rapidly, making him head of the firm's newly formed editorial department. He had started out in charge of design, and it was Gant who picked out the young illustrator James Broom-Lynne to produce for *A Question of Upbringing* the first in a series of bold, grainy, instantly recognizable dust jackets that made successive volumes of the *Music of Time* look quite unlike other novels.

Frere took key decisions (like whether or not to suppress the overall series title) but Gant oversaw production, setting up with Tony what became a long-term habit of going through the text together. "When work was to be done on a Powell manuscript," said a colleague, "he would crank up, all too often literally, the old banger he so enjoyed driving, and set off for the Powell house, bringing his gaiety and wit with his blue pencil." In future Heinemann acquired rights to Tony's novels as he wrote them, taking over in the course of the next few years his five pre-war novels as well, and finally completing the set with *John Aubrey and His Friends* in 1959. More than quarter of a century later Tony said with a hyperbole entirely out of character that Gant was a publisher in a million.

A Question of Upbringing is at first sight deceptively simple and transparently clear, like spring water, with strong and suggestive currents moving beneath the surface. It is extremely funny, sometimes disturbingly so. Violet's brother Edward read it at home at Pakenham Hall soon after it came out. He was approaching fifty, weighed more than twenty-eight stone, and nearly died laughing, according to his wife Christine: "He was speechless, choking, purple in the face, rolling on the old sofa in the drawing-room here & breaking the springs, & his tongue was rolling outside his mouth. Anyone who didn't know him, or the book, would have thought he was very ill indeed. Whenever he seemed to have recovered for a moment, he had a relapse again, like hiccups. It was wonderful to watch him."

The book's trajectory is roughly Tony's own—school, university, a first foot in the door of the London scene—observed and recorded by a relatively colourless narrator called Nicholas Jenkins, who seems to have little else to do. "I know Jenkins is awful, but think he's more to be pitied than blamed," Tony told Violet, who was the first (though by no means the last) to complain about his lack of identity. Tony explained that colourlessness was the point. He needed a neutral narrator as a focus for bringing people and events into view. The flavour and complexity of the *Dance* in its early volumes is in large part due to everything that happens being seen in double focus, through the eyes of a narrator in his forties who looks back to a less experienced, far more naïve and much younger self moving jerkily towards an adult understanding of people and events. The book is full of vignettes like this child's-eye view of Jenkins's housemaster:

He climbed up on to the fender, and began to lift himself by the edge of the mantelpiece. I thought for a moment that he might be going to hoist himself right on to the shelf; perhaps lie there.

Jenkins functions as an astute and observant eye trained on his contemporaries as they begin to assert their own identities at school, and afterwards to jockey for position at university. The second volume of the series, *A Buyer's Market*, sees a whole generation repositioning in business, the arts and the media: Widmerpool filling in time with a firm of City solicitors, Stringham working in some unspecified capacity for the industrial magnate, Sir Magnus Donners, their careers interweaving in a jostling crowd of young opportunists like the egregiously smooth Mark Members, and his opposite number J. G. Quiggin ("Quiggin sat sourly on the extreme edge of the sofa, glancing round the room like a fierce little animal, trapped by naturalists . . . He had something of the angry solitude of spirit that held my attention in Widmerpool"). An exchange between two schoolboys lays down what turns out to be a lifelong pattern when Widmerpool admonishes Jenkins for his furtive admission that he reads books, and might even write one himself:

> "It doesn't do to read too much," Widmerpool said. ". . . By all means have some familiarity with the standard authors. I should never raise any objection to that. But it is no good clogging your mind with a lot of trash from modern novels."

Even as a teenager Widmerpool closes down possibilities. Stringham opens them up. Insouciant, elusive, intractable, impossible to pin down and utterly indifferent to the rich and privileged milieu into which he was born, Stringham parts company with Jenkins at the end of the book—"The path had suddenly forked"—as arbitrarily as Widmerpool converged on him at the start. The two might be said to represent in Jenkins's life the same incompatible principles as Muggeridge and Orwell in Powell's. There is no specific resemblance in character, background or circumstances but these two, perhaps more than any other of Tony's friends, embodied in his life the twin poles of power and imagination.

"Mr. Powell's purpose is, like [Balzac's] *Comédie humaine*, to convey the whole character of an epoch," Muggeridge wrote on the jacket flap of *A Question of Upbringing*. Neither yet realized that for them too the path was about to fork. Tony became from now on increasingly absorbed by the creative and imaginative imperatives of the *Dance*, while Muggeridge started a ten-year affair with Lady Pamela Berry that drew him inexorably in the opposite direction. Pam was by Muggeridge's account not particularly pretty or clever or nice, but she possessed power, inextinguishable vitality and a husband who was the *Telegraph*'s editor-in-chief, and son of the proprietor, Lord Camrose. "She personified the world in which Malcolm was now embroiled—the world of politics, power, high society and wealth," wrote Muggeridge's biographer. His radio broadcasts had already brought him national fame, and his TV career was about to take off. "Malcolm's voice comes over the air like an infuriated east wind," said John Heygate, listening to the *Critics* on Sunday morning, "disgusted with almost everything and almost invariably loathing his fellow critics. I simply admire it." Countless listeners agreed with Heygate that without Muggeridge the *Critics* or *Any Questions* was "like an army dinner without the sauce bottle."

Tony used the interval between his book's delivery and its publication to produce another long *TLS* feature on Marcel Proust as "a great comic writer," paying special attention to the construction of a single ambitious extended work exploring contemporary political and social developments in twelve successive volumes. Powell was evidently working out his own blueprint in this piece with its emphasis on technical problems, on the intrinsic importance of humour, and in particular its beautiful, unexpected final definition that surely confirms he was thinking as much about the work still stretching ahead of him into the future as about the *Remembrance of Things Past*: "a novel that curiously resembles a poem in the manner in which its cadences carry the ebb and flow of the imagination and the will."

A Question of Upbringing was published on 22 January 1951. A few days later Tony called Violet to the window in Chester Gate to watch the book's opening scene re-enacted: "In the road outside, a hole had been dug and the workmen had lighted a brazier beside it. Deliberate snowflakes were falling, hissing as they hit the brazier." Reviewers were generally appreciative, especially John Betjeman in the *Telegraph*, who found Powell as funny as Waugh or Max Beerbohm ("He never seems to laugh. He leaves that to the reader"). Nobody noticed a darker undertow except Christine Longford, who said, watching her husband's convulsive reaction, that the book struck deep: *"All his past life arose & looked him in the face."* Tony interrupted work on the sequel to take a short break with Violet in Spain in May, otherwise writing steadily at home, often alone while she took the children to stay with their cousins. *A Buyer's Market* starts in a dusty sales room crammed with junk off the Euston Road: discarded canvases, battered suitcases, random rolls of linoleum and odd bits of furniture, "items not to be tolerated in any inhabited dwelling finding each its own level in these expansive, anonymous caverns, where, making no claim to individual merit, odds and ends harmonize quietly with each other, and with the general sobriety of background." It might be a definition of human life itself as portrayed in the *Dance*.

The book's opening pages raise questions of style, scope and purpose posed by the painter of the wildly ambitious and crudely executed canvases, Edgar Deacon, an elderly, offbeat, increasingly crucial figure who threads in and out at unexpected moments on various levels of every subsequent volume of the *Dance*, binding its disparate elements together. A glimpse of his dismal canvases encapsulates for the narrator on page one the constant interchange at the core of the *Dance*: "They made me think of long-forgotten conflicts and compromises between the imagination and the will, reason and feeling, power and sensuality . . ." This is the point where Jenkins and his contemporaries confront the adult world, and make their first heady bargains with girls. As he finds himself drawn inexorably into the complexities of grown-up ambiguity and compromise, Jenkins's growing fascination with those ruled by power and the will—Widmerpool above all—evolves in parallel with his slow realization that, for all his reservations about the painter's work, he, too, like Deacon, belongs unconditionally on the side of the imagination and the arts.

Hurrying to meet a publisher's deadline at the end of the year, Tony was already beginning to realize he'd entered himself in a race against time. He had no way of knowing at this stage how many volumes lay ahead, or how long the sequence would take to complete. From now on for almost exactly quarter of a century, he produced a novel roughly every two years, balancing a perpetual demand for new invention against complicated emerging patterns, catching up with the future while keeping pace with the past in a dance that often felt more like a pursuit. "From the very beginning I was painfully aware of the necessity of speed."

The whole family left for a seaside holiday at Lee that summer, returning on 21 August to learn that Constant Lambert had died the same day. He had grown to look more and more like a bulky, battered and debauched Roman emperor, obliged to rely on drink to sustain him in a losing battle against exhausting work schedules, relentless travelling and undiagnosed diabetes mellitus. A brash new administrator at the Royal Opera House, Covent Garden, had sacked him as conductor after the war, causing such uproar among dancers and musicians that Constant was rapidly reinstated, but further clashes, together with his own considerable loss of confidence, forced him to resign as musical director six months later. He made a second, happier marriage to the painter Isabel Delmer, and moved with her into a flat at 197, Albany Street just round the corner from the Powells. Even as neighbours he and Tony saw little of one another but they talked regularly, two or three times a week often late at night on the telephone. Constant, who had always had a mysterious knack of conjuring up inexplicable phenomena, made his last intervention in Tony's life when the phone rang just before midnight the day after he died. Violet and Tony both knew it was Constant before each of them realized that in fact it could not be. When Tony picked up the receiver, the line clicked and went dead.

Lambert had conducted his masterpiece, *Summer's Last Will and Testament*, for the last time in July. "I remembered the words 'Come, come, the bells do cry, I am sick, I must die. Lord have mercy on us!'" said a fellow conductor: "And I thought of his setting of these words and I had the awful feeling of a man really destroying himself, taking no care, making himself ill with overwork and worry." Constant was forty-six years old, almost exactly the same age as Tony, who was never able to fill the blank space left in his life. Varda, too, had died at the beginning of the year, taking an overdose of drugs alone in the house in the country she shared with her husband, Dennis Proctor. Although the marriage had apparently been going badly, he was distraught: "I could do nothing with her," he said. She and Tony had rarely met since their parting nearly twenty years earlier, but he had seen enough before that to recognize what was bound to happen when "the terrible devils of self-destruction took their final revenge."

His own life was overdue for uprooting. Tristram had started as a boarder at a prep school called Sandroyd School, but even in term-time Chester Gate was barely big enough to contain its floating population of children, relations and friends. The spare room on the top floor was occupied for long periods by Violet's niece, Frank's eldest daughter, Antonia Pakenham. Mary Clive came to stay whenever she was in London, and there were frequent visits from other nieces and nephews. As a child of ten or eleven Julia's son, Ferdy Mount, remembered his uncle Tony lying full length on a Regency chaise longue, brooding perhaps on how to set up in the early volumes of the *Dance* a base sufficiently broad, strong and flexible to support a still uncertain number of instalments to come. "I always think of him reclining thus like Mme Récamier," wrote Ferdy (who ended up writing novels himself), "with a favoured cat strolling impertinently across his cavalry-twill trousers throughout our long conversations over the next fifty years . . ." Antonia, who had watched her uncle sit down to work every morning as soon as the table was cleared after breakfast, decided to become in due course a writer too: "Somehow I began equating writing, discipline and a good life."

Antonia found particular support and sympathy from her Aunt Violet. In the large and obstreperous tribe of Pakenhams, both of them were throwbacks to Lady Jersey. Like her great-grandmother, Antonia would eventually make a career in her own right as a dazzling socialite who knew everyone, went everywhere, read every book as it came out and entertained not only the top politicians but the leading authors of her day. For the moment she was filling in the gap between leaving school at seventeen and going up to Oxford with a job in a West End shop. Her plan was to earn enough money to launch herself as a debutante on the London season in spite of stiff opposition from her mother. "Elizabeth did not understand that her frivolity was my serious glamour," Antonia said long afterwards. Chester Gate was a taxi ride from the nightclubs, hotels and hotspots where Antonia wanted to be, unlike the Pakenhams' family house in far-away Hampstead Garden Suburb, where her mother was fully occupied by six younger siblings as well as by the demands of her own socialist convictions and her role as the wife of a minister in the

Violet photographed by her niece Antonia Pakenham:
"No one was dull in Violet's company."

post-war Labour government. Her girlhood had made Antonia feel
"like a feral child . . . brought up by wolves."

Violet by contrast was endlessly tolerant, inquisitive and kind. She
had been a young debutante in London herself, keeping an energetic
nightlife secret from her own mother, and she listened attentively
every morning to her niece's gossip about the parties she'd been to
and the people she'd met the night before: "No one was dull in Violet's company . . . There was something infectious about Violet's
enthusiasm." Antonia's mother, Elizabeth Pakenham, had played the
part of a big sister to Violet, providing a role model she now in turn
offered her niece. They visited art galleries together, often with Tristram in tow. Tony too liked Antonia, who became in some sense for
both Powells the daughter they never had. They opened a door on
the world of books and writers to which she essentially belonged,
welcoming her at their parties and accepting her into their household

on easy terms as an equal. "Inclusion at last in the London whirl!" she wrote: "This was my first reaction to the generosity of my aunt."

The need for some measure of escape from that whirl was beginning to press hard on Tony. An increase of 150 per cent in the annual ground rent at Chester Gate, coinciding with completion of *A Question of Upbringing*, prompted thoughts of a move to the country. Waugh read the book "with huge delight and admiration" as soon as it came out, writing at once to propose a weekend at his Georgian house in Gloucestershire with a staff of eleven and four acres of garden ("We freeze and starve but you'd find an affectionate welcome"). Soon he was suggesting likely properties, and urging the Powells to move in as neighbours. Tony's Aunt Vi had died at the start of the war, leaving what remained of her trust fund to her husband in his lifetime, but with his death in 1950 the money reverted to Tony. On the strength of this windfall of just over £17,000 the Powells started serious house-hunting. In the summer of 1951, while Violet took the boys on a tour of Irish relations at Pakenham Hall and Dunsany, Tony finished *A Buyer's Market* and embarked on a terrific programme of house clearance, emptying cupboards, sorting the contents and throwing out junk: "After settling this I propose to reorganise the whole of the civil service, & rebuild the area around St. Paul's with my own hands."

By the following spring, he and Violet had found nowhere they could afford within a hundred-mile radius of London and, after inspecting around forty houses, were about to give up looking when Julia Mount rang with a favourable report on a place called the Chantry. It lay on the edge of the watery Somerset levels just south of Frome within easy reach of the Mounts at Chitterne and the Waughs at Piers Court, a couple of hours' drive from the Drus, who had just moved to another handsome, dilapidated manor house at Timberscombe on Exmoor in the far south-west of the county. The Chantry was a rundown Georgian property with outhouses and stables standing in dense matted shrubberies so overgrown that passers-by often refused to believe there could be a house at the end of the pot-holed drive. It included a small neglected lake largely silted up with mud, an uncut hayfield opposite the front door, and twenty-two acres of land rented out to a local farmer. Water had until recently been pumped up from the lake by an ancient water-wheel. Even so, the price would have been beyond anything the Powells could hope to raise if growing fears of another war, strengthened by Russia's recent acquisition of an atom bomb, had not depressed the property market. After several nerve-wracking offers and counter-offers, they finally bought the place cheap partly because of the war scare, and partly because the owner, Wing Commander Barraclough, took a strong dislike to the rival buyer who had made a slightly higher bid.

In the middle of negotiations Pryce-Jones left the *TLS*, and Tony lost his job. The London estate agent who had insisted he could easily sell the Chester Gate lease for a substantial sum turned out to have miscalculated. The first two reviews of *A Buyer's Market* in June struck Violet as "so terrible a lesser man might have abandoned the project." Unemployed, with no capital and no further income coming in from reviews, Tony had already started the third novel in the sequence when the practicalities of a move forced him to break off. The Powells took possession of the Chantry on 15 July 1952, moving in with two small boys, a huge second-hand refrigerator (which had already exploded in a blast of toxic gases at Chester Gate, and now developed a steady throb punctuated by occasional loud screams on reaching the country), and many boxes of books that remained unpacked on the stone floor of the basement for so long they grew whiskery streamers of mould.

Tony went first with the furniture, taking Albert in a cat basket, and leaving Violet to follow after a last night alone at Chester Gate. "From all around, the night was rent by cats keening the loss of Albert," she wrote, "until with the summer dawn I rose to take my departure to a new life." Severely schooled as a small child never to complain or grumble, she permitted herself a muffled cry only half a century later, looking back in her memoirs to "the house that I had often wished to be engraved on my tombstone because I felt its inconvenience would be the direct cause of my death." Violet had lived briefly in Oxfordshire as a child but Tony, who had never known anything except urban life, had no idea how or whether he would take to the country. All he had to go on was the lesson he had learned by default from Aubrey that the paramount need for a writer was stability, seclusion and a workplace free from the noise, the expense, the intrusions, and the unceasing social demands of London life.

9

1953–59

The Chantry stood on sloping ground so that the front door beneath a small pillared porch on the north side opened into the hall at ground level, but the south-facing drawing room on the far side of the hall looked out from the first floor across a broad stretch of grass at the back of the house to woods beyond. There was a dining room on one side, and a small sitting room or study for Violet on the other. Tony worked upstairs in a bedroom that faced into a yew tree because he found the unfamiliar sight of wooded hills and fields disturbing.

Unassuming, compact and gracefully proportioned, the house suggested the same "curious mixture of wit, austerity and reserve" as its new owner. A previous occupant had added electricity but no heating. Water came from a well liable to run dry in summer. An extension tacked on to one side of the house between the wars as a Roman Catholic Mass centre (Evelyn Waugh was not impressed) had been clumsily converted into a kitchen with the chapel bell and cross still hanging above the door. Steep steps at the other end of the hall led down to the original kitchen in the basement, a gents' lavatory and a playroom for the boys. Upstairs were four bedrooms and a bathroom. Their furniture was scanty and previous owners had painted the interior pink throughout, but the Powells were pleased with their new house. Tony's American publisher—Robert Vanderbilt, a New York bookshop owner preparing the first US edition of *Venusberg* and *Agents and Patients*—was ecstatic. "The high point of our trip has been our trip to Somerset . . . ," he wrote to Violet soon after the move: "The whole day was constant elation, as almost no

The Chantry seen from the south

day ever was, and no moment, joke or thing, treacle pie, grotto, John, or the fierce cat that looked peaceable enough to lie down with lambs, can easily be singled out as climactic."

The glory of the Chantry was its grottoes, built at the same time as the house by the original owner, a local ironmaster called James Fussell, who made money out of agricultural edge tools, and spent it on the exuberant revival of eighteenth-century grotto-building that became a craze in Somerset among early-nineteenth-century industrialists. Fussell commandeered an abandoned ironworks below his house, transforming the mine into a labyrinth of ruined archways, stone chambers, columns, caves and cells linked by underground passageways with a curving Gothic frontage set into the side of a natural amphitheatre, watered after rain by a little stream that trickled down through tiered arcades to feed the lake in the valley bottom. The whole complex was part mine-working, part romantic folly with druidic overtones and art-nouveau embellishment: "even in Bristol there was nothing on this scale or of this oddity," wrote Somerset's latest garden historian.

Tony dug out Fussell's strange conglomeration single-handed from a shroud of ivy, brambles, laurel and elder, discovering in the process a separate smaller grotto and a secret garden so choked and overrun that nobody knew it was there when he bought the property. He even composed a minor variation of his own on the same theme: Albert's Grotto, hollowed out in a sunny sheltered spot below the house with a chimney-pot in the middle topped by a miniature bust of Apollo, and named for the companion who had given up his old streetwise lifestyle to reposition himself in old age as a country-garden cat.

Tony shifted rocks, built dry stone walls, lit bonfires and dismantled the innumerable glass panes of the Chantry's two collapsing greenhouses. A man with a tractor came to mow the field opposite the front door, and the Drus drove over at intervals with bill-hooks and diggers, offering physical back-up and practical suggestions. The pace and scope of clearance was prodigious. Tony slashed, scythed and chopped so energetically that his rapid turnover in gardening gloves and tropical army-surplus boots became a family joke. All through that first year and the next, he and Dru compared notes as they fought back the jungle growth advancing on their respective homes. "Spurred on by your example I took to the shrubbery and hacked and cut my way through an area that would have daunted Stanley and Livingstone," Alick wrote competitively: "Come very soon and see the results as I need an audience to do my best work."

The man on the tractor was the local communist, employed for odd jobs by neighbours like Waugh's future biographer, Christopher Sykes, and Katherine Asquith, the widowed daughter-in-law of a former prime minister who lived a mile or so away at Mells with her faithful companion, Monsignor Ronald Knox. "I must say that my heart goes out to the poor man," Dru said of Tony's handyman, "with you at one end of his beat and Ronnie, Chris & Katherine at the other. His experience of suffering should be wide & deep." A communist in Frome can't have had an easy life at a time when national feeling against the party had been whipped to fever pitch by the press over the Burgess and Maclean spy scandal, but Tony was in no position to employ a gardener. Tristram was due to start at Eton in the New Year, John was booked into a small private school in Frome, and the lease on Chester Gate remained unsold. Although Colonel Powell helped with school fees, Tony was overwhelmed again by "financial struggles owing to the hideous expensiveness of everything." On Alick's advice, the Powells stocked their new cellar by importing a hogshead of claret direct from France and bottling it at home, borrowing a corking machine from the Asquiths at Mells. They bought a ponderous twenty-year-old Humber Snipe that looked like a pre-war village taxi and, driven erratically by Tony, struck awe into drivers coming the other way. Money was tight, and looked like getting tighter. "We must meet," said Dru, whose approach to the rising cost of living was philosophical, "and bang our heads against the wall somewhere or other."

Tony's manic attack on the Chantry's neglected garden was in part practical necessity, in part perhaps an essential displacement activity. He had made a start before leaving London on the third instalment of the serial novel in which he hoped to explore an area so simple and obvious it had been largely ignored by his contemporaries: "One of the most difficult things to realise when one is young is that all the awful odds and ends taking place round one are, in fact, the process of living." Tony's aim was to pin down that process by designing a structure sufficiently flexible to contain the turbulent, shifting and disruptive nature of life itself. But for the moment the novel-writing engine had stalled, and it was not until winter clamped down on outside activity that he managed to restart it. By the beginning of January 1953 he had written "about 25,000 words of volume three"—probably the first two chapters in draft form—when Malcolm Muggeridge offered him a job.

He had just become editor of *Punch*, and wanted Tony at his side as literary editor. The proposal was unthinkable at first. *Punch* had long since turned its back on its great iconoclastic founding fathers of a hundred years before, the merciless Victorian humorists who had entranced Tony as a child. In the first half of the twentieth century the magazine had squandered its accumulated goodwill, becoming a byword for everything Malcolm most abhorred. It was timid, stuffy, backward-looking and predictable, conformist in approach and banal in execution, with a dismal reputation and a fast dwindling readership. Only pure perversity could have made Muggeridge accept a post for which he was totally unfitted. He was admittedly provocative—and innately satirical—but he had none of the qualities of a good editor. Rash, opinionated, inconsistent, with a short attention span and a low boredom threshold, he had neither stamina nor experience in that line, and no clear vision of the future.

But he was exceedingly persuasive, and he proposed paying Tony

£1,500 a year (the equivalent of more than £30,000 in today's money) for two or three days' work a week with an extra fee for any review he undertook on top of that. Malcolm guaranteed complete autonomy on the books pages, and pointed out the almost limitless potential for improvement of a paper that, as Tony said, had already reached rock bottom. He agreed to take up Malcolm's offer in March, far enough ahead to get well into the next chapter of his novel first. In the meantime he paid a couple of visits to the *Punch* offices in Bouverie Street, a few minutes' walk away from the old Varda Bookshop on High Holborn, and dined afterwards with Malcolm to plot revolution. They discussed the possibility of persuading Nancy Mitford to contribute a regular feature—"Mr. Punch's French Letter"—and pooled suggestions about what to do with *Punch*'s existing staff ("it does not seem possible at present to take them into a back room and pistol them at the base of the skull, anyway in bulk," Tony explained to Bob Vanderbilt, "but no doubt liquidations will take place one way or another").

Tony's aim was to reverse the paper's "long and obstinate tradition of active philistinism." It had never had a literary editor before, nor anything like adequate book coverage, and he was in no mood to compromise: "the books I myself thought deserved attention would in future be reviewed in *Punch*." He kicked off with a lead article on an anthology of Kipling's poems chosen by T. S. Eliot, translated into French, published in Paris and reviewed by himself under the headline "*Bottes, bottes, bottes.*" Bewildered readers were treated the week after to his assessment of Alfred de Vigny's military thinking, followed the next week by "An Austrian Proust," in which Tony came to grips intellectually and aesthetically with the modernist Robert Musil. Every so often he carried the offensive into what must once have been *Punch* readers' home ground with an attack on some literary grandee, such as J. B. Priestley (Tony's review of his novel *The Magicians* made Priestley hopping mad).

Probably no book gave Tony a greater jolt than Gerald Reitlinger's *The Final Solution*, which arrived on his desk in April. It came from Vallentine Mitchell & Co., a small specialist publishing house that had brought out Anne Frank's diary the year before. Reitlinger's subtitle was *The Attempt to Exterminate the Jews of Europe, 1939–1945.* This was the first comprehensive history of the Holocaust, an authoritative and meticulously researched study that would remain for decades the definitive account. Reitlinger had spent the last four years assembling and collating material, tracking down documents in many languages, going through official German archives, scrutinizing transcripts of the Nuremberg trials, interviewing witnesses and reading the first-hand testimony of survivors.

Muggeridge, dropping in at Woodgate the year before with a friend called Tosco Fyvel, had found Gerald hard at work, sitting alone in his study between two paraffin stoves: "No more visitors, spongers, parties, travels . . . Second wife has left him, first (Varda) lately committed suicide. Tosco said afterwards that writing the history of the annihilation of the Jews was an act of atonement for his efforts not to be a Jew." Reitlinger himself said he had begun the work as a way of coping with the breakdown of his second marriage. His daughter had been three years old when he began and, when he finished, he inscribed his manuscript: "To Venetia that one day she may read and know the tragedy of her race." When she was old enough to question him about it, he said simply: "*Some* bloody Jew had to write it."

Reitlinger describes the very nearly indescribable events and actions of his story clearly and succinctly with extraordinary poetic and imaginative precision. "Like the aerial bomber, the bureaucrat does not see his kill," he writes of Hitler's civil service. In a footnote to a passage describing living human bodies stirring and jerking their limbs in a Nazi killing pit, he quotes a line from the *Aeneid* that he and Tony must have construed as schoolboys, where Virgil imagines the dead or dying as they cross the river of oblivion to the underworld: "*Tendebantque manus ripae ulteriorae amore.*"* Reitlinger's tone is rational and measured. He writes without evident emotion, revealing only rarely the depth of feeling beneath the dispassionate surface of his sombre, detailed and studiously objective account. His wit is pertinent and sharp, his images as powerful as his narrative grip. "After May, 1945," he writes on the last page, "the whole apparatus of National Socialism resembled a tangle of burnt rafters, blackened, soaked and ill-smelling, under which crawled persecutor and victim, no longer very distinguishable . . ."

* They reached out their hands to the far bank in longing (Virgil, *Aeneid*, Book VI, l. 314)

The Final Solution was widely ignored on publication by both critics and readers. It was too soon for most people to begin to face a European genocide virtually impossible to confront at the time. Collective amnesia blocked it out. Max Beloff, reviewing Reitlinger's book in the *Jewish Chronicle*, said that although there was ample evidence to prove the existence of Hitler's death camps, "public opinion outside Jewry nowhere accepts the fact." The few mainstream papers to acknowledge the book at all included the *Manchester Guardian* ("an unendurable horror"), and *Punch*. "In so far as it is possible to bring a detached and sardonic manner to such a horrible subject, Mr. Reitlinger does so," Tony wrote in a brief notice, singling out for emphasis "the illogicality, incompetence and futility shown by the Germans as much as their fiendish cruelty."

Three years later Reitlinger produced a sequel, *The SS: Alibi of a Nation*, published this time by Heinemann presumably at Tony's insistence. Reitlinger rewarded him with a copy of his first book, inscribed: "To Tony Powell who has read at least part of this monstrous thing (sorry, the whole of it)—Gerald Reitlinger 12.5.56." The bracket was added as an afterthought above the line, apparently in answer to protests from Tony. Already working on the final volume of what turned out to be a trilogy, Gerald had become a hermit, shut up alone at Woodgate, seldom leaving the house, seeing almost no one, getting up from his desk only in the evenings to listen with his housekeeper to the nine o'clock news on the radio.

He had moved a long way from his hospitable heyday but the few friends he still saw found in him an unaccustomed sweetness and good humour, as if some inner pressure had been lifted from him. Among the few were Eve Disher and her ex-boyfriend, the film-maker Sir Arthur Elton, both of whom knew Gerald from art-school days in Chelsea before the war. Elton's new young wife was charmed by the courtly kindness of her husband's old friend. Eve herself made a lively portrait of him in the 1950s, looking old and grizzled (he was five years older than Tony) with three of his blue-and-white Iznik plates hanging on the wall beside him. The portrait is affectionate and unsparing, on the one hand exploring the sitter's tight lips, thinning hair, bushy eyebrows and pebble glasses while, on the other, strongly conveying the warmth and depth of the painter's feelings for him.

Tony's own parallel withdrawal to the country was a decidedly more sociable affair. The Powells made new friends, and entertained old ones at the Chantry most weekends. They exchanged drinks with near-neighbours: the Sykeses, the Asquiths, Lord Bath at Longleat and Violet's closest childhood friend, Ty Mac-Rae, who turned out to be living near Mells with her second husband. Evelyn Waugh, who remembered the house at its dingiest between the wars—"I shall be very curious to see how wealth & taste have transformed it"—came regularly with his eldest son on outings from Downside School, or for dinner with his wife Laura.

The first to sign the Chantry visitors' book was Osbert Lancaster, pocket cartoonist of the *Daily Express*, who arrived with his wife Karen for a weekend in October, bringing hot news from London's social swamps and jungles. Osbert, who had produced an elegant animated dust jacket for the Vanderbilt edition of Tony's pre-war novels, looked like a character from one of his own cartoons in loud check suits, double-breasted waistcoats and yellow boots. With his booming voice, pop eyes and bristly moustache—"half Balkan bandit, half retired brigadier"—he matched Tony in ruthless wit, penetration and executive urbanity. He belonged to the small band of people—Constant Lambert, Violet herself, Malcolm Muggeridge and Alick Dru—Tony relied on to examine and explore with him what was going on around them as it happened.

The Mounts made frequent contact, the two sisters picking up their old close relationship and talking on the telephone nearly every day. Old Mrs. Maydwell from Chantry Grange saw her chance and seized it, conscripting Violet to replace her in the Mothers' Union, the Chantry Women's Institute and the local branch of the Conservative Association. Violet, "thrown into the pond of village life . . . to sink or swim," adapted easily and fast, settling down on the parish council, attending fetes, whist drives and skittle matches, taking her turn to present prizes afterwards in the corrugated-iron hut (heated only by councillors bringing their own electric fires) that served as Chantry's village hall. Over the next decade and more she proved a wily, shrewd and vigorous operator on Frome Rural District Council, infuriating commercial developers and taking on all comers in a long-running battle for conservation and co-ordinated planning, actively promoting both long before either had secured a regular place on the national agenda.

Tony returned to his novel on the few working days left over each week from *Punch*. He had added another five thousand words before getting stuck again in April but by autumn he had reached halfway, quickening his pace that winter, and handing a completed draft in February 1954 to Violet, always his first reader at this provisional stage. In *The Acceptance World* he sharpened and concentrated his focus. By the end Jenkins has lost his tentative air, published his first book, and stepped forward—or more precisely slightly to one side—to take on an increasingly authoritative role as presenter of the *Dance*. Relationships shift and buckle. Widmerpool's career pursues a rising curve, Stringham's its steep decline; Members loses ground to Quiggin, each jostling the other in the political correctness stakes against a background of economic depression and 1930s protest marches. Degenerates of an older generation are strongly represented by the seductive delinquent Dicky Umfraville, and the clairvoyant Mrs. Erdleigh whose aura, at once bogus and commanding, well conveys the faintly sinister occult authority that exerted a compulsive grip on people like Maud Powell after the First World War (Osbert Lancaster said his mother's life was full of Mrs. Erdleighs too). Like Mr. Deacon, both became strands threading through the emerging pattern of the *Dance*.

But the core of the book is Jenkins's passionate affair with Templer's younger sister, a girl called Jean Duport whose "grave gothic beauty," ironic intelligence and frank sensuality clearly derive initially from Tony's encounter twenty years before with Marion Coates. Like Marion, Jean has an unfaithful and absconding husband regarded by her lover with a mix of scorn and dread. She generates the sexiest passages in the *Dance* with erotic undercurrents intensified by being touched on, rather than rubbed in. The scene where Jean opens the street door to her lover with nothing on certainly impressed the Irish government, whose censor banned the book on publication as obscene. Violet, who had met and liked Marion before the war, recognized her immediately as Jean's model, singling out her affair with Jenkins as especially moving. But the reason she was so touched by the narrator's account of his involvement was that she knew her own part in it was as great as Marion's. The general outline of the fictional liaison followed Tony's relationship with Marion and Wells Coates. So did its abrupt ending with Jean on the verge of returning to her husband (except that in fact the sexes were reversed, and it was Tony who left Marion without warning for Violet). But the equally abrupt start of the affair, its electric undertow and painful aftermath, came from Violet. More than almost any other of Tony's books, *The Acceptance World* held a personal significance for her ever after:

> It begins with a prophecy of a love affair [she wrote at the end of her long life] and ends with the ominous prospect of a break-up between the lovers. The first stitch of this pattern had been sewn in the opening chapters of . . . [the] *Dance*, and threads of the same romance would suddenly glitter in all but one of the later volumes.

Violet had been very young when she met and married Tony at a stage when her knowledge of boys still came largely from her brothers, or from shy and inexperienced dancing partners like Alick Dru (remembered from her debutante days as a first-rate ballroom dancer), and the charming elusive asexual Hamish Erskine, who captivated Nancy Mitford. Violet's first five years of marriage, disrupted by the anxiety and pain of repeated miscarriages, had been followed by another five years of war, which meant almost continuous separation. At some point in the stretch she spent living apart from her husband in Oxford, or Belfast, or Petersham, she fell in love with another man. She never said who he was, when or where the affair started or how far it got, but she told Sonia Orwell that "he was the love of her life." Perhaps he was married like herself, perhaps one or other of them had second thoughts, perhaps the war itself swept them in different directions: at all events Violet's role as wife and mother exerted in the end a greater pull. Some time later Tony found out what had happened, probably in 1946 when he plunged into a black hole of depression, exhaustion and almost insane overwork.

His discovery caused them both much pain but, by the time he came to write *The Acceptance World*, whatever storms had shaken their marriage a decade earlier had been resolved between them. The book deals in the narrator's words with "the ecstasies and bitterness of love": on a personal level Violet was clearly implicated in both, particularly in the paroxysms of jealousy that make the narrator feel, here and at intervals throughout the *Dance*, as if he were successively chained to a corpse, gripped by red-hot pincers and being brutally beaten up: "I felt as if someone had suddenly kicked my legs from under me, so that I had landed on the other side of the room . . . with all the breath knocked out of me."

The deadpan knockabout side of Tony's writing, handled more subtly here and with far greater emotional impact, goes back to episodes like Pringle's mock-suicide in *Afternoon Men*, or the chained and naked man being tortured on a London pavement in *Agents and Patients*. His reluctance to ratify borders between the comic and the serious went down well with a new generation of writers emerging in the 1950s. "I would rather read Mr. Powell than any English novelist now writing," said Kingsley Amis, reviewing *The Acceptance World* on publication. As literary editor of *Punch*, Tony had contacted him on the strength of the first review he ever wrote, even before he shot to fame with *Lucky Jim*, and the two quickly became friends. Three years later the same happened with V. S. Naipaul, a penniless young West Indian trying and failing to make his way in London as a writer when he received a note out of the blue from Tony. Naipaul's professional career in the UK began when Tony fixed him up with a weekly fiction column on the *New Statesman*, then the most prestigious of British weeklies, at the start of what turned out to be another life-long friendship. Thirty years after they first met, Naipaul re-read *The Acceptance World* and was bowled over by it all over again: "So original; so rich; so beguiling; so classical; so full of wisdom and gentleness and passion," he wrote to Tony, describing the scene where the narrator falls in love with Jean in the back of her brother's car: "The drive to Templer's house in the snow—there is in the language and the images the wonder and magic of a sonnet by Shakespeare . . . I do not know how you managed to pack so much into such a short space."

Tony had barely finished his first rough draft of the novel when his mother fell and fractured her thigh bone at the age of eighty-seven. Her death two months later devastated her husband, who was seventy-one and had for years seemed older than she was. Cosseted

Brigadier Gerard, drawn by
Tony for his son John during
bedtime readings of *The Exploits
of Brigadier Gerard* by Arthur
Conan Doyle

and protected for more than half a century, he had no experience of adult life without her, and apparently no experience in managing his own affairs. Tony found to his cost that his mother's responsibilities now devolved on him. Colonel Powell began arriving for weekends at the Chantry and his son, depositing him afterwards back at his residential hotel, marvelled yet again at his father's ability to antagonize people whose support and tolerance he desperately needed. Money was a further worry. His father's constant grumbling about the exiguous purchasing power of his army retirement pay made Tony reluctant to accept even the offer of a drink for fear the expense might be beyond his meagre means. An abominable parent and a grossly self-indulgent husband, Colonel Powell capitalized on the role of doting grandfather, presenting the boys with alarmingly extravagant gifts, tips and treats. Tristram, in his second year at Eton, received a cine camera complete with state-of-the-art projector. For John, starting his first term at Sandroyd School aged eight in the summer of 1954, there was a giant teddy-bear, and a ventriloquist's dummy in the shape of Archie Andrews, currently one of radio's greatest hits.

John's departure disoriented Violet, whose priority for the last fourteen years had been her children: "Suddenly with no child in the house, I felt like a mare whose foal had been taken to market." She and Tony took a fortnight's Italian holiday in May to console her and distract him from his father's problems. In June he was guest of honour at a party for his first French translation, *Une Question d'éducation*, given by his publisher in Paris, where he got good advice from Nancy Mitford, and headlines from the French announcing the arrival of UN PROUST ANGLAIS. He spent the rest of the summer revising and retyping *The Acceptance World*, taking a week off from *Punch* for a final push at the end of July, and delivering the typescript in August to the managing director of Heinemann, who astounded him by taking it home and reading it right through overnight. "I think he really does like it," Tony wrote dubiously to Violet, in Ireland with the boys at Pakenham Hall. All of them spent the first week of September beside the seaside at Lee.

In October Muggeridge took on a second job as interviewer for a new and still experimental news programme called *Panorama* on BBC TV. He had spent nearly two years stirring things up at *Punch*—"You felt some life crackling behind the desk," said another hardened provocateur, Claud Cockburn, "as though someone had thrown a firecracker into a mausoleum"—but the old regime was proving harder to overthrow than he had expected. He was the first outsider *Punch* had ever had as editor, and his intrusion was bitterly resented. He poured out new ideas and brought in fresh people ("Almost everybody you had ever heard of turned up in the pages"), but he was always better at rocking the boat than steering it. Tony rarely and reluctantly attended the monthly conferences where in theory policy was formulated and problems sorted out. In practice they were power struggles with the editor confronting snipers, undercover opponents and last-ditch resistance fighters on a rising swell of jealousy and rancour. Muggeridge gave as good as he got at these sessions, buoyed up by his horror of ever becoming part of the establishment—or only, as he said, "in the sense that Lear's Fool was part of his court."

If Muggeridge gave him practical lessons in power politics at *Punch*, Tony himself spruced up its appearance, recommending fewer cartoons of higher quality, inserting drawings in the lead book review, and generally promoting changes in the art department more clear-cut and decisive than seemed possible elsewhere on the paper.

One of his first big surprises was how few of the senior staff apparently grasped that "the magazine was at least intended to make people laugh." He urged Malcolm to replace the cruder cartoonists ("I do beg you to steer clear of Topolski") with artists of more character and bite, himself recruiting a brilliant young newcomer called Mark Boxer, who got his first professional job on *Punch* through Tony. In a major battle to preserve the paper's original cover by Richard Doyle, Tony was forced to admit defeat, but he succeeded in persuading Malcolm to create the new post of art editor, and to instal Adrian Daintrey in it. He even roped in Osbert Lancaster: "particularly pleased," wrote Malcolm, who had so far courted Osbert without success, "because, being a worldly individual, it's a very good sign that he should want to appear in *Punch*. He's waited eighteen months to see how the wind was blowing."

On the book pages Tony built up an unusually wide range of contributors, scouring the little magazines for young unknowns, often taking on characters too reclusive, or too innately disruptive, to suit other editors for long. Many of them became his friends. The first was Jocelyn Brooke, whose novel *Mine of Serpents* Tony had reviewed a few years earlier in the *TLS*, marking him down at once as a writer to watch. But Brooke beat him to it with a long appreciative assessment of *Afternoon Men* (one of Heinemann's recent reissues) in *Time and Tide* at the start of 1953. He had been a twenty-three-year-old in his first job with a bookshop in the City when the book originally came out, and he never forgot the instant buzz at a Bloomsbury sherry party: "My dear, it's the party novel to end *all* party novels . . ." For Brooke, *Afternoon Men* scotched for ever the romantic myth of the party-goers of the period, who suddenly looked as lewd and drab as real human beings, "the squalid fag end of the Bright Young People, the post-slump survivors of circa 1930 . . . every effect is scrupulously underplayed, the flat, colourless prose suggests perfectly the muzzy fatigue of the morning's hangover." He had never read anything like it and, analysing the book twenty years later, he finally worked out what made Powell so extremely funny, and so different from other comic novelists:

It wasn't Stein and Hemingway so much as Mr. Eliot who seemed to be lurking in the background. The laconic, curiously empty dialogue, with its deliberate repetitions, achieves a compulsive interior rhythm which almost suggests *Sweeney Agonistes* . . . "Birth, copulation and death" . . . the theme is never stated but it is implicit in almost every paragraph . . . One would hardly guess . . . that *A Buyer's Market* was by the same author . . . yet the later novels seem to me to retain . . . something of the same quality: one feels in all Mr. Powell's work a sense of inward desolation, a dead-centre of emptiness.

Brooke was a serious naturalist specializing in orchids, with a secondary passion for fireworks and a keen interest in the army. Tony wrote at once to thank him, and ask if he would review military memoirs as a corrective to "the Private Pipeclay–Colonel Haversack sort of stuff" that *Punch* traditionally favoured. The two had never met but they began writing one another the kind of letters that Tony used to exchange with Heygate before he lost interest in writing novels. Brooke was next after Violet to read the first draft of *The Acceptance World*, and make suggestions. At the end of the year Tony proposed an alternative ending for Brooke's next book, *Private View*. An appealing, melancholy homosexual, Brooke had by this time largely withdrawn from the literary world, living at home with his mother and his former nanny just outside Hastings on the south coast, where his family ran a wine merchants business. He and Tony had a strong affinity as writers, and a growing admiration for each other's work, but it wasn't until Brooke spent a weekend at the Chantry in the spring of 1956 that he could bring himself to call Tony by his Christian name. "It's a long time since I've been so well dined, wined, sunned and aired," he wrote afterwards to Violet: "I do so love your house—I should write the most elegant Augustan prose if I lived in it."

In every literary sphere except the act of writing, Brooke was passive and professionally inert, incapable of promoting himself or his work, so Tony did it for him, publishing his reviews and championing his books in *Punch* as they came out, finding him new outlets, and enthusiastically promoting his work over the next three decades in private and in print. Brooke was not the only of his contributors he did this for: nurturing other writers' talent was a process he enjoyed,

and the breadth and variety of his contributors show how good he
was at it. He had given the young Francis Wyndham his first books to
review on the *TLS*, later kick-starting a distinguished career by getting him a job on the *Observer*. At *Punch* he approached both Amis and
Naipaul before either had made any sort of name, and he published
a series of brilliant short stories by Inez Holden, some of the best
work she ever did. He also rediscovered Alfred Duggan, Hubert's
elder brother who, after a spectacular career of drink, debauch and
gambling, reinvented himself in the 1950s as an outstanding historical
novelist: "the unbelievable—as so often—had taken place. Alf Duggan had begun a new career."

Of all the *Punch* reviewers who made inroads on Tony's time and
patience, probably the most exorbitant was Julian Maclaren-Ross, who
supplied a steady flow of stories, feature articles, accomplished paro-
dies and authoritative book reviews. He had erupted from nowhere
on to the London scene with a string of remarkable books that came
out in quick succession after the war. Tony picked out his distinctive
qualities—"shape, life and staying-power"—from the first magazine
story he ever published in 1946. It was followed the year after by what
has remained his best-known novel, *Of Love and Hunger*, about his
short stint as a vacuum-cleaner salesman. "It proves that in economy
of phrase and neatness of characterisation American writers can be
rivalled at their own game," Tony wrote crisply in the kind of review
it is a pleasure to write as well as to receive.

Maclaren-Ross was a literary editor's dream, and nightmare. Tall,
pale and dandified, he wore dark glasses in all weathers and carried a knobbed cane, said to be for self-defence in case of assault by
the burly editor of the *Observer*'s book pages, John Davenport. His
knowledge of films and books was impossible to fault in Tony's view.
He spent his afternoons at the cinema and read every new novel as it
came out, buying and reading it on the same day so he could flog it
to a second-hand bookshop the day after, and buy another one. His
industry was prodigious, and his routine exacting. He lived in Fitzrovia hotels, shuttling according to his means between the Imperial on
Russell Square ("I could never afford it myself," said Henry Yorke),
and a basement room at the cut-price Hotel Cora a few streets away.
He drank morning and evening all through pub opening hours, gen-

erally in the Wheatsheaf on Rathbone Place, returning to his lodgings at closing time to write until 3 a.m. "He composed orally, like Homer," said a colleague, describing how he settled with a notebook in the hotel lounge after his fellow residents had gone to bed, "and took down his own story as if it were from his own dictation." His copy was sharp, clean and to the point, utterly reliable and invariably on time, written in a minute, exquisitely legible, non-cursive hand as artificial and fastidiously disciplined as his entire persona.

He had two disadvantages. The first was that, as soon as he started calling regularly at the *Punch* office, a crowd of duns and bailiffs turned up to wait for him on the steps outside. Maclaren-Ross was chronically destitute. Creditors pursued him at all times. He travelled exclusively by taxi on the grounds that "taxis provided a security, denied to the man on foot, against bailiffs serving writs for debt." Endless credit, unpaid bills, unearned advances and ongoing royalties for unwritten books were his sole means of support. He was expert at extracting loans from friends like Tony, who could not spare the money, and from editors intimidated by the menacing implication that failure to pay over yet another fee for an article not yet delivered threatened the very existence of his next book. His instincts were belligerent and abrasive. Tony did what he could to extract him from troubles mostly of his own making, negotiating on his behalf for a grant from the Royal Literary Fund, and persuading the literary editor of the *Daily Telegraph* to take him on in spite of the fights he picked, a habit that made him hard to help even for "those determined he should not starve to death."

The second drawback was that Maclaren-Ross could be a crashing bore. Like everyone who knew him, Tony came to dread his interminable monologues. His ring at the door at Chester Gate, or his voice on the telephone at the Chantry, meant being cornered for an hour or more with no hope of escape. He submitted a two-page business schedule of pieces he proposed to write for *Punch*, set out under six main headings with countless subsections, and accompanied by stern instructions to "*take up the points one by one with the Editor, & let me know the decision in your next.*" His colossal ego had struck Tony the first time they met and, though he was at best both stoical and brave, at worst he was a domineering bully.

When he fell in love in 1954 with a girl who drove him by his own account to the brink of madness, he told Tony that her name was too sacred to mention, passing it instead across the bar of the Wheatsheaf on a folded slip of paper. The name scribbled on his note was Sonia Orwell. Sacred she may have been to Maclaren-Ross, but his devotion took the form of harassment and intimidation. He moved lodgings to be near her, proclaimed his feelings for her at length in public, pestered her friends at home in writing, barged into her office at *Horizon* and hung around outside her flat, waiting for her to come out. Stalking Sonia took up a high proportion of his time for years, and might easily have sabotaged a less indomitable personality than hers.

Maclaren-Ross died at the age of fifty-two in 1964. However much he owed to Tony's unfailing generosity, he paid it back posthumously by appearing, barely disguised, in the tenth instalment of the *Dance* as X. Trapnel, a novelist with a chaotic lifestyle, uncompromising ambition and invincible panache. Maclaren-Ross belonged along with Lambert and Dru to the small group of people transposed more or less directly from fact to fiction in the *Dance*. Another was Adrian Daintrey, who saw himself in the painter Ralph Barnby, the narrator's shrewd and sceptical companion in the early volumes: "My pride at (unless I'm mistaken) recognising some resemblance to myself in one of the characters is enhanced by relief at appearing in such a comparatively flattering light." This was written when *The Acceptance World* came out in May 1955, a point when a good many of Tony's friends were beginning to feel nervous, like Daintrey, as the scale and reach of the *Dance* became clearer. Davenport in the *Observer* recognized it as "the most exciting experiment in post-war English fiction." V. S. Pritchett identified Powell's "hard-headed English comedy" as precisely what was needed at a point when the novel itself seemed to be losing ambition and narrowing its scope: "The subject is society in disintegration, living on its discount bills, financial and moral, and feeling the teeth of time . . . Where the whole charade is going to lead one cannot tell, but one cannot miss a page of it."

Reviewers beginning to acknowledge the emergence of a specifically Powellian identity made fewer dismissive comparisons to Proust. "I'd have written this series if he'd never existed," Tony insisted, pointing out that admiration was an entirely different thing from imitation. The Powells underlined the point with what Violet called a "Homage à M. Proust holiday," taking their sons abroad for the first time in September to a tiny pension on the Channel coast at Cabourg, Proust's Balbec, first visited by Tony ten years earlier in the final stages of the war. Since then a small memorial had been put up to Proust in the municipal garden opposite the Grand Hotel, still exactly as he described it although the brothel had long gone. Back at the Chantry they found a postcard waiting for them, showing a monolithic tower of rock rising from a beach in Portugal: "This is pretty impressive, no? And when you get tired of looking at it, you can always turn round & look at a hill. And when you get tired of that, there's plenty of sport to be had, going round the house with the DDT spray. And then you get your homeward vouchers out & read them attentively. Still, I've got nice & brown & that's something. All the best Kingsley Amis."

Tony settled down to work on the fourth volume of the *Dance* at the Chantry in the room with no view, making slow progress and grumbling that he had produced only fifteen thousand words by the end of the year. He was fifty in December. "Each recriminative decade poses new riddles . . . ," says his narrator on reaching the same age in the *Dance*: "One's fifties, in principle less acceptable than one's forties, at least confirm one's worst suspicions about life, thereby disposing of an appreciable tract of vain expectation, standardised fantasy, obstructive to writing, as to living." What was originally planned as three volumes or a little over had grown to eight or nine by now. This was the first book Tony started writing at the Chantry, and it established a pattern that lasted to the end of his writing life. He wrote every morning, then switched to hauling rocks, cutting paths and clearing grottoes ("Not of course *flowers*," wrote Dru, whose taste like Tony's was severely French, "but *such* buildings, *such* diggings") in the afternoon. The two activities were complementary. "After a late lunch, he potters and trundles and works in his large garden . . . ," reported an interviewer, who caught precisely Tony's intonation and turn of phrase: "After tea he returns to his typewriter, which is kept upstairs on an old light-green bed-table, and there he aims to complete his stint for the day."

The daily stint was roughly three hundred words, which he wrote straight on to the typewriter, going over what he had put down, add-

Violet with Tristram and John on the rocks at Lee

ing and revising at least twice, producing in a good week a thousand words at most. Each week consisted normally of two working days. The other three were spent at the *Punch* offices in London. Weekends were mostly taken up with friends. Tony never changed the provisional arrangement of the small bedroom where he worked on an upright chair at a flimsy table designed for a quite different purpose, almost as if he hoped to catch himself or his imagination unawares. "'Writing is something like weight-lifting,' Mr. Powell said, and he added, without understatement this time, and expressing all the secret love and fear of that consuming craft: 'It's a terrible job.'"

By late summer 1956, when the family spent their usual week beside the seaside at Lee, he was nearly halfway through his new novel. His life and Violet's had been overshadowed for the past nine months by the threat hanging over her sister Julia Mount, who had cancer. The youngest of the six Pakenham siblings and always by far the closest to Violet, Julia managed her illness as quietly and composedly as everything else she ever did. "It was hard to believe that someone so rose pink and golden haired could be fighting a losing battle," said Violet, describing her still in her early forties "as beautiful as she had ever been" right up to the day they said goodbye at the end of August. Violet had agreed to take a break in Venice organized by their elder sister Mary Clive with Tristram and Mary's two children, while John stayed with a friend from school. Tony, who had never properly got the hang of family holidays, accepted an invitation of his own to sail down the Adriatic on a cruise to the Greek islands with Antonia, her contemporary Francis Wyndham, and a school friend of her brother's called Laurence Kelly. Both holidays went wrong at the last minute. Mary pulled out when her son George contracted acute appendicitis, and Tony's companions also cancelled one by one: Antonia on account of her sudden engagement to a Tory politician called Hugh Fraser, Francis in favour of a more attractive invitation elsewhere and Laurence because, as a Life Guardsman in the reserve, he risked involvement in any prospective military action against the regime in Egypt, which nationalized the Suez Canal that summer to the consternation of the Western powers.

The Powells went ahead anyway, overlapping briefly in Venice, where Tony joined his wife and son at the Pensione Seguso in the early hours of 10 September with a day to spare before boarding his boat that night. They visited a Delacroix retrospective put on as part of the Venice Biennale and attended a party at the Palazzo Polignac, enjoying their explorations so much that he was sad to have to cut them short so soon. The SS *Aegeon* had started out as a Canadian lake steamer, big enough to hold around two hundred passengers of mixed nationalities, many of them transacting regular business in Corfu, Athens or Rhodes. Tony's original companions had been replaced by another of Violet's nieces, Pansy's daughter Henrietta Lamb, and her friend Marigold Hunt. The two girls were up for anything, starting with an expedition to the walled mediaeval city of Dubrovnik that required a visa check: "a scene took place rather as if the university rugger match were played in the Black Hole of Calcutta," said Tony, whose great aim was to do nothing.

His old habit of working steadily through the summer holidays had been suspended only long enough to replenish his energies for a further work session. To the girls he was a friendly uncle, entertaining and appreciative, listening patiently to stories of their exploits, leaving sightseeing to them, and luxuriating himself in sun, sea and the excellent local wine served on board ship. "As a matter of fact I just lie on the deck all day, not even reading, among a lot of barnacles & binnacles & things . . . ," he told Violet: "Already I feel as if I had been away for about a thousand years."

He went ashore at Corfu, where the former governor's palace made him feel at home, "like a chunk of Regent's Park (Cumberland Terrace) in greyish yellow stone." In Rhodes he marvelled at the ramparts, dismissing the heavily restored old town as a tourist trap: "The rest of it is like Beverly Hills." When the Greek navy put into port, the place filled up with handsome sailors who danced with the girls, and picked Marigold—small, pretty and extremely lively—as their queen for the night before any of them realized she was British. Britain's imperial attitude to Cyprus in the 1950s was deeply unpopular with Greeks, whose potentially explosive response alarmed the captain of the *Aegeon* as much as it amused Tony. He roared with laughter, referring to Marigold ever after as Miss Greek Navy. Perhaps she distracted him from a telegram he received on the third day of the cruise, announcing Julia's death, news he had been expecting that still came as a painful shock. "I felt terribly upset about it . . . ," he wrote at once to Violet: "Knowing how awful I feel myself, I am afraid you must find it a frightful blow, darling, as I really can't claim to have been more than very fond of her in a general way, and she did play such a large part in your everyday life."

By the end of September he was back at the Chantry, sufficiently restored to resume work on his book. "Coming down here helped," said Violet. Israeli, French and British troops attempted unsuccessfully to reverse the Suez situation by invading Egypt in late autumn, making it virtually impossible for Britain to protest when Russian tanks almost simultaneously rolled into Budapest. Soviet control, brutally affirmed by the crushing of the Hungarian Revolution, now closed off Eastern Europe as Amiel had foreseen in the passage on Russian despotism picked out by Tony a decade earlier.

In December 1956, Nina Hamnett jumped or fell from her window, impaled herself on the railings below and died in hospital a few days later. In more than quarter of a century since she and Tony parted, she had made virtually no change to her lifestyle. Increasingly battered, lame, often in pain, as hard-up as she was indomitable, she remained well into her mid-sixties a familiar fixture in the bars of Fitzrovia, still working intermittently, and still drinking with successive generations of young men. She painted Julian Maclaren-Ross, and designed a jacket for his third collection of short stories. Jocelyn Brooke reviewed her last book, *Is She a Lady?*, published the year before she died. So did Tony, both of them agreeing that her writing reproduced exactly "her breathless, slightly raucous and quite unmistakeable voice . . . bustling and self-important as ever, unbuttoned, inconsequent, sometimes boring yet holding one's attention by its sheer, unquenchable vitality."

Over the next two decades the Chantry became a powerhouse, its layout and routines evolving round production of the *Dance*. The downstairs drawing room, where Violet mercilessly dissected the first draft of each volume as soon as Tony finished it, took on aspects of an engine room. It was in fact a library with white-painted bookshelves filling two whole walls, and invading a third on either side of the chimney-piece. The elderly chaise longue, where Tony lay full length to process and ponder the workings of his novel, stood opposite the fire, drawn up at right angles to a deep, soft, squashy sofa. The impression of a workplace, however unconventional, was reinforced by the powerful striped wallpaper selected by Violet and designed by Edward Bawden, its tone and texture a strange mix of coal, asphalt and rough-cast concrete. Interrogated by Sonia Orwell as to why on earth she chose it, Violet said simply: "Because I love my husband." Floor-length velvet curtains, a couple of armchairs and the wood fire burning brightly in the elegant Regency grate made the room comfortable and welcoming while the multicoloured book bindings lining the walls, and reflected in a big, gilt-framed mirror above the fireplace, added warmth and gaiety.

Pink-painted interiors throughout the house gradually receded in the next few years before a tide of rich pattern and strong colour. A luxuriant deep red paper with stylized urns and trophies in the hall continued up the shallow curving staircase, giving way to blue on the first-floor landing. The small square bedroom where Tony worked was papered in soft plum-red, the spare room in green with a scattering of red stars. Violet picked a graceful design of flower-and-ribbon garlands on a pale blue paper for the light and airy bedroom she shared with Tony, installing delicate Victorian watercolours of Naples on the walls and a flounced white dressing-table beside the big bay window. Roman fountains decorated the bathroom with water spouts and thrashing dolphins straddled by muscular sea-gods. John slept next to his parents in the east-facing end bedroom until he was eleven, when he moved upstairs to a room next to Tristram's in the attic.

Tony commandeered the east room at this point as his work space, choosing another of Bawden's forceful wallpapers striped in jagged black, white and ropes of chalk-green ivy. Ravening insomnia still wrecked his nights, lying in wait for him in the small hours, making his fitful sleep so twitchy that in the end he was forced to move his bed into his workroom too. Here he wrote books and articles for the rest of his life on a narrow army-issue camp table squeezed into a corner between cabinets with a lifetime's accumulated images on the walls, going back to military prints and hunting scenes inherited from his Powell and Adcock grandfathers, Picasso's tiny drawing of his mother picked up in student days, and a page of sketches by Michael Ayrton of Constant Lambert conducting on gruelling wartime tours.

Violet became an adept at local auctions and house sales, starting with a successful bid of £1 for a set of five railway engineers, miniature marble busts of Victorian pioneers in Roman togas that stood on top of the bookshelves in the library. She put a second-hand billiard table in the old basement kitchen, and organized ancestral Pakenham games of slosh. Portraits of Wellses, Dymokes and even dimmer ancestors proliferated. Busts multiplied indoors and out. Wyndham Ketton-Cremer supplied a pair in plaster—Antinous and the Roman emperor Caracalla—to fill two tall alcoves in the dining room. Henry Bath at Longleat presented Violet with a larger-than-lifesize stone head of the emperor Caligula because he said it was lopsided, regretting his generosity too late when he found it was highly valuable.

A steady stream of guests passed through the Chantry. Cyril Connolly brought his new wife, the beautiful emaciated Barbara Skelton, who reminded Tony of the vamp with cavernous black eyes and chalk-white skin in cartoons by Charles Addams, himself thought to have numbered among Barbara's many lovers. She was one of three girls said to be able to make or break a London reputation in the 1950s (the other two were Sonia Orwell and the Irish novelist Edna O'Brien). Any ambitious young man hoping to make a name in journalism or the book world was likely to get nowhere unless he could boast of having slept with at least one, preferably all three. Of all his actual and potential wives, Connolly rated Barbara bottom for spirituality but top for sex appeal and, although he didn't say so, she was in a class of her own for raising hell.

"Rage seems to have presided over their ill-starred marriage from the beginning," wrote an obituarist when she died. By her own account, asking the Connollys to stay was like entertaining a couple of battling kangaroos, but their weekend at the Chantry passed off relatively smoothly to the surprise of all concerned, including Barbara herself, who accosted Violet at a party afterwards with her usual truculence: "I hear we behaved so well when we stayed with you that we may even be asked again." Violet was mystified because Barbara's partner at this party was the publisher George Weidenfeld. "How could George resist her?" asked Antonia, who worked for him. "Who could resist her? Barbara was sinuous and sensual with a curving figure like a Modigliani sculpture. Beneath her long hair peeped out a small, almost childlike face: a bewitching naughty child." Connolly divorced her in 1956 on grounds of adultery with Weidenfeld, who promptly married her and published her first novel, divorcing her a few years later on grounds of adultery with Connolly.

The Connollys were followed by a visit from L. P. Hartley, a hospitable Somerset neighbour who lived with a succession of increasingly eccentric manservants just outside Bath, and often drove literary houseguests over for lunch at the Chantry. This time it was Elizabeth Bowen and Eddy Sackville-West, "four novelists . . . seated at the same table," said Violet, describing their strenuous expedition afterwards down to the lake and along its banks, "a nature reserve of tangled thickets and stagnant pools where brontosaurus and pterodactyl might be expected to roam." The Hartley and Powell households got on well, apart from a slight coldness caused by a couple of unfortunate notices in *Punch*, when Tony's attempts to pick reviewers likely to respond favourably to Leslie's novels misfired badly. Jocelyn Brooke was so dismayed by fellow critics' wildly overpraising *The Perfect Woman* that he went too far in the opposite direction, and the same thing happened two years later when Julian Maclaren-Ross savaged *The Hireling*.

Kingsley Amis caused no such problems, spending a weekend at the Chantry with his wife Hilly that spring, and inviting the Powells back to stay with them in Swansea on what turned out to be the start of a regular exchange of visits between Somerset and Wales. The young Amises were relieved to find the Powells' regime as simple and unpretentious as their own, and completely disarmed when

Tony with Kingsley and Hilly Amis, one on each side
of their friend Philip Larkin, who first told them to
read Powell

Violet treated their small urban house in Swansea with old-fashioned country-house courtesy, leaving ten shillings for the bed-maker (happily pocketed by Hilly) on her mantelpiece. Kingsley had read his first Powell novel at Oxford on the recommendation of his friend Philip Larkin, and "immediately recognised a talent and a way of looking at the world utterly congenial to me." Tony for his part found *Lucky Jim* immensely funny, saluting Amis in *Punch* as the most promising young novelist to emerge for years with an underlying commitment to the art of writing, heightened by "more than a touch of Swiftean horror . . . at the goings-on of human beings, particularly their sexual antics."

In the public mind the pair of them conveniently embodied opposing sides in an acrimonious flare-up, sparked by John Osborne's *Look Back in Anger* in 1956, between angry dynamic go-ahead young men and their stubborn obsolete obstructive elders. At the end of 1957 the BBC arranged for Amis to interview Powell in what was clearly meant to be a head-on confrontation: "lower-class malcontent . . . having a good go at somebody whom he would see as an upper-class git," was Kingsley's guess at the intended programme. In the event their companionable studio discussion of the latest volume of the *Dance* was interrupted by the producer, explaining disgustedly that was not at all what he had in mind only to be cut short in turn by

Tony: "'We don't care what you want. We're going to do what we want. And if you don't like it, we're walking out this minute. Now.' What impressed me about this utterance, even more than its style and content, was its placid, conversational delivery . . . ," Amis wrote more than thirty years later: "that short speech of Tony's knocked all the fight out of the producer."

1957 was the year mains water pipes finally reached the Chantry. The engineers laid an open trench across the entrance to the drive and knocked off for the weekend on a Friday night when Harry and Rosie d'Avigdor-Goldsmid were coming to stay. Violet had known Rosie from debutante days. Harry, a faithful fan of Tony's, was a bullion broker descended from two great Jewish banking dynasties. A handsome and commanding personality with "an almost Renaissance range and depth of abilities," a sardonic wit and an outstanding war record, he had inherited his father's baronetcy at the beginning of the war together with Somerhill, a Jacobean pile in Kent eclipsed in size only by the Sackville-Wests' at Knole. Energetically restored to its original splendour, the house now stood among shaven lawns, beech trees and bluebell woods, its greenhouses "hung with incomparable nectarines," the dark panelled rooms indoors glowing "with Sisleys and Vlamincks and enormous Rothkos." A stream of guests from the more glamorous echelons of politics, business, society and the arts filled Somerhill at weekends. "Harry and Rosie Goldsmid entertained there on a scale the house cannot have experienced since the Earl of Essex's widow . . . in 1613," wrote Violet's nephew Ferdy Mount, a close friend of the Goldsmids' daughter Sarah.

Violet herself remembered dancing in the ballroom at Somerhill with Harry, who left her briefly to whirl Elizabeth Taylor round the floor, reporting sadly on his return that "Miss Taylor was too much in love with Michael Wilding for any impression to be made on her." Harry, a former deputy lieutenant and high sheriff of Kent, was now Tory MP for Walsall South. The two families had got to know each other in the spring of 1948, when the Powells borrowed a cottage in Kent and the Goldsmids invited them over for a first taste of Somerhill's munificent hospitality ("After six years of wartime austerity one could feel very grateful for a bucket or two of champagne"). Tony had already begun *A Question of Upbringing*, and Harry followed the sequence with close attention from the start. He was himself a mag-

Harry d'Avigdor-Goldsmid with his family
at Somerhill (Sarah is on the left) in the years
when he became prime business consultant to
the *Dance*

nate comparable in wealth and stature, if not in temperament or character, with Sir Magnus Donners of Stourwater Castle, at one point
Widmerpool's employer in the *Dance*. Harry read *The Acceptance
World* in proof, and acted intermittently as a kind of business consultant on successive books. "Goldsmid's knowledge of the City, the
complexities of financial dealings, especially on their comic side, was
of incalculable value to me," Tony wrote long afterwards. For almost
twenty years Harry offered advice, checked proofs and made suggestions, becoming progressively more fascinated by the movement of
the *Dance*. "I am very proud to have been the least of your collabora-
tors . . ." he wrote of the current novel: "now that I am 'on the team'
I feel my responsibilities very keenly."

At Lady Molly's was finished in July 1957, the same month that
Evelyn Waugh published *The Ordeal of Gilbert Pinfold*, which Tony

considered probably the best thing he ever wrote. As West Country neighbours the two families saw more of one another in the 1950s. Violet, driving the boys to visit their Clive cousins at Whitfield in school holidays, often broke her journey at Piers Court in Stinchcombe with the Waughs. Once Evelyn threatened to give his children away to Lady Violet, who was taken aback when, far from protesting, they piled eagerly into her car and had to be forcibly extracted. The younger Waughs dined in the servants' quarters behind a red baize door for fear their presence at table might annoy their father, who was said on one occasion to have been so infuriated by their noise that he burst through the baize door shouting, "Let there be no laughter in my house." Violet feared another outburst when John joined the others with the servants and made them roar with laughter, but to her relief Evelyn contained himself. He had moved with his family earlier that year to Combe Florey in Somerset, just over an hour's drive from the Chantry. "Alick has a theory that the slump in properties on the Wiltshire border will now lift, as the fear is over," Tony wrote to Violet, as soon as Waugh's new neighbours heard the news, "and they will rise in value . . . Gloucestershire too, I suppose." He and Evelyn now sometimes coincided on the train from London, travelling back to Somerset together on the Paddington to Plymouth line.

Pinfold is a barely fictionalized account of an appalling experience three years earlier when Evelyn, a veteran insomniac like Tony, booked a passage alone on a cargo boat sailing for Rangoon, and found himself tormented night and day by threatening voices that disturbed him so deeply he feared madness or demonic possession. The doctor he consulted on his return diagnosed hallucinations, caused by the large quantities of bromide he took to make him sleep. On his recovery he described exactly what had happened in *Pinfold*, "the most searching of Waugh's works," said Tony: "the 'voices' on the boat seem to me to make a sequence unequalled in their combined funniness and macabre horror." Waugh in his early fifties—"stout and splenetic, red-faced and reactionary"—had by now perfected his chosen persona, a kind of burlesque country gentleman with cigar and ear-trumpet, dressed in grey bowler hat and spongebag tweeds of the loudest check, looking as Tony said like "a prosperous bookie on the way to Newmarket." On the face of it the two had little in common. Their circles barely overlapped. Waugh made a point of heartily disliking two of Tony's closest friends, Alick Dru and Malcolm Muggeridge ("Your galloping major is not to be expelled from Pratt's," wrote Evelyn, who had hoped he might be, "it is thought he would get the club talked about in undesirable quarters").

Professionally speaking, their careers had run parallel from the start, when Powell's early books were often dismissed as imitation Waugh by people who failed to read them closely. If Waugh won hands down in terms of popularity and sales, Tony of all people understood what it cost him in loneliness, self-doubt and annihilating depression. "I am delighted to hear *Pinfold* made you laugh," Evelyn wrote: "It is so much a slice of autobiography that I find it impossible to judge." Tony admired above all in Waugh a relentless honesty, quite different from his own but no less exacting, and the ability to carry off a tour de force like Pinfold's voyage: "a really brilliant piece of technique, I thought." What captivated Waugh was the fluidity of the *Dance*, and the way its characters generate warmth and a mysterious living energy quite unlike the brilliant hard glitter of his own creations.

"I had been looking forward to it like seven days' leave, and read it without interruption," he wrote on publication of *At Lady Molly's*, which remained ever after his favourite volume of the series. "In the opening pages I felt the void of Widmerpool really aching—I could not have borne another page's delay of his entry. Did you intend him to dominate the series when you introduced him in the first volume?" Tony had been as surprised as anyone, according to Violet, when Widmerpool showed signs of taking on a momentum of his own. Harry Goldsmid even suggested killing him off at this point but Widmerpool overruled him, acquiring in the end, like Shakespeare's Falstaff or Dickens's Mr. Micawber, an identity beyond his fictional origins, becoming even for people who had never read the *Dance* the essence of a harsh, officious and manipulative greed for power.

In *At Lady Molly's* Jenkins has moved on from a dead-end publishing job to a low-grade film company ("It may lead to something better," says Widmerpool severely: "If you are industrious, you get on. That is true of all professions, even the humblest"). Marriage looms for his contemporaries, several of whom have already tried it without conspicuous success. Even Widmerpool turns up with a formidable fiancée at a seedy party given by Lady Molly Jeavons, one of those shambolic gatherings that galvanize the *Dance* at intervals. War, omnipresent for this generation, puts down markers in the person of Widmerpool's prospective brother-in-law, General Conyers, and Lady Molly's husband, Ted Jeavons, an unemployed ex-soldier first encountered polishing cars at the Olympia Motor Show (he was immediately singled out as a remarkable invention by Elizabeth Bowen). At the Jeavonses' party Jenkins first comes across the Tolland family, headed by the socialist peer Lord Erridge, known as Erry, a gaunt ungainly narcissist dressed like a tramp with a retinue of spongers and left-wing hangers-on orchestrated by J. G. Quiggin. It is after a meal of bangers and mash with these two at the Tollands' dilapidated country seat that Nicholas Jenkins first sets eyes on Erry's younger sister, Isobel, a meeting that looks back to Violet's unexpected arrival at Pakenham Hall more than twenty years before:

> Would it be too explicit, exaggerated, to say that when I set eyes on Isobel Tolland I knew at once that I should marry her? Something like that is the truth . . . it was as if I had known her for many years already; enjoyed happiness with her and suffered sadness . . . I remember chiefly a sense of tremendous inevitability, a feeling that fate was settling its own problems, and too much reflection would be out of place.

This is as close as the *Dance* ever comes to direct autobiography: Isobel figures in subsequent volumes less as a character in her own right than as a faint but perceptible source of warmth and generosity in the narrator's hinterland.

Critical response when the book came out in October reflected a division that persisted in readers of Powell's *Dance* between, on the one hand, those who found it too uneventful, too low key, altogether too lacking in conventional drama or plot line and, on the other, those who recognized the tone and texture of life itself. In the autumn of 1957 nothing provoked more violent argument at the nation's dinner tables, according to a contemporary commentator, than "the Suez crisis . . . and the novels of Anthony Powell. He is an unexpectedly mild person to have this explosive effect . . . Yet—far more, for example, than Iris Murdoch, Kingsley Amis, John Osborne or any of the other young writers—there is a quality of such strong individuality about

Anthony Powell that his novels can divide [a dinner table] with the sudden fierceness of a civil war."

Tony had been made a CBE the year before ("I hope it doesn't block you for a knighthood," wrote Waugh. "That is what one really needs"), and he won the James Tait Black Prize for *At Lady Molly's*. His publisher's advances, creeping very slowly upwards, had now reached £500, a third of what he earned in a year from part-time attendance at *Punch*. The atmosphere in Bouverie Street was becoming increasingly strained by this time. Muggeridge had steadily lost interest in the paper as his TV career consumed more and more time and energy, releasing inner tensions that "coursed like electricity through the *Punch* office . . ." The old easy-going days when he and Tony swapped stories, laid plans and made one another laugh had long gone. "I could sense an immediate buzzing in my own nerves on crossing the threshold of the editor's door," said Tony. A series of editorial lapses and misjudgements culminated in a relatively trivial disagreement with the proprietors, who finally sacked Muggeridge in the late summer of 1957.

Although the paper almost immediately reverted to its traditional stuffiness and predictability, the books pages were initially unaffected. This was the point at which Francis Wyndham submitted some unpublished short stories by V. S. Naipaul, whose first novel was about to come out from André Deutsch: "That's *just* what we want," said Tony. He published a favourable review of *The Mystic Masseur* in *Punch*, and wrote to suggest a meeting, explaining over lunch that he recognized in Naipaul's novel an unforced lyricism present in every serious writer's earliest work. "I was twenty-five and awkward, poor in London, with one book published," Naipaul wrote long afterwards: "For a reason I couldn't understand . . . he offered his friendship." Naturally suspicious and mistrustful, Naipaul was baffled not only by Tony's tact and kindness but by the trouble he took to make his professional career financially viable, finding him work, recommending him for a BBC traineeship, intervening on his behalf with literary editors. Looking back fifty years later, Naipaul celebrated Tony's innate genius for friendship:

He delighted in his friends, saw them all as special, liked as it were to walk round them, to see all sides of their character; and he did so

Vidia Naipaul in the late 1950s, when Tony
served as his gateway to literary London, as well
as becoming a close friend

without malice. The absence of malice was the great revelation . . .
I loved the Tony who was like John Aubrey, the collector of people
and their oddities, the man who seldom censured, and thought that
people and especially his friends made the world glamorous . . .
This was the England I had wanted to find, and had given up looking for. The "lyrical quality" of a first book: I had never heard any
literary judgement so profound spoken so easily; there was a depth
of civilisation there. And there was that depth, too, in Tony's attitude to people. I consciously began to copy that: it became part of
my own personality.

Himself an expert on slight and rebuff, still unfamiliar with the
financial stringency of the British book world, Naipaul was dismayed
to discover that Tony's high literary reputation was no guarantee of
earning power, and shocked by the contemptuous way he was treated
by his new editor at *Punch*. The cartoonist Bernard Hollowood, formally appointed to succeed Muggeridge, was a throwback to the old
regime, a trained economist and mediocre draughtsman with minimal

sense of humour, who took a dim view of the book pages, reversed Tony's innovations, and frequently remarked in public that he could fill the review columns himself. Tony had no choice but to put up with him. Any review he wrote himself generated extra income on top of his salary and, as he explained to Bob Vanderbilt, he stepped up contributions in the summer of 1958 in order to repay a substantial sum borrowed from his publisher to buy a field, earmarked otherwise for commercial development next to the Chantry. "That was a job full of humiliation for him," said Naipaul.

Tristram had left Eton in the spring, departing for Aix-en-Provence to spend three months with a local family brushing up his French. At the end of May his parents drove down through France to visit him in a new, pale blue Austin Cambridge, spending three weeks on the kind of leisurely journey they most enjoyed, putting in "some fairly heavy eating and drinking on the way," and stopping as always to watch the *flâneurs* in striped blazers on the front at Cabourg. In August Tony attended his first literary conference, organized for the Société Européenne de Culture in Venice by a high-powered fixer called Umberto Campagnolo. "The meetings are nonsensical & boring beyond all guessing," Tony reported briskly, but he enjoyed the absurdity of being momentarily swept up in Venice's international high life. When Alan Pryce-Jones left his bathing-suit behind at a party, it was returned to him in Harry's Bar by Lady Diana Cooper. The multimillionaire Don Carlos de Bestegui showed delegates round his elaborately restored Palazzo Labia, a baroque building with a vast high-ceilinged ballroom frescoed by Tiepolo. "It was more like Sir Magnus Donners at Stourwater than you can imagine," wrote Tony, describing the tour for Violet as well as the drinks party that followed, given by Victor Cunard of the shipping dynasty, "now reduced to about four rooms, only one with a painted ceiling." Fifteen years later this visit had a sequel, when Tony invented a sumptuous Tiepolo fresco of his own on the ceiling of an imaginary Venetian palace in *Temporary Kings*, the penultimate volume of the *Dance*.

That autumn he went back to work on the fifth volume, moving slowly as usual in these early stages, breaking off to lunch with Kingsley Amis, who wanted Tony to meet Philip Larkin, already a poet to be reckoned with, and a close reader of the *Dance*. They swapped gossip, cracked jokes, drank a lot, and Larkin took photographs, posting a couple to the Chantry afterwards: "In the small one I fancy you & K look like father & son on Speech Day. You've just tipped him a fiver." The two of them got on well, sending one another copies of their respective books and exchanging letters intermittently for the rest of Larkin's life, a correspondence based on mutual admiration and a growing affection that co-existed, as always on the poet's part, with the sneering derision he trained on his friends behind their backs. If Tony suspected that Philip called him a horse-faced dwarf with Kingsley in private, it didn't stop him enjoying their company, and including both in the circle of his friends, reinforced over the next decade as his family began to split up. John started his first half at Eton that September, and Tristram was about to leave for Oxford. Violet had begun work on a memoir of her childhood with encouragement from Tony.

Nothing had prepared either of them for what happened next. In the first week of December Bernard Hollowood sacked his literary editor on the grounds that the paper could no longer afford him. "I thought it might amuse you that I am leaving *Punch* in the New Year," Tony wrote to Jocelyn Brooke: "It is really rather a relief, though a bore to have to reorganise one's affairs." All his later accounts of what happened strike the same dry, casual, even flippant note, a trick Tony had learned early to control the helpless rage and misery that in his father always remained ungovernable. His immediate reaction had been unguarded anger, bitterness and shock. "He took it very badly," said Paul Johnson, then a young leader-writer on the *New Statesman*, who witnessed his distress that day: "he hadn't seen it coming, and he couldn't understand what had hit him." For once Tony was knocked off balance with nothing to fall back on and no hold on the future. "He got very drunk," said Paul, who spent the evening with him: "I more or less put him to bed. I felt very sorry for him that night."

Tony was a first-rate editor. In the past eight years he had made *Punch* a force to be reckoned with in the book world, and it had given him in return a London base for social life as well as a practical outlet for his habitual generosity to other writers, especially struggling young unknowns. It also solved his financial problems. This sharp reminder of the precariousness of the freelance life came a week or two short of his fifty-third birthday. He had no capital, his mother's legacy had largely been expended on refurbishing the house, and his father showed no sign of regulating expenditure in line with the exigencies of his army pension: if anything in his mid-seventies Philip Powell intensified his running feud with the hotel manageress, whose ability to tolerate his truculence, and the friction he caused with fellow residents, was almost at an end.

Immediate offers of help came from Tony's publisher and from the *Daily Telegraph*. Heinemann's proposal to make him a literary adviser came to nothing, but he remained in his new job as one of the *Telegraph*'s lead reviewers for more than quarter of a century. Slowly he remade his life. He still went up to London a couple of times a month to pick through the review copies, and lunch with friends at the Travellers. "I would see him grow abstracted, slightly hunched, deeply melancholy," Naipaul said of these meetings. In the months that followed Tony abandoned his old compartmentalized schedule divided between the capital and the country, switching each week from the ceaseless commotion of his office to the solitude and silence of his writing regime at home. Now he worked at the Chantry to a different rhythm, breaking off once a fortnight for the short sprint of a review before returning to the disciplined marathon of the *Dance*.

The new book, *Casanova's Chinese Restaurant*, was completed in November 1959, and recognized at once by Violet as "an infinitely touching memorial to Constant Lambert." At the time of Lambert's death eight years earlier, Tony had made "absolutely Herculean efforts to produce a biography," realizing after three prospective biographers shelved the book in turn that his only practical alternative was to do it himself in fictional form. Perhaps he remembered Lambert's joke, when conducting a concert before the war in Budapest, that he couldn't decide whether to dress "in a cloak & slouch hat as a character from William Le Queux [romantic author of spy thrillers]," or to wear his own clothes and go as a character out of one of Tony's books.

The character at the centre of *Casanova's Chinese Restaurant* is the conductor and composer Hugh Moreland, who has Lambert's looks and background, his idiosyncratic humour and many of his eccentric tastes. Moreland's voice—wry, sharp and funny—discussing life and art, power, death and the human condition permeates the later stages of the *Dance* much as Ralph Barnby's pithier and more pungent comments thread through the early volumes. He operates within a musical community that parallels Lambert's London circle of musicians, chief among them the misogynist Maclintick, a brilliantly grotesque, ultimately tragic character incorporating traits from both Philip Heseltine and the *Manchester Guardian*'s fierce, morose, heavy-drinking music critic, Cecil Gray. The stormy trajectory of Moreland's marriage to the actress Matilda Wilson—a forceful and engaging personality who more than holds her own in the male-oriented world of the 1930s—is replayed in a harsher, wilder key by Maclintick's squalid ménage with his hair-raising wife Audrey.

But Moreland himself comes most powerfully alive in a friendship with the narrator that re-creates the deep and strong affinity between Lambert and Tony from the days when they frequented Maxim's Chinese restaurant in Wardour Street together, and first heard the song—"strong and marvellously sweet"—sung by a crippled girl working her beat in that corner of Soho. *Casanova* begins with memories of listening with Moreland to the street-singer, and ends with a trip he and Jenkins once took together on a fairground ghost railway that became for both a graphic image of everyday life, and later by extension of the *Dance* itself:

> slowly climbing sheer gradients, sweeping with frenzied speed into inky depths, turning blind corners from which black, gibbering bogeys leapt to attack, rushing headlong towards iron studded doors, threatened by imminent collision, fingered by spectral hands, moving at last with dreadful, ever-increasing momentum towards a shape that lay across the line.

On 2 December 1959 the Powells celebrated their silver wedding with a party at the Travellers for more than a hundred people from sixteen to well over seventy years of age, virtually everyone they knew who was not too befuddled by drink (like Henry Yorke, now a confirmed alcoholic), or geographically too remote (like John Heygate, ensconced with a third wife on his Irish estate), to make the journey. Tony said the party passed in a flash so that before he knew it he was helping to sweep out the club at 1:30 next morning, and laying the tables for breakfast. "I only wish, like parties one has heard of in Monarchist Russia or was it China, that it had gone on for several days to enable one to fully explore all the vistas which it opened up," wrote Adrian Daintrey, recalling the great elegiac party at the end of Proust's novel: "I thought Gerald definitely brought an atmosphere of *Time Regained* to the whole scene, with his snowy hair . . ."

A few days later the manageress of the Morshead Hotel at Richmond rang with an ultimatum, demanding the immediate expulsion of Lieutenant Colonel Powell. Tony was given a week's grace to organize his transfer on doctor's orders to a nursing home, a far from straightforward transaction over Christmas given the shortage of available funds and his father's bitter resistance to the move. On the last day of the year, Violet travelled up to London to break the news to her father-in-law, who pre-empted alternative plans for his future by dying the same day. He was buried on 4 January in the churchyard at the Chantry. Walking back from the funeral Tony heard a muffled explosion from a neighbouring quarry that sounded, as he said to Tristram, like Grandfather being received in the next world.

Unpredictable to the last, Colonel Powell had formed a habit during his long retirement of dropping in, sometimes several times a day, to see his bank manager, who had for many years made cautious share and gilt-edged investments on his behalf. When Tony paid a routine visit to Mr. Winch of the Westminster Bank in Curzon Street, he learned that he stood to inherit under his father's will, in trust for Tristram and John after his death, £174,350 4s 6d (the equivalent, even after paying tax at 55 per cent, of more than £1.5 million in today's money). This was the last thing he had anticipated. Presumably his father had extracted a miser's satisfaction from the contrast between sham penury and secret wealth. Perhaps there was an underlying element of compensation, conscious or not, for his lifelong derogation of Tony.

"It was a pleasure to his friends to be with this new, relaxed man, to see the old melancholy drop away . . . ," wrote Vidia Naipaul, describing Tony's response to his father's death. Financial security stabilized his life, and opened up possibilities for the *Dance*. Over the next two years as he worked on the sixth volume, Tony for the first time openly envisaged expanding the sequence to twelve novels with the next one marking the halfway point. "The old magic works again," Evelyn Waugh wrote when it came out, defining the *Dance to the Music of Time* in a single image that has never yet been bettered:

> The life of the series is generated within it . . . Less original novelists tenaciously follow their protagonists. In the *Music of Time* we watch through the glass of a tank; one after another various specimens swim towards us; we see them clearly, then with a barely perceptible flick of fin or tail, they are off into the murk. That is how our encounters occur in real life. Friends and acquaintances approach or recede year by year . . . Their presence has no particular significance. It is recorded as part of the permeating and inebriating atmosphere of the haphazard which is the essence of Mr. Powell's art.

10

1960–75

T he *Dance* had no written blueprint but at some point, probably round about the time he moved to the Chantry and revised his novel's scope and scale, Tony began filling a second scrapbook. His first, *Dream Memories*, had served as prelude to his early books, and this new red scrapbook opens with what looks like a declaration of intent: a dwarfish puppeteer in curled wig and brocaded coat presenting on a raised stage at his back a performance called "Powell's puppet show."

The showman was Tony's formidable namesake, Martin Powell, said to be so popular in the 1770s that he could lure whole congregations out of St. Paul's Church in Covent Garden: pasted above him, slightly off centre, is a tiny snapshot of Tony himself in peaked cap and military greatcoat. Sticking scraps on to almost any surface had been a craze among bright hard-up young things before the war, a characteristically English nursery form of surrealism: the Powells decorated a scrap screen together at the start of their marriage; Evelyn Waugh covered a coal scuttle in his own early days as a married man. Tony's pre-war dust jackets relied on a more sophisticated use of cut-outs, and two decades later he was still at work with glue and scissors, sprucing up a filing cabinet or the spare-room wardrobe in odd moments at the Chantry.

Collage seemed to clear his mind, offer new possibilities, sometimes even to throw up patterns that anticipate developments in the *Dance*. A brutal eighteenth-century brothel scene to the left of Powell's puppet show is balanced on the right by a nubile naked girl on a Fragonard-style swing and surmounted by two flirting couples, the

"Powell's puppet show"

probing pointed toe of one of the lovers encroaching suggestively on the rape about to take place in the bedroom below: a rococo extravaganza that foreshadows Peter Templer's performance as Lust at the end of one of Donners's dinner parties, the last of several tableaux played out against tapestries representing the Seven Deadly Sins at Stourwater Castle in *The Kindly Ones*. This particular charade in the autumn of 1938 is broken up by the arrival of Widmerpool in military uniform, an absurd, incongruous, faintly menacing reminder of the inevitability of war in the aftermath of the Munich Agreement.

The red scrapbook continues conventionally enough with a double-page spread of snapshots showing the battlefields of Normandy after the Allied landings in 1944. Prosaic black-and-white scenes of wastage, blasted tree-trunks, chunks of twisted metal, are neatly aligned in pairs and pasted in above a pre-Raphaelite costume drama enacted by a cast in brightly coloured velvets, rearing and plunging in poses of extravagant mourning, grief or shock. The combination of fake emotion and authentic devastation is quintessentially Powellian. In one form or another it permeates the *Dance*, producing some of his subtlest and most startling effects.

As a novelist he excels at the cross-cutting, overlapping, interleaving techniques of collage, relishing its disconcerting and expressive power in sequences like the Seven Deadly Sins tableaux, or in the entire complex construction of *The Kindly Ones*, where memory rakes back and forth, expanding and contracting, telescoping past and present as it ranges over both world wars in the pivotal central movement of the *Dance*. "I want to make the outbreak of war something of a watershed," Tony told John Heygate, "this being the sixth volume and half way." *The Kindly Ones* starts with a flashback to the narrator's childhood in the summer of 1914. Impending catastrophe is presented in double focus, viewed in hindsight by the middle-aged narrator, and seen simultaneously with a child's piercing clarity by his younger self, eight years old when a minor incident in the Balkans sets in motion a process that will lead over the next four years to the end of the known world.

Nicholas Jenkins at Stonedene, like the young Anthony Powell at Stonehurst, registers the responses of his parents and their friends together with a gathering sense of unease articulated by the local crank, Dr. Trelawney, arriving with a pack of white-robed disciples as Dr. Oyler used to do in Tony's youth on Ludshott Common. Trelawney's rhetorical gibberish about loosening the bonds of Time and Space underlines the blank reaction of virtually everyone else present to news of an obscure assassination in Sarajevo. Almost quarter of a century later, Trelawney resurfaces in the second half of the book, reduced by time and chance to little more than a vagrant member of "the proud, anonymous secretive race that dwell in residential hotels," living from hand to mouth without followers or resources:

> All was changed. Even the beard, straggling, dirty, grey, stained yellow in places . . . had lost all resemblance to that worn by the athletic, vigorous prophet of those distant days. Once broad and luxuriant, it was now shrivelled almost to a goatee . . . His skin was dry and blotched. Dark spectacles covered his eyes . . . His smile was one of the worst things about him.

This encounter with Trelawney washed up in a shabby seaside boarding house is one of the most memorable of Powell's many transformation scenes. Still intoning prophecies of doom in a

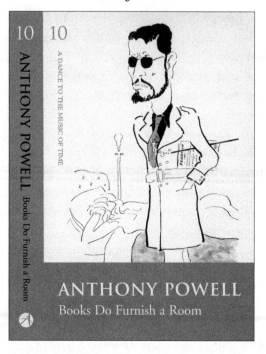

Dr. Trelawney was one of the very few characters transferred, like X. Trapnel (above), more or less directly from fact to fiction in the *Dance.*

drug-induced rant—part Mithraic, part classical, wholly bogus—Trelawney becomes, even in his shrunken state, once again a harbinger of war, like Widmerpool, in October 1938.

"To the novelist, the characters in his novel are known as those in a dream are known," said Tony, "the texture too complicated to be explained." Crude and reductive attempts to pair individuals in the *Dance* with real-life models exasperated him, although inevitably in fiction, as in dreams, characters take shape from a starting point in real people. A few survived the transfer more or less intact. Barbara Skelton reappears as the fearsome Pamela Flitton, for instance, and Julian Maclaren-Ross as the novelist X. Trapnel, a vigorous figment who makes his original look pallid by comparison: "it is Trapnel who seems the master figure," said Walter Allen, "and Julian whom he inspired."

Many, probably most, characters are multiple in origin. The popu-

lar and prolific Edwardian man of letters, St. John Clarke, who epitomized vanity, bathos and complacency to the young Jenkins, was
based by Tony's own account on a combination of Hugh Walpole,
Logan Pearsall Smith and the Anglo-Irish veteran Sir Horace Plun-
kett. Others rely on involuntary borrowings—a dash of Bowra in
the power-mongering don Sillery, hints of Muggeridge in the hack
journalist, Lindsay Bagshaw—not always obvious at the time even
to the novelist. But surface likeness lends neither reality nor depth. If
Hugh Moreland owes something to Constant Lambert, Ralph Barnby
to Adrian Daintrey, Jean Duport to Marion Coates, all of them rely
for their energy and their opaque, many-layered individuality on
"invention, imagination, the creative instinct." Or, as Evelyn Waugh
succinctly put it, "the life of the series is generated within it."

The more powerful the creation, the more complex and mysterious its origins. Widmerpool's roots run deep and wide. In the summer before the war, when Tony was filling in time with odds and ends
of genealogical research, he lunched with a man called Alan Bishop,
whom he met while ferreting about among Westminster's parish
records. "He is too extraordinary," he reported to Violet at Dynevor:
"He tells me he thinks of nothing but making a career. I think he's
really a character out of one of my books who wants to be put back."
Bishop was in his early thirties, diligent but dull, with a second-class
degree from Keble College, Oxford, and little to show for it but a
handful of ill-paid, short-term jobs that led nowhere. He was unpopular, friendless and solitary, "a rum sort of character, impenetrable,
remote . . . no gossip or small talk at all." His looks were as unprepossessing as his manner. He was thickset and coarse-featured with a
fixed expression, and something about his stubborn certainty transfixed Tony.

In fact Bishop's post-war career went nowhere. He became a humble Reader in paleography at Cambridge, specializing in a subsection
of early mediaeval codicology, achieving neither a university post
nor a college fellowship, "his advance blocked by total lack of diplomatic skill or interest in other people." His reaction to a PhD student
who submitted a learned article suggests that what caught Tony's
attention was an authentic whiff, at once absurd and paranoid, of
the will to power. "The title alone . . . will get it into bibliographies.
You should be very far from satisfied with this degree of accept-

ability," was Bishop's discouraging advice to a future mediaeval scholar: "or with anything short of *complete control over your readers' minds.*"

Bishop's own impact on readers' minds, in his lifetime or afterwards, probably depends on that single brief encounter in 1939 when Tony recognized him as a character waiting to be put back into a book, where he belonged. His was the first of many contributions feeding into Kenneth Widmerpool like tribute streams into a river. Denis Capel-Dunn, Tony's principal at the Cabinet Office in 1943, was a prime source, and so was his commanding officer in military liaison, Colonel Carlisle. Other more or less improbable influences suggested at one point or another include Harold Macmillan's attorney general, Sir Reginald Manningham-Buller; a later Tory prime minister, Edward Heath; and Tony's brother-in-law Frank Pakenham, who succeeded to the family title as Lord Longford on Edward's death in 1961. To the end of both their lives Frank insisted, in spite of Tony's flat denials, that he was the model not only for the down-at-heel socialist peer, Lord Erridge, but for Widmerpool as well.

Further input came from Gerald Reitlinger, whose career, like Widmerpool's, was viewed in startlingly different lights by his professional peers on the one hand, and his dismissive old friends on the other. To people who had attended his parties before the war, Reitlinger still seemed a ludicrously gauche and ineffectual outsider, physically clumsy, sexually null and socially tone-deaf, harbouring ambitions impossible for anyone to take seriously. His neighbour, Malcolm Muggeridge, saw him as both preposterous and pitiable, shut up at Woodgate like a hermit, pulling his blinds down earlier each day: "Now the early afternoon, soon after lunch, until the time comes that they are never pulled up at all. Gerald in the shadows with his Ming china, accumulating sales room information about the shifting price of pictures . . . He spoke to me yesterday from his solitude with a note of desperation in his voice, like a man desperately breaking out from a prison in which he knew he was incarcerated for ever."

By any objective standard, Reitlinger's achievements were formidable by the early 1960s. Having completed a trilogy that defined the field of Holocaust studies for years to come, he was currently working on a second pioneering three-part study that for the first time subjected the economics of the art market to meticulous historical analysis. His own collection had no rival, whether for its superlative quality, its uniquely systematic documentation or its breathtaking extent. By now it filled every corner of his house from the dining room richly hung with Japanese polychrome, the bedrooms decorated with blue-and-white ware from China and Korea, the stairwell lined from top to bottom with sixteenth- and seventeenth-century Swatow plates, and even the bathroom stocked with Iznik plates, to the overflowing room originally fitted up with floor-to-ceiling glass cases as a museum on the first floor: "On the chimney piece, in the fireplace, on the covered-over Russian billiard table . . . along the window sill in serried ranks, there were vases, bottles and bowls."

Reitlinger's circle, in so far as he had one, now consisted of fellow specialists and collectors who recognized in him, alongside his passionate commitment to oriental porcelain, a pervasive and ironic humour based on what Sir Alan Bullock called his "varied, if sceptical experience of human nature." A key element in that experience had evidently been the miscellaneous weekend guests so indiscriminately assembled in his pre-war heyday at Woodgate, where Muggeridge remembered first meeting Tony at "such a house-party as the Stourwater one . . . These gatherings were like a curtain-raiser in preview of the *Dance to the Music of Time*." If so, they belonged to the more ramshackle end of the narrator's spectrum. The comfortlessness of Woodgate, and its host's decidedly primitive housekeeping, could not compete with the hospitality of Sir Magnus Donners, who entertained at Stourwater on the same lavish scale as Harry and Rosie Goldsmid at Somerhill.

Tony had dedicated *Casanova's Chinese Restaurant* to them and, when he set to work on *The Kindly Ones*, Harry sent him regular memos, setting out in minute detail with bullet points possible developments for Widmerpool's career. 1961 was the year Goldsmid became chairman of the Anglo-Israel Bank but nothing distracted him from Magnus Donners's business dealings: "This is priority 1 in my affairs." It was Harry who had been responsible for Widmerpool's job as manager of the pension fund at Donners Brebner ("into this department were shifted the duds who had failed to make it elsewhere"), and for his subsequent fiasco over commodity investment ("I would think that Donners would not dream of telling an ass like Widmerpool the real reason for his chrome purchases, namely expectation of war"). Tony built up over time an extensive team of consultants—Benjamin Britten advised on the music world in *Casanova*, Basil Boothroyd on the mindset of Welsh bank clerks for *The Valley of Bones*—but none so nearly blurred the bounds of fact and fiction as Harry Goldsmid, who identified unreservedly with his fictional counterpart, assuming Donners's personality, viewing plot developments through his eyes, even speaking authoritatively in Donners's voice. "I felt nervous about chrome," he wrote on receiving his finished copy, "but you have handled the incident with the trained negligence of the *Financial Times* commodity report."

Donners admittedly has a darker manipulative and predatory side, contributed partly perhaps by Sir George Sitwell, Osbert's father, whose brooding presence oppressed his children's guests at Renishaw before the war. Sir George's unnerving remarks about mediaeval painted chambers ("strange . . . very strange . . . rather horrible at times") convey the same ghoulish relish as Sir Magnus's insistence on touring the dungeons with his Stourwater house party ("*this is where we should put the girls who don't behave*"). The Sitwells were currently in vogue again, especially Edith, encrusted in jewellery, bedizened in brocade, a major celebrity in her sixties and seventies at parties and on platforms, radio and TV. "She's become a mixture of the Blessed Virgin Mary and Queen Elizabeth," said Ivy Compton-Burnett. Osbert achieved a more dubious notoriety as one of D. H. Lawrence's models for Sir Clifford in *Lady Chatterley's Lover*, itself on trial at the start of the sixties for attempting to deprave and corrupt the British public. Tony attended the trial as a witness for the defence. "I envy you *Lady Chatterley*," wrote Graham Greene, smarting over his rejection by the legal team, but Tony was relieved when the case collapsed without his intervention, finding the book for all its impact on sexual liberation didactic, implausible and impossible to defend in strictly literary terms.

He himself aimed to reach the *Dance*'s halfway point by the end of 1961. For a decade now he had produced a book every other year, barely missing a morning at the desk, starting a new novel while his publishers read the typescript of the one before it, often halfway through the next before they got round to publishing the last. The pace was gruelling but necessary, given that each fresh instalment was part of the same whole. One of his strategies for dealing with his tough schedule was to leave the country as often as he could. After his father's death, he and Violet had decided to spend their unexpected fortune largely on foreign travel, starting immediately in the spring of 1960 with a fortnight at sea, cruising through the Mediterranean via Sardinia and Sicily, down the northern coast of Africa and crossing back again to Greece, where they walked the Sacred Way to the Temple of Apollo at Delphi as they had done on their honeymoon nearly thirty years before.

The cruise was laid on by a small adventurous family firm in Market Harborough founded by W. F. Swan, who ran each cruise with his son Ken as a highly enjoyable party for between two and three hundred people on a small comfortable ship with excellent food, a convivial atmosphere and a great deal to do. Swan Hellenic organized almost daily excursions to view the monuments and ruins of classical antiquity, many of them recently excavated and still barely known in these years of post-war austerity when a strict travel allowance of £50 per person made abroad more or less off limits for the British tourist. Passengers were entertained on board by relays of lecturers, headed by the archaeologist Sir Mortimer Wheeler, one of TV's earliest household names, like Malcolm Muggeridge. Wheeler's innate showmanship, combined with an expertise both scholarly and practical, made him an even match for the most eminent of his fellow lecturers, who on this occasion was Maurice Bowra. Any lingering ill-will between Maurice and Tony evaporated when the two sat side by side on the coach, talking all the way from Milan to join their ship at Genoa. Fellow passengers included former neighbours from Chester Gate, Elizabeth and Christopher Glenconner with their twelve-year-old daughter, Catherine, who was an old friend of the Powells' son John (John's elder brother Tristram, in his last year at Oxford, found himself fully occupied elsewhere).

This first cruise was such a success that the Powells booked another the year after, taking Antonia with them this time and sailing from Venice down the Adriatic, along the western coast of Greece, past Crete to Beirut, where they caught a small plane inland to Petra. Swan's passengers entered the narrow gorge of red rock on horseback, and followed that with the scarcely less spectacular temple of Jupiter at Baalbek in the Lebanon, before returning by sea via Cyprus and the Greek islands through the Corinth Canal to Olympia and the western Mediterranean. Travel was tonic and stimulant for Tony. Voyages like these replenished his energy and gave perspective, making it easier for him to pace himself.

He seems to have started writing *The Kindly Ones* the day after he got back from his first cruise, breaking off ten days later to sit for a drawing by Augustus John. Shuffling and mumbling in his early eighties, lonely, deaf, irascible as ever and attended by his surviving harem, John relished Tony's company and did his best to prolong the sittings. This must have been one of his last portraits (he died just over a year later), but he caught in his sitter the abstracted look of inner concentration that signals a book in progress. *The Kindly Ones* was just over halfway through when Tony broke off again for a second cruise, interrupting himself a third time at the beginning of October to visit the United States for the first time since his dismal days in Hollywood in 1937.

He had accepted an invitation from Dartmouth College in New Hampshire on condition that he was neither required to lecture nor to play any part in arrangements for the trip. He spoke to staff and students, lunched with the president, gave a radio talk and fitted in a visit to Amherst (where he agreed to give a talk on Stendhal). As soon as he decently could, he moved south to Ithaca in New York State, where Arthur Mizener, his first American fan and subsequently a friend, was professor in the English faculty at Cornell University. The plan was to stay with Arthur and his wife Rosemary, while investigating the possibility of John becoming a student at Cornell on leaving school. The Mizeners made the most of their distinguished guest. Wholly unused to the efficiency, effusiveness and unconditional generosity of American hospitality, Tony was admired and entertained on a scale unthinkable at home. Parties were given in his honour. Reverential fans were mustered. Mindful of his reluctance to speak in public, Arthur laid on an informal gathering of well-behaved young people who had read his books, and whose eagerness disarmed him: "you discovered a Winston Churchill hidden away in yourself," his host said afterwards, "and had a lovely time talking to students." A slot was organized for John, and someone introduced Tony to an obscure junior faculty wife called Alison Bishop, said to be lecturing herself in some humble backwater of the English department. Her impact was striking: "After ten minutes' conversation, I saw that undoubtedly one would hear more of this supposedly shy girl."

Little, Brown, Tony's publishers in the US, had started him off at the Ritz in Boston, and for the end of his stay a fortnight later they put him up at the St. Regis in New York, giving another party for him in consultation with his American agent, Dorothy Olding. He flew back to London on 21 October, recharged and ready for work as soon as he reached the Chantry. His first cruise had precipitated the opening pages of *The Kindly Ones* and, after his return from America eighteen months later, he completed his typescript in five weeks flat, handing it to Violet to read on 27 November 1961. Her job was to assess consistency and structure, and she gave incisive notes. "Galsworthy once said of his wife that she was the best natural critic a man ever had," Violet said darkly, "you might say that I was the worst natural critic a man ever had." Her own first book had come out the year before, a stoically detached account of being brought up by a cold-hearted mother as the third of four unwanted daughters. For all the unsparing harshness of its subject matter, and an occasionally jerky narrative technique, *Five Out of Six* has a warmth and humour that make it unexpectedly beguiling, "like certain Post-Impressionist pictures," said Jocelyn Brooke, "Berthe Morisot, for instance."

Tony started at once on volume seven. This was the point when he finally made up his mind to allocate three books to the Second World War, and complete the entire sequence in twelve volumes. From now on he was in a tearing hurry, painfully aware of both the risk and the necessity of taking time off. He wrote the first chapter of his next book while correcting proofs of *The Kindly Ones*, which came out in June with a dedication to the most meticulous of Tony's proofreaders, Wyndham Ketton-Cremer. "One of your very best . . . ," said Wyndham: "How vividly you bring back all that hellish unease of 1938/9." After much urging, Tony had agreed to join him on the board of the National Portrait Gallery in London. Wyndham himself had by now reached the stage in his late fifties when a full-bottomed peruke would, as Tony said, have suited both his looks and his position as a conscientious, old-fashioned village squire at Felbrigg, where the Powells still stayed with him each summer.

The next instalment of the *Dance* covers the opening months of inaction and delay when war materialized in slow motion, ending with the fall of France and the intervention of Fascist Italy on the German side in June 1940. Dispatched to join the Welsh Regiment, Jenkins, like his author, stands out by age and origin as a misfit in a company of hastily recruited young Welsh miners officered by local bank clerks. The humdrum concerns of these hymn-singing Welsh soldiers, their humour, simplicity and tolerant acceptance of their imported English subaltern, give a new flavour, both mundane and moving, to the *Dance*. The novelist Alan Judd singled out the shambolic, beer-swilling outsider, Lieutenant Bithel: "a wonderful invention and done in a masterly, musing way." Olivia Manning—like Judd, a fellow chronicler of the same war—picked Jenkins's company commander, Captain Gwatkin, a former branch bank manager whose romantic dreams of military servitude and grandeur end wretchedly in failure. "That vision of him in a cape & flat tin-hat as something of the Shakespearian wars will always remain with me," she wrote to Tony when the book came out.

Unlike most war novels, *The Valley of Bones* conveys with apparently effortless directness the feel and texture of army life among the ranks at the lowest, least pretentious level. After three months Jenkins leaves briefly for an officer training course at Aldershot, laid on for civilians by a British army ill prepared for war, let alone for the mass military conversion of a conscript population. The shambolic unwieldy obstinacy of the entire manoeuvre is captured in a Powellian image of dreamlike unreality:

We were operating over the dismal tundra of Laffan's Plain . . . Lumbering army reconnaissance planes buzzed placidly backwards and forwards through grey puffs of cloud, ancient machines garnered in from goodness knows what forgotten repository of written-off Governmental stores, now sent aloft again to meet a desperate situation. The heavens looked like one of those pictures of an imagined Future to be found in old-fashioned magazines for boys.

But, in spite or perhaps because of a trajectory closely following the author's own, *The Valley of Bones* was a hard book to write. The altered landscape of the war itself, the rapid switches of pace and personnel, the constant fluctuation and adjustment between private and public life, imposed new kinds of strain. Tony took his title from a passage in the biblical book of Ezekiel, describing how difficult it is to breathe life into dry bones. "I have done about 15,000 of a new one, but in great agony," he told his agent at the end of March 1962, reporting six months later that he was well over a third of the way through, "but still in great agony." Bouts of unremitting mental and imaginative effort alternated with physical exertion as Tony criss-crossed England and the continent with Violet all through that agonizing year. They took a three-week motoring tour down through France to Collioure and the Spanish border in April, and embarked at the beginning of September on another long haul up through England to stay with the Glenconners at their family home in the Scottish borders. In late autumn, when Tony was halfway through the book, they set out for the third time, flying this time to Malaga in Spain to spend a week with another former neighbour from Chester Gate, Gerry Wellesley, Duke of Wellington, on his ancestor's estate outside Granada.

Tony finished *The Valley of Bones* in June 1963, and dedicated it to the Mizeners. He was immediately immersed in preparations for a play based on *Afternoon Men* that had been under discussion for two years, and suddenly looked as if it might be about to open at the New Arts Theatre Club. In the end he and Violet flew off to join a pre-booked Greek cruise on 22 August, missing the play's first night, which had been postponed at the last minute. It was a disaster, according to Arthur Mizener, who found the script clumsy and humourless, the direction crude and the acting lamentable. The chief attraction was the chic and sexy Pauline Boty: a charismatic Pop artist, the epitome of London's swinging-sixties style, she was completely out of place in a play so strongly rooted in the 1930s, and in any case hopelessly miscast as Powell's loutish Lola. So was James Fox, acutely conscious of his blond patrician good looks in the role of the ironic, observant, quintessentially unromantic Atwater. The production was panned by critics and ran four weeks to virtually empty houses. "Almost nobody laughed," said Mizener.

But on his return from Greece Tony was captivated, partly by hearing actors speak his dialogue aloud, partly by the leading lady, Georgina Ward as Susan Nunnery, an exquisite sixties dolly bird who couldn't act but begged him to write another play with a good part in it for her. Tony promptly obliged with two. He had never thought of the theatre as much more than a feeble substitute for art and books but he enjoyed the momentary glitz and glamour that came with it, and he welcomed the brief respite it provided, turning out two play-scripts that winter which made no demands whatsoever on the imaginative and creative powers that shaped the *Dance*. For the next few years they did the rounds of theatrical managements, including the West End's virtual despot, H. M. Tennant, who toyed desultorily with one of them ("they are muttering about Peggy Ashcroft and Ralph Richardson") to no practical effect. "My heart was in my boots," said Violet, "but then a very interesting thing happened. Tony was rather entranced at hearing his own words spoken on stage, and it had a striking effect on the *Dance*. It tightened the whole thing up in the last part. It kind of freshened him up."

Afternoon Men closed on 19 September 1963. On the same day the Goldsmids' elder daughter, Sarah, was drowned at sea while sailing with her boyfriend in a boat belonging to Violet's nephew, Paddy Pakenham (who was the sole survivor). She was twenty-one years old. "Harry Goldsmid's life was utterly, irretrievably laid waste," Tony wrote long afterwards. The Goldsmids commissioned in Sarah's memory a stained-glass window for their local church in Kent from Marc Chagall (over the next twenty years he filled all of the twelve windows in Tudeley village church with blazing coloured glass). At the time, Harry plunged more furiously than ever into external activity, reading the proofs of *The Valley of Bones* in November, and pondering fresh outlets for Widmerpool's aggression.

Harry was responsible for Widmerpool's appointment as DAAG— deputy assistant adjutant general—a job of minimal importance with maximum potential for causing trouble, fomenting rows and conducting feuds at Divisional Headquarters in Northern Ireland, where the Welsh Regiment receives its military training. "Perhaps . . . the post of DAAG will have to be abolished or renamed like Rillington Place & Flat 13," said Harry, when he read the next instalment of the *Dance*. Jenkins spends twelve months as Major Widmerpool's administrative assistant ("No one but a tireless creator of work for its own sake would have found an assistant necessary in his job"). His experience of dispersal, destruction and death in *The Soldier's Art*, the conduct of the war and the havoc it brings to the lives of everyone he knows, are all filtered through the lens of Widmerpool's indefatigable, unceasing daily grind of bureaucratic intrigue and manipulation.

In February 1964, the Powells flew to Cairo to join a cruise organized by the enterprising R. K. Swan, who had taken over his father's firm with ambitious expansion plans. After a disappointing first night at the Cairo Hilton (where Violet objected strongly to belly dancers in the night club performing for Westerners in prim silk pyjamas), this Nile cruise proved an unforgettable experience at a time when Egyptian tourism was still officially restricted and small-scale. It included the Pyramids and the ancient sites of Abydos, Karnak, Luxor and Abu Simbel, already threatened by the rising waters of Colonel Nasser's Aswan High Dam. "The German firm of temple removers is moving more slowly than the Russian firm of dam builders," Violet reported ominously in her journal. She had packed a box of coloured chalks, and started drawing again for the first time in twenty years: bold fast incisive sketches ("there is nothing like a Nile river boat for sharpening up one's drawing technique") of people and places that filled the first of many travel sketchbooks. "We had a marvellous time in Egypt & I've never felt better in my life," Tony wrote to David Higham on 3 March, the day they got back and Heinemann published *The Valley of Bones*.

He got a nasty jolt when he read Malcolm Muggeridge's review the same day in the London *Evening Standard*. Malcolm had given up drink, smoking, sex and Pamela Berry on his sixtieth birthday the year before, converting with maximum publicity to a life of abstention, continence and piety. From that day on he used all available media outlets to denounce everything he had once promoted, complaining bitterly meanwhile when members of the public recognized him on the street ("It's like being accosted as a prostitute," he said complacently, "but then appearing on TV is the vilest form of degradation"). This new self-righteous Malcolm had booked himself in for a night at the Chantry a month after his sixtieth birthday. "I long for hours & hours of talk," he wrote, "it seems an eternity since we were together."

The upshot of their talk was the opposite of what either might have expected. Twenty years earlier Malcolm had defined for Tony the two essential types of human achievement, one based on disproportion, the other on proportion: "The former is passionate, active, restless, glittering; the latter is serene, durable, satisfying." Now each of them in his different way had fulfilled that prophecy. Malcolm's career never glittered more brilliantly than in the early 1960s, when Tony once more demonstrated his durability by publishing the seventh volume of the *Dance*. The disparity proved too much for his old friend. Malcolm's review began by dismissing the book's "inherent drabness," and went on to deride the *Dance* itself: "It is a kind of social accountancy, and not much more enlivening than the financial sort." He contrasted Powell unfavourably with Waugh, singling out in particular the character of his narrator: "his snobbishness . . . is quiet, steadfast, as it were Anglican in its flexibility and tenacity. It is Snobbishness Ancient and Modern . . . the Thirty-Nine Articles of Snobbishness . . ."

This was a strange charge, given that in the days when the pair used to talk non-stop together, snobbery had been one of Malcolm's favourite topics. "I have often thought it would be interesting to attempt an Anatomy of Snobbishness," he told Tony, confessing that he himself had once vehemently denied being related to a Muggeridge who sold gents' clothing in Newcastle (the outfitter was in fact his brother Douglas). But what took Tony's breath away was the brutality of the review's last paragraph, where Malcolm, who had compared him to Balzac at the outset of the *Dance*, now contrasted him with Stendhal, whose neglect by his contemporaries had been reversed by posterity:

> We, Mr. Powell's contemporaries, have proved less recalcitrant, and done him proud. Will posterity be correspondingly less amenable? See in his meticulous reconstruction of his life and times a heap of dust? Despite a strong personal partiality, honesty compels me to admit it might.

For Tony this was a stab in the back from the least expected quarter. He never entirely got over the shock of being publicly betrayed by one of his closest friends. Olivia Manning diagnosed jealousy on the part of a failed novelist, and advised paying no attention. Long afterwards Violet, who had witnessed at first hand Tony's disbelief and pain, described with formality and restraint what still seems the only rational explanation for Muggeridge's outburst: "it was with *The Valley of Bones* that Powell began to be more generally recognised as a formidable writer and that is why Malcolm Mugg., who was not so recognised, was provoked to sabotage." Malcolm himself claimed later that he couldn't understand, and later still that he couldn't even remember, what he had done to upset his old friend. The two remained on civil terms in public and in private, but intimacy and trust were at an end between them.

Tony left the country a month later to celebrate the four hundredth anniversary of Shakespeare's birth at a book festival in Japan, where he found with pleased surprise that *Casanova's Chinese Restaurant* was an English textbook at Kyoto University, while Tokyo students learned the language from *At Lady Molly's*. The British Council could hardly have designed a better antidote. Tony was one of three writers picked for export as, in his own words, "anthropological specimens of that trade." The other two were Alan Pryce-Jones, and a Cambridge don called Muriel Bradbrook who proved equally congenial. Tony enjoyed everything about his three weeks in Japan from his companions to his punctilious hosts and their landscape, finely disciplined like a Japanese print. Even the wine and the slaughterous Tokyo traffic amused him.

He spent the rest of the year working on *The Soldier's Art*, breaking off only once for a week in Spain in mid-September. He and Violet stayed with Bill and Annie Davis, hospitable American expatriates who ran their house overlooking the sea on the coast of Andalusia as among other things a luxurious rest home for sections of the British book world. The Powells, who had stopped off there two years earlier on the way to stay with Gerry Wellington, returned happily to La Consula, a capacious Italianate palace with marble floors, shady arcades and terraces festooned with vines and lilies, standing behind high iron gates in semi-tropical groves of acacia, palm and avocado. The Davises had thrown a flamboyant party at La Consula for the sixtieth birthday of Ernest Hemingway, who was Bill's favourite writer until he switched to Powell. Bill read voraciously, collected books on a heroic scale, and was passionately addicted to the *Dance*. "If I could receive a new book of yours every winter month, this place would not be so bad," he told Tony, planning to "compile *A Readers' Handbook to Powell: an Index-Guide*" (he never did), and going to great lengths to obtain the *Daily Telegraph* in Spain every other Thursday for the sake of Tony's book reviews ("the best now being done").

This Spanish excursion marked the moment of loss and liberation that comes when children finally move out. John left school and sailed for the US on 2 September 1964, to enrol at Cornell University. Tristram was now a TV producer, opening up new territory with a BBC documentary, *In the Shadow of Cain: Writers of the 1940s*, which included the sole surviving fragmentary recording of Maclaren-Ross in action. After more than a decade of strenuous activity, Tony had effectively completed the heavy clearance at the Chantry and, on his return from Spain, he moved indoors and started papering the walls. In the mornings he worked on *The Soldier's Art*, which was nearly halfway through, and in the afternoons he laboured to produce a monstrous collage of a size and surrealistic disturbance beyond anything he had so far attempted. It started with a couple of French recruiting posters for the First World War, and slowly grew to cover the walls, pipe-work, cistern and ceiling of the basement boiler room with what Ferdy Mount called "a scrap mural of almost Sistine proportions." Tony cut human figures out of ads, catalogues, Christmas cards and especially the *Sunday Times*'s brand-new colour magazine, sticking them together in a seething jumble: incoherent, shapeless, meaningless, and pulsing with raw energy as if he had simply emptied out the contents of his imagination on to the space in front of him.

Above the main boiler pipe a crowd of women of all kinds and ages swarm round William Shakespeare. *The Retreat from Moscow* takes place on a smaller pipe below. There are French writers above the basin in the gents' lavatory, and two Elizabethan nursing mothers below the elegant bare legs of Poussin's Rinaldo, fast asleep in a pair of gold silk shorts underneath one of the recruiting posters. Proust's pale face above the mirror is sandwiched between the Byzantine Empress Theodora on one side, and Joseph Stalin on the other. A second image of Proust looks down dispassionately from the far wall. To the right of the boiler, Henri Matisse and his wife in *The Conversation*, Picasso's absinthe-drinker and a couple of Gauguin's Polynesians all somehow meld with the row of Jacobean stone children kneeling above them, the porcelain baby doll, the 1960s fashion model, and the girl with half-open blouse and rope-soled sandals reclining underneath in a display without limits, hierarchy or borders, like the sea.

As the tide of images rose up the walls, Tony climbed on chairs, and brought in ladders. He worked in great bursts that drained his energy, stopping only to rest his arms and back. There is something elemental, even horrifying about the scale and impact of this torrential outpouring. It may have started as a physical outlet to offset intense mental concentration. Possibly the methodical, largely mindless work of clipping, sorting, filing and pasting scraps increased the artist's grip on the unmanageable flood of images surging through his brain. Tony said collage was good for the nerves. He also said that while you worked on it, just as when you wrote non-fiction, "you could think about other things." The boiler-room collage seems to have functioned, like gardening, as a means of disarming the conscious mind so as to gain access to turbulent, unplumbed depths below.

Alison Bishop, who published three novels under her maiden name of Alison Lurie before paying the first of many visits to the Chantry, saw the basement collage as a giant metaphor for Powell's own ongoing novel. This riotous display is a great deal more dishevelled than Poussin's *Dance to the Music of Time*, but both follow the gyratory principle that holds individual figures in place in the novel, imparting both control and freedom to characters revolving at uneven speeds in unpredictable patterns, massing together, careering apart, stumbling, colliding, occasionally spinning out of control. Time in Poussin's painting is calm and composed. Tony insisted that the difference between a painter's time and a writer's time was that the first was motionless and fixed, the second essentially unstable, "far less relaxed, indeed appallingly restless." Time in Powell's work is perpetually on the move, treacherous and disruptive, always liable to shatter an illusion or dislodge a prop concealing or protecting sometimes painful realities.

Visitors escorted down precipitous stone steps at the Chantry to view the vast invasive basement sprawl often found it a hard test to pass. Most were flabbergasted, some baffled, others frankly appalled. A few recognized themselves uneasily among the crowd. "Yes, not a bad likeness," was all Lord Bath could bring himself to say, preoccupied perhaps by his own even more ambitious scheme for rival attractions at Longleat. Driving over to lunch with the Baths was one of the Powells' favourite ways of entertaining weekend guests, even before the installation of a zoo. "I bought 25 lions . . . which Henry Bath wanted for the opening of his Safari Park at Longleat in 1966," wrote their friend Lees Mayall, a diplomat in Ethiopia at the time, with a house in Wiltshire where he planned to spend his retirement as a neighbour.

Apart from Violet, the person best placed to grasp the boiler room's importance for the *Dance* was probably Tony's editor at Heinemann, Roland Gant. But Gant, a supporter of the sequence from the start, had left the firm in 1957 after a cataclysmic upheaval when Heinemann sold its major shareholding to an investment consortium called Thomas Tilling. Four years later the Tilling Group bought the firm outright and discovered on close inspection that its prestigious acquisition was on the verge of bankruptcy. For all his literary flair and confidence, Frere had squandered the firm's resources through financial fecklessness, long-term mismanagement and over-rapid, underfunded expansion. His job was handed over to executives with no experience of or interest in books. Graham Greene and many other authors moved elsewhere at this point, along with Heinemann's more enterprising staff.

Leaving was not an option for Tony with the first six books of the *Dance* in Heinemann's hands already, and another on the way. Without Gant and Frere, he lost his backing in the firm, itself demoralized and weakened by internal feuds. From now on he found his work neglected, undervalued or ignored. He experienced at first hand Jenkins's conviction that publishers despise books and those that write them: "After all, they think, if authors can do that, anybody can." Heinemann's chairman Dwye Evans did what he could to keep things ticking over, but at least three of Tony's books got virtually no editorial attention within the firm. His angry complaints were as ineffectual as his threats to leave. Tilling installed its own managing director to oversee emergency reconstruction, replacing him once financial stability had been restored with Charles Pick, a hard-headed, book-trade virtuoso of no literary pretension whatsoever, unlike Frere. Tony had no choice but to sign Heinemann's new contract with advances this time of £1,000 for each of his next three novels.

At the end of 1965 Pick succeeded in luring Gant back as the firm's editorial director in time to take delivery of *The Soldier's Art*. Gant's return transformed Heinemann's internal ethos. Exceedingly well read and intellectually sure-footed with a reputation as an editorial genius in the trade, he possessed every quality Pick lacked. Together they made an outstanding team. Never close to Dwye Evans and unable to warm to Pick, Tony thankfully resumed his old easy companionable relationship with Roland, who had continued unofficially to look over his books in typescript. They shared a similar sense of humour, a broad range of esoteric interests and, professionally speaking, unqualified respect for one another's abilities. Roland's first move was to propose lunch at the Garrick. He handled Tony's affairs with speed, energy and skill, reading *The Soldier's Art* as soon as he got it in early February 1966, checking, correcting and marking up the manuscript over a single week, reading it through again at the weekend, and sending it immediately to press with plans to publish in early autumn.

From now on he rigorously scrutinized each successive manuscript, providing with the help of what Tony called his "international detective service" meticulous verification not only of facts and dates but—invaluable for the wartime volumes—the nuances of French, German, Belgian, Dutch and Polish names, phrases and military procedure. He and Tony edited each book together in the course of marathon phone calls and joint sessions at the Chantry, where both greatly enjoyed the ritualistic drama of Roland's comings and goings in his vintage Riley. "When I travel in that car I intend my departure to be rather like that of a 1918 pilot boarding a Sopwith Camel," he explained with satisfaction after a slight hitch in the performance: "The fur collar and the firm handshake . . . were somewhat cancelled out by the recalcitrant old mother Riley refusing to fire on the first swing of the prop!"

Gant's efficiency was as impressive as his acceleration and, as Heinemann rapidly became profitable again under Pick's vigorous new management, the two of them abolished Tony's prime grievance by ensuring that the entire expanding sequence of the *Dance* remained available and in print. Partly educated in France, by choice and instinct a Parisian intellectual, Gant had no problem with the concept—intrinsically alien to British publishers—that twelve books published over quarter of a century could be separate instalments of the same novel. Violet said Tony's rapport with his publisher reminded her of "the couple in the *New Yorker* cartoon, when one of them protests: 'You're always on the cat's side!'"

Cats played an integral part in life at the Chantry. Albert had died at a ripe age and been succeeded by a brown Burmese incumbent, brother of the Burmese champion, "a very self-possessed character" by the name of Kingsplay Flixey Fum. Tony insisted that Fum was the most intellectual, if not the most intelligent of all his cats. He was certainly one of the most cordial, greeting guests with gravity and charm, putting them at their ease with throaty purrs, and "talking to each of them for just the right time." In the intervals of daily business on the hunting field and afternoon siestas in the drawing room, he presided purposefully over morning work sessions in Tony's room upstairs.

P. G. Wodehouse, a keen fan of the *Dance*, told Tony he had six cats in his New York household. The two made contact through Wodehouse's step-grandson, Edward Cazalet, who reported that his grandfather possessed every Powell novel except *What's Become of Waring* so Tony posted him a parcel. "It was the thrill of a lifetime when I opened it and found *Waring*," wrote Wodehouse, who finished the book at a single sitting: "I enjoyed every line of it. And had the usual Why-on-earth-didn't-I-think-of-that feeling I always get when I read your books." A few years later Tony sent him signed copies of the three latest volumes of the *Dance*. "As usual I am absolutely stunned by their artistry," wrote Wodehouse: "I study the stuff under a microscope, and I still can't see how you do it."

The admiration was mutual. There is a strong streak of Wodehouse in Powell's delicate slapstick, his hair-trigger placing of an adverbial phrase and the deadpan absurdity he can give to perfectly ordinary situations. They share the same fondness for ludicrous similes that are at the same time strangely apt: Jenkins as Mephistopheles unexpectedly floored by Faust in *The Valley of Bones* for instance or, three books later, Widmerpool letting himself into his cheerless London flat with a rare twinge of apprehension:

No one seemed to be about. Widmerpool listened, his head slightly to one side, with the air of a Red Indian brave seeking, on the tail of the wind, the well-known, but elusive, scent of danger.

The most striking difference is that Wodehouse's stories take place in an English Arcadia untroubled by social disintegration, world war or twentieth-century genocide, where Powell's are firmly anchored in the real world. "The great historical happenings of the time— depression, Nazism, Communism—are persistent off-stage presences without distorting or violating the fabric of the narrative," wrote the American historian Arthur Schlesinger, Jr., exploring the ways in which Powell reinvigorates the increasingly etiolated tradition of English social comedy by rooting it again in contemporary actuality.

A whole generation of younger writers took advantage of this reconnection, chief among them Kingsley Amis, who said that even a pre-publication extract from a Powell novel was "enough to make me do my *Music of Time* reader-reaction act half a dozen times: laughter signified by a cessation of breathing & a kind of seated bow." His fellow addict, Philip Larkin, found the military aspect of *The Soldier's Art* as fascinating as it was funny. "I'm greatly honoured to have a copy personally inscribed by you," he wrote to Tony on 7 September 1966, sending an astute appreciation, "but this hasn't prevented my reading it at breakfast, or in the bath, in the most disrespectful and eager way."

Publication on 12 September was overshadowed by a simmering row that finally boiled over into the *Evening Standard* under the headline POWELL AND PENGUINS, accompanied by a grim-faced picture of the author. The first six volumes of the *Dance* had been published in paperback by Penguin with covers by Osbert Lancaster but, after Tony had twice reminded them to sign Osbert up again for the cover of *The Valley of Bones*, he got a curt note saying Lancaster had been dropped without consulting or informing either him or his author. This was one of the rare occasions when Tony gave way, like his father, to a paroxysm of rage. "People are going down on their knees to have jackets by Osbert Lancaster!" he wrote to David Higham: "He only does them because he is a personal friend of mine. And then just a cock-a-hoop letter saying they had decided to make a change . . . I have some experience of publishers but this beats everything!" Higham sent a soothing reply ("You couldn't have more reason to be indignant"), and Tony relieved his feelings in a

A 1920s party: one of Osbert Lancaster's early book jackets that perfectly caught the mood of the *Dance*

brisk exchange with Penguin's chief editor, the brilliant but imperious Tony Godwin, one of a band of high-profile sixties whizz-kids brought in by Penguin to institute a drastic overhaul in all departments, including cover policy.

Godwin, who had a temper as hot as Tony's, pointed out that poor sales put him in no position to demand special treatment. Tony in turn accused Godwin of incompetence, ineptitude and the blatant inefficiency of his sales department. "Reading your three letters . . . ," wrote Godwin, "makes me wonder whether you really want to continue with a publisher that you seem apparently so to dislike, or at any rate, of which you seem so intolerant." He got the expected answer no, and shortly afterwards made Tony even angrier by ensuring that a full report, complete with extracts from his letters supplied by himself, appeared in the *Evening Standard*. Godwin complained about Powell's condescending attitude; Penguin's legendary chairman, Allen Lane, denied all knowledge of the affair; and Gant at Heinemann set about disentangling Powell's books from Penguin.

Part at least of Tony's fury came from loyalty to Osbert, whose wife had died suddenly of a heart attack two years earlier, leaving him wretchedly depleted and distressed. Osbert came to stay at the Chantry after the funeral, and Violet said that Karen Lancaster was the only person she missed as much as her sister Julia. The experience drew Tony and Osbert closer, and soon things started to look up for both of them. Osbert married again, and Tony's paperbacks were swiftly transferred on greatly improved terms to Fontana, who paid £1,000 for *The Soldier's Art* (Penguin had paid £300 for each book a decade earlier), and another £5,000 for the other seven volumes: "a real sock in the eye for master Godwin," David Higham wrote to Tony at the end of September.

Tony was already preoccupied with his next book. Two friends and fellow novelists, both almost exact contemporaries, died in 1966. Jocelyn Brooke was just short of sixty when he was found dead in his Kentish cottage in October, a notable writer who had never made the mark Tony thought his books deserved. On Evelyn Waugh's death six months earlier, his reputation had taken a steep posthumous downturn. "Even among his acquaintances there was a loud noise of worms turning," wrote his son Auberon. Evelyn, worn out at sixty-three, had been sinking slowly deeper into misogyny and gloom. Tony had reviewed his last book, the autobiographical *A Little Learning*, trying to counteract what was then an increasingly prevalent public image of Waugh as a frivolous and over-rated minor writer, perhaps also to combat his old friend's terminal depression: "Over and over in the book one is impressed by the author's innate seriousness, his indomitable determination." The day after Tony's review came out, he and Violet hijacked Evelyn on the train from London, carrying him off for a night at the Chantry. "It is very rare for anything unexpected to happen to me these days," Evelyn wrote afterwards, "still rarer something unexpected and pleasant."

Now that he was dead, the sniping at him intensified. Obituaries were grudging and denigratory. Tony's dismay increased a few years later when gossipy and disobligingly frank extracts from Waugh's diaries in a Sunday paper caused consternation among all who knew him. People mentioned in these sensational snippets felt Waugh had betrayed them, and disgraced himself. "His sinister meanness and invariable desire to wound suggest to me almost a psychopath," wrote an agitated friend, Freddie Birkenhead, "and that, I believe is what he was." Bewildered admirers and vindictive rivals dismissed

Waugh as a malicious lightweight. When Christopher Sykes's biography appeared in 1975, Tony responded with approval and relief to its shrewd, affectionate, clear-sighted portrait, but publication of the *Diaries* in book form immediately afterwards whipped up something approaching mass hysteria among the London literati. In these years when Waugh was subjected to every kind of slight and barb, Tony's view of him never wavered. "Surely the time has come to abandon trivialities," he wrote sternly in the *Daily Telegraph* when the furore about the diaries first arose, "and treat him as a great writer."

In November 1966, Tony left with Violet to spend a month travelling round India and Pakistan in a party led by Mortimer Wheeler ("immensely enjoyable . . . though very energetic," he told Dru). Invigorated as always by foreign travel, he was back at the Chantry ready to start his next book by early December. *The Military Philosophers* closely follows the time he spent in an obscure subsection of military liaison at the War Office, handling on the most prosaic, peripheral level the consequences of havoc and destruction in Central and Eastern Europe. It covers the years from the Japanese capture of Singapore to the final London Blitz of flying bombs, ending with a visit to the ravaged plains of northern France, and a momentary encounter after the Victory service in St. Paul's with Jean Duport, now remarried to a high-powered South American diplomat. In the opening pages Charles Stringham is reported missing after the battle for Singapore.

Jenkins's friendship with Stringham was effectively over by the end of the first volume but he remains a powerful presence in the *Dance*, drinking and drifting slowly downwards, dissolute and sardonic, last seen early in the war as a private soldier in a Mobile Laundry Unit about to be posted to the Far East. For all his elusiveness a particular aura still clings to Stringham, a residual memory of the slight, self-contained, commanding boy who looked like the young Emperor Alexander in Veronese's painting. His death in a Japanese prisoner-of-war camp, confirmed in the end by Widmerpool (who had organized the posting in the first place), is one of many tricks played by time in *The Military Philosophers*. Another is the narrator's chance meeting with Jean, first seen as an awkward schoolgirl with a tennis racket, later as the kind of beauty painted by Rubens or Delacroix, a source of great joy and even greater bitterness to Jenkins, who now finds her unrecognizably transformed into a cosmopolitan sophisticate, "only just short of a perfect stranger."

There is perhaps an indefinable slackening of pressure in the *Dance* at this point, something almost imperceptible in *The Soldier's Art*, slightly more evident in *The Military Philosophers*, probably inevitable given the exigencies of war. Too many of the military characters stick too closely to their real-life counterparts, a literal transcription that makes the fictional figments oddly lifeless. Dru is more or less directly transposed as the philosophical David Pennistone, whose outstanding administrative efficiency and phenomenal intellect never entirely ring true. Pennistone retains "the slightly fleshless air of a character taken straight from life," as Tony said of Guy Perron in Paul Scott's *Jewel in the Crown*.

Other, more fully realized characters come energetically alive. Poignant memories of prolonged exposure to bureaucratic blockage, procrastination and preclusion—"arguing, delaying, encumbering, hair-splitting"—take memorable shape in the civil servant Blackhead, whose obstructive genius finds unprecedented scope in daily efforts to frustrate the war effort. Mr. Blackhead descends directly from Mr. Child, Duckworths' accountant who went mad in 1931, and had to be removed by ambulance from the office in Henrietta Street. He owes something also to Dru's colleague at the War Office, Major Bradfield, whose stupendously long dull minutes lie behind Blackhead's masterpiece: "three and a half pages on the theory and practice of soap issues for military personnel, with especial reference to the Polish Women's Corps." In *The Military Philosophers* this dissertation is returned with a terse request that drives Blackhead almost insane: "Please amplify. D. Pennistone, Maj. G. S."

This purely fictional episode delighted Dru. "I felt tempted to send you a card on finishing the proofs with 'Please expand—Pennistone, Maj. G. S.,'" he wrote, adding a characteristically metaphysical postscript of his own that in turn delighted Tony: "I hope you will continue & perhaps catch up with life & go through the time barrier into the future." Much as he appreciated Blackhead, Dru thought Charles Stringham's niece, the devastating Pamela Flitton, the best thing in the book, a view widely shared by all who knew the original of this scarily accurate portrait, including Barbara Skelton herself. "Dear Tony, I am suing naturally," she wrote: "in the meantime can you advise me a good publisher for my new novel?" Roland Gant, recommended by Tony, wisely passed her on to Alan Ross, who was rash enough to publish her book, which had to be withdrawn immediately when one of Barbara's innumerable ex-lovers threatened to sue.

What made Tony far more apprehensive was the reaction of the officers he had used as models, especially his commanding officer, Colonel Carlisle, portrayed with relish and precision as the unctuous and ingratiating Captain Farebrother. He had taken risks on the assumption that Carlisle never opened a book, and was shocked to get a letter from the colonel saying he had read *The Military Philosophers*, and suggesting they meet for lunch. A postcard of William Blake's *God Judging Adam* arrived for Dru with a note on the back from Tony, identifying himself as the naked penitent with bowed head, and Carlisle as the ferocious greybeard enthroned on a flaming chariot with his Book of Judgement. But in this instance Blake's prophetic vision turned out to be a false alarm. The colonel was well pleased with his reflection in the book, having chosen to see himself as the dashing First War hero Major Finn, VC (who was by Tony's own account a faithful rendering of Carlisle's deputy, Major Ebenezer Kerr).

Tony gave himself a break on completion of the three war novels. For almost two decades he had kept up his schedule, allowing himself to deviate only once when he interrupted the sequence just over halfway through for a theatrical excursion that led nowhere. By the time he finished *The Military Philosophers*, delivering the manuscript to Gant at Heinemann on 20 March 1968, he was exhausted. He had been working continuously since 1950 on what he insisted was a single novel, driving himself so hard it sometimes seemed his only escape hatch was foreign travel. Gaps between ending one novel and starting the next were growing longer. His old enemies, gloom and sloth, hovered so close at his back that it was late autumn before he began work on a sequel. When Alison Lurie read his horoscope a year later, she picked out specific incidents from his past, all of them vague enough to cover many eventualities apart from the entry for 1969: "Slowdown—illness—depression." Tony confirmed her diagnosis, noting that the things she specified generally happened a year

A page from Violet's 1967 diary recording
the visit to Odessa on the Black Sea, newly
opened to Westerners by Soviet Russia

earlier than the date she gave, and that she tended to downplay his
setbacks and reversals ("I think you let the Native off rather lightly in
some of the more afflicted aspects").

He corrected proofs of his book in June and left with Violet to
spend an undemanding ten days on a canal boat in Sweden, moving
slowly from Gothenburg to Stockholm, where they visited his publishing house and inspected Descartes' grave in a church opposite.
Travel was more than ever restorative, especially by water. One of
the best things about Swan cruises was the range of distractions they
provided, starting with a passenger list that nearly always included
people the Powells had come across, or could track down in one connection or another. Once on board ship the only decisions that had to
be taken were whether or not to attend a lecture, or join a sightseeing
expedition. On a Swan tour in 1967 (when Russia relaxed its restric-
tions on Western travellers) they had steamed through the Darda-
nelles to Istanbul, and round the top of the Black Sea, stopping at

Odessa, Crimea, and on the western slopes of the Caucasus to pay respects to Mikhail Lermontov. Tony pictured Pechorin, the hero of our own time, a military philosopher in his own right, taking a trip from Pyatigorsk on the far side of the mountains to the seashore where Swan's ship put in: "Streaks of sunlight, penetrating the leaves of the forest, brilliantly lighted up an extraordinary kaleidoscope of variations on the colour green. We sat in the woods picnicking, drinking a bottle of Turkish wine brought from the ship . . ."

In late August 1968, the Powells took another boat up the west coast of Scotland to visit Antonia and Hugh Fraser with their growing family on the island of Eilean Aigus near Inverness. Tony worked his way that summer through *The Great Terror* by Robert Conquest, who had been trying for years with small success to counteract the blanket approval and support still extended by the West to Soviet Russia. On the Powells' bus tour round Odessa the year before the Ukrainian guide had started on his standard propagandist patter at the grave of the unknown sailor only to be sharply corrected by one of the passengers, seconded by Tony ("the guide under-estimated the ferocity of the English when they see their tea growing ever more remote," Violet wrote in her diary).

But the Communist regime in Russia was still by and large accepted in Britain as essentially well-meaning and forward-looking, if possibly misguided on certain points, a view heavily buttressed by intellectual amnesia and ideological suppression of anything approaching Soviet reality. Conquest's history of Stalin's purges in the 1930s was the latest in a series of sobering accounts, and the one that finally began to turn the slow tides of opinion. Tony recommended the book to Dru, "if you can take it." *The Great Terror* explores the tyranny— "silent as darkness, rigid as ice, insensible as bronze, decked with an outer amiability and glittering with the cold brilliance of snow"— predicted a century before by Henri-Frédéric Amiel. Tony met Bob Conquest through their mutual friend Kingsley over regular weekly lunches at Bertorelli on Charlotte Street in the late sixties and seventies. In 1990, when the opening of Soviet archives provided documentary evidence that amply justified Conquest's conclusions, Kingsley suggested calling the new revised edition *I Told You So, You Fucking Fools*.

In the spring of 1969 Tony broke off again from his current novel for a cruise round the eastern Mediterranean. In late autumn there was a month's art-treasure tour of southern India, starting in Ceylon and ending up at a dinner party given by the Nizam in his palace at Trichinopoly, with a last night in Pondicherry, where Tony said the back streets reminded him of Arles. Between trips the Powells' first grandchild was born, Tristram's daughter Georgia (he had married a painter called Virginia Lucas the year before). John, who had inherited his grandfather's financial acumen, was now working for a firm of City stockbrokers.

The usual procession of friends, relatives and neighbours streamed through the Chantry. "I can't tell you how much we enjoyed every minute and every item of our weekend," wrote Georgia Sitwell, who came to stay with Sachie: "From the lavender bags to the caves, the pictures and the furniture, the company and the conversation, everything, especially the atmosphere you two and son produce, is an enchantment." Kingsley Amis, who brought his second wife, the novelist Elizabeth Jane Howard, said the same in a different key: "I've never enjoyed myself more with my clothes on, as a soldier might say." The American ambassador, David Bruce, came often with his glamorous wife Evangeline. So did Jilly Cooper, an addict of the *Dance* from the age of fourteen, currently the *Sunday Times* correspondent on sex, marriage and housework. "Like Dr. Barnardo's," Tony said of Chantry hospitality, "no one is ever turned away."

Alison came regularly, marvelling at the stoicism of British hosts who saw no reason to let pouring rain prevent a scheduled summer picnic: "we went anyhow with umbrellas and parkas and ate the elaborate lunch (roast chickens, white wine, apple tart, linen napkins, etc.) in what . . . looked like a bamboo bus shelter. It was very cold and wet but they did not seem to notice this at all." Tony's forecast when they first met had proved correct. Leaving behind the academic world of Ithaca along with her husband and three sons, Alison reinvented herself as a novelist on annual trips to England, assuming as she said a different personality—confident, appreciative, entertaining, "an aspect of myself I far prefer"—with a growing circle of writers as friends in London, impressed and intrigued by her lopsided grin, her elegant long legs and her sudden enigmatic arrivals apparently out of nowhere for a month or two in summer.

Back in Ithaca in the winter months of 1969, she cast Tony's horoscope, consulting the moon and planets whose findings might have been predicted by anyone who knew him: love of social life and the arts, intellectual courage, endurance, a capacity for hard work, a successful marriage and many friends with a "fire-air emphasis" on energy, originality and intellectual creation. "May be introspective and moody at times," she conceded in what was otherwise a wholly favourable reading: "May take up projects which are difficult to complete." Tony, who was wrestling with the latest instalment of the *Dance* ("in my usual state of turmoil with number 10"), maintained ever afterwards that Alison was a witch, always a high compliment from him.

For more than ten years now he had reviewed regularly for the *Telegraph*'s literary editor, Herbert Ziman, "an Homeric Bore, perhaps captaining the English team," but also the best-read man even Tony had ever met. On alternate Saturday mornings he gutted a book for Ziman at the *Telegraph*. "They held a lifetime's thought about an extraordinary range of writers," said Naipaul, who greatly admired the clarity and directness of these reviews. Tony himself claimed that, without them, he would "go bankrupt from buying books, or mad from having nothing to read." His next novel depicts with fearful authenticity the small, highly specialized professional enclave inhabited by those who read, write and review books. Its title comes from an alcoholic all-purpose journalist known for reasons not entirely clear as Books-Do-Furnish-a-Room Bagshaw, currently editing a small impoverished left-wing weekly called *Fission*.

Jenkins, picked by Bagshaw as his third choice to run the book section, surveys the big beasts of the book world, among them Nathaniel Sheldon "who had probably never read a book for pleasure in his life. This did not at all handicap his laying down the law . . . with brutal topicality in the literary column of a daily paper." At the opposite extreme is X. Trapnel, a genuine writer whose flamboyance masks punitive self-abnegation in pursuit of the kind of deathless masterpiece that seldom ends, then as now, in anything but anticlimax. Trapnel runs away with Widmerpool's new wife, the former Pamela Flitton: "it is interesting . . . to see how the monstrous Pam drains the colour from the previously monstrous Widmerpool," wrote Harry Goldsmid when the book came out. "Most of the reviewers . . . failed to spot how minor a bogy Widmerpool becomes when confronted

Alison Lurie on one of many summer visits to
the Chantry: Tony said she was a witch.

with the horrific Pam." After a brief spell of camping out with Trapnel at the brink of destitution, the vengeful Pam destroys her lover's
novel and returns to her atrocious marriage, leaving Trapnel physically and emotionally unfit to face the squalor of his future. "With
you, both the horror and the joke reside well back of a very quiet
surface," Arthur Mizener once wrote to Tony, contrasting the *Dance*
with the surface sensationalism of American novelists like Norman
Mailer.

The grotesquerie and pathos of the literary scene have rarely been
better caught than in *Books Do Furnish a Room*. Tony dedicated the
novel to Rupert Hart-Davis, a man of letters in the urbane Edwardian sense, dedicatee of twenty-one other books, pillar of the London
Library, secretary of the Literary Society (William Wordsworth's
dining club to which Tony also belonged), and founder of his own
small publishing house which he sold to the Tilling Group, retiring in

his late fifties to a Yorkshire cottage with five studies, one for each of the books he happened to be writing or editing at any given time. He invited the Powells to stay, and corrected Tony's proofs "with precision and severity" at Marske in Swaledale. "I seem to have known Hart-Davis scarcely less than I do now," Tony wrote in the fourth volume of his memoirs, "now perhaps scarcely more than then."

Another of Tony's proofreaders, Wyndham Ketton-Cremer, died at the end of 1969 as unostentatiously as he had lived, leaving a private joke for Tony on page 340 of his last book, *Norfolk in the Civil War*, in the shape of a Norfolk man called Henry Widmerpool, a Royalist rent collector who carried on doggedly extracting money all through those cataclysmic years. Kenneth Widmerpool himself—the fictional master figure, as Walter Allen put it—reaches his high point in *Books Do Furnish a Room* as an ambitious post-war MP and parliamentary private secretary, wooed simultaneously by the Labour Party and the City, with a peerage in the offing and power within his grasp, his career threatened only by his wife's marauding instinct for ransack and dereliction. The book was completed in May 1970, and came out the following January to a largely cordial reception except in the *New Statesman*, where Philip Larkin panned it, dismissing the entire sequence as a failure for good measure. Tony was surprised and hurt. "You've gone on writing novels," Kingsley explained bluntly, "and he hasn't."

This marked the start of what Tony called his final trilogy, and from now on the *Dance* moved fast with no further block or hesitation. The first faint signs of volume eleven had started stirring at the back of his mind well before the tenth was published. "I can't quite get started," he wrote cautiously to Alison on 13 October, returning from a fortnight in Persia with Violet, "though feeling less utterly without ideas than when we set out for Iran." He consulted Harry Goldsmid in November about possible dealings for Widmerpool with communist Eastern Europe, and checked with American friends—Alison, the Mizeners and the Davises—on the authenticity of the two Americans in his book. All through 1971 he worked steadily, stopping only to refresh his memory with a week in Venice in May.

Two thirds of the new book, *Temporary Kings*, takes place in Venice where an international literary conference in the summer of 1958 provides the background for converging people and events, actual, imaginary, and recounted by X. Trapnel's prospective biographer, the American academic Russell Gwinnett. Trapnel himself has died after dropping out of his familiar world, abjuring even the pubs that had always been his habitat: "The roving intelligentsia of the saloon bar—cultural nomads of a race never likely to penetrate the international steppe—professional topers, itinerant bores, near-criminals, knew him no more." The first of two great climactic gatherings takes place in the course of a visit to the Bragadin palazzo beneath a Tiepolo painted ceiling of Powell's own invention: "Miraculous volumes of colour billowed, gleamed, vibrated, above us." The fresco depicts the Lydian King Candaules exhibiting his naked wife to his friend Gyges. Beneath it a sightseer gazing intently upwards turns out to be Pamela Widmerpool in a patterned shirt of crimson and peacock-blue: "These colours might have been expressly designed—by dissonance as much as harmony—for juxtaposition against those pouring down in brilliant rays of light from the Tiepolo; subtle yet penetrating pinks and greys, light blue turning almost to lavender, rich saffrons and cinnamons melting into bronze and gold."

Powell uses the sumptuous fabric of Tiepolo's fresco to counterpoint, in a series of increasingly sordid and brutal disclosures, the voyeurism of the Widmerpools' home life. Conflicting testimony from various more or less unreliable witnesses describing the confrontation between the couple in Venice suggests some kind of assault perpetrated by Widmerpool, provoked beyond bearing by his wife, a scene paralleled by a similar collision enacted above them on the ceiling between Tiepolo's three painted personages in a pillared bedchamber that seems somehow to have floated free from whatever palace it was part of:

> The skill of the painter brought complete conviction to the phenomena round about . . . Meanwhile, an attendant team of intermediate beings—cupids, tritons, sphinxes, chimaeras, the passing harpy, loitering gorgon—negligently assisted stratospheric support of the whole giddy structure and its occupants, a floating recess perceptibly cubist in conception . . . "Who's the naked man with the stand?" asked Pamela.

This whole extended passage is a bravura performance by a writer with a practised eye who has looked long and hard at Tiepolo, especially at his mastery of different levels of reality, real or imagined, grafted on to or opening out of one another with a technical assurance not unlike Powell's own strategy in the *Dance*, where flashbacks or retrospects materialize through retrospects, juxtaposed like the painted frames surrounding real doors and windows in Tiepolo's actual or invented Venetian wall paintings.

Back in London rumours circulated by his wife claim that Widmerpool's involvement with the Communist bloc included espionage as well as trade (one of the many experts Tony initially consulted was a keen admirer of the *Dance*, the immensely popular thriller-writer Dennis Wheatley, who had worked, like Tony, in Churchill's underground bunker in the Second World War). Narrowly averted scandal fails to terminate Widmerpool's career. Pamela ends hers with a lurid self-inflicted death.

Temporary Kings, for all its extravagant energy and excess, is permeated by mortality. A chance acquaintance at a reunion dinner describes Stringham's last days in a Japanese labour camp. Hugh Moreland—like Stringham, an adept of the power of the imagination rather than the will—slowly succumbs to sickness, money troubles and loss of confidence. The book that had started with Trapnel's disintegration and death ends with Moreland's physical collapse. Jenkins's grief as he leaves the hospital for the last time, knowing that he will never have with anyone again the kind of conversations he had with Moreland, probably comes as close as the *Dance* ever comes to the borderland of fact with fiction. In the summer of 1972, as *Temporary Kings* neared completion, Tony wrote a memoir of Constant Lambert as he had done earlier for George Orwell. Brilliant, subtle and penetrating like its subject, his portrait lacks only the haunting depth of feeling that informs the final chapter of *Temporary Kings*.

The novel was completed by late November 1972. In the New Year the Powells left for South America to spend a month travelling through Mexico and Guatemala, recording the trip in Violet's sketchbook, which includes an exuberantly coloured scene of sex and violence signed "Diego Riviera Powell." When *Temporary Kings* came out a year later, it was reviewed by the new director of the Ashmolean Museum in Oxford, David Piper, transfixed not so much by the author's affinity with Tiepolo as by Widmerpool's growing stature in popular mythology. "In him Powell has isolated—and named for ever—a recurring elemental irritant of human intercourse. Everyone has their Widmerpool . . . Who is your Widmerpool?—awesomely, whose Widmerpool are you?"

For years the Chantry supplied a lifeline for footloose friends like Miranda Christen, newly emerged as Miranda Wood from her second marriage—"a 23 year long ghastly mistake"—to a former sergeant in the British army. "Rocks of Gibraltar," she wrote of Violet and Tony, "amongst the shifting sands of my own and practically everyone else I know's experiences in matrimony." She had finally taken her last slow boat to Australia, returning to settle in a tiny flat off Baker Street in London, where Tony fixed her up with a job as personal assistant to the political buccaneer Woodrow Wyatt. After more than three freebooting decades in Sumatra, Java, Perth and Papua New Guinea, she had stockpiled the contents of the autobiographical novel—*Pickle My Bones* was its current title—that had been in the offing ever since she and Tony first laid plans at Duckworths for their respective futures. "The way we used to function at Henrietta Street remains my ideal," she wrote to him at the end of her long life, "though I didn't know it at the time."

Another of the same rackety tribe was Bobby Roberts, who had confounded all who knew him by marrying a rich wife and going to ground in Hampstead. John Heygate was a third, now a widower alone again at Bellarena, sinking into "the particularly helpless semi-decay that overcomes Irish houses," in Violet's words, a "quality of mildewed despair . . . also apt to overtake the inhabitants." As the balance of his mind, never particularly stable, became increasingly precarious, Heygate paid regular visits to the Londonderry asylum, or "the Derry Mental" as he called his second home, threatening to produce an autobiography of his own, and watching over Tony's progress, in periods of sanity, with proprietary approval spiked by flashes of resentment.

In these final stages when the *Dance* drew towards its close, Violet built her own career, specializing in neglected or forgotten women authors and starting with Maude Ffoulkes, a prolific Edwardian ghost-writer whose position in the shadows prompted inevitable comparison with the author's own role in the background of the

Violet and Tony at the Chantry with Lord Bath's Caligula

Dance. Violet's phenomenal memory for plots and people had been as invaluable to Tony as his professional experience now proved for her. Their son John once accidentally interrupted a session in the library when Tony was taking Violet's latest book to pieces: "I never heard anything so excoriating in my life," he said afterwards. "You wait until I get going on your father's," Violet replied sternly. Her intricate knowledge of the byways and side roads of the English novel, her vast network of human contacts—alive or dead, in fact or fiction—her shrewd grasp of motive and behaviour, and her formidable faculty for what she called continuity made her a collaborator in the sense that, without her, the *Dance* could hardly have taken the form it did. Her memory was, in Tristram's words, "*the right arm, as it were, of my father's imagination.*"

She also ran the Chantry. Someone from the village came to clean, and for many years there was a first-rate cook called Mrs. Dodd in the school holidays. A couple occupied the lodge at the front gate in return for mowing the grass and keeping an eye on the house when the Powells were away, and there were tenants in the old coach house, made habitable by the late sixties and renamed The Stables. Violet oversaw all these arrangements, organized the social calendar, kept house and entertained the grandchildren (Georgia, who was five in 1973, had acquired a brother Archie, who was three). In the 1950s she also conducted a running battle, ably assisted by John Betjeman, against efforts by the rector—"the local iconoclast," said Violet—to rip out the box pews and eliminate the rood screen in Chantry church. Both Powells fought the various quarry companies extracting Mendip limestone, whose rapacity closed down local roads and footpaths, polluted the atmosphere by blasting, and poisoned streams and rivers, including Chantry lake, with toxic effluent.

For twenty-five years work took everything Tony had to give. He alternated between intense absorption—when he found it impossible to judge the overall impact of his novel because of "the hypnotised state one gets into, when writing"—and the absolute detachment he recognized in Tiepolo's self-portrait in the Palazzo Labia: "the painter stands in the background watching the proceedings rather sardonically." His general position came perhaps closest to the standpoint of Nicolas Poussin, who observed at a critical juncture of the civil wars in seventeenth-century France, a decade or more after he had finished his own *Dance to the Music of Time*: "It is a great satisfaction to live in a century in which such great events take place, provided one can take shelter in some little corner and watch the play in comfort." The Chantry was that place for Tony.

Hearing Secret Harmonies, the twelfth and final novel in the sequence, begins and ends at the Chantry. It is, as one of its closest readers pointed out, the most pastoral of them all, and the one that brings the narrative to the point where it catches up with life in the early 1970s. It starts with an episode based on an actual encounter eight years earlier, when a band of bedraggled drop-outs with a horse-drawn caravan turned up at the Chantry in a rainstorm, barefoot and wringing wet. One of them was the Glenconners' daughter, Catherine Tennant, known to the Powells from childhood, who asked permission to camp out in the paddock. In the end she and her two companions spent the night indoors, supplying prototypes for the travellers in the opening pages of *Hearing Secret Harmonies*. Reversing his child's-eye view of the adult world in the central section of *The Kindly Ones,* Jenkins now trains his dispassionate and attentive eye on the social, sexual and civic counter-culture of a new generation in the 1960s. Malcolm Muggeridge had hit the headlines in 1968 with a notorious address as Rector of Edinburgh University, denouncing the student body as slothful, licentious and drug-fuddled, an episode reflected and inverted by Widmerpool who, in his capacity as the chancellor of a red-brick university, endorses student revolt with unconditional enthusiasm.

Milder shocks of this sort recur throughout. The book is laced with familiar figures in whom the dimly discernible outlines of younger and more vigorous selves can still be traced, "like a footpath lost in the brambles and weeds of an untended garden." Scorpio Murtlock leads an increasingly sinister cult, playing variations on a theme introduced by Dr. Trelawney forty years before. Mr. Deacon falls due for posthumous rehabilitation, his vast, unwieldy, ill-constructed canvases disinterred from junk-piles and waste-tips to adorn the walls of a go-ahead London gallery. Bob Duport turns up in a wheelchair pushed by his ex-wife Jean, herself now smoothly translated into a Latin American presidential consort, at the Bosworth Deacon private view. "The astonishing thing is the way you make old age happen . . . ," wrote Arthur Mizener: "I am saving up Duport's description of Widmerpool as a chateau-bottled shit to use on some specially significant occasion—perhaps an English department meeting." The sequence turns full circle, returning to the first of what Tony called the interior images that haunt the novelist's imagination. Widmerpool, who had advanced out of mist and drizzle as a schoolboy twelve books earlier, now concludes the *Dance* by disappearing back into the creative void. "In the last and—to me—infinitely sad pages of *Hearing Secret Harmonies,*" wrote Paul Scott when the book came out, "he is still there, running."

The book had been interrupted as Tony neared its halfway point at the beginning of 1974, when his son John succumbed to severe and incapacitating depression. The brutal severity of his collapse deeply disturbed both parents, appalled by his suffering and by their helplessness to intervene. "This awful melancholia . . . really does seem to be the scourge of the age," wrote Tony, who had himself been subject intermittently to the same scourge all his life. He consulted friends who gave what comfort they could. Naipaul explained with sympathy and feeling that he had himself survived a similar crisis at the same age. Alison diagnosed inner conflict caused by malign planetary activity, forecasting an imminent conjunction of the moon and Saturn "which should steady the mind and provide new opportunities," and advising an immediate retreat to the country. Tristram saw his brother through the worst phase of crack-up and disintegration until, after medical treatment had restored some sort of equilibrium, John could return to the quiet and seclusion of the Chantry.

For Tony writing had always held at bay the intolerable pressures of unreason and black despair. He returned to his unfinished novel, ending the last chapter in late November with an autumn bonfire, a kind of sequel to the workmen's bucket of burning coke that set the *Dance* in motion twenty-five years before. *Hearing Secret Harmonies* was revised, retyped and finally delivered on 1 December. Tony had won the W. H. Smith Prize a month earlier, accepting a cheque for £1,000 with a graceful reference to Ivy Compton-Burnett's imaginary fan, who said the only way to express sufficient appreciation would be with a thousand-pound cheque. David Higham took him out for a celebratory lunch at the Etoile. "I can at least begin to imagine what it must feel like for you to have really finished the *Music of Time*," wrote Arthur Mizener: "a radical transformation of life . . . shocking, I'm sure, whether good or bad." Tony himself felt too dazed to think clearly. "You should . . . be very proud," wrote Alison, "like someone who has built a city."

Hearing Secret Harmonies was published on 8 September 1975. BBC TV screened a film about the *Dance* that night, and a portrait gallery of key characters, specially commissioned from Osbert Lancaster, appeared in that week's *Sunday Times*. "My only sadness was occasioned by the thought that it would be the last," wrote Osbert, "—though quite why it should be I don't know—think of Balzac!" At Heinemann's lunch party on publication day Tony sat between two reigning beauties of the book world, Antonia Fraser and Jilly Cooper. "Will he be Lord Powell of Llangwyllogefyn or plain Sir Anthony?" Heygate asked on a postcard to Miranda Wood (Tony refused the knighthood offered him at this point by the Thatcher government): "I think they will probably revive the ancient Dukedom of Chantry."

Tony said he was still too close to the workface to be able to step back and judge what he had done. Fellow practitioners set to work to pin down the essence of his achievement. "My own guess is that, within the English tradition, he is pre-eminent," wrote Paul Scott, who published the final volume of his *Raj Quartet* that year. "The world remembered by Nicholas Jenkins is in many ways better established, more publicly accessible, more objectively *there*, than the worlds we ourselves remember," wrote Michael Frayn. Kingsley Amis closed the book with a sombre feeling, "like the sadness that descends when the last chord of a great symphony fades into silence."

Almost a year after he finished the last instalment, Tony was still struggling to detach himself fully from the hypnotic dreamlike state in which he wrote the *Dance*, a state he found it almost impossible to describe, saying that the material in the end controls itself, or alternatively that he was sometimes "conscious of an external force taking over the job, something beyond the process of thought, conscious planning, or invention." Perhaps he looked back to T. S. Eliot, who had tried to define what a modern novel might be in an essay published the year after Tony first read *The Waste Land* as a sixteen-year-old schoolboy. Certainly Eliot's prescription—"One can be classical in tendency by doing the best one can with the material at hand"— might have been a blueprint for the novel in twelve volumes that Powell finally completed just over half a century later. In *A Dance to the Music of Time* he found the way Eliot suggested, "a way of controlling, of ordering, of giving a shape and a significance to the immense panorama of futility and anarchy which is contemporary history."

POSTSCRIPT

"S hort and slightly stooped," wrote an American fan, describing his first sight of Anthony Powell at the Chantry in 1976: "I noted his full head of grey hair, his up-tilted nose, and wide mouth. He was wearing a red, open-collared shirt, tan drill trousers and low-cut beige chukkha-type boots." In town he wore a battered suit and tie. Apart perhaps from the red shirt, both outfits were practically uniform at the time for writers of his generation. He never wore anything else when I knew him. At our first meeting I was still in my twenties, over-awed by the prospect of meeting a writer I'd been bowled over by at eighteen or nineteen. *A Dance to the Music of Time* changed my life, as it did Jilly Cooper's when she was even younger. Michael Frayn described how it felt in the heady 1960s to stumble on Anthony Powell for the first time:

> It was like discovering a complete civilisation—and not in some remote valley of the Andes or the Himalayas, but in the midst of London, in the midst of my own life. It altered my perception of the world . . . I began to see in my own life the kind of patterns which were emerging in Jenkins's life; glimpsed how tremendous changes prepared themselves unseen beneath the surface of the apparently immutable course of events, and then quite suddenly deflected one's life into some new course, apparently no less immutable. Another world had been superimposed upon my own, refracting and reflecting it.

Exposure to Powell's *Dance* for people who grew up watching its complexities unfold was both intoxicating and unsettling. Halfway through the sequence, I left university and got my first job as a waitress in a fast-food joint on the Tottenham Court Road, later moving one street westward to work as an office dogsbody at the *Spectator*. Both were seedy spots but neither half so real to me as the imaginary pubs in the same neighbourhood frequented by X. Trapnel, or the dingy junk-shop on a side street where Edgar Deacon kept male por-

Hilary Spurling on the jacket flap of her
handbook *Invitation to the Dance*, 1977

nography under the bed at the back. We met in fact, not fiction, in
the basement dining room of the *Spectator*'s old premises at number
99, Gower Street in the autumn of 1969. I had graduated to the books
pages by then, but I couldn't figure out what made Mr. Powell accept
an invitation to lunch from the young, unknown literary editor of an
obscure, small-circulation weekly.

Long afterwards I realized why he came. He was currently working on *Books Do Furnish a Room*, re-creating the fractious and fre-
netically competitive journalistic end of the literary world that he'd
belonged to himself until he was sacked by the editor of *Punch*. Presumably he wanted to dip his toe in it again. All I can remember now
is that I invited a few close friends, including Jim Farrell (who had
just finished writing *Troubles*, the novel that made his name), but not
Auberon Waugh, Evelyn's eldest son, who was the paper's political
correspondent. I remember Bron as a tall shambling friendly figure
hurrying up Gower Street, always with books under his arm and
papers stuffed into the pockets of his long shabby overcoat, but I

didn't know him well, certainly not well enough to guess how he felt about his father's old friend Anthony Powell.

Less than a year after that convivial lunch party at the *Spectator*, I got the sack myself (or rather I resigned before I could be dismissed on the day the proprietor sacked the editor, who was Nigel Lawson). Losing my job seemed a good moment to become a real writer so, on the strength of a publisher's advance of £50, I started work on my first biography. I was already married to a fellow writer, and we scraped a living from then on as jobbing freelance reviewers. Tony helped by asking me to write a kind of handbook or glorified index to the *Dance*, which I did, as soon as the sequence was finished.

These were the years when we got to know the Powells, dropping in at the Chantry in our ancient sports-car whenever we visited my family in the West Country. The pattern was always the same. We arrived for lunch and then walked round the lake, returning around four o'clock to find Violet seated bolt upright on the sofa in the library with a tea-tray on the low table in front of her, and shelves of reference books within easy reach of her right hand. Tony occupied the chaise longue opposite the fireplace. Here they capped and recapped each other's stories, checked dates and sources, bounced ideas, jokes and memories off one another. Their antiphonal exchange was so unlike anything I'd ever heard before that I jotted down a random scrap of dialogue:

TONY: *Is* it Ella Wheeler Wilcox?
VIOLET: Or Robert W. Service?
TONY: Certainly not Robert W. Service.

It wasn't always easy to tell if the characters darting in and out of the Powells' lifelong conversation were real or imaginary. It was often just as hard to say if Tony agreed with Violet's view, or if she were voicing his. He would start an anecdote which she corrected and he then continued, incorporating her twists, embellishments and polishings as he went along. Violet was sceptical, humorous, infinitely discreet and endlessly inquisitive. Her interest in the strangeness of human nature was inexhaustible, like her husband's, and the contents of her mind were finely catalogued and constantly surprising. He drew on them as a novelist today might use the internet. Books surrounded them on shelves and in stacks on the floor, with newspapers on the low table and the TV "tucked away like an animal" in the basement.

Throughout the 1970s and '80s a steady stream of journalists, editors, academics, biographers and TV or radio programme-makers turned up at the Chantry to quiz Tony about the early lives of his contemporaries in a generation that was fast thinning out. John Heygate sent a last affectionate letter at the end of 1975, and shot himself three months later, leaving instructions for a slap-up funeral to be laid on for his friends at Bellarena. Alick Dru died the year after, marvelling to the end at Tony's stamina and strength ("His energy does appal me: he is Balzac & Saint-Simon combined"). In 1978 Gerald Reitlinger accidentally set fire to his house at Beckley, watching in horror as Woodgate and its contents were reduced to the kind of smoking ruin he had himself described on the last page of *The Final Solution*: "After May, 1945, the whole apparatus of National Socialism resembled a tangle of burnt rafters, blackened, soaked and ill-smelling, under which crawled persecutor and victim, no longer very distinguishable . . ." Nobody was hurt and curators from the Ashmolean Museum drove down at once to salvage the collection, but the shock of his loss was so great that Reitlinger died a few weeks later without fully comprehending that his incomparable pots had miraculously survived, stained by smoke and soot but essentially intact, ready to be moved to the museum. He had already made provision for their transfer on his death, a gift that meant the Ashmolean possesses to this day one of the finest collections of oriental porcelain anywhere in the world, East or West.

Writing obituaries took up increasing amounts of Tony's time, and he spent longer still on the incisive portraits of old friends that largely fill his memoirs. He still wrote every morning ("it is awfully difficult to know what to do otherwise"), following up the *Dance* at intervals of a year or two with four successive instalments of these entertaining and instructive memoirs in which he himself barely figures. "I have absolutely no picture of myself," he said when someone asked him why, "never have had." It was nearly a decade before he produced another novel. *O, How the Wheel Becomes It!* is short, slight and as cryptic as its title (taken from Ophelia's mad scene in *Hamlet*). It revolves around G. F. H. Shadbold, an octogenarian man of letters living in the country with two demanding cats and a resourceful, energetic, younger wife, who also writes. Shadbold's own literary output is negligible but his memories of long-forgotten professional rivalries and ancient love affairs give him a modest standing as a relict of the 1920s, "a band decreasing in number, expanding in amnesia and incoherence."

Having become a standby in TV films about household names like Orwell, Betjeman and Waugh, Tony featured in one of his own in 1983, the year the book came out. The high point of his novel is Shadbold's interrogation at the hands of a famously abrasive TV celebrity called Rod Cubbage: "His eyes protruded. His tone was that of a bullying counsel cross-examining in a criminal case of an unusually degrading kind." Outmanoeuvred and ignominiously upstaged by Cubbage, Shadbold ends up being sidelined by the arrival of an ageing beauty with whom he once had an unrequited love affair. "*O, How the Wheel* came over to me as a book about age," Vidia Naipaul wrote to Tony, "creative minds in old bodies, funny, serious, stoical, capturing something special of you both as a man and as a writer." *The Fisher King*, published three years later, is an even flimsier fable set on board a cruise ship steaming round the British Isles (as Swan Hellenic's ship had done in 1979 with the Powells aboard). The central figure is a fashionable photographer with a domineering personality and a pitifully crippled body, who decides after various minor intrigues to give up taking photos. Tony was eighty-two at the end of 1987, and resolved on 31 December to write no more novels. "There is never any lack of material," he said, "only energy to handle what is on offer."

Contemporaries found their own solutions to the same predicament. Adrian Daintrey retired to congenial quarters in the Charterhouse in Smithfield, Philip Larkin read right through the *Dance* ("I am simply racing through it," he wrote to Tony the year before he died: "My only regret is that it is so short"). Osbert Lancaster, growing increasingly deaf, forgetful and short-tempered, expressed his feelings in a last letter to Tony, signing off with a drawing of himself dressed in his robes as a City of London liveryman, bristling with outrage from his wild eyes to the pompoms on his shoes. When New York's *Hudson Review* gave Tony its Bennett prize of $1,500, he spent it on drink, distributing magnums of champagne and crates of

Osbert Lancaster's self-portrait in civic robes from his last
letter to Tony

claret to his innumerable friends, including his agent, his publisher
and a small contingent still toiling at the literary workface, like us.
The Ingersoll Foundation in Chicago picked him for its T. S. Eliot
prize, and in 1988 the Heath government made him CH, or Companion of Honour, an "eminently respectable order," as he said, noting
with satisfaction that most people had never heard of it. Whenever
he won an award or published a book, Tony gave a lunch party at a
round table in a London restaurant, remembering perhaps the gaiety
and good humour of lunches fifty years before at Castano's in Greek
Street. He told me that every writer starts out with a drawer full of
talent: some drawers are deep, some shallow, and you never know
which yours is until you put your hand in it for the last time, and find
it empty.

He still consumed books on a heroic scale (Tony said the only
other advantage of old age was that you lived to see "the end of a
few contemporary stories"). He read or re-read Homer, Dante, Virgil (who defeated him with the *Aeneid*), Proust, Balzac, Dostoevsky,
and Shakespeare above all. The journals he started keeping in 1982
record him reading a Shakespeare play most days, treating the characters exactly as he treated real people. He saw nothing odd in Hamlet ("only too like many persons one has known"), singled out Jessica
in the *Merchant of Venice* as "one of Shakespeare's most attractive
girls," and identified strongly with Macbeth ("anyway in his rumi-

native moods"). *Julius Caesar, Coriolanus* and *Antony and Cleopatra* were probably his favourites among the tragedies with *As You Like It* ("particularly the girls talking to each other") the comedy he liked best. Every so often he caught disconcerting hints of the playwright's private life, confirming a personal note in the sadistic streak shared by the *Tempest*'s Prospero with the Duke in *Measure for Measure*, and speculating about the implications of the couplet in *All's Well That Ends Well*: "War is no strife/To a dark house, and a detested wife."

His own next book was a selection of the reviews he had contributed once a fortnight for almost as long as anyone could remember to the *Daily Telegraph*. "Our nearest thing to Aubrey's *Brief Lives*," said John Bayley, noting the liveliness, the hidden learning and "the serene air of calculated dishevelment" in these lucid, pithy, unpretentious pieces. Professor Bayley was not the only academic critic to find their judgement of other writers sharper and deeper than "all the theoretical pronouncements of modern academic criticism." But Tony's reviewing came to an abrupt halt in the spring of 1990, when *Miscellaneous Verdicts* reached the *Sunday Telegraph*'s chief book reviewer, who was Auberon Waugh. "His review was one long insult," wrote Vidia Naipaul: "It was horribly unfair . . . you felt it was something he had waited a lifetime to write. It was not at all about the literary pieces in the book. It was not even about Tony's novels. It was about an idea of Tony . . . There was an explosion."

Bron by his own account had grown up under a barrage of taunts and merciless disparagement from his father, whose admiration for Tony's writing was so intense that no adverse comment was allowed in the Waugh household. After an upbringing that left him with "the instincts of a street fighter," as one of his friends said, Bron went out of his way as an adult to savage successive volumes of the *Dance*. His autobiography, published after his father's death, contains a scary portrait of Evelyn as a monstrous egoist who regarded all his sons, and this one in particular, as rivals to be snubbed, derided and put down. Even in his own distress, Tony recognized Bron's response as essentially vicarious, the vengeful product of a largely loveless childhood. "Unbalanced though he was with grief and rage," wrote Vidia Naipaul, "Tony's explanation of Bron's behaviour held something of his old generosity." But, whatever its origins, the violence of this latest unprovoked attack was devastating. Tony resigned immediately from the *Daily Telegraph*. The editor, Max Hastings, was appalled. A long-term admirer of the *Dance*, he drove down himself to the Chantry but Tony remained implacable. Nothing Max could say lessened his sense of betrayal by a paper for which he had reviewed, in Shadbold's phrase, up hill and down dale for nearly half a century, including the year he spent after the war writing its fiction column.

The situation was painful for me, too, because by that time I was also working for the *Telegraph*'s book section, contributing the lead piece in alternate weeks with Tony. His precipitate departure caused anger and distress on both sides, especially on the books page. It seemed to me one way of defusing the situation might be for the paper to make a traditional gesture of regard for one of its oldest and most illustrious contributors, perhaps in the shape of a portrait. Tony was already modelling for a head by the sculptor William Pye, so I suggested buying a cast, and the editor agreed. Rodrigo Moynihan had painted Tony five years earlier as an eightieth birthday present from his friends and admirers, who clubbed together to pay for it as Henry James's supporters had done before them, commissioning John Singer Sargent to paint the novelist at seventy in 1913. But Sargent turned out to be the better bet. Moynihan produced a decidedly anaemic portrait, and so did Henry Mee, who persuaded Tony to sit for him two years later. "Powell undoubtedly looks a shade battered, perhaps even recent subject of physical assault . . . ," Tony said of this second canvas, possibly seeing it as a premonition of his treatment at Bron's hands. Neither portrait comes anywhere near the power and presence of the bust the *Daily Telegraph* acquired from Pye at the end of 1991.

The problem was where to put it. The paper had recently exchanged its venerable art deco building in Fleet Street for streamlined new premises in the UK's tallest office block, number 1, Canada Square in Docklands, where nobody wanted a massive bronze bust, least of all the new literary editor who had caused the trouble in the first place, and now looked likely to have Powell's head standing in his office "as a permanent reproach." In the end it took up a position outside the editor's door. Almost at once it became the paper's central landmark, a means of taking bearings and navigating the identical corridors radiating out from the hub of this vast anonymous white-walled office complex. The bust, probably the only unique and absolutely individual object in the building's entire fifty storeys, spent its first few weeks perched on a filing cabinet with an office memo taped to its forehead: "Some day my plinth will come." A second cast stood in the dining-room window at the Chantry, facing down the long polished table to Tony's place at the far end. Violet told me that, whenever she rushed past it from the kitchen to answer the telephone in the hall, the bust was so uncannily lifelike that—although it was three times lifesize and cast in greenish bronze—she more than once mistook it for her husband.

It had seemed a good idea at the time to extend the impressively eccentric collection of busts at the Chantry by adding one of its owner, but it never occurred to me that it might aggravate the disobliging reputation that clung to Powell in these years. He had somehow come to stand for everything dull, conventional and socially exclusive to a younger generation who had never read him, and being cast in bronze only confirmed his supposed stuffiness and pomposity. Vidia Naipaul, who had written with such subtlety and feeling about the third volume of the *Dance*, read six more volumes after Tony's death and promptly reversed his view, characterizing the sequence as irredeemably trivial and clumsy. From a man who had received nothing but admiration and affection from Tony in his lifetime, this posthumous offensive is not easy to explain. It struck much the same note of grievance and personal affront as previous attacks by Muggeridge, Larkin and Bron Waugh, all actual or failed novelists, presumably obscurely threatened by the sheer scale and ambition of Powell's achievement. "Anthony Powell was the most European of twentieth-century British novelists," Tariq Ali wrote, responding to Naipaul in an essay that places Powell alongside his peers, Stendhal, Balzac, Musil and Proust: "We need to dispense with the blinkered view that his *Dance to the Music of Time* is a novel sequence that can be enjoyed only by English 'toffs' or readers of the *Daily Telegraph*."

But the popular myth of Powell as an arch-Tory and snob's snob was a miasma almost impossible to dislodge, as Philip Larkin said when he and his girlfriend found themselves "preceded, accompanied and followed by a guard of honour of flies" on West Country walks after their only visit to the Chantry. By the time I reached London in the early 1960s, it was already becoming almost a badge of political correctness in literary circles to disparage the *Dance*. "It's elitist, class-ridden, an English upper-class comedy of manners written by a snob," Ian Rankin said of his first attempt to read *A Question of Upbringing*. This was the standard view, one that could not long survive even the most cursory reading of the sequence, but it was as if people had mysteriously agreed it wasn't worth the trouble. Rankin's response was unusual only in that he persevered, coming in the end to count himself among the *Dance*'s greatest admirers. "Reading it is like a great creative master-class," he said: "I re-read it every couple of years."

The generally negative response was, if anything, reinforced by publication of the memoirs. With the death of Malcolm Muggeridge in 1990, Tony became virtually the sole survivor of his literary generation. Mannerisms and turns of thought that had once been completely normal were growing less and less familiar. There were complaints about Powell's old world attitudes, his clothes, his accent, even the way he pronounced his name. Three volumes of *Journals* made things worse. Even a keen admirer like Hugh Thomas deplored the author's apparent determination to portray himself "as dim, provincial, insular." Tony's habitual tactics with interviewers confirmed the stereotype. He made no attempt to hide his irritation with journalists' often banal and endlessly repeated questions, claiming that he kept a set of stock responses ready to hand out in return, like a soldier who saves himself trouble by setting aside part of his kit for inspection only. Interviewers, already irritated by the way he looked or talked, naturally took offence at his brusque manner, and resented his perfunctory or unhelpful answers.

In fact Tony was exhausted. The miseries of old age—physical frailty, memory loss, lack of concentration—steadily overhauled him in his late eighties. "It's like being punished for a crime you did not commit," he said. He no longer went to London, rarely entertained guests at the Chantry and became increasingly reluctant to leave the house himself, even in a wheelchair. Movement was difficult. People tired him. Talking wore him out. The last conversation of any length I had with him was in 1993 or 1994, when he was almost ninety. I had just come back from a summer spent in the south of France doing research for a biography of Henri Matisse, a subject Tony strongly

He was a captivating friend, and the best listener
I ever met.

advised me to avoid. Now I had stumbled on a secret history that
placed the painter at the heart of the sensational Humbert trial, billed
by the press in 1901 as the greatest scandal of the century. I had told
no one my story, which Tony assured me would be safe with him
because his short-term memory no longer functioned.

Before showing me upstairs to his bedroom, Violet had warned
me that half an hour was as much as he could manage but, when I
got up to go after thirty minutes, Tony told me curtly to carry on.
He was as intent as I had ever seen him, listening with concentration,
pouncing on salient detail and cross-examining with forensic skill.
When I finally came downstairs an hour and a half later, Violet was
furious. I explained that I couldn't repeat my story to her or anyone
else because I hadn't yet told Matisse's immediate descendants, who
knew only that their family skeleton had been so successfully hushed
up that nobody any longer had the faintest inkling what it was. "Must
be sex, crime or money," Violet snapped. She was right on two out
of three counts, but her antennae were so acute that it seemed to me

she was quite capable of piecing the whole affair together if I told her which two of the three she'd got right.

For some reason I remember their reactions as vividly as if it were yesterday. Tony's absorption was as characteristic as Violet's indignation. He was the best listener I ever met, and in these last years I saved up gossip and stories for him because there was nothing else I could give him that he liked so much. He was a captivating friend, generous, affectionate, consoling and often absurdly funny. His braying laugh, Violet's occasional acerbity and underlying sweetness, made visits to the Chantry still a pleasure unlike any other, no matter what problems now lurked beneath the surface. "They were obviously a happily married couple," as Tony himself said of the Macbeths.

It had been agreed between us that I would one day write his biography but, when Tony suggested we make a start before it was too late, the experiment proved a miserable failure. It was my fault, not his. He was perfectly willing to answer whatever I asked, but I was too preoccupied elsewhere to formulate the right questions, or follow them up with anything like professional rigour. Afterwards I had to write and explain that it was impossible for me to think of him in the cold, even clinical light essential for any biographical attempt, and that I couldn't even try to treat him as a subject without establishing some sort of temporal perspective. "I only wish I could give it to you," he wrote sadly in reply.

For a decade or more he had been aware of shadows lengthening: "a masked and muffled figure loiters persistently at the back of every room," he wrote at the end of the last volume of his memoirs, "as if waiting for a word at the most tactful moment." By the 1990s he was showing symptoms of the progressive and degenerative disease that eventually killed him. He remained at home with his family about him. Tristram and Virginia with their children had taken over the renovated Stables. Violet and John looked after Tony in the house itself, doing what they could to discourage visits from reporters, eventually from friends as well. The doctor and the district nurse called regularly. Repeated stays in the Bath Clinic left Tony sometimes too drained and depleted even to read Shakespeare. He was drawn to Justice Shallow in *Henry IV, Part 2*, the quavery, confused and garrulous provincial magistrate who finds himself no longer able in his eighties to get up to London: "perhaps my favourite character

Anthony Powell: clay head by William Pye

in Shakespeare," Tony said of Robert Shallow, "a very interesting figure."

A more comprehensive likeness, first pointed out by Ferdy Mount, is the figure in the right-hand-bottom corner of Poussin's *Dance to the Music of Time*:

> If you subtract Time's whiskers and ignore his nakedness, there is something about the figure—his ironic smile, the way he watches the figures dancing with such amused detachment while plucking his lyre—which recalls Powell's relationship to those around him.

Tony died of cerebro-vascular disease on 28 March 2000. His sons scattered his ashes from a boat on Chantry lake and, at a memorial service in the Grosvenor Chapel in London, Antonia's second husband, Harold Pinter, read the passage from the bible about Ezekiel in the valley full of bones. Violet died just under two years later.

For her Pye's bust of Powell had been a comfort, as it afterwards became for me. We had installed a third cast at the bottom of our long

London garden, beneath an ancient pear-tree in an untidy tangle of comfrey, cranesbill and spurge. If I look out of the first-floor window in my workroom, I can see its ever so slightly asymmetrical features looking back at me: observant, amused and sceptical, even faintly sardonic: the face of a man who had, as he himself once said of Shakespeare, "an extraordinary grasp of what other people were like."

NOTES

Abbreviations

Works by Anthony Powell

Novels

AM *Afternoon Men*, 1931
Vbg *Venusberg*, 1932
FVD *From a View to a Death*, 1933
A&P *Agents and Patients*, 1936
WBW *What's Become of Waring*, 1939
OHWB O, How the Wheel Becomes It!, 1983

DMT/Dance *A Dance to the Music of Time*:

QU *A Question of Upbringing*, 1951
BM *A Buyer's Market*, 1952
AW *The Acceptance World*, 1955
ALM *At Lady Molly's*, 1957
CCR *Casanova's Chinese Restaurant*, 1960
KO *The Kindly Ones*, 1962
VB *The Valley of Bones*, 1964
SA *The Soldier's Art*, 1966
MP *The Military Philosophers*, 1968
BDFR *Books Do Furnish a Room*, 1971
TK *Temporary Kings*, 1973
HSH *Hearing Secret Harmonies*, 1975

Non-fiction

JA *John Aubrey and His Friends*, revised edn., 1988 [1948]
IS *Infants of the Spring. The Memoirs of Anthony Powell*, vol. i, 1976
MD *Messengers of Day. The Memoirs of Anthony Powell*, vol. ii, 1978
SAG *The Strangers All Are Gone. The Memoirs of Anthony Powell*, vol. iii, 1980
FMT *Faces in My Time. The Memoirs of Anthony Powell*, vol. iv, 1982

J1 *Journals 1982–6*, 1995
J2 *Journals 1987–9*, 1996
J3 *Journals 1990–92*, 1997

MV *Miscellaneous Verdicts. Writings on Writers 1946–89*
UR *Under Review. Writings on Writers 1946–90*
WN *A Writer's Notebook*, 201
SP *Some Poets, Artists & "A Reference for Mellors,"* 2005

Works by Violet Powell

FOS *Five out of Six*, 1960
WFC *Within the Family Circle*, 1976
DP *The Departure Platform*, 1998
SiS *A Stone in the Shade*, 2013

General

AP Anthony Powell
APS Anthony Powell Society
APSN Anthony Powell Society Newsletter
CA Chantry Private Archive
DMM *Like It Was: The Diaries of Malcolm Muggeridge*, 1981
DT *Daily Telegraph*
HA Heinemann Archive, HRC
HRC Harry Ransom Humanities Research Center, Austin, Texas
MJM an unpublished memoir by Martha James, daughter of Irene Hodgkin and
    Tristram Hillier
MWA ts autobiography by Miranda Wood (said by its author to be the novel she
    called *Pickle My Bones*: in fact a direct transcript from life with only the
    names changed), priv. coll.
PFA Powell Family Archive
PMB *Pack My Bag. A Self-Portrait* by Henry Green [Henry Yorke], 1940
SL Stephen Lloyd, *Constant Lambert. Beyond the Rio Grande*, 2014
VP Lady Violet Powell, née Pakenham

Chapter 1

3   "All his character points . . .": JA 34
3   "If ever I had been good for anything . . .": JA 12
3   "It was this powerful visual imagination . . .": JA 31
4   genealogical knitting: To H. Spurling; for a family tree, see IS xi; for family
    origins, IS 2–22; & for a fuller account, AP, "The Powell Family of Lowes
    and Clyro in Radnorshire, and Brilley in Herefordshire, 1581–1800," *Trans-
    actions of the Radnorshire Society*, 1940
4   his grandmother refused: IS 35
4   "an unappeasable fox-hunter": KO 36
5   to avoid being treated: IS 27

5 Adcock was once mistaken: IS 30–31

6 "guests came for a week . . .": IS 34

7 smeared by the master of the Belvoir: IS 36; KO 36, information from J. Powell

7 "nerve-wracked, despondent . . .": IS 35

7 "an unusual man . . .": IS 29

8 "lands won with an admixture . . .": JA 246

8 Llyr of Crugeryr: See IS 5–6; & AP, "The Powell Descent from Llewellyn Crugeryr & the Princes of Deheubarth," *Transactions of the Radnorshire Society*, 1960

8 "Their pleasures and . . .": JA 131

9 His mother moved house: IS 1

9 "the area . . . imparts . . .": BM 273–4

10 "rumoured to be able . . .": SiS 90; for a fuller account of the Wells-Dymokes and their ancestors, see IS 13–27

11 AP's parents' courtship: IS 38; & information from VP

13 "It would be impossible to believe . . .": VP to HS

13 AP's parents' marriage: Information from VP; & see IS 38–9

14 "I was brought up . . .": AP interview, "Talk of the Town," *New Yorker*, 3.7.65

14 "the unhappy gift . . .": IS 177

15 "I have sometimes wondered . . .": IS 40

16 "a kind of innate spite . . .": IS 29

17 "My father always came first . . .": IS 38

17 "My father really hated clarity": KO 45

17 "coping skilfully . . .": IS 86

18 happiest time: IS 51

18 ten years off her age: E.g., 1911 census

18 "A white belted . . .": Barbara Ker-Seymer/AP, 17.10.76

19 "I cannot remember a time . . .": IS 43

19 "Now the truth came . . .": IS 46

20 "where, beside the kneeling elephant . . .": BM 18

20 "Walking there was not at all . . .": WBW 63

20 "a long, low Noah's Ark . . .": KO 5; see also IS 51, 53–4, and 84–5 for photo. Stonedene, long since demolished, bequeathed its name to Stonedene Close, part of the characterless suburban infill now covering the hill, bisected by the B3002. The fictional name Stonehurst came from a neighbouring house that once stood on the site of what is now 15, Stonehill Road

21 Straker-Squire: Several records were broken at Brooklands by the prototype, including the Flying Mile at 95 mph in 1910

21 Philip Oyler: 1880–1973, founder of the progressive Marshin School at Hadley Down, Hants. See J2 102

21 Ludshott Common: Renamed Grayshott Common in KO, and subsequently acquired by the National Trust

21   she sometimes woke: IS 55

22   "Vi has always been . . .": IS 39

22   the divorce decree became final: 21.7.13: I am grateful to John Powell for sharing with me Sarah Taylor's research into this affair; its repercussions in the *Grey River Argus* of Greymouth, New Zealand

22   "completely at ease . . .": IS 39

22   "a life entirely enclosed . . .": KO 23

22   "Life seemed all at once . . .": IS 57

23   "My dear mummy . . .": AP/Maud Powell, n.d. (Nov. 1914)

23   "standing in the middle . . .": Basil Hambrough, IS 86

24   "the unpleasantness of some boys . . .": IS 58

24   "This boy shows . . .": Peter Ustinov, *Dear Me*, 1977

24   "a kind of shanty town . . .": IS 61

24   "a child's . . . protective forgetfulness": IS 63; for AP's account of New Beacon, see IS 61–8

24   smashed the much-prized watch: AP/Maud Powell, 18.6.17

24   "the wickedness of boies": JA 40

25   "'I was exceedingly mild . . .": JA 39

25   "an ever rolling stream . . .": IS 63

25   "sparse grey hair . . .": IS 62

25   "a language that passed . . .": IS 63

25   "nothing much short . . .": IS 61

25   "I think I bashed him": AP/Maud Powell, 4.3.17

26   stinking ham: PMB 41

26   "as prisoners . . .": PMB 49

26   "At first we paid attention . . .": PMB 83

27   "malignant ghosts . . .": PMB 46

27   "Sometimes on icy football fields . . .": AP, "The Wat'ry Glade," Graham Greene (ed.), *The Old School. Essays by Divers Hands*, 1934, p. 150

27   killed the headmaster: IS 70

27   "I should be unwilling . . .": IS 65

27   like the witch: PMB 19; IS 62

27   "he can talk . . .": R. Byron, *Letters Home*, ed. Lucy Butler, 1991, p. 8

27   "like professional narrators . . .": IS 67

27   "I have been inventing . . .": AP/Maud Powell, 4.3.17

27   improvising a novel together: IS 67–8

28   a tiny inkwash of the artist: AP/Maud Powell, 13.3.17

28   "a touch of M. de Charlus": J3 115

28   first school report: 2.8.16 (CA)

29   Pontifex & Shanks: Jeremy Treglown, *Romancing. The Life & Work of Henry Green*, 2000, p. 102

29   "We were well brought up . . .": PMB 14

29   "ragging his father . . .": IS 67

30   "a powerful narcotic . . .": SAG 47

30 "The end of the war . . .": Arthur Waugh, *One Man's Road*, 1931, p. 364; & see Alan Pryce-Jones, *The Bonus of Laughter*, 1987, p. 23

30 "an almost solid phalanx . . .": IS 85

30 "You can tell me nothing . . .": Information from VP

31 a slow-moving disaster: VP, SiS 2

31 Lilette McCraith: IS 34

31 acknowledged . . . as Jessie's lover: J3 22

32 more like his mother: AP/VP, 27.11.39

32 Jessie finally sent for: IS 35

32 Shakespeare: J2 15; J3 7, 85

32 "When she opened the door to us . . .": CCR 108

33 "Small, wiry, aggressive . . .": SA 120

Chapter 2

34 Daytrip to Eton: DMM 288 (entry for 22.7.48)

34 he even played Post in a Ram: J2 80, Greene (ed.), "The Wat'ry Glade," op. cit., 159

35 cruelly teased for: Treglown, *Romancing*, op. cit., 36

35 "There was far more liberty . . .": PMB 93

36 "He does not make . . .": A. M. Goodhart, 27.7.20 (CA)

36 "possibly what is due . . . ," "his mind and tastes . . .": Ibid., 7.4.23 & 2.8.23 (both CA)

36 "There was always a fuss . . .": IS 72

37 "I am having rather beastly . . .": AP/Maud Powell, Sunday, Nov. 1920

37 "A. M. Goodhart's was not merely . . .": IS 75

37 "being always prepared . . .": Ibid.

37 the lost umbrella had now turned up: DMM 24.3.50; for a reconstruction of the Braddock alias Thorne incident, based on this affair in DMT, see Jeffrey Manley, "Follow the Eton Wick Road," APSN, no. 42, pp. 10–15

37 "a deplorable figure . . .": Hugh Cecil, "My Father at Eton," *David Cecil*, ed. Hannah Cranbourne, 1990, p. 20

38 "an acknowledged star . . .": IS 76

38 "sleet: wind: sultry heat": QB 3

38 "Homer metamorphosed . . .": IS 125

39 slow and unacknowledged transition: See Michael Meredith, "A Question of Upbringing and the Eton Experience," APS, *Conference Proceedings*, 2001, pp. 19–27; I am grateful to Mr. Meredith for much further information, & for a tour of the school

39 Goodhart had studied music: For his subsequent musical career, see W. B. Henshaw, *Biographical Dictionary of Organists*, pp. 2003–15

39 ban on drama: See Michael Meredith, *The Hundred Years of Eton Theatre*, privately printed, Eton, 2001

40 revival of *The Beggar's Opera*: 5.6.20 at the Lyric Theatre, Hammersmith,

with Frederick Ranalow as Macheath; ran for a ground-breaking 1,463 performances

40 on *Desert Island Discs*: BBC Radio 4, 16.10.76

41 "I remember thinking . . .": AP/VP, 3.11.39

41 "the most loathsome form . . .": IS 78

41 "At the time . . .": QU 28

41 *The Loom of Youth*: IS 76

42 "Sex was a dread mystery . . .": PMB 47

42 David Cecil: IS 80; J1 58

42 "One drank the milk . . .": AP, "The Wat'ry Glade," op. cit., 159

42 officer cadets in horn-rimmed spectacles: Ibid., 160

43 "It was a long low room . . .": PMB 171

43 "among the byways . . .": IS 81; for Sidney Evans (1846–9), see Meredith, "A Question of Upbringing and the Eton Experience," op. cit.; & Sidney Evans, *The Drawing Schools, Eton College*, 1983

43 "Here . . . we had what came . . .": PMB 172

44 "'What did the headmaster say?'": Footnote to Harold Acton's obituary, DT, 28.2.1994

44 a scene from *Macbeth*: "A Question of Upbringing and The Eton Experience," op. cit., p. 20; J1 276

44 "to sound the trumpet . . .": IS 117; *Eton Candle*, vol. 1, Mar. 1922, was the only issue

44 a rakish Napoleonic guardsman: *Colonel Caesar Cannonbrains of the Black Hussars*, see IS 117

45 Acton's first book of poems: IS 118

46 Tony's illicit picture-books: *L'Art decoratif de Léon Bakst* (*The Decorative Art of Léon Bakst*), Maurice de Brunoff, Paris, 1913

46 "It was nothing less than a disaster . . .": IS 81

46 prize for English literature: Goodhart's reports, 31.3.21 & 20.12.21 (CA)

47 "She and I . . . seem . . .": IS 87

47 "arriving at the house . . . more calming than wine lists": IS 90

47 "the occasional sweep . . .": IS 88

48 "the kingdom of art . . .": IS 88

48 "I assure you I know . . .": C. Millard/AP, 15.3.22

48 "I . . . passed it over . . .": Ibid., 28.2.22

48 "He was the first . . .": IS 90

49 Oscar Wilde bibliography: Published 1914 under the pseudonym Stuart Mason

49 "For those who live . . .": IS 93

49 full-length oil portrait: By Harper Pennington, now in Los Angeles (the NPG still has no portrait of Wilde)

49 "I should have thought . . .": IS 93

49 "an exceptionally talented . . .": C. Millard/AP, 5.4.22

50 "Millard's talk . . .": IS 91

50 "You are a great . . .": IS 93

50 "something wan and starved . . .": Oscar Burdet in Montgomery-Hyde, *Christopher Sclater Millard (Stuart Mason), Bibliographer & Antiquarian Book-dealer*, NY, 1990, p. 22

50 "I was brought face to face . . .": IS 94

50 "I am glad that my mother . . .": IS 95

51 "to me a picture . . .": IS 48

52 "even tennis parties . . .": IS 144

52 "My father used to say . . .": IS 143

52 "For A.D.P . . .": IS 144

52 a lengthy assessment: By V. Larbaud, first published April, 1922, reprinted *Criterion*, no. 1, 1922

52 "It's all very like reviewing . . .": AP/VP, 23.8.50

53 "he is a great friend . . .": A. M. Goodhart school report, 7.4.23 (CA)

53 "lively, obstinate, generous . . .": QU 9

54 "Like a man effortlessly . . .": QU 56

54 "come to deliver . . .": IS 169

55 "the stuff is like autumn leaves . . .": James Knox, *Robert Byron. A Biography*, 2003, p. 49

55 "indefinable air . . .": QU 191

55 "letting himself out of . . .": PMB 181

55 "The pinnacles, the turrets . . .": AP, "The Wat'ry Glade," op. cit., 161

55 last time he ever: AP/VP, 26.12.39

55 one-way ticket: Knox, *Robert Byron*, op. cit., 27

55 "days at school . . .": QU 2

56 "Money did not come into it . . .": PMB 171

57 "too young to enter the war . . .": John Heygate, *Talking Pictures*, 1934, p. 282

57 "Men and women . . . *You never caught up with them* [my italics. HS]": IS 147–8

58 "I think Byron scarcely knew . . .": J3 143

58 Venusberg and Helsinki: IS 171–2

59 AP in Finland: Visiting cards, postcards, photos and newspaper clipping (CA); see also IS 172–4

60 *Desert Island Discs*: BBC Radio 4, 16.10.76

60 *Hunters in the Snow*: DP 114

61 prostitutes he met: PMB 184

61 virginity remained intact: Cyril Connolly, *Enemies of Promise*, 1938, p. 227

61 Lulu, who worked for Zelli's: IS 177

61 "How little I liked . . .": IS 189

61 always with him: IS 182

62 "One left reeling": Hugh Lloyd-Jones (ed.), *Maurice Bowra. A Celebration*, 1974, p. 49

62 looked like Humpty-Dumpty: IS 178

62 "He passed all Maurice's . . .": Leslie Mitchell, *Maurice Bowra. A Life*, 2009, p. 171

62 "Everything about him . . . open snobbishness . . .": IS 180

63 "The idea that Bowra himself . . .": IS 189

63 Marcel Proust: IS 194, MD 115 (AP read the first 3, not 6, at Oxford: vols. 4, 5 & 6 came out in 1928 & 1929)

64 "a most awful, dreadful . . .": Henry Green, *Blindness*, 1926, p. 34

64 "perhaps the greatest . . .": IS 52

64 "the unadorned style . . .": IS 161

64 "Irrelevancy means so much . . .": Tchekhov's *Cherry Orchard*, Henry Yorke/Neville Coghill, 8.4.25; Treglown, *Romancing*, op. cit., 58; although AP said little about Chekhov, he certainly read the plays at this point, and came in the end to rate Chekhov with Dostoevsky as one of the twin poles of modern Russian literature, see WN 4 & IS 174

65 the General Strike: IS 95–6

65 Congress of Vienna: IS 196–7

65 "*I now saw in a flash* . . ." (my italics): IS 150

65 Henry's novel: Treglown, *Romancing*, op. cit., 159–60

66 "invaluable hints , , ,": MD 6

66 "A published novel . . .": IS 194

66 It was Balston: IS 146 & 197; see also MD 4 & 182, FMT 157

66 "I feel you need a word . . .": M. Bowra/H. Yorke., n.d., Treglown, *Romancing*, op. cit., 299, n. 89

66 discovered Richard Burton: MD 114

67 "Now come tidings . . .": WN 5; & HSH 271–2

Chapter 3

68 "All publishing houses . . .": MD 18

68 plum-coloured suit: Tom Bishop/AP, 7.6.78

68 "decaying fruit . . .": Tom Bishop/AP, 6.6.78 & MD 8

69 "Dust was everywhere . . .": MD 14

69 half tipsy: M. Wood/AP, 19.3.39

69 "a natural enemy . . .": Arthur Waugh, *One Man's Road*, 1931, pp. 464–5

69 "close to detesting . . .": MD 9; for an official history of his firm, see John Joliffe, *Woolf at the Door. Duckworth: One Hundred Years of Bloomsbury Behaviour*, 1998

69 Jonathan Cape . . . left in 1920: See Joliffe, *One Man's Road*, op. cit., 464–5

69 Balston as Cape's successor: Basil Liddell Hart/AP, n.d., & MD 9

69 "Even to a boy's ears . . .": Tom Bishop/AP, 6.6.78

70 He had joined the firm . . . : Basil Liddell Hart/AP, n.d.

70 a good deal of platitude: WN 17

70 "one of the firm's most lucrative . . . Galsworthy stood there . . .": MD 76

71 "literary agents . . .": WN 15

71 "you patiently interviewed . . .": Tom Bishop/AP, 6.6.78

71 "He did not listen . . .": AM 39–40

71 nothing taught him more: MD 75

71 "mice- and beetle-infested . . .": T. Bishop/AP, 6.6.78

72 *The Green Hat*: MD 2

72 £120,000: A. S. Frere, Introduction to Cassell's 1968 reprint of *The Green Hat*

72 "above a mean lane . . .": Michael Arlen, *The Green Hat. A Romance for a Few People*, 1924, p. 3

72 "a kind of tarts' barracks": MD 16

72 "an airing-cupboard . . .": MD 3

72 wooden prop: AP, "I Was a Territorial," *Night and Day*, 8.7.37

72 Bumble Dawson: MD 15

73 "the Market's air . . .": MD 2

73 "for purity": Arlen, *Green Hat*, op. cit., 47

73 "She was a woman . . .": Ibid., 268

73 "in the burning darkness . . .": Ibid., 56

73 *Saturday Market*: See Jane Stevenson, *Edward Burra: Twentieth-century Eye*, 2007, p. 147 (Burra took the shopfront from his home town of Rye)

73 "I liked living there . . .": AP, "I Was a Territorial," *Night and Day*, 8.7.37

74 "de-Oxfordification": Ibid.

74 "I felt that if the Gunners . . .": MD 25

74 "impelling an iron-mouthed . . .": MD 26

74 "I should like to meet . . .": WN 6 (identified by AP in pencil in his copy)

74 "I used to wonder . . .": Mary Clive, *Brought Up and Brought Out*, 1938, p. 195

75 "bored with boredom": Arlen, *Green Hat*, op. cit., 111

75 "In her day she must . . .": MD 53

75 modern equivalent of the tavern: AP/Malcolm Muggeridge, 21.8.45

76 "*Why* aren't you going? . . .": Dig Biddulph/AP, 19.12.26

76 "Do write and tell me": Ibid., 24.11.26

76 "an ordeal of the most gruelling order": IS 187 & Lloyd-Jones (ed.), *Maurice*; op. cit., 95; see also C. M. Bowra, *Memories 1898–1939*, 1966, p. 195

76 Georgia Sitwell: WN 19 (place and person identified by AP in pencil in his copy)

76 parting with Duggan: IS 196

76 "Hopeless inferiorities": AP/H. Yorke, n.d. [Oct. 1927]

76 "I still can't understand . . .": D. Biddulph/AP, 6.1.27

76 twenty thousand words of another: Treglown, *Romancing*, op. cit., 69

76 He read extracts: H. Yorke/AP, 4.9.28 & 13.10.28

77 "Publisher talking . . .": WN 3

77 "Ah, you're buying experience . . .": WN 11

77 "courtly old bores": WN 13

77 "I am so bored . . .": Chekhov, *Ivanov*, Act 2; see WN 4

77 "the dreadful monotony . . .": AP/H. Yorke, 28.8.27

77 "almost suicidal": John Knox, *Robert Byron*, 2003, pp. 122–4

77 "The last thing on earth . . .": Interview with Lynn Barber, *Sunday Times Magazine*, 8.3.92

78 "the most *ravishing* young women . . . I shall have to . . .": AP/H. Yorke, n.d. [autumn 1927]

78 "those years seemed . . .": Alec Waugh, *My Brother Evelyn and Other Portraits*, 1961, pp. 18 & 191

78 Duckworths' advance: Joliffe, *Woolf at the Door*, op. cit., 50; but see MD 23

78 "Balston will never . . .": Alec Waugh, *My Brother Evelyn*, op. cit., 188

78 "too ashamed to mention": Ibid., 191

78 "Oh, Tolstoy and all that": MD 62

78 *Picaresque*: MD 21

78 "I have done another chapter . . .": E. Waugh/AP, n.d. (autumn 1927)

78 Evelyn claimed: MD 21–2

79 "books—their writing, editing . . .": MD 19

79 "a thrusting youngster . . .": MD 20

79 "This was the period . . .": MD 19

80 "a shattering blow": MD 28

80 A sketch of Tony reading: See Nina Hamnett, *Is She a Lady?*, 1955, p. 128; another of her portraits is reproduced in MD 86

80 "his first grown-up affair": Peter Quennell, see Denise Hooker, *Nina Hamnett. Queen of Bohemia*, 1986, pp. 187 & 272, n. 22

80 "*elle est vraiment putain . . .*": Hooker, *Nina Hamnett*, op. cit., 112 & 268, n. 29

81 "the same kind of gutless half-wit . . .": Nina Hamnett, *Laughing Torso*, 1932, p. 7

81 Nina had an income: Hooker, *Nina Hamnett*, op. cit., 28

81 "I let them get on with it . . .": Ibid., 112 & 268, n. 27

81 John Banting's surrealist nude: Hamnett, *Is She a Lady?*, op. cit, 66; reproduced in Hooker, *Nina Hamnett*, op. cit., 210

81 "my little Etonian": Hooker, *Nina Hamnett*, op. cit., 187 & 272, n. 21

82 "a well-dressed young Englishman . . .": Hamnett, *Laughing Torso*, op. cit., 270

82 "murky shows": Dig Biddulph/AP, 6.1.27

82 Nina suggested drawing Tony: MD 42

83 mice in her studio: Hamnett, *Laughing Torso*, op. cit., 38

83 Nina exuberantly drunk: Maurice Richardson, see Michael Barber, *Anthony Powell. A Life*, 2004, pp. 64 & 304, n. 30

83 "her light, savant and malicious . . .": *Vogue*, April 1928; see Hooker, *Nina Hamnett*, op. cit., 187

83 "It seems that Nina Hamnett . . .": To Gerald Yorke, 22.2.29; John Symonds, *The King of the Shadow Realm. Aleister Crowley, His Life & Magic*, 1989, p. 490

83 "a liberal education": Alec Waugh, *The Best Wine Last*, 1978, p. 182

83 "Finding a way of killing Sunday afternoons . . .": Hamnett, *Is She a Lady?*, op. cit., 5

83 She introduced him: See MD 54 & Hooker, *Nina Hamnett*, op. cit., 187

84 Betty May: MD 79–81; and see Hooker, *Nina Hamnett*, op. cit., 45

84 Alfred Duggan: MD 80

84 Death of Loveday: Betty May, *Tiger Woman. My Story*, Duckworth, 1929, pp. 181–4 & 188; Hamnett, *Laughing Torso*, op. cit., 176

85 "Please, please . . .": MD 81

85 "We are taking no risks . . .": AP/H. Yorke, 19 Oct. [1928]

85 Simpson's in the Strand: MD 83

85 "the wildest stories . . .": Tom Driberg, *Ruling Passions*, 1977, p. 84

86 money into Crowley's bank account: H. Yorke/AP, 13.9.28; & see Symonds, *King of the Shadow Realm*, op. cit., 419, 420, 433, 437 & 442–3

86 "Love is the Law . . .": MD 82

86 "strangely caught together . . . the hard life of a mage . . .": MD 83

86 Rainbow Edition: The first 6 volumes came out in 1929, starting with *Prancing Nigger*, followed in 1930 by 2 more, & the last 2 in 1934; Duckworth simultaneously published a more conventional, 2-volume New Collected Edition; & see MD 75

87 "they do not like . . .": To his mother, 29.4.28; see Knox, *Robert Byron*, op. cit.

87 "a rather amusing young woman . . .": AP/H. Yorke, 28.8.27

87 Stendhal: MD 115

87 Lermontov: MD 117–18

87 strongest single influence: Laurence Kelly to HS, 21.11.12

88 "his luminous brutal prose . . .": MD 112

88 James Joyce: MD 111

88 "purposeless exchanges . . .": MD 110

88 "*The Enormous Room* seemed . . . Cummings really . . .": *Punch*, 1.3.84; cutting of an undated interview with AP pasted into Varda's 1930 reissue of *The Enormous Room*; see also MD 109

88 *Decline and Fall*: MD 102–6; Alec Waugh, *My Brother Evelyn*, op. cit., 193; *The Early Years of Alec Waugh*, 1962, p. 203

89 commissioned a novel: *The Old Expedient* (1928) by Pansy Pakenham; & *In England Now* (1932) by Hans Duffy [pseudonym for Mary Pakenham]

89 *Frost in May*: MD 95–6

89 Inez Holden: MD 23–4; information from Ariane Banks; see also memoirs in the *London Magazine* by AP (Oct./Nov. 1974) & by Celia Goodman (Dec./Jan. 1994)

89 "We were at the Holdens . . .": E. Waugh/AP, n.d. [Oct. 1927]; & see Mark Amory (ed.), *Letters of Evelyn Waugh*, 1980, p. 25. Cachets de Faivre were popular painkillers

89 "the sort of woman . . .": WN 16; see Vbg 38

89 "a nature altogether unused . . .": MD 24

90 "I must not be . . .": Edith Sitwell/AP, 11.2.39

90 "Every time the public . . .": Hamnett, *Laughing Torso*, op. cit., 105

90 "They exult in a scrap . . .": Sarah Bradford, *Sacheverell Sitwell. Splendours and Miseries*, 1993, p. 12

90 "tall fair attenuated . . .": MD 36

90 "Give my love to Nina . . .": O. Sitwell/AP, 27.11.28

91 "after us like a fox . . .": Victoria Glendinning, *Edith Sitwell. A Unicorn among Lions*, 1981, p. 169

92 living on a volcano: Bradford, *Sacheverell Sitwell*, op. cit., 188

92 "a colourless young man . . .": Ibid., 187

92 no room for him: WN 19 (place and person identified in Chantry copy in AP's hand)

92 Tony later came to think: MD 161

92 Thomas Joyce: Hooker, *Nina Hamnett*, op. cit., 186

92 "Among the writings of the three . . .": MD 36

92 "I wish you . . .": E. Sitwell/AP, n.d. [summer 1928]

92 "just the bare luxuries . . .": Philip Ziegler, *Osbert Sitwell*, 1998, p. 80

93 "could feel competitive . . .": MD 37

93 "If I had not known . . . An atmosphere . . .": O. Sitwell/AP, 26.2.2

93 "at least 800 pages long . . .": Ibid., n.d. [1929]

93 "Each set frightens . . .": Ibid.

94 damages and costs: Ziegler, *Osbert Sitwell*, op. cit., 127

94 "preferably in a form twice as large . . .": William Chappell, review of *The Lamberts* by Andrew Motion, 1986 (unidentified cutting, CA)

94 "At seventeen . . .": SL 217

95 a musical contribution: MD 57

95 "Lambert was the first . . .": MD 59

95 "With them there seemed always . . .": MD 59

95 "no less elderly, stuffy . . .": MD 5

95 "Sir George is the strangest . . .": MD 165

95 "Will you have one drink?": MD 58

95 "He carried about . . .": SL 241

95 "the only francophil English composer . . .": Driberg, *Ruling Passions*, op. cit., 165

96 "the best professor . . .": Hamnett, *Laughing Torso*, op. cit., 21

96 Collins's Music Hall: Ibid., 6

97 known and disliked: Adrian Daintrey, *I Must Say*, 1963, pp. 66–7

97 "I take women . . .": WN 39

97 Henry Yorke never forgot: H. Yorke/AP, 23.1.36

97 "eternity of boredom": CCR 15; & see J1 143

98 sailors' brothels: A. Daintrey/AP, n.d. [1970s]; this visit was April 1930 (Daintrey/AP, 27.4.30)

98 "Daintrey suddenly rapped . . .": AP, catalogue pamphlet for Daintrey exhibition, Sally Hunter Fine Art, Feb. 1988

98   "These we studied . . .": MD 90

98   "The band should be . . .": PMB 185

99   "I do not regret . . .": MD 31

99   "a Comus-like rout": Peter Quennell, *The Marble Foot. An Autobiography, 1905–38*, 1976, p. 162

99   "He built her up . . .": Hamnett, *Laughing Torso*, op. cit., 187 & 272, n. 22

100 massive wooden bulwark: AP, "I Was a Territorial," *Night and Day*, 8.7.37; & see MD 106

100 33, Tavistock Square: MD 107–8 & 191

100 "*Barnard Letters* . . .": MD 108

100 urban pastoral: MD 155

100 dry run for the *Dance*: MD 109

100 Enid Firminger: see MD 142–4; my account owes much to Enid Firminger's stepdaughter, Martha James, and to her highly informative memoir about the family and its background

100 Reginald Firminger: Mary Poole and her daughters moved in with Firminger and took his name, the two girls remaining at first in his Wimbledon house after their mother's death, when Enid changed her name to Firminger by deed poll, presumably for legal reasons (*London Gazette*, 27.3.25). I am grateful to P. L. Dickinson for this and much other information about the Firminger family

101 easily the loveliest: Barbara Wadsworth, *Edward Wadsworth. A Painter's Life*, 1989, p. 157

101 Osbert Sitwell . . . told a story: MD 143

102 "He hoped that . . .": AM 96

102 boxing match: AM 133–44

102 "Fear has much . . .": WN 97

102 "A most violent passion . . .": R. Burton, *The Anatomy of Melancholy*, Part 3, Everyman, 1932, p. 264

102 a joint party: J. Heygate/AP, 23 Mar., n.d. [1937]; & see MD 125–6, J1 84

103 dinner at Boulestin's: WN 18 (place and people identified by AP in pencil in his copy)

103 by a telegram: 26.7.29 (CA)

103 angry husband . . . buying a revolver: J. Heygate/AP from Ulm, 26.7.29, and Verdun, 28.7.29

103 the first person to spot: MD 124

103 showdown in Henrietta Street: For the contract & its public termination see MD 4 & 182

104 terms of his own: MD 183

104 a pair of drawings: Both portraits reproduced in MD between 86 & 87

105 "a weedy-looking young man . . .": AM 2

105 one of the best books: Jeremy Warren, "Nicolas Poussin's Painting, *A Dance to the Music of Time*, in the Wallace Collection," APS *Conference Proceedings*, 2003, p. 26.

105 "a company of giddy-heads . . .": MD 114 & MV 8
105 "These meetings with painters . . .": MD 43

Chapter 4

106 "I always rejoice . . .": Barber, *Anthony Powell*, op. cit., 84
106 "I thought I had . . .": AP/Jocelyn Brooke, 12.1.53
106 advice of Constant Lambert: MD 156
106 Toulon: Date & personnel of this Toulon holiday are hard to establish because different accounts (by AP himself, William Chappell, Tristram Hillier, Hillier's daughter Martha James, & Burra's biographer Jane Stevenson) rely on overlapping memories of successive Toulon summers in 1928, 1930 & 1931. AP suggests 1930, MD 15 (his passport shows an earlier French holiday, arriving Saint-Malo 10 August 1928, & departing Dieppe 2 September, but, even if he had gone to Toulon that year, he would have missed the Burra crowd, who did not arrive until late September); Stevenson, following Hillier, gives 1928 but includes visitors from 2 years later (including Barbara Ker-Seymer & Frederick Ashton)
107 Irene Hodgkins: Irene Rose Georgiana Hodgkins was known as Irene-Rose by her family, Hodge at art school, Irene or Georgiana by later friends; MJM
107 "the people are . . .": 9.10.28, Edward Burra, *Well, Dearie! The Letters of Edward Burra*, ed. William Chappell, 1985, p. 46
107 *Midnight Follies*: Information about Hodge from her daughter, Martha James
107 first boyfriend: Jane Stevenson, *Edward Burra. Twentieth-century Eye*, 2007, p. 89
107 "hardened hustlers . . .": Burra, *Well, Dearie!*, op. cit., 27
107 "appeared neatly . . .": WBW 144
108 always fancied him: J1 17
108 "a small, sleek and vivacious . . .": Barbara Ker-Seymer obituary, *Independent*, 3.6.93
108 series of these flappers: Roland Gant correspondence, 1982, HA
108 since they were both twelve: J1 277
108 "busy photographing Miss Modern . . .": Stevenson, *Edward Burra*, op. cit., 87
108 "He spoke rarely . . .": MD 157
108 "always his deepest pleasure": Burra, *Well, Dearie!*, op. cit., 45
108 the local gendarme: WBW 150
108 "Salome dancing . . .": W. Chappell/AP, 4.1.77
109 "Nobody could get . . .": 2.7.81
109 *Rio Grande*: See William Chappell (ed.), *Edward Burra. A Painter Remembered by His Friends*, 1982, pp. 60–1; & SL 210, nn. 10 & 11
109 "the same kind of buzz . . .": Chappell (ed.), *Edward Burra. A Painter Remembered*, op. cit.
109 Tony watched Burra: B. Ker-Seymer/AP, 10.3.83

109 "one of the most unusual . . . He would sit . . .": MD 157

110 A battered sailing boat . . . : For this episode, see Tristram Hillier, *Leda and the Goose*, 1954, pp. 95–7; Burra, *Well, Dearie!*, op. cit., 45; & MD 158–9

110 "caked with seasalt . . . so astonishingly beautiful . . .": Hillier, *Leda and the Goose*, op. cit., 96

111 "At Victoria I lost . . .": Ibid., 97

111 "He circled round her . . .": AM 26

111 as if the pit: AM 211

111 left the others dancing: MD 158

111 Hodge's post: Irene Hodgkins/AP, 22.8.30

111 caught a plane: J1 49

111 stunted troglodyte: MD 73

111 Pansy Pakenham . . . second novel: *August*, 1931

111 *God's Failures*: AM 66

112 "who could do anything awful enough . . .": B. Ker-Seymer/Roland Gant, 15.12.82, HA

112 Morris Minor: MD 102

112 "This driving complex . . .": J. Heygate/AP, 4.3.31

112 Misha Black: MD 184

113 finally unhinged Mr. Child: My account of this incident is based on MD 73, & on contemporary correspondence: T. Balston/O. Sitwell, n.d., in Joliffe, *Woolf at the Door*, op. cit., 47; and E. Sitwell/T. Balston, n.d. (dated 10.3.31 by Balston) & 16.5.31 in "Edith Sitwell's letters to Thomas Balston," ts (CA). Child reappears briefly transacting business with Harold Acton and Hector Winkle in Duckworth correspondence, Jan.–Apr. 1936, HA

113 "I suppose I am generally . . .": J3 95

113 Waugh . . . travel book: *Remote People*, Nov. 1931

113 "The trouble with your novel . . .": Evelyn Waugh (née Gardner)/AP, 29.5.31

113 "the aura of journalism's lower slopes . . .": AM 33

113 "I am fortunate . . .": J. Heygate/AP, 4 Aug., n.d. [1931/2] (Oliver Harbord was the relevant character in *Decent Fellows*); my account of the Pease and Roberts episode is based on this letter

114 "My dear Fotheringham . . .": AM 61

114 "The Hole in the Elephant's Bottom": MD 93

114 Bobby had extravagant ambitions: My account based on MD 93–5, & letters to AP from J. Heygate, Miranda Wood, and Roberts's first wife, Diana Beaufort-Palmer

114 "Some sort of beachcombing bagmannery": Bobby Roberts/AP, 5.9.44

114 "a richly comic figure . . .": MD 94

115 "Could one introduce . . .": J. Heygate/AP, 4.10.33

115 "Dear Mr. Powell . . .": J. O'Rorke/AP, n.d. [1931]

115 *Hay Fever*: J1 192

115 Their affair seems: J. O'Rorke/AP, 7 Aug., Friday, n.d. [1931 added by AP]

115 Sainte Maxime: MD 159

115 "It seems quite . . .": J. O'Rorke/AP, 7 Aug., Friday, n.d. [1931 added by AP]

115 "Darling—what is . . .": J. O'Rorke/AP, n.d. [Aug. 1931]

116 architect from New Zealand: For Brian O'Rorke's professional career, see John Maxton-Graham, *Liners to the Sun*, 2001; for his character & marriage, see Seton Lloyd, *The Interval. A Life in Near-Eastern Archaeology*, 1986, p. 16; & Barbara Wadsworth, *Edward Wadsworth. A Painter's Life*, 1989, p. 204

116 "rather sparkling hardness": Vbg 32

116 "surprised and rather shaken": Vbg 34

116 Cocteau: MD 159; others included Brian Howard, Bunny Rogers & Sophie Fedorovich

117 Hotsy Trackles: Burra, *Well, Dearie!*, op. cit., 27

117 "in the war she . . .": J. Heygate/AP, 4 Aug., n.d. [1931]

117 printmaker: Jean Varda (Yanko Vardas), well known later in the US as a glass mosaicist

117 "the only difference . . .": C. Lambert/AP, 1.5.30

117 Foreign Legion: E. Burra/AP, p.c, 30.9.31

117 Arles: Enid Firminger, MD 160

117 "I didn't play tennis . . .": J. O'Rorke/AP, 7.8.31

117 "Who is that very good looking . . . It is awful . . .": J. O'Rorke/AP, n.d. [1931]

118 Tony reported: J. Heygate/AP, 7.7.31

118 "I hope your dinner . . .": J. O'Rorke/AP, Harrods Writing Rooms, n.d.

118 "perhaps he will . . .": Ibid., 18.8.31

118 "I hope this isn't so": E. Heygate/AP, n.d. [winter 1931/2]

118 "You are tramping . . . Well, I have had . . .": J. O'Rorke/AP, n.d. [1931]

119 "that wry Baltic idyll": *New York Herald Tribune*, n.d., HA

119 "Lushington was examining . . .": Vbg 109–10

119 "My misadventures . . .": AP/Barbara Wadsworth, 5.4.32; APSN, no. 25, p. 5

119 Salaman offered him: MD 192

120 Varda . . . had been writing a novel: D. Varda/AP, 12.3.31 & 22.3.31; MD 92–3

120 John Rodker: See B. Wadsworth, *Edward Wadsworth*, op. cit., 142

120 T. S. Eliot: Eliot/D. Varda, 29.7.27 & 30.8.27, *The Letters of T. S. Eliot*, vol. 3, *1926–27*, ed. Valerie Eliot & John Haffenden, 2012, pp. 591–2 & 668–9

120 It was left to *Vogue*: Rebecca West, see Lisa Cohen, *All We Know. Three Lives*, 2012, p. 249

120 "The celebrated West End mannequin . . .": *Vogue*, 1924: I am greatly indebted to Patric Dickinson for photographic images, and for exhaustive research into Varda's family origins, her Paris interlude and her theatrical career

120 man's sense of humour: IS 96

121 Cochrane had plans: *Arthur Machen & Montgomery Evans: Letters of a Literary Friendship 1923–1947*, ed. S. S. Hassler & D. M. Hassler, 1992

121 the Beautiful Varda: IS 96

121 *Ordo Virtutum*: I am grateful to Patric Dickinson for locating a review of this production by John Francis Hope, *New Age*, 18.12.19

122 two infant daughters: Joan by Sonia Cohen, b. 1915, & Camilla by Mary Butts, b. 1920.

122 a young minder: Diana Beaufort-Palmer, later briefly married to Bobby Roberts, D. Beaufort-Palmer/AP, n.d. [1970s]

122 Captain Turle: Charles Edward Turle (1883–1966), master of the *Resolution* (O. Sitwell/AP, 25.1.33)

122 "the beautiful and stormy Varda": MD 92

123 "She was unfortunately . . .": MD 93

123 "varda bookshop": B. Wadsworth, *Edward Wadsworth*, op. cit., 142; IS 97; & R. Shead, *Constant Lambert*, 1973, p. 76

123 "all the lunatics in London . . .": IS 97

124 one of Varda's: Justin Clarke-Hall, who married Varda's younger sister Adelaide in 1933, moving the bookshop to 222, Shaftesbury Avenue and setting up under his own name at 3, Cecil Court the year after (information from Patric Dickinson)

124 "I laughed . . .": D. Varda/AP, 17.1.31 (dated by AP)

124 "Set in this stormy . . .": "*Pax imperatrix*," 1890 ("England" swapped for "Varda")

125 character out of Dostoevsky: FMT 25

125 double-jointed walk: AM 84

125 Groucho Marx. "Yeah . . .": I am grateful to Venetia Bell for this episode, & much further information about her father

126 "bugger heaven . . .": Stevenson, *Edward Burra*, op. cit., 81

126 "He was intended . . .": AM 111

126 One of his former girlfriends: Lucy Norton, Stevenson, *Edward Burra*, op. cit., 80

126 "enquiring if *I had* everything . . .": D. Varda/AP, 15.11.32

127 one of the finest collections: David Piper/AP, n.d., 1978, & Michael Rogers of the British Museum, J3 62; Reitlinger's collection now forms the core of the ceramic holdings of the Ashmolean Museum, Oxford

127 virulently anti-Semitic: See R. Byron, *The Station, Athos, Treasures & Men*, 1931, p. 39 *et passim*

128 Duckworths came closer: See Joliffe, *Woolf at the Door*, op. cit., 57–8

128 "It seems to me that . . .": T. Balston/AP, 7.6.32; & see MD 191

128 "long rickety blue sofa": FMT 2, n.d. [1930]

128 tugging at the back: MD 108

128 "The dammed up reserves . . .": MD 185

129 forced to resign: MD 153

129   radio play: J. Heygate/AP, 23.4.30

129   fiction editor at *Harper's Bazaar*: E. Heygate/AP, 6.2.32

129   "little Evelyn seemed . . .": J. Heygate/AP, 31.1.46

129   "we have got . . .": E. Heygate/AP, 22.3.31

129   UFA: Universum-Film Aktiengesellschaft. For this venture and Heygate's involvement, see Chris Wahl, "Inside the Robots' Castle: UFA's English-language Versions in the Early 1930s," *Destination London: German-speaking Emigrés and British Cinema, 1925–50*, ed. Tim Bergfelder and Christian Carnelli, 2013; & Geoff Brown: "I Am Also a Camera: John Heygate and Talking Pictures," *Film History*, vol. 20, issue 2, 2008

129   "more money to spend . . .": J. Heygate, *These Germans. An Estimate of their Character Seen in Flashes from the Drama 1918–39*, 1940, p. 93

130   grease-stained motoring coat: John Heygate, *Talking Pictures*, 1934, p. 219 (supposedly a novel, this is in fact a direct account of Heygate's time at UFA with AP as the fictional "Rightlaw"; the same is true of Heygate's *Motor Tramp* (1935), and *These Germans*, op. cit., where AP figures under his own name)

130   "I can see you both . . .": E. Nightingale (formerly Heygate)/AP, 26 March, n.d. [1976]

130   "I knew that he was . . .": Heygate, *Talking Pictures*, op. cit., 278

130   good and bad points of the extras: Ibid., 224

130   his recent affairs: J. Heygate/AP, 23.7.32

131   "They bid each other . . .": Heygate, *These Germans*, op. cit., 73

131   "They were afraid . . .": Ibid.

131   "an absolute Royal Academy . . .": Ibid., 71

131   no Nazi marches: MD 128

131   "two great bodies of troops . . .": Heygate, *These Germans*, op. cit., 113

131   cheap pension: *Talking Pictures*, op. cit., 231

132   "When you approach . . .": Wahl, "Inside the Robots' Castle," op. cit., 54, n. 52

132   "a series of derelict streets . . .": Heygate, *Talking Pictures*, op. cit., 39

132   "infested with prostitutes . . .": MD 128

132   "they read like . . .": Constant Lambert/AP, 16.8.32

133   beauty, intelligence and wit: Shead, *Constant Lambert*, op. cit., 25

133   their romantic story: MD 122–3

133   Flo's origins remained uncertain: Andrew Motion, *The Lamberts: George, Constant and Kit*, 1986, p. 187; & SL 144

133   Lady Cardigan: IS 33

133   "Mama don't make me . . .": D. Varda/AP, 7.10.32

134   "Send me news of Varda . . .": J. Heygate/AP, 11.11.32

134   "I thought Varda . . .": J. Heygate/AP, 6.12.32

134   "Picture of Olga . . .": Wyndham Lloyd/AP, 2.11.35

135   semi-pornographic fantasy: D. Varda/AP, 14.2.33

135   Captain Teach: Pseudonym of Gerald Reitlinger (1885–1951), see MD 172

135 fought throughout: FVD 70

135 "it seems only yesterday . . .": FVD 216

136 *Drag Hunt Ball*: D. Varda/AP, p.c., 9.1.33

136 first draft: MD 108

136 "both of us too drunk . . .": *The Diaries of Evelyn Waugh*, ed. Michael Davie, 1976, entry for 12.6.30, p. 314

136 "Tony dear . . .": D. Varda/AP, Monday n.d. [end 1932]

136 Pat Herdman: MD 186 & J2 6–7

136 schoolgirl sister: J1 102

136 Boxing Day meet: J2 7

137 probably the only novel: Information from Lord Gowrie, whose stepfather was Mary Herdman's brother

137 "The butler stood . . . For a moment . . .": FVD 9 & 201

137 "'I like the little man . . .": KO 142

Chapter 5

138 ". . . a Race whose Thought . . .": AP, *Caledonia. A Fragment*, 1934, p. 6; see also MD 175

138 "Fewer such statesmen . . . *ambient* Wireless": Ibid., 10

138 Castano's: See MD 167–9; J1 41–2; & MV 326

138 buskers: MD 169–70

139 gagged and chained: A&P 5–9

139 how he felt about his marriage: A&P 15; & E. Nightingale/AP, 14.1.36

139 "Replace this Race . . .": *Caledonia*, 11

139 *bouts-rimés*: MD 175

140 nude bathing: W. Chappell/AP, 12.1.81

140 "this place is nothing . . .": Burra, *Well, Dearie!*, op. cit., 69

141 "I hope it will be nice . . .": D. Reitlinger/AP, Fez, 14.2.33; all further quotes in this para from ibid.

141 "Perhaps I was . . .": Ibid., 10.3.33

141 "I seem to have . . .": Ibid., 20.3.33

141 "scabrous old bore": Ibid., n.d. [April 1933]

141 "Goodnight my precious . . .": Ibid., 10.3.33 (*dot* is French for dowry)

142 "Trilby and Svengali": G. du Maurier, *Trilby*, 1895

142 she had commandeered: G. Reitlinger/AP, 26.7.33

142 motoring holiday in Spain: See MD 193–7 for AP's account of this trip

142 "Here is an idea . . .": G. Reitlinger/W. Lloyd, 15.8.33

143 "A strong and threatening . . .": MD 194

143 meagre allowance: G. Reitlinger/AP, 26.7.34 & n.d. [Aug. 1933]

143 "Has either of them . . .": J. Heygate/AP, n.d. [20.8.33]

143 Constant Lambert . . . in Saragossa: MD 195

143 "*It's no good* . . .": SL 419

144 Misha Black: See MD 184

144   only novelist: *Harper's Bazaar*, 1933; Barber, *Anthony Powell*, op. cit., 85

144   "I would rather . . .": J. Betjeman/AP, 27.7.39

144   "It is the kind . . .": E. Sitwell/T. Balston, n.d. [April 1934]

144   "I am afraid you are . . .": J. Heygate/AP, n.d. [20 Aug. 1933]

144   John Wesley: Sermon 67, see A&P flyleaf

144   "post-war types . . .": A&P 2

145   "in a spirit of . . .": A&P 87

145   "one of the worst . . .": A&P 26

145   "Tell me about . . .": J. Heygate/AP, 20.8.33

146   hung in a hospital: Wadsworth, *Edward Wadsworth*, op. cit., 201

146   in *The Times*: Letters page, 12.6.33

146   "young and poetical . . .": M. Coates/Wells Coates, n.d. [1940s] (I am grate-
      ful to Julia Elton for access to this correspondence)

146   Napoleonic campaign: Ibid., 16.9.30

146   apartment in Doughty Street: Sherban Cantacuzino, *Wells Coates. A Mono-
      graph*, 1978, p. 91

146   Lawn Road Flats: See Fiona MacCarthy, "Jack Pritchard and the Hamp-
      stead of the Thirties," *View from a Long Chair. The Memoirs of Jack Pritchard*,
      1984

146   affair with Molly Pritchard: M.Coates/Wells Coates, 15.7.32

147   "I am a gobbler . . .": 11.7.31

147   "for whom I once had . . .": To HS

147   Born in China: I am grateful to the late Laura Cohen for much information
      about her parents and grandparents; see also Laura Cohen, *The Door to a
      Secret Room. A Biography of Wells Coates*, 1999

148   "Under capitalism . . .": Maurice Goldsmith, *Sage. A Life of J. D. Bernal*,
      1980, p. 67

149   the most joy . . . : M. Coates/Wells Coates, n.d. [Aug. 1937]

149   "I have been . . .": Ibid., n.d. [April 1932]

149   "grass-green-greying . . .": M. Coates/Wells Coates, n.d. [July 1931]

149   "Do not imagine . . .": Ibid.

149   loved and envied: M. Coates/Wells Coates, 11.7.31

149   "There was that same . . .": BM 216

150   evenings together: AP, 1934 appointment diary

150   "I am glad to hear . . .": J. Heygate/AP, 27.1.34

150   "on re-reading . . .": Ibid., 15 Feb., n.d. [1934]

150   explained frankly: M. Coates/Wells Coates, n.d. [Aug. 1937] & 13.1.38

150   *Femmes d'Alger*: AW 58

151   "Do write me 500 words . . .": J. Heygate/AP, 18.4.34

151   she undoubtedly recognized . . . change in the atmosphere: Information
      from Marion's daughter, Catherine Chamier

152   "all Gerald Duckworth's . . .": MD 198

152   Milsted took advantage: Joliffe, *Woolf at the Door*, op. cit., 60

152   complaining that a charwoman: Bradford, *Sacheverell Sitwell*, op. cit., 228

152 "one of the worst days . . .": E. Sitwell/AP, 28.3.44, "Letters of Edith Sitwell to Thomas Balston," ts, ed. John Ehrstine & Thos. Rand, Washington State University, CA.

152 "reprints of a few staples . . .": MWA

152 Typical titles: By, respectively, Isobel Macdonald, Christina Whitbread & Godfrey Winn

153 one of his authors: Pansy Lamb

153 "an enormous gothicky . . .": Ferdinand Mount, *Cold Cream*, 2008, p. 63

153 Nationalist bastion: WFC 90

153 never met either of them: FMT 4

154 "the right sort . . .": Elizabeth Longford, *The Pebbled Shore. The Memoirs of Elizabeth Longford*, 1986, p. 153

154 "thrilled at the prospect . . .": E. Pakenham/AP, 4.8.34

154 "it might be about . . .": C. Longford/AP, 13.8.34

154 "I could fill . . . 4 feet 3 inches . . .": AP/Maud Powell, 30.8.34

154 made a mistake: FMT 9–10

154 Aztec look: FMT 7

155 a gossipy inquisitive audience: Information from the late Terence de Vere White; see also FMT 10; & Christopher Fitz-Simon: *The Boys. A Biography of Micheál MacLiammóir & Hilton Edwards*, 1994, p. 144

155 party at Pakenham Hall: AP/Maud Powell, 30.8.34

155 Horace Egosmith: Beckett was initially drawn to the theatre by writing a speech (subsequently dropped) for this character, see Deirdre Blair, *Samuel Beckett. A Biography*, 1978, p. 235

156 a journalist by profession: Theatre critic of the *Irish Independent*, see Mary Manning Howe Adams obituary, *Irish Times*, 8.7.99; & *Enter Certain Players: Edwards-MacLiammóir and the Gate, 1928–78*, ed. Peter Luke, 1978, pp. 35–9

156 "But O Tony . . .": M. Manning/AP, 23.9.34

156 Lionel Dymoke: AP/Maud Powell, 30.8.34

156 dropping hints: M. Manning/AP, 23.9.34

156 "You're an awfully companionable cad . . .": Ibid.

156 Dublin gossip: Information from the late Terence de Vere White

157 "the shock of the icy water . . .": DP 112

157 "The coat was pale-ginger . . .": H. Lamb/AP, 2.2.38

157 cleaning his brushes: WFC 235

157 another portrait session: FVD 139

157 atmosphere of the house: FMT 12

158 "There was something . . .": Julia Tomlin, reported in B. Ker-Seymer/AP, 10.9.34

158 "never did we reach . . .": WFC 236

158 panics and discomforts: FOS 65

158 "Darling Tony . . . By the way . . . novel with jokes": VP/AP, Thursday, n.d. [13 Sept. 1934]

159 "Now take my case . . .": J. Heygate, *Motor Tramp*, 1935, pp. 20–21

159 "Undoubtedly it was . . .": FMT 13

159 "midnight to the milkman's round": Maurice Richardson, "The Bottle-Party Belt," *Night and Day*, no. 1, 1.7.37

160 how many parties: WFC 132

160 "the melancholy songs . . .": WFC 142

160 inconceivably squalid: IS 89 & J3 127

160 Smokey Joe's: WFC 162

160 "Violet went to . . .": Mary Clive, "Mary Countess of Longford," ts with corrections by VP in the possession of Lady Rachel Billington

160 the London Ladies: WFC 178–9

160 "a . . . way of life which . . .": WFC 31

161 "Lady Violet's bad enough . . .": Information from the late Henrietta Phipps

161 stockings and buttoned boots: Clive, *Brought Up and Brought Out*, op. cit., 66–7

161 to go to school: Queen's College, Harley Street (autumn term, 1927), & St. Margaret's, Bushey (1928–9). See FOS chaps. 14, 15 & 16

161 posed for her naked: WFC 176

162 the LSE: WFC 159–60, 163 & 167–9

162 never tasted wine: WFC 75

162 powdered footmen: WFC 177

162 "I've Told Ev'ry Little Star": WFC 176

162 she was dying: Clive, "Mary Countess of Longford," ts, op. cit.; & see WFC xi, 181–2, 204–5

162 alibis and excuses: WFC 75 & 178

162 caught pneumonia the following spring: WFC 225–8

163 "I took my place . . .": VP, *Margaret Countess of Jersey*, 1978, p. 181

163 "a semi-stranger . . .": SiS 15

163 "the neurotic, semi-invalid . . .": Clive, "Mary Countess of Longford," ts, op. cit.

163 "skull-cracking collisions": FOS 218

163 compulsive need: WFC 30

164 "My mother closed . . .": SiS 31

164 large, cheerless, rented houses: North Aston Hall, Oxfordshire, VP, *Margaret Countess of Jersey*, op. cit., 182–3; & Peverel Court, near Aylesbury, Bucks, WFC 1–3

164 her eight small grandchildren: VP, *Margaret Countess of Jersey*, op. cit., 173

164 "Grandmamma was a mother . . .": Information from Georgia Powell

164 a third of the sum: Waugh, *The Best Wine Last*, op. cit., 17

165 "In my family . . .": WFC 152 (VP's sisters, Pansy & Mary Pakenham, pseud. Hans Duffy; her aunt Christine Longford; & her Uncle Lord Dunsany)

165 they met once more: AP appointment diary, 24.10.34

165 one of her daughters: Catherine Chamier

166 She herself went on: Wells Coates/M. Coates, 1.6.40; & information from her daughters, the late Laura Cohen and Catherine Chamier

166 "where you can behold . . . Get down to it . . .": M. Manning/AP, 23 Sept., n.d. [1934]

167 "There will be few . . .": *Now and Then*, 1934 (CA)

167 "While not believing . . .": J. Heygate/AP, 5 Nov., n.d. [1934]

167 Lambert published: *Music Ho! A Study of Music in Decline*, 1966 [1934], quotations from pp. 60, 190 & 200 respectively

168 "Lady Vi [R] introducing Mr. Powell . . .": C. Lambert/AP, Aug. 1936

168 Cecil Beaton: AP edited his *Book of Beauty* in 1930

168 Beaton wedding: AP appointment diary, 4.11.34; the wedding dress is now in the Victoria & Albert Museum

168 "Three Times a Bridesmaid . . .": Undated cutting in VP's photo album

168 two columns . . . under the name of Mary Grant: Clive, *Brought Up and Brought Out*, op. cit., 225–6; FWC 217; & FMT 23–4

168 The wedding itself: FMT 17–18; WFC 238; VP, *Margaret Countess of Jersey*, op. cit., 187; for All Saints, Ennismore Gardens, see Keith Marshall, APSN, no. 57, winter 2014

169 Lamb was tipsy: VP/AP, 2.1.40

169 Heygate threatened . . . : J. Heygate/AP, 17 Nov., n.d. [1934]

169 "a poky little room . . .": Ibid., 22 Nov., n.d. [1934] (Heygate gives the Bridge Hotel, AP the Orleans Arms, FMT 18, presumably the same place, since both claimed to have hosted Louis Philippe)

169 the worst crossing: FMT 19

169 the Sacred Way: SiS 8–9

170 "little developed since . . .": FMT 20

170 "across the island . . .": Ibid.

170 a coffee pot: MD 169

170 edition of *Caledonia*: MD 175

Chapter 6

171 "all silver grey . . . tall blonde girl . . . a thirtyish man . . .": MWA

171 velvet pantsuit: Miranda Wood, née Hayward/AP, 17.1.79

172 "living breathing . . .": MWA

172 "Birmingham discovery": J. Heygate/AP, 23 Oct., n.d.[1935]; see also J1 150

172 for the job of secretary: M. Hayward/AP, n.d. [autumn 1935]

172 "an old man . . .": MWA

172 "our daily . . .": MWA

173 "A Woman's Point of View": *Evening Standard*, 28.2.36, 18 & 25.6.35 & 3.7.35

173 Marion Coates: AP appointment diary

173 Dennis Proctor: AP/VP, 11.9.39; & see Dennis Proctor obituary (by John Bullard), *The Times*, Sept. 1983

174 "heavy thuds . . .": FMT 26 (the ballet was *Apparitions*, premiered March 1936)

174 house manager: MD 96 & SAG 5

174 "When the little, golden-skinned . . .": William Chappell, *Fonteyn. Impressions of a Ballerina*, 1951, p. 13

175 "A simple message . . .": C. Lambert/AP, 11.6.35

175 "in case anyone . . . Do you think . . .": Ibid., 15.8.35; & AP/VP, 24.1.42

175 country weekends: AP, 1935 appointment diary

176 "Yours Gerald . . .": G. Reitlinger/AP, n.d. [22 Aug. 1934]

176 "Mr. & Mrs. Sponge's . . .": DP 178 (cf. R. S. Surtees's *Mr. Sponge's Sporting Tour*, 1853)

177 "well content to drift . . .": Wyndham Ketton-Cremer, *Thomas Gray*, 1935, p. 18

177 tie-wig: IS 164

177 "To the end of his days . . .": IS 163

177 preference for boys: VP/AP, 16.7.40

178 "O dearie me . . .": SL 212

178 "a distinctly uncomfortable . . .": To HS

178 "painted and powdered . . .": Pauline Gray, *Cecil Gray. His Life and Notebooks*, 1989, p. 26

178 "While I do not defend . . .": Cecil Gray, *Musical Chairs, or Between Two Stools. The Life and Memoirs of Cecil Gray*, 1948, p. 76

178 Philip Sainsbury: D. Varda/AP, 17.1.31; P. Sainsbury/AP, Christmas, 1936

179 "A sort of modern . . . :" J. Heygate/AP, 15 May, n.d. [1935]

179 "Nothing has changed . . .": J. Heygate/AP, n.d. [1935]

179 "the Hitler Jugend . . .": J. Heygate/AP, n.d. [16.10.35]

179 "But Aryans . . .": Ibid., n.d.

179 "The news of your tragedy . . .": H. Lamb/VP, 11.12.35

179 Violet wept: VP/AP, 17.8.38

179 "Dies Irae": SL 225

180 On re-reading: J2 121

180 "I am advertising . . .": J. Heygate/AP 12 Jan., n.d. [1936]

180 "though I must say . . .": E. Heygate/AP, 14.1.36

180 "isn't it funny . . .": D. Varda/AP, n.d. [1936]

180 "He could only stare . . .": A&P 156

181 "The male gorilla . . .": A&P 154

181 "a torpedo-shaped . . .": A&P 9 & 31

181 substantial money: Selina Hastings, *Evelyn Waugh*, 1994, p. 352

181 "It sometimes looked . . .": MWA

181 "more than orientally . . .": FMT 34

181 *Shorter Oxford* . . . : A. G. Lewis/AP, 22.10.36

181 "I believe him . . .": E. Sitwell/G. Duckworth, 9.11.36, Duckworth Archive

182 "There is no . . .": G. Duckworth/E. Sitwell, 11.11.36, ibid.

182 "I'm going . . .": AP/VP, 20.8.36

183 "the pellucid northern light . . .": FMT 33

183 "He seemed much . . .": MD 119

183 The wife of one: VP, ts of talk on this Russia trip for Frome Women's Institute, n.d. (CA)

184 "one of the great slaughters . . .": MD 119

184 Teddington Film Studios: FMT 35–6

184 "Teddington seemed to . . .": FMT 36

185 "ghastly interior misery": FMT 43

185 Tommy Phipps: See Joyce Grenfell, *Joyce Grenfell Requests the Pleasure*, 1976, p. 220

185 "terrible fascination . . .": AP/VP, 8.1.40

186 seizing the hand-brake . . .": FMT 38

186 "weariest of . . .": FMT 47

187 The cheerful competent cook: FMT 22 & 46

187 Bosola: FMT 23

188 "I suppose one oughtn't . . .": AP/VP, 8.8.38

188 "He wasn't actually . . .": AP/VP, 18.8.38

189 Eve Disher: Obituary, DT, 30.12.91; and information from Julia Elton

189 "Eve . . . felt really devastated . . .": DP 206

189 Eve never showed: Other work of hers was shown in public at Hartnoll & Evans in 1976, and at Foyles Art Gallery in 1987 (she was 62 and 73 respectively); Elton's portrait is at Clevedon Court, Bristol, and Reitlinger's in the Ashmolean Museum (see Chapter 9 below); the two of VP priv. coll. Chantry)

189 David Jones: See J3 8

190 "like the final labour . . .": FMT 40

190 *The Boy from Barnardo's*: FMT 40–43; & see Walter Allen, *As I Walked Down New Grub Street*, 1981, p. 98

190 "melancholy miles . . .": AP/M. Muggeridge, 14.5.46

190 "terrible place": AP/VP, 26.2.40; for AP's account, see FMT 47–54

191 Warner Groat: This and other engagements from AP's appointment diary

191 "a picture by . . .": FMT 63

191 "shake-those-feet . . .": *Night and Day*, 12.8.37, reprinted more or less verbatim in FMT 54–6

191 *The Spanish Earth*: *Night and Day*, 19.8.37; & see FMT 56–8

191 9460, Wilshire: AP/J. Heygate, n.d. [1937 from US]; Rex Evans/AP, 20.5.38

192 "Without wine . . .": FMT 59

192 "It would be Hans . . .": MD 43

192 big movies: *Camille* with Greta Garbo, 1936; *Zaza* with Claudette Colbert and Bert Lahr, 1938

192 Scott Fitzgerald: FMT 61–8

192 all of them dismayed: See Lisa Colletta, "Powell, Waugh and Hollywood," APS *Conference Proceedings*, 2003, p. 234

192 Edward VIII: FMT 69

192 "I have almost come . . .": AP/M. Muggeridge, 15.4.46

193 "as possibility became . . .": FMT 72

193 "without even the . . .": FMT 73

193 "the feeling that . . .": Quoted in Lynn Barber interview, *Independent*, 8.3.92

193 "my awful bag . . .": AP/VP, 7.4.40

193 "some sort of a . . .": FMT 74

193 "Architectural purity . . .": G. Reitlinger/AP&VP, 9.11.37

193 "Now what about . . .": M. Hayward/AP, 11.11.37 & 26.4.38

194 "dark red in the face . . .": WBW 1

194 recognized himself: B. Hambrough/AP, 28.1.39

194 gibbering with fury: IS 86, & see Chapter 2 above, pp. 23–4

194 comic masterpieces: VP/AP, 22.7.39

194 "he had only entered . . .": WBW 9

194 faithful portraits: L. P. Hartley, *Weekly Sketch*, 22.3.39

194 "a noise like . . .": WBW 28

194 "mad but with . . .": Hartley, *Weekly Sketch*, op. cit.

195 "he looked every inch . . .": WBW 68

195 "real life was lived . . .": WBW 134

195 unanimously rejected. M. Wood/AP, 9.9.37

195 "I now know what . . .": MWA

195 Oxford University Press in Bombay: MW/AP, 10.11.36, & MWA

196 "with or without . . .": MW/AP, 11.11.37

196 SS death-list: Information from Venetia Bell

196 "Horst Wessel Song": SP 321

196 "It was a . . .": M. Muggeridge/AP, 24.1.39

197 Tranby Croft: FMT 24–5

197 "the home of . . .": FMT 81

197 Flo told Violet: Meredith Daneman, *Margot Fonteyn*, 2004, p. 108

197 "he was, early on . . .": Ibid., 102

197 Rows with Flo: Ibid., 132

198 "You know the ballet . . .": W. Chappell/AP, 21.5.84

198 "very wild . . .": AP/VP, 10.8.38

198 "a very ominous . . .": AP/VP, 6.8.38

198 "So this afternoon . . .": AP/VP, 8.8.38

198 "I could walk . . .": AP/VP, 10.8.38

199 consulted Graham Greene: AP/VP, 6, 8 & 18.8.38

199 Cassell: AP/VP, 18.8.38; & see FMT 74

199 "Darling don't be sad . . .": VP/AP, n.d. [17 Aug. 1938]

199 "There was a fearful . . .": AP/VP, 22.8.38

199 "I've been ill . . .": VP/AP, 23.8.38

200 "I rushed upstairs . . .": AP/VP, 20.8.36

200 "Nothing is sadder . . .": VP/AP, 18.8.38 (*Rien n'est plus triste qu'un nain enragé*)

200 "I had to curl . . .": AP, "Mr. Orioli & Others," *Spectator*, 5.9.38 [review of G. Orioli, *The Adventures of a Bookseller*]

200 "horrible shrill screech": FMT 86

200 the basement sitting room was made gas-proof: FMT 73

200 "Its mother . . .": MWA

201 "abominable snow women": VP/AP, 23.12.39

201 scrappier and more prosaic: FMT 88–9

201 Edward Lear: MW/AP, 7.3.76

201 "His genius . . .": AP, "Books of the Month," *New English Review*, Aug. 1947

201 "the oddness of the . . .": FMT 88

201 "Mr. Waugh carries . . .": Hartley, *Weekly Sketch*, 22.3.39

201 "She spoke as . . .": VP, *Margaret, Countess of Jersey*, 1978, p. 188

201 "I must not be . . .": E. Sitwell/AP, 11.2.39

201 in the Rhineland: M. Wood/AP, 19.3.38

202 "the racking international . . .": FMT 75

202 Cassell's copies: FMT 74 & AP/VP, 24.2.41

202 1813 edition: VP/AP, 22 July, n.d. [1939]

202 "You can hardly . . .": VP/AP, 28 July, n.d. [1939]

202 volunteer nurse: VP/AP, 21 July, n.d. [1939] & 7.9.39

202 "only too appropriate . . .": FMT 90

202 Violet's doctor: FMT 92

203 "I *know* I'm glad . . .": VP/AP, 5 Sept., n.d. [1939]

203 filling sandbags: AP/VP, 8.8.39

203 "He really might never . . .": AP/VP, 5.9.39

203 "mournfully polishing . . .": M. Muggeridge, review of *Hearing Secret Harmonies*, 1975 (CA clipping, no source)

203 "Like hell I should": AP/VP, 9–11.10.39

203 "I don't think . . .": AP/H. Yorke, 4.9.28

203 "so underlined . . .": VP/AP, 13.10.39

203 "real dwarfs' boots . . .": AP/VP, 13.10.39

204 an ambulance: AP/VP, 11.9.39

204 "the Squire is liable . . .": B. Hambrough/AP, 16.10.39

204 "Do you want . . .": AP/VP, 8.1.40

204 "My darling, I miss . . .": VP/AP, 23.10.39

204 *Spectator* competition: 22.11.39

204 Château Malfoutueux: *New Statesman*, 30.11.38

205 private's uniform: M. Muggeridge, *Chronicles of Wasted Time*, vol. 2, *The Infernal Grove*, 1973, p. 81

205 "He looks an absolutely . . .": AP/VP, 24.11.39

205 "If I was . . .": AP/VP, 22.11.39

205 "I think we shook . . .": AP/VP, 22.11.39

206 "the Squire may make . . .": AP/VP, 3.12.39

206 "*Je te couvre* . . .": AP/VP, 5.12.39

206 "Darling I can't tell . . .": VP/AP, 11.12.39

206 "when I sometimes . . .": AP/VP, 12.12.39

206 "the curious, dreamlike . . .": VP/AP, 5.1.40, & AP/VP, 6.1.40

206 Gort: General Gort, CIGS

Chapter 7

207 as George Orwell said: "The Limit to Pessimism," *New English Weekly*, 25.4.40, qu. D. J. Taylor: APS *Conference Proceedings*, 2003, p. 35

207 "an absolutely hammer-and-tongs . . . I wondered . . .": AP/VP, 9.10.39

207 a rude rhyme: AP/VP, 3.12.39, & VP/AP, 5.12.39; published *New States-man*, 17.2.40, & Kingsley Amis (ed.), *The Oxford Book of Light Verse*, 1978 (W. H. Auden's *The Dog beneath the Skin* & Christopher Isherwood's *Mr. Norris Changes Trains* were key documents of the late 1930s)

207 in his diary: Peter Parker, *Isherwood. A Life*, 2004, p. 455

208 "on the boggy shores . . . looks like the sort . . . exactly like the one . . .": AP/VP, 19.12.39

208 Browning automatic: AP/VP, 22.12.39, & AP/R. Mount, 23.12.39

208 "talkative, good-natured . . .": FMT 98

208 "I don't expect . . .": AP/VP, 12.12.39

208 "elderly to . . .": FMT 97

208 his sympathies lay: AP/VP, 1.4.40 & 15.4.40

208 "I hope to . . .": J. Heygate/AP, 4.3.40

208 "Sooner or later . . .": AP/VP, 2.1.40

209 pay off his overdraft: AP/VP, 19.2.40

209 "There's Powell . . .": AP/VP, 31.12.39

209 "I think it must . . .": VP/AP, 2.1.40

209 dwarf with gritted teeth: 24.1.40

209 like children: AP/VP, 8.1.40

209 "when we meet . . .": AP/VP, 6.1.40

209 "in spite of . . .": AP/VP, 21.2.40

209 a complaint: AP/VP, 25.4.40

209 "playing Red Indians . . .": AP/VP, 9.1.40

209 "like the White Rabbit . . .": AP/VP, 22.12.39

209 "inspecting lavatories . . .": AP/VP, 4.4.40

210 casting his bobble-cap: AP/VP, 30.1.40

210 "go off into . . .": AP/VP, 9.2.40

210 "You should have . . .": AP/VP, 16.2.40

210 "a running commentary . . .": AP/VP, 26.12.39

210 "It will pass . . .": J3 157

210 Horace Probert: J2 174, AP/VP *passim*, & FMT 105

211 Penn-Jones: AP/R. Mount, 23.12.39

211 "long experience . . .": AP/VP, 26.12.39

211 "As I lay . . .": VP/AP, 23.12.39

211 "He is in some ways . . .": AP/VP, 19.2.40
211 "The poor old boy . . .": AP/VP, 15.4.40
211 "the most ghastly . . .": AP/VP, 8.1.40
211 "Any groundwork . . .": J. Heygate/AP, 4.3.40
212 "I know it's . . .": AP/VP, 8.1.40
212 "like the *second* . . . : AP/VP, 12.1.40
212 "an awful little tick . . .": AP/VP, 22.1.40
212 "this regiment . . .": AP/VP, 17.1.40
213 "My life has been . . .": AP/VP, 25.5.40
213 "I thought we . . .": AP/VP, 29.2.40
213 "the awful boredom . . .": WN 96
213 "My darling, I hope . . .": VP/AP, 4.3.40
213 "Does she know any? . . .": VP/AP, 3.11.39
213 "Bit of bombing . . .": VP/AP, 6.4.40
213 her grandmother: VP/AP, 4, 11 & 25.3.40
214 "He throws red tape . . .": VP/AP, 29.6.40
214 "I do feel rather sorry . . .": VP/AP, 7.3.40
214 "The awful thing . . .": VP/AP, 17.4.40
214 an elaborate hoax: AP/VP, 12.4.40
214 becoming a father: FMT 105
214 Violet was radiant: Maud Powell/AP, 7.5.40
215 "difficult to believe . . .": AP/VP, 5.5.40
215 it was a week . . . : VP/AP, 5.5.40
215 Gosford Castle: AP/VP, 18.4.40 & 6.5.40; & see FMT 105
215 "like Edward . . .": AP/VP, 13.5.40
216 "all the ghastly . . .": H. Lamb/AP, May 1940
216 "I had to stop . . .": VP/AP, 10.5.40
217 "Poor old Miranda . . .": VP/AP, 10.5.40
217 an impersonal situation report: AP/VP, 24.5.40
217 "My childhood . . .": DP 111
217 her first film: Gwyneth Lloyd, later Heygate, starred in British Gaumont's *Wild Boy*, 1934
217 "I've just remembered . . .": VP/AP, 31.5.40
217 "I have a lot to say . . .": VP/AP, 14.3.40
217 "I would give the world . . .": AP/VP, 23.6.40
218 "I shot Mussolini . . .": AP/VP, 16.5.40
218 playing soldiers: AP/VP, 2.7.40
218 "Though he himself . . .": AP/VP, 3.7.40
218 "the great qualification . . .": AP/VP, 26.7.40
218 "to see if the All Clear . . .": VP/AP, 15.8.40
218 "The weather is like . . .": VP/AP, 7.8.40
218 "By the way has . . .": AP/VP, 31.7.40
219 "Peter Quennell . . .": VP/AP, 9.8.40
219 "the Great Nurse War": VP/AP, 31.7.40

219 "He not only beats her . . .": VP/AP, 11.7.40

219 "in the case of . . .": AP/VP, 17.7.40

219 "the theory that . . .": AP/VP, 15.4.70

219 "you realise of course . . .": AP/VP, 17.8.40

219 "one of the least distinguished . . .": FMT 105

220 "I am now doing . . .": AP/VP, 2.8.40

220 "nightmare of cheerlessness . . .": SA 19

220 "Either Dennis Thomas . . .": Jo Grimond, *Memoirs*, 1979, p. 94

221 "The syllabus . . . all the dons . . .": AP/VP, 12.1.41

221 "bracicephalous populations . . .": AP/VP, 23.1.41

221 Goronwy Rees . . . Rowena Fayre: AP/VP, 7.2.41

221 Geoffrey Dennis: AP/VP, 15.1.40; & see FMT 116–20 & VB 25–8

221 Freddy Ayer: AP/VP, 7.2.41

222 "always causes everyone . . .": AP/VP, 13.2.41

222 Andrew Gow: FMT 114–15; & SP 318

222 Muggeridge met him: AP/VP, 3.2.41

222 "a colossal dish-up . . .": AP/VP, 27.1.41

222 Juliet O'Rorke . . . "one of those houses . . .": AP/VP, 3.2.41

222 "You manage to . . .". AP/VP, 19.1.41

223 "make up his mind . . .": IS 146

223 Renewed threats: AP/VP, 11.8.41

223 sabotaging his son's: AP/VP, 31.7.40

223 "I don't think . . .": AP/VP, 31.7.41

223 "Bedlam in a . . .": Artemis Cooper, *Patrick Leigh Fermor. An Adventure*, 2012, p. 12

223 "He isn't much . . .": AP/M. Muggeridge, 1.8.42

224 "I can't decide . . .": AP/VP, 17.8.41

224 "I wish you were . . .": AP/VP, 21.8.41

224 Adrian McLaughlin: AP/VP, 9.8.41

224 "Osbert has already . . .": AP/VP, 9.8.41

224 Evelyn Waugh: AP/VP, 5.8.41

224 "infinitely more . . .": M. Muggeridge/AP, n.d. [Dec. 1941]

224 "I look like . . .": AP/VP, 17.8.41

224 "You speak of . . .": AP/VP, 30.8.41

225 "I don't mind Arthur . . .": AP/VP, 16.8.41

225 "seems nice as . . .": AP/VP, 9.8.41

225 Edouard Manet: *A Bar at the Folies Bergères* (Courtauld Institute of Art, London), & *Mademoiselle Victorine in the Costume of an Espada* (Metropolitan Museum, New York), SiS 27 & 102

225 semi-detached suburban house: 55, Lauderdale Drive, Petersham, Surrey

226 "I really can't quite . . .": AP/VP, 10.9.41; for Alick Dru, see FMT 137–45

226 "lethal quickness": FMT 139; & see MD 61

226 "I really cannot endure . . .": A. Dru/AP, 16.4.48

226 "The violets burst out . . .": AP/VP, 13.11.41

226 "I feel rather . . .": AP/VP, 6.11.41

227 "an armour-plated . . .": FMT 141

227 "a Frenchman translated . . .": FMT 138

227 to read Petrarch: AP/VP, 21.1.43

227 his only published book: *The Journals of Søren Kierkegaard*, trans. & ed. A. Dru, 1938

227 "I particularly admired . . . I had the impression . . .": P. Wilkinson/AP, Jan. 1977

228 Polish Independent Parachute Brigade: See Patric Delaforce, *Monty's Rhine Adventure. War and Peace, September 1944, NW Europe*, 2014, p. 176

228 "I hardly exist . . .": AP/VP, 30.9.41 & 10.10.41

228 "I think he now realises . . .": AP/VP, 7.10.40

229 "an empty, dark city . . .": Muggeridge, *The Infernal Grove*, op. cit., 103–4

229 "calming to the spirit . . .": FMT 147

229 Jo and Laura Grimond: AP/VP, 27.12.41

229 Widow Lloyd: AP/VP, 9.1.42

229 Reitlinger: AP/VP, 27.12.4

229 Waugh: AP/VP, 30.9.41

229 Connolly . . . "all quite enjoyable . . .": AP/VP, 9.10.41

229 "quite inconceivably boring . . .": AP/VP, 24.1.42

230 "Ballad of LMS Hotels": C. Lambert/AP, 25 Sept., n.d. [1942]; & see SL 305

230 *Arthur Towle*: Controller of LMS Hotel Service in WW2, SL 305

230 *Keep the Aspidistra Flying*: IS 130

230 "hitting back at . . . annoying them": G. Orwell/AP, 8.6.36

231 "one lean and ugly . . .": DMM 331

231 "working-class life . . .": J54

231 "a friend for whom . . .": *Punch*, 15.7.53

231 "We cannot win the war . . .": Part I of *The Lion and the Unicorn*, 1941, reprinted in *Collected Essays, Journalism & Letters of George Orwell*, vol. ii, *My Country Left or Right, 1940–43*, ed. Sonia Orwell & Ian Angus, 1968, pp. 94 & 109; for revolutionary blueprint, see pp. 94–103

231 "It will crush . . .": Ibid., 102

231 "It seems to me . . .": AP/VP, 10.10.41

232 Victor Chocquet: IS 131

232 "one of those fiercely . . .": AP/VP, 10.10.41

232 "Always put them . . .": IS 138

232 a dismal failure: FMT 184–5

232 ten thousand letters: FMT 172

233 "He became a kind of cult": FMT 145

233 "an altogether phenomenal . . .": FMT 150

233 "like an immensely genial troll": Description of Dempster, Bradfield's fictional alias, MP 25

233 "as really it was . . .": AP/VP, 6.2.43 (Wolfit's *Lear* opened in Jan. 1943, at the St. James's Theatre, Piccadilly)

233   "What a work! . . .": A. Dru/AP, n.d. [1948]

233   the Papal Bun . . . "people used actually . . .": FMT 155–6

234   on the direct intervention: FMT 157 (Churchill was minister of defence)

235   "unrivalled knowledge . . .": "Denis Capel-Dunn—An Appreciation" by V. F. W. C-B. [Victor Cavendish-Bentinck, chairman of JIC, later 9th Duke of Portland) & E. I. C. J., *The Times*, 25.7.45, reprinted APSN 56, autumn 2014

235   "My [attention] . . . was . . .": MP 53

235   "an immense, wiry . . .": MP 184

235   "to get through . . .": AP/VP, 7.7.45

235   purely materialistic: Hugh Massingberd, "A Hero of Our Club. Anthony Powell at the Travellers 1930–2000 (Part 1)," APSN 8, autumn 2002

235   "a squat figure . . .": James Allason, "Widmerpool Goes to Ground: Capel-Dunn in the Cabinet War Rooms," APSN 29, winter 2009

236   Young Bloody: James Allason, "Powell in Clubland," APSN 43, summer 2011

236   "it was impossible . . .": MP 12

236   "in so far . . .": AP/Ulf Brandell, 1974, "Powell–Brandell Letters," APSN 34, p. 6 ('Identification subsequently spotted by Desmond Seward in *Brooks's: A Social History*, eds. Philip Ziegler & D. Seward, 1991)

237   "They are rocking . . . How, as I say . . .": MP 105 & 107

237   He sacked Tony: FMT 158

237   "my nerves wouldn't . . .": Allason, "Powell in Clubland," op. cit.

238   1st Polish Armoured Division: See Peter Wilkinson & Joan Bright-Astley, *Gubbins and SOE*, 1993, p. 179

239   *Luxemburger Wort*: AP's column ran monthly in 1946 and twice monthly in 1947, tailing away to only 2 columns in March and April, 1948; for his dealings with the Grand Duchy, see FMT 166–7

239   "small but dapper . . .": Auberon Waugh, *Will This Do?*, 1991, p. 21

239   Pig-Walloper: Ibid., 110; & see Amary (ed.) *Letters of Evelyn Waugh*, op. cit., 442

240   "This Regency villa . . .": DP 1

240   "I think we are . . .": AP/VP, 16.7.45

240   "The landscape reminded them . . .": DP 2; & FMT 146

240   "We went for a walk . . .": FMT 147

240   making a desultory start: AP/VP, 17.7.44

240   "an agreeable, fairly intelligent . . .": JA 9

240   "I think you need not . . ." (my italics): J. Heygate/AP, 12.9.42

241   "I saw some stuff . . .": AP/VP, 25.6.44

241   windows had been smashed: AP/VP, 19.7.44

241   "One morning . . . from my bed . . .": DP 3

241   Even Tony was reduced: FMT 170; & MP 158

241   "Already a stylised figure . . .": FMT 171

242   "Each cough . . .": H. Lamb/AP, 23 Dec., n.d. [1943]

242 Revolution threatened . . . in Belgium: FMT, 174–7
242 "The Bun seems . . .": AP/VP, 7.7.45; & see FMT 159–60
242 he begged her: AP/VP, 19.7.45
242 "'Overlord' will be . . .": AP/VP, 4.7.45
243 "I got syrup . . .": AP/VP, 28.7.45
243 "It gives one . . .": AP/VP, 30.7.45
243 "How many latch-keys . . .": AP/VP, 20.7.45
243 "What do you do . . .": AP/VP, 30.7.45
243 "calling down . . . anathema . . .": FMT 182
243 "It was like lying . . .": AP/VP, 10.7.45
243 "more suitable to an adventure story . . .": FMT 177
243 "one of the tragedies . . .": FMT 177
244 Okulicki's arrest: Noted under 1945 in "War Dates," a ts list compiled by AP for use when working on vols. 7, 8 & 9 of the *Dance* (CA)
244 "Big Brother": FMT 161
244 see him in Prague: AP/VP, 24.7.45
244 "He has brought her . . .": AP/VP, 16.7.45
244 "We can only hope . . . heart attack": FMT 162; & information from John Powell
244 "I think Alick's despair . . .": AP/VP, 4.8.45
244 Victory service: AP/VP, 19.8.45
244 "the little pimp . . .": AP/VP, 24.7.45
245 two long articles: "Henri-Frédéric Amiel," *Cornhill*, Dec. 1945 & Jan. 1946, reprinted in AP, MV 413–29
245 "They would bring us . . .": FMT 187, MV 428–9
245 "line upon line . . . looks exactly like . . .": AP/VP, 1.9.45
245 cleaning the silver: AP/VP, 6.9.45
245 "Whether you will ever get back . . .": A. Dru/AP, 28.7.45
245 The depression that engulfed: FMT 189; & M. Muggeridge/AP, 5.11.45
245 productive years: Miriam Gross interview, *Observer*, 15.12.85
246 "the agonising, futile longing . . . like jealousy . . .": M. Muggeridge/AP, 5.6.42
246 equally agonizing certainty: AP/M. Muggeridge, 15.4.46

Chapter 8

247 ten years to work out: AP interview, *New York Times*, 3.7.65
247 "human beings behaving": AP/Jocelyn Brooke, 6.4.64
247 "I knew all at once . . .": FMT 214
247 "The one thing certain . . .": FMT 215; see Jeremy Warren, "Nicolas Poussin's Painting *A Dance to the Music of Time* in the Wallace Collection," in APS, "Anthony Powell & the Oxford of the 1920s," Proceedings of the 2nd Biennial Conference, 2003, pp. 25–33
248 "somehow serene and clear": DMM 379

248 "This amalgam . . .": FMT 191

248 typewriter stopped functioning: T. S. Eliot/VP, 21.11.45

248 agreed with Muggeridge: DMM 209

248 "genealogical potterings . . . novel-writing machine . . .": FMT 195

249 "his presentation of life . . .": JA 66 (for an authoritative update on Aubrey, see Ruth Scurr, *John Aubrey. My Own Life*, 2015)

249 "Here is the face . . . : JA 115 (portrait drawing by William Faithorne)

249 "He contemplated . . .": JA 11

249 "the good and evil . . .": JA 13

250 "bomb-defaced weary . . .": FMT 196

250 "How absolutely awful . . .": AP/G. Reitlinger, 29.12.45

250 Venetia Digby: Information from Venetia Reitlinger

250 "most lovely . . .": *John Aubrey, Brief Lives and Other Selected Writings*, edited with an introduction by Anthony Powell, 1949, pp. 47–8

250 just too soon: Lady Jersey died 22.5.45

250 "I felt her loss . . .": DP 156

250 "strange, red little . . .": DMM 209

251 *Strand* magazine: AP/M. Muggeridge, 6.5.46

251 David Higham: D. Higham/AP, 11.2.46; & AP/M. Muggeridge, 14.5.46 & 15.4.47

251 obligation to Cassell . . . secured offers: D. Higham/AP, 2.5.46 & 10.2.50; & AP/M. Muggeridge, 6.5.46

251 "by no means so . . .": FMT 199

251 "I wish to God . . .": G. Greene/AP, 16.12.40

251 "Of course, his prayer . . .": M. Muggeridge/AP, 2.5.46

251 "except possibly . . .": AP/VP, 22.11.39

251 "one of the really . . .": D. Jerrold/AP, 27.9.48

252 from *The Forsyte Saga*: DMM 261

252 "I have seldom signed . . .": G. Greene/AP, 27.5.46

252 Tony took him: AP/M. Muggeridge, 15.4.46

252 "I will cheerfully . . .": VP/AP, 30.10.39

252 back-up and babysitting: Information from VP

252 "looking like St. Christopher . . .": VP to HS

252 "managed to dress . . .": AP/M. Muggeridge, 8.2.47

252 massive clasp-knife: IS 141

253 "I can't say it has . . .": AP/M. Muggeridge, 3.7.46

253 "rather like Christian . . .": AP/M. Muggeridge, 28.12.46

253 "I think the crofter . . . I know that if . . .": G. Orwell/AP, 8.9.47

253 "They draw me as . . .": M. Muggeridge/AP, 2.5.46

254 "Actually I think . . .": M. Muggeridge/AP, n.d. [late 1945]

254 a slender, slant-eyed beauty: J1 151

254 stamp collection: M. Christen/AP&VP, 3.3.46

254 "years of book . . .": MWA

255 "she wants agents . . .": AP/VP, 14.3.46

255 "We peacetime deadbeats . . .": B. Roberts/AP, 5.9.44

255 sipping surgical spirit: M. Muggeridge/AP, n.d. [Oct. 1945]

255 his sexual advances: M. Wood/AP, 21.9.77

255 "Bobby was sheer bliss": M. Wood/AP, 20.6.78

255 "the author can . . .": DT, 15.2.47

255 "Mr. Neville Shute . . .": DT, June 1947

255 "His striking dialogue . . .": DT, 15.11.46

256 "Let them—like the *Bridge* . . .": *Spectator*, 7.6.46

256 *Novels of High Society from the Victorian Age*: Benjamin Disraeli's *Henrietta Temple*, G. A. Lawrence's *Guy Livingston* and Ouida's *The Moths* selected and introduced by AP, Pilot Press, 1947

256 *Luxemburger Wort*: AP's *Brief aus London* ran from May 1946 to May 1948

256 British Communist Party: AP, "Die kommunistische Partei in England," *Luxemburger Wort*, 4.7.46; & see J1 234–5

257 dry rot: DP 16

257 "the wave . . .": DP 16

257 Jane Asher: DP 7

257 "That little girl . . .": J1 170; & see DP 7

257 Even the policeman: DP 14

257 "It sounds as if . . .": VP/AP, 10.11.39

258 "He hardly ate . . .": AP/VP, 13.4.47

258 "the gnome I caught . . .": AP/VP, 15.4.46

258 "When my obituary . . .": AP/VP, 14.4.46

259 "Having a real . . .": AP/B. Hambrough, p.c., 24.8.46

259 "I just wanted . . .": J. Heygate/AP, 7.5.46

259 Dru . . . diagnosed: A. Dru/AP, 3.9.46

259 "I am very worried . . .": Quoted in AP/M. Muggeridge, 28.12.46

259 "I don't know when . . .": AP/M. Muggeridge, 28.12.46; see Chapter 9, pp. 11–12

259 took fifty minutes: AP/M. Muggeridge, 28.12.46 (the guest was John Hayward)

259 cold weather: AP, *Luxemburger Wort*, 7.2.47

259 the Glenconners: AP/M. Muggeridge, 9.4.47

260 seriously ill: AP/M. Muggeridge, 14.4.47 & 16.5.47

260 he confidently predicted: *Luxemburger Wort*, 23.1.47 (19.1.47 was the day Poland went to the polls)

260 "a gang of Russian-nominated . . .": *New English Review*, Feb. 1947

260 "poor old Miroslav . . .": AP/M. Muggeridge, 28.5.47

260 "a permanent dent . . .": IS 141

261 "I was riveted . . .": MWA

261 retailed the plot: AP to HS

261 He told Tony: G. Orwell/AP, 29.11.47

261 expecting a third child: AP/M. Muggeridge, 16.4.47

261 "I have put your works . . .": A. Dru/AP, 13.9.47

261   a visit with Violet: AP/M. Muggeridge, 28.12.46

262   "Everything at the moment . . . stockbrokers' heaven": A. Dru/AP, 8 July 1947

262   "Like Kierkegaard . . .": A. Dru/AP, 22.9.46

262   "Violet, I presume . . .": A. Dru/AP, 3.10.47

262   "I went out earlier . . .": A. Dru/AP, 19.3.47

263   "The whole thing . . .": A. Dru/AP, 9.3.48

263   "a faint but perceptible . . .": FMT 207

263   Alick Dru had been urging: A. Dru/AP, 22.11.46 & 29.5.47

263   its writ ran: A. Pryce-Jones, *The Bonus of Laughter*, 1987, p. 152

263   "lively dialogue . . .": This and subsequent quotations in the same para from AP's first article, *TLS*, 13.9.47

264   "the lives and . . .": *TLS*, 29.11.47

264   "it would give . . .": *TLS*, 8.11.47

264   "concise, witty . . .": *TLS*, 30.12.47

264   "little old peer . . . Oh I don't . . .": AP/M. Muggeridge, 28.12.46

264   collected editions: G. Orwell/AP, 8.3.48

265   "all much funnier . . . It is, in fact . . .": AP/M. Muggeridge, 30.7.46

265   "a last gasp . . .": AP, "Marcel Proust," *TLS*, 18.8.50

265   "I have begun it . . .": AP/M. Muggeridge, 8.2.47

265   "I can't say . . .": AP/M. Muggeridge, 8.12.46

265   assumed they were brothers: AP/VP, 21.8.45

265   "It will be wonderful . . . ": M. Muggeridge/AP, 5.4.47

266   "Alone I cannot . . .": M. Muggeridge/AP, 30.3.46

266   "I wish you were . . .": M. Muggeridge/AP, 5.5.41

267   "memory . . . enigmatic . . .": QU 3

267   "I used to walk . . .": Muggeridge, *The Infernal Grove*, op. cit., 253

267   the novel he published: *Affairs of the Heart*, 1949

268   "the sombre demands . . .": QU 3

268   In March: G. Orwell/AP, 8.3.48

268   "I suppose . . .": G. Orwell/AP, 25.6.48

268   "a perception of . . .": G. Orwell, *The Collected Essays, Journalism and Letters of George Orwell*, vol. iv, *In Front of Your Nose*, 1945–50, ed. Sonia Orwell & Ian Angus, p. 443

268   Greene's work: AP, "West African Rock," *TLS*, 29.5.48

268   "They all thought . . .": DMM 276

269   white with rage: J3 105

269   "It's a bloody boring . . .": FMT 201; for this incident, see FMT 200–202, & DMM 298

269   an immediate release: AP/G. Greene, 12.11.48, & G. Greene/AP, 14.12.48

269   protestations from Douglas: D. Jerrold/AP, 27.9.48

269   "Jerrold . . . could bring . . . Jerrold's capacity . . .": FMT 200–203

269   "<u>I BEG</u> . . .": P. W. L. Powell/AP, 4.9.48

270 "Things may buck up . . . : P. W. L. Powell/AP, 8.9.48

270 Cresset Press: *Brief Lives and Other Selected Writings by John Aubrey*, edited and with an introduction by AP, 1949; see FMT 202–3

270 rejected Jerrold's overtures: AP/D. Jerrold, 28.10.48, & D. Jerrold/AP, 29.10.48

270 overruled Higham: D. Higham/AP, 8.10.48, 15.10.48 & 9.11.48

270 "a more morbid . . .": AP/M. Muggeridge, 9.4.47

270 "I love anything . . . it's a ghastly . . .": G. Orwell/AP, 15.11.48

270 "How about you? . . .": G. Orwell/AP, 2.2.4

271 "I am not sure . . .": DMM 324

271 "or if not in bed . . .": G. Orwell/AP, 11.5.49

271 "When I told this . . .": DMM 330 (the publisher was Fred Warburg)

271 to read both of them: G. Orwell/AP, 11.5.49 & 6.6.49

271 George told her: Hilary Spurling, *The Girl from the Fiction Department. A Portrait of Sonia Orwell*, 2002, p. 96

272 "old Wodehousian side": IS 141

272 "all the time . . .": DMM 368

272 a Church of England funeral: See IS 141–2, & FMT 220–21

272 Fifty or sixty people: AP/J. Heygate, 7.4.50

272 "The Lesson . . .": FMT 221

272 "We are . . . more than . . .": D. Jerrold/D. Higham, 13.1.50

272 to be handed over: DMM 363 (the handover took place on 8.12.49)

272 Greene's confirmation: AP/G. Greene, 12.11.48; & G. Greene/AP, 14.12.48

273 almost identical terms: Contract dated 28.2.50, HA

273 "the world's . . . amateur champion . . .": John St. John, *William Heinemann: A Century of Publishing*, 1990, p. 255

273 "He didn't like . . .": Ibid., 254

273 "the firm's ideal . . .": Ibid., 295

273 "it is ten years . . .": D. Higham/AP, 10.2.50

273 "at least a . . .": D. Higham/G. Greene, 20.10.48

273 "soft-pedal . . .": A. S. Frere/AP, 1.5.50 & 2.1.51; initially the overall series title was *The Music of Time*, becoming *A Dance to the Music of Time* only with *Temporary Kings* in 1973 (but see FMT 216)

274 Falcon and Grey Walls Press: See R. Gant, "Paul Scott," *Bookseller*, 11.3.78; & Hilary Spurling, *Paul Scott. A Life*, 1985, pp. 176 & 178 *et passim*

274 "either a professional Scot . . .": T. G. Rosenthal, R. Gant obituary, *Independent*, 29.3.93

274 Frere promoted Gant: St. John, *William Heinemann*, op. cit., 329

274 James Broom-Lynne: R. Gant/Philip Mann, memo 15.4.75, HA

275 "When work was . . .": T. G. Rosenthal, op. cit.

275 publisher in a million: J1 251

275 "He was speechless . . .": C. Longford/VP, Easter [25 March] 1951

275 "I know Jenkins . . . ": AP/VP, 23.4.52

276 "He climbed up . . .": QU 223

276 "Quiggin sat sourly . . . He had something . . .": QU 180 & 205

276 "'It doesn't do . . .": QU 134

276 "The path had suddenly . . .": QU 229

277 Pam was by Muggeridge's account: Richard Ingrams, *Muggeridge. The Biography*, 1995, p. 172

277 "She personified . . .": Ibid., 173

277 "Malcolm's voice . . . like an army dinner . . .": J. Heygate/AP, 2.4.50 & 13.4.50

277 "a great comic writer . . . a novel that curiously . . .": AP, "Marcel Proust," *TLS*, 8.8.50

277 "In the road outside . . .": DP 4

278 "He never seems . . .": J. Betjeman, DT, 26.1.51

278 "*All his past life* . . ." (my italics): C. Longford/VP, Easter [25 March] 1951

278 "items not to be . . . They made me . . .": BM 1

279 "From the very . . .": J2 162

279 A brash new administrator: David Webster, see SL 355 & 362–3

279 his last intervention: AP, "A Memoir," in Shead, *Constant Lambert*, op. cit., 26; & FMT 222

279 "I remembered the words . . . : SL 388

280 "I could do nothing . . .": Jean Rollason, "A Link Broken, Part 2," APSN, no. 31, 2008; Varda Proctor died 21.2.51

280 "the terrible devils . . .": MD 93

280 "I always think . . .": Mount, *Cold Cream*, op. cit., 68

280 "Somehow I began . . .": A. Fraser, *My History*, 2015, p. 208

280 "Elizabeth did not . . .": Ibid., 201

281 "like a feral . . .": Ibid., 115

281 "No one was dull . . .": Fraser, *My History*, op. cit., 207

282 "Inclusion at last . . .": Ibid.

282 An increase of 150 per cent: A. Dru/AP, 3.11.50

282 "with huge delight . . . We freeze and starve . . .": E. Waugh/AP, 12 & 16.3.51

282 "After settling this . . .": AP/VP, 27.8.51

282 the Chantry: SAG 22; further information from John Powell

282 refused to believe: SAG 24

283 fears of another war: DP 15 & 17; & information from VP

283 Wing Commander Barraclough: SAG 22

283 "so terrible . . .": Fraser, *My History*, op. cit., 49; (VP's was a disproportionate reaction to the minor reservations obligatory at the end of enthusiastic notices by Philip Toynbee [*Observer*, 22.6.52] & J. W. Lambert [*Sunday Times*, 22.6.52]; subsequent reviews were uniformly good)

283 second-hand refrigerator: DP, 63–4 (workmen at Chester Gate had appropriated the original fridge)

283 "From all around . . . the house that . . .": DP 16

Chapter 9

284 woods beyond: DP 17

284 "curious mixture . . .": Mark Girouard, see Harry Mount, *Country Life*, 27.10.2005

284 Mass centre: E. Waugh/AP, Oct. 1952; & information from John Powell

284 "The high point . . .": Robert Vanderbilt/VP, 22.9.52; AP and R. Vanderbilt, *The Acceptance of Absurdity. Anthony Powell & Robert Vanderbilt. Letters 1952–1963*, ed. J. Saumarez Smith & J. Kooperstein, 2011, p. 31

285 "even in Bristol . . .": Timothy Mowl & Marion Mako, *Historic Gardens of Somerset*, 2010, p. 158; & see SAG 24–5

286 bill-hooks and diggers: A. Dru/AP, 31.7.53

286 family joke: See John Powell, APSN, no. 33, pp. 3–5

286 "Spurred on . . .": A. Dru/AP, 30 Sept., n.d. [1952]

286 the local communist: Information from J. Powell

286 "I must say . . .": A. Dru/AP, 1.9.52

286 "financial struggles . . .": AP/J. Heygate, 9.1.53

286 On Alick's advice: A. Dru/AP, 25.8.52, 1 Sept., n.d. [1952] & 4.6.53

287 Humber Snipe: AP/J. Heygate, 9.1.53; & DP 15

287 "We must meet . . .": A. Dru/AP, 21.12.52

287 "One of the most . . .": WN 81; & see CCR 212

287 "about 25,000 . . .": AP/J. Heygate, 9.1.53

287 Muggeridge offered him: SAG 47–9

288 £1,500 a year: R. G. Price, *A History of Punch*, 1957

288 rock bottom: AP/R. Vanderbilt, 26.1.53; AP and Vanderbilt, *The Acceptance of Absurdity*, op. cit., 49

288 Nancy Mitford: Ibid., 50

288 "it does not seem . . .": Ibid., 49

288 "long and obstinate . . .": SAG 53

288 AP's reviews of Kipling, de Vigny and Musil: *Punch*, 11, 18 & 25 March 1953

288 hopping mad: AP and Vanderbilt, *The Acceptance of Absurdity*, op. cit., 66

289 the definitive account: See David Luck, "Documents: Reitlinger and 'How many?'," *Jewish Social Studies*, vol. 41, no. 2 (spring 1979), Indiana University Press; & Alan Bullock, "Gerald Reitlinger: A Portrait," *Eastern Ceramics and Other Works of Art from the Collection of Gerald Reitlinger*, ex. cat., Ashmolean Museum, 1981, pp. 9–12

289 "No more visitors . . .": M. Muggeridge, 22.3.52, DMM 433

289 "*Some* bloody Jew . . .": Information from Venetia Bell, née Reitlinger

289 "Like the aerial bomber . . .": G. Reitlinger, *The Final Solution*, 1953

289 living human bodies: Ibid., 206

289 "After May, 1945 . . .": Ibid., 482

290 "public opinion . . .": See David S. Wyman & Charles H. Rozenveig, *The World Reacts to the Holocaust*, 1996, p. 621

290 "an unendurable horror": Ibid.

290   "In so far as . . .": AP, *Punch*, 6.5.53
290   become a hermit: Information from Venetia Bell
290   Elton's new young wife: Margaret Elton ts
290   a lively portrait: *Gerald Reitlinger* by Eve Disher in the Ashmolean Museum
291   "I shall be very . . .": E. Waugh/AP, Oct. 1952
291   swamps and jungles: FMT 218
291   "half Balkan bandit . . .": Hugh Casson quoted in Richard Boston, *Osbert. A Portrait of Osbert Lancaster*, 1989, p. 125
291   "thrown into the pond . . .": DP 37; see also 38–9, 52–3 & 105
292   returned to his novel: AP/J. Heygate, 1.4.53 & 8.10.53; & DP 39
292   getting stuck: AP/J. Heygate, 1.4.53; & AP/D. Higham, 24.4.53
292   had reached halfway: AP/J. Heygate, 8.10.53; & DP 39
292   completed draft: DP 45
292   full of Mrs. Erdleighs: O. Lancaster/AP, n.d. [1968]
292   "grave gothic beauty": KO 180
292   Irish government: Office of Censorship of Publications in Eire; see DP 66 (the ban was lifted in 1963, D. Higham/AP, 8.10.63)
292   as Jean's model: Information from VP
292   singling out: DP 45
293   "It begins . . .": DP 18
293   Alick Dru: FMT 139
293   Hamish Erskine: DP 86
293   "the love of her life": Information from the late Sonia Orwell
293   Tony found out: Information from Tristram Powell
293   "the ecstasies . . .": AW 212
294   chained to a corpse: AW 1
294   red-hot pincers: ALM 68
294   "I felt as if . . .": KO 178
294   "I would rather . . .": K. Amis, *Spectator*, 13.5.55
294   Tony had contacted: K. Amis, *Memoirs*, 1991, p. 150; & K. Amis/AP, 24.3.54
294   received a note: V. S. Naipaul, *A Writer's People*, 2007, p. 35
294   Tony fixed him up: V. S. Naipaul/AP, 28.10.57
294   "So original; so rich . . .": V. S. Naipaul/AP, 13.10.86; & see Naipaul, *A Writer's People*, op. cit., 36–9 for a change of heart
295   "Suddenly with no child . . .": DP 46
296   his publisher in Paris: René Julliard/AP & VP, 13.6.54
296   Nancy Mitford: N. Mitford/AP, 2.5.52 & 28.6.58
296   UN PROUST ANGLAIS: Headline of article by Michel Mohrt, *Arts*, 16–22.3, 1955 (*Une Question d'éducation*, pub. 1954; *Les Mouvements du coeur* [*A Buyer's Market*], pub. 1955)
296   "I think he . . .": AP/VP, 12.8.54 (the managing director was Dwye Evans)
296   *Panorama*: Richard Ingrams, *Muggeridge. The Biography*, 1995, p. 171
296   "You felt some life . . .": Ibid., 165
296   "Almost everybody . . .": Ibid., 323

296 "in the sense . . .": DMM 449; & see SAG 60

296 more clear-cut: Ingrams, *Muggeridge*, op. cit., 168

296 "the magazine was . . .": SAG 60

296 "I do beg you . . .": Ingrams, *Muggeridge*, op. cit., 164

297 Mark Boxer: J2 123

297 cover by Richard Doyle: SAG 61–2

297 "particularly pleased . . .": DMM 470; & see J2 123

297 See AP, Introduction to Jocelyn Brooke, *The Orchid Trilogy (The Military Orchid, A Mine of Serpents, The Goose Cathedral)*, 1981, p. 2

297 "My dear, it's the party . . . fag end of . . . It wasn't Stein . . .": J. Brooke, "Wauchop Agonistes," *Time & Tide*, 17.1.53

298 "the Private Pipeclay-Colonel . . .": AP/J. Brooke, 23.1.53

298 make suggestions: J. Brooke/AP, 23.3.54

298 alternative ending: AP/J. Brooke, 14.12.54

298 "It's a long time . . .": J. Brooke/VP, 29.5.56

298 Francis Wyndham: Information from F. Wyndham

299 "the unbelievable . . .": IS 165

299 "shape, life and staying-power": AP, *Spectator*, 5.4.46 (the story was "The Swag, the Spy and the Soldier" in *New Writing*, no. 26, spring 1946)

299 "It proves that . . .": AP, *TLS*, 24.10.47

299 in case of assault: Walter Allen, *As I Walked Down New Grub Street. Memories of a Writing Life*, 1981, p. 156

299 impossible to fault: SAG 6

299 every new novel: Allen, *As I Walked Down New Grub Street*, op. cit., 156

299 "I could never . . .": SAG 9

299 cut-price Hotel Cora: Geoffrey Favell/AP, 22.11.82

299 "He composed . . .": Allen, *As I Walked Down New Grub Street*, op. cit., 154

300 a crowd of duns: SAG 55

300 "taxis provided . . .": BDFR 121

300 friends like Tony: AP/VP, 23.8.50, 31.8.51, 22.2.55, 8.3.55 & 4.6.56; & Julian Maclaren-Ross, *Selected Letters*, ed. Paul Willetts, 2008, pp. 113 & 174

300 Royal Literary Fund: AP/VP, 23.8.50 (Maclaren-Ross subsequently applied himself at regulation three-year intervals)

300 *Telegraph* to take him on: AP/J. Maclaren-Ross, 2.5.56

300 "those determined . . .": AP, review of Maclaren-Ross's *Memoirs of the Forties*, DT, 30.9.65

300 Tony came to dread: AP/VP, 25.8.48

300 a two-page business schedule: J. Maclaren-Ross/AP, 19.11.54; & see Julian Maclaren-Ross, *Selected Letters*, op. cit., pp. 189–93 for a not entirely accurate version of the text

300 colossal ego: SAG 6

300 Sonia Orwell: See Maclaren-Ross, *Selected Letters*, op. cit., 177; & AP/Ulf Brandell, 1991, APSN, no. 34, spring 2009, p. 8

301 "My pride at . . .": A. Daintrey/AP, 4 May, n.d. [1955]

301 "the most exciting . . .": *Observer*, 15.5.55
301 "hard-headed English comedy . . .": V. S. Pritchett, *Bookman*, April 1955
301 "I'd have written this series . . .": AP to Serrell Hillman, see "Proust from the Other Side," *Summary*, vol. 1, no. 1, autumn 1970, p. 124
301 "Homage à M. Proust . . .": VP/Alison Lurie, 15 Dec., n.d.
301 a small memorial: See FMT 170
302 "This is pretty . . .": K. Amis/AP, 7.9.55
302 only fifteen thousand words: AP/J. Heygate, 18.12.55
302 "Each recriminative decade . . .": TK 224
302 three volumes: D. Higham/G. Greene, 20.10.48
302 eight or nine: AP interviewed by Angela Paine, *Books & Bookmen*, Nov. 1957
302 "Not of course . . .": A. Dru/AP, 29.7.53
302 "After a late lunch . . .": Humphrey Clinker, "Powell's England," *Books and Art*, vol. 1, no. 2, Nov. 1957
302 The daily stint . . . a thousand words: AP, *Books & Bookmen*, op. cit.
302 provisional arrangement: See Chapter 4, p. 122
302 "'Writing is something . . .": AP interviewed by Adriaan van der Veen, English translation of "An Introduction to Anthony Powell," *Nieuwe Rotterdamse Courant*, enclosed in A. van der Veen/AP, 20.4.60
303 beside the seaside: DP 79
303 nearly halfway: AP/J. Heygate, 27.9.56
303 "It was hard . . . as beautiful . . .": DP 72 & 80
303 Both holidays: See DP 79
304 in Venice: AP/VP, 3.9.56; & see DP 86–7
304 "a scene took place . . .": AP/VP, 11.9.56
304 To the girls: Information from Henrietta Phipps & Marigold Johnson
304 "As a matter . . .": AP/VP, 11.9.56
304 "Already I feel . . .": AP/VP, 14.9.56
304 "like a chunk . . .": AP/VP, 11.9.56
304 "The rest of it . . .": AP/VP, 14.9.56
305 alarmed the captain . . . Miss Greek Navy: Information from Marigold Johnson
305 "I felt terribly . . .": AP/VP, 12.9.56
305 "Coming down here . . .": VP to HS
305 Nina Hamnett: Died 16.12.56
305 Julian Maclaren-Ross: Geoffry Favell/AP, 22.11.8; & see Denise Hooker, *Nina Hamnett. Queen of Bohemia*, 1986, pp. 235 & 242
305 both of them agreeing: J. Brooke/AP, 16.11.55
305 "her breathless . . .": J. Brooke, *Time and Tide*, 3.12.55
306 "Because I love . . .": Information from the late Sonia Orwell
306 the east-facing end bedroom: I am grateful to John Powell for a guided tour of the Chantry
307 railway engineers: DP 23–4
307 billiard table: DP 28

307 Busts multiplied: Information from John Powell
307 Charles Addams: J2 140
307 one of three girls: Information from Pail Johnson
307 top for sex appeal: B. Skelton, *Tears Before Bedtime*, 1987, p. 83
307 "Rage seems . . .": B. Skelton obituary, DT, 29.1.96
307 battling kangaroos: Skelton, *Tears Before Bedtime*, op. cit., 83
307 "I hear we . . .": DP 66
308 "How could . . .": Fraser, *My History*, op. cit., 252
308 first novel: B. Skelton, *A Young Girl's Touch*, 1956
308 "four novelists . . .": DP 64
308 "a nature reserve . . .": SAG 25
308 misfired badly: SAG 54
308 "immediately recognised . . .": Amis, *Memoirs*, op. cit., 150
308 saluting Amis: *Punch*, 3.2.54
308 "more than a touch . . .": SAG 159
309 "lower-class malcontent . . .": Amis, *Memoirs*, op. cit., 151; Amis misremembered the year as 1955: in fact the interview was recorded 25.11.57 to coincide with publication of *At Lady Molly's* (K. Amis/AP, 21.11.57)
309 "'We don't care . . .'": Ibid., 152
310 "an almost Renaissance . . .": Keith Joseph, "Sir Henry d'Avigdor-Goldsmid," DNB 31
310 "hung with incomparable nectarines": Pryce-Jones, *The Bonus of Laughter*, op. cit., 170
310 "with Sisleys . . .": Mount, *Cold Cream*, op. cit., 200
310 "Harry and Rosie Goldsmid entertained . . .": Ibid., 200
310 "Miss Taylor was too . . .": DP 10
310 "After six years . . .": FMT 219
310 "Goldsmid's knowledge . . .": FMT 219
311 "I am very proud . . .": H. Goldsmid/AP, 13.12.57
311 the best thing: MV 317 & MD 21
311 Evelyn threatened: DP 31
312 "Let there be . . .": DP 122
312 "Alick has a . . .": AP/VP, 3.9.56
312 "the most searching . . .": MD 21
312 "the 'voices' on the boat . . .": MV 317
312 "stout and splenetic . . .": Hastings, *Evelyn Waugh*, op. cit., 567
312 "a prosperous . . .": MD 8
312 "Your galloping . . .": E. Waugh/AP, 20.10.57
313 "I am delighted . . .": E. Waugh/AP, 3.7.57
313 "a really brilliant . . .": AP/R. Vanderbilt, 23.8.57, & *The Acceptance of Absurdity*, op. cit., 89
313 "I had been . . . In the opening . . .": E. Waugh/AP, 20 Sept., n.d. [1957]
313 killing him off: H. Goldsmid/AP, 13.12.57
313 "It may lead . . .": ALM 52

314 by Elizabeth Bowen: Information from VP

314 "Would it be . . . I remember . . .": ALM 136 & 203

314 "the Suez crisis . . .": Humphrey Clinker, *Books and Art,* vol. 1, no. 2, Nov. 1957

315 "I hope it doesn't . . .": E. Waugh/AP, n.d.

315 "coursed like electricity . . . I could sense . . .": SAG 65

315 sacked Muggeridge: See Ingrams, *Muggeridge,* op. cit., 180

315 "That's *just* what . . .": Information from F. Wyndham

315 "I was twenty-five . . .": Naipaul, *A Writer's People,* op. cit., 35

315 BBC traineeship: Patrick French, *The World Is What It Is: The Authorized Biography of V. S. Naipaul,* 2008, p. 183

315 "He delighted . . .": Naipaul, *A Writer's People,* op. cit., 48–9

316 Bernard Hollowood: Ibid., 57

317 fill the review columns: Ibid., 57

317 to Bob Vanderbilt: 24.6.58, AP and Vanderbilt, *The Acceptance of Absurdity,* op. cit., 95

317 "That was a job . . .": Naipaul, *A Writer's People,* op. cit., 57

317 "some fairly heavy . . .": AP/J. Brooke, 29.5.58

317 "The meetings are . . .": AP/VP, 24.8.58

317 Lady Diana Cooper: AP/VP, 26.8.58; & SAG 170

317 Palazzo Labia: SAG 169–71

317 "It was more like . . . now reduced . . .": AP/VP, 31.8.58

317 Tiepolo fresco of his own: TK 42–3, 76, 82–9 & 96

318 "In the small one . . .": P. Larkin/AP, 27.9.58

318 horse-faced dwarf : see J3 211 & 221

318 Bernard Hollowood sacked: AP/J. Heygate, 28.2.59; SAG 65 & DP 142

318 "I thought it might . . .": AP/J. Brooke, 12.12.58

318 "He took it . . . He got very drunk . . .": Information from Paul Johnson

319 "I would see him . . .": Naipaul, *A Writer's People,* op. cit., 62

319 The new book: AP and Vanderbilt, *The Acceptance of Absurdity,* op. cit., 101

319 "an infinitely touching . . .": DP 205

319 "absolutely Herculean . . .": AP/D. Higham, 10.9.71; & SL xi–xiv

319 "in a cloak . . .": SL 208

319 Hugh Moreland: For a detailed comparison of Lambert with Moreland, see SL Appendix 9.

320 "strong and marvellously sweet": CCR 1

320 "slowly climbing . . . a shape that lay across the line": CCR 229

320 silver wedding: DP 208–9; & AP and Vanderbilt, *The Acceptance of Absurdity,* op. cit., 101

320 in a flash: AP/Wyndham Lloyd, 6.1.60

321 "I only wish . . .": A. Daintry/AP, 2.12.59

321 an ultimatum: P. W. L. Powell/AP, 25.12.59

321 death of Col. Powell: VP/AP, 31.12.59; & see DP 207, & SiS 1

321 Grandfather being received: Information from Tristram Powell

321 share and gilt-edged investments: Information from John Powell

321 routine visit: SiS 2; I am grateful to Patric Dickinson for a copy of this will

321 "It was a pleasure . . .": Naipaul, *A Writer's People*, op. cit., 62

321 expanding the sequence: AP/D. Higham, 21.3.61, HRC

322 "The old magic . . .": E. Waugh, review of KO, *Spectator*, 29.6.62

Chapter 10

323 "Powell's puppet show": Frontispiece of *A Second Tale of a Tub, or the History of Robert Powell the Puppet-show-man*, 1715: a political skit aimed at Robert Harley, Earl of Oxford, ousted as chief minister that year

323 coal scuttle: Hastings, *Evelyn Waugh*, op. cit., 177

325 "I want to . . .": AP/J. Heygate, 2.5.61

325 "the proud, anonymous . . .": KO 149

325 "All was changed . . . His smile . . .": KO 186 & 190

326 "To the novelist . . .": IS 53

326 "it is Trapnel . . .": Allen, *As I Walked Down New Grub Street*, op. cit., 171

327 St. John Clarke: Sources identified to me by AP

327 "invention, imagination . . .": MD 60

327 "the life of . . .": E. Waugh, review of KO, *Spectator*, 29.6.62

327 Alan Bishop: T. A. M. Bishop, 1907–1994, thanked by AP in the preface to JA: I am particularly grateful to Patric Dickinson for help in tracking him down

327 "He is too . . .": AP/VP, 22.7.39

327 "a rum sort . . . his advance blocked . . .": David Ganz, "T. A. M. Bishop," *Proceedings of the British Academy*, vol. iii, *Lectures and Memoirs*, 2000, pp. 393–412

327 "The title alone . . ." (my italics): Ibid.

328 Denis Capel-Dunn: Identified by Desmond Seward in *Brooks's: A Social History*, 1991; see Chapter 7, p. 35

328 Widmerpool as well: J3 219; but see his disclaimer a week after AP's death, DT, 4.4.2000 (he died a year later)

328 "Now the early afternoon . . .": DMM 538

328 three-part study: *The Economics of Taste. The Rise and Fall of Picture Prices, 1760–1960*, 1961; *The Rise and Fall of Objets d'Art Prices since 1750*, 1963; & *The Art Market in the 1960s*, 1970

329 His own collection: I am indebted for this assessment to Sheila Vanker, Senior Curator of Chinese Art, and Francesca Leoni, Jameel Curator of Islamic Art, Ashmolean Museum, University of Oxford

329 "On the chimney piece . . .": Richard de la Mare, "Gerald Reitlinger: Collector," *Eastern Ceramics and Other Works of Art from the Collection of Gerald Reitlinger*, ex. cat., Ashmolean, 1981

329 "varied, if sceptical . . .": Bullock, "Gerald Reitlinger: A Portrait," *Eastern Ceramics*, op. cit.

329 "such a house-party . . .": M. Muggeridge, review of HSH, 12.9.75

329 "This is priority . . .": H. Goldsmid/AP, 24.3.61

329 "into this department . . .": H. Goldsmid/AP, 17.5.58

329 "I would think . . .": H. Goldsmid/AP, 28.3.61

330 Benjamin Britten: B. Britten/AP, 2.1.59 & 19.3.60

330 Basil Boothroyd: SAG 57

330 "I felt nervous . . .": H. Goldsmid/AP, 4.5.62

330 "strange . . . very strange . . .": MD 164

330 *"this is where . . ."*: BM 198–201 (AP's italics)

330 "She's become . . .": Victoria Glendinning, *Edith Sitwell*, op. cit., 296

330 one of D. H. Lawrence's models: Ziegler, *Osbert Sitwell*, op. cit., 139

330 "I envy you . . .": G. Greene/AP, 5.12.60; (AP attended the trial 27–8.10.60)

330 implausible and impossible: SAG 72

331 cruising through: 2–17 April 1960: dates & destinations from AP diary

331 Swan Hellenic: SiS 5–11; & Colin Stone, "Swan Hellenic Refines the Art of Discovery Cruising," *Prow's Edge Cruise Magazine*, n.d.

331 Bowra: IS 191–2

331 sailing from Venice: 15 April–1 May 1961; AP diary & SiS 18–23

331 Petra: AP/J. Brooke, 2.5.61

332 day after he got back: AP/D. Higham, 21.4.60

332 Augustus John: MD 46; & see SiS 37. AP sat on 28 & 30 April

332 just over halfway: 50,000 words, AP/J. Heygate, 2.5.61

332 Dartmouth College: FMT 215–16; SAG 95–6 & 99–101

332 Arthur Mizener: AP reviewed his life of Scott Fitzgerald. *The Far Side of Paradise*, TLS, 23.11.51; for their subsequent friendship, see SAG 94, 96 & 103–4; & DP 169–71

332 "you discovered . . .": A. Mizener/AP, 23.10.61

332 Alison Bishop: See Alison Lurie, below *passim*

332 "After ten minutes' . . .": FMT 104

333 completed his typescript: SiS 42

333 "Galsworthy once said . . .": VP to HS

333 "like certain . . .": J. Brooke/AP, 4.5.61

333 twelve volumes: SAG 116

333 the first chapter: AP/Dwye Evans, 5.3.62, HA/HR

333 "One of your . . .": W. Ketton-Cremer/AP, 2.4.62

333 full-bottomed peruke: IS 165

334 "a wonderful . . .": Alan Judd, "Anthony Powell's War Trilogy," APS *Conference Proceedings*, 2003, p. 86

334 "That vision . . .": O. Manning/AP, 20.3.64

334 "We were operating . . .": VB 123–4

334 his title: Ezekiel 37:3

335 "I have done . . .": AP/D. Higham, 30.3.62, HRC

335 "but still in great . . .": AP/D. Higham, 13.9.62

335 motoring tours: 10–30 April, Collioure, Figeac, Beynac in the Pyrenees; 4–12 Sept., Glen; 19–29 Oct., La Torre, Molino del Rey: AP 1962 diary

335 June 1963: AP/D. Higham, 10.4063, HRC

335 AP foresaw completion of VB in 2 months in AP/D. Higham, 10.4.63, HRC

335 under discussion: AP met Margery Vosper, Higham's theatre agent, & dined with the impresario Michael White 7.11.60 & 21.12.60, AP diary

335 *Afternoon Men*: see SAG 106–15

335 a disaster: A. Mizener/AP, 9.10.63

335 "Almost nobody . . .": A. Mizener/AP, 9.10.63

335 by the leading lady: Information from the play's director, Roger Graef

335 obliged with two: *The Garden God* & *The Rest I'll Whistle*, published as *Two Plays* 1971 with set designs by Osbert Lancaster

336 theatrical managements: AP/VP, 6.10.66, Hilton Ambler (D. Higham Associates)/Binkie Beaumont (H. M. Tennant), 7.11.69; & see SAG 117–24

336 "they are muttering . . .": Roland Gant/Osbert Lancaster, n.d. (Nov. 1969)

336 "My heart was . . .": VP to HS

336 "Harry Goldsmid's . . .": FMT 219

336 pondering fresh: H. Goldsmid/AP, 4.11.63 & 22.12.64

336 "Perhaps . . . the post . . .": 21.5.66; H. Goldsmid/AP (10 Rillington Place, scene of John Christie's serial murders in 1940s, subsequently demolished; Henry Holt, *The Murder in Flat 13*, published 1935)

336 "No one but . . .": SA 21

337 belly dancers: SiS 57

337 "The German firm of temple removers . . .": SiS 42

337 "there is nothing . . .": Ibid., 58

337 "We had a marvellous . . .": AP/D. Higham, 2.3.64, HRC

337 Muggeridge's review: *Evening Standard*, 3.3.64

337 Muggeridge's conversion: Ingrams, *Muggeridge*, op. cit., 92–4

337 "It's like being . . .": Mount, *Cold Cream*, op. cit., 71

337 "I long for . . .": M. Muggeridge/AP, 27.4.63

337 "The former is passionate . . .": M. Muggeridge/AP, 2.5.46

338 "inherent drabness . . . It is a kind . . . his snobbishness . . .": *Evening Standard*, 3.3.64

338 "I have often . . .": M. Muggeridge/AP, 30.3.46

338 "We, Mr. Powell's . . .": *Evening Standard*, 3.3.64

338 stab in the back: J3 91

338 Olivia Manning diagnosed: O. Manning/AP, 20.3.64

338 "it was with . . .": Mount, *Cold Cream*, op. cit., 70

339 Malcolm himself claimed: Ingrams, *Muggeridge*, op. cit., 199

339 Japan: 11 April–4 May, see SAG 125–7, 129–30, 132–7

339 at Kyoto . . . while Tokyo: AP/D. Higham, 5.5.64, HRC

339 "anthropological specimens . . .": AP/D. Higham, 5.5.64

339 La Consula: See FMT 26; & SiS 72–5

339 "If I could . . .": Bill David/AP, 6.3.64

339 "compile *A Readers' Handbook* . . . the best . . .": Bill David/AP, 24.10.66

340 *Writers* documentary: SAG 13

340 nearly halfway: AP/D. Higham, 11.12.64

340 It started: Information from John Powell

340 "a scrap mural . . .": Mount, *Cold Cream*, op. cit., 70

341 good for the nerves: AP, "A Room of My Own," *Observer*, 1.4.84

341 "you could think . . .": AP to HS

341 a giant metaphor: A. Lurie, "Up Jenkins," *Summary*, vol. 1, no. 1, autumn 1970

341 "far less relaxed . . .": HSH 33

341 "Yes, not a bad . . .": Information from John Powell

341 "I bought 25 lions . . .": Lees Mayall, *Fireflies in Amber*, privately printed 1989, p. 14 (this sale had to be cancelled because of transport problems)

342 cataclysmic upheaval: Information from Roland Gant & Harry Frere; see also St. John, *William Heinemann*, op. cit., 419–22

342 Jenkins's conviction: TK 74

342 at least three: CCR, KO & VB

342 His angry complaints: AP/D. Higham, 21.4.60, 22.2.61, 4.9.61, 18.9.61, 29.9.61, 3.10.63 & 9.10.64, HRC

342 Pick & Gant: Information from T. G. Rosenthal, and personal experience; & see St. John, *William Heinemann*, op. cit., 437

342 *The Soldier's Art*: R. Gant/AP, 11.2.66 & 17.2.66

343 "international detective . . .": AP/R. Gant, 31.1.70, HA

343 "When I travel . . .": R. Gant/AP, 18.9.71

343 "the couple in . . .": St. John, *William Heinemann*, op. cit., 341

344 "a very self-possessed . . .": AP/VP, 31.8.5

344 the most intellectual: SAG 23

344 "talking to each . . .": AP/VP, 5.9.58

344 "It was the thrill . . .": P. G. Wodehouse/AP, 16.11.67

344 "As usual I . . .": P. G. Wodehouse/AP, 24.1.73

344 Jenkins as Mephistopheles: VB 191

344 "No one seemed . . .": BDFR 175

345 "The great historical . . .": Arthur Schlesinger, Jr., "Anthony Powell: The Prosopographer as Novelist," *Summary*, vol. 1, no. 1, autumn 1970, p. 67

345 "enough to make . . .": K. Amis/AP, 4.4.60

345 "I'm greatly honoured . . .": P. Larkin/AP, 7.9.66

345 POWELL AND PENGUINS: *Evening Standard*, 8.9.66

345 a curt note: SAG 92

345 "People are . . .": AP/D. Higham, 28.7.66, HRC

345 "You couldn't have . . .": D. Higham/AP, 8.8.66, HRC

346 poor sales: Anthony Godwin/AP, 8.8.66

346 incompetence, ineptitude: AP/D. Higham, 28.7.66, & A. Godwin/AP, 24.8.66

346 "Reading your three . . .": A. Godwin/AP, 24.8.66

346 supplied by himself: O. Lancaster/AP, n.d. [Sept. 1966]; & see *Evening Standard*, 8.9.66

346 Violet said that Karen: SiS 81

347 "a real sock . . .": D. Higham/AP, 29.9.66, HRC

347 "Even among his . . .": Waugh, *Will This Do?*, op. cit., 188

347 "Over and over . . .": AP, DT, Oct. 1964; see MV 312

347 hijacked Evelyn: SiS 79–80

347 "It is very rare . . .": E. Waugh/AP, 14.9.64

347 "His sinister . . .": Lord Birkenhead/Osbert Lancaster, 11.7.73, attached to O. Lancaster/AP, 16.8.73 (CA)

347 approval and relief: For AP's review of C. Sykes, *Evelyn Waugh. A Biography*, 1975, see MV 315–17

348 "Surely the time . . .": Review of *Evelyn Waugh and His Friends*, ed. David Pryce-Jones, DT, 1973, see MV 313

348 "immensely enjoyable . . .": AP/A. Dru, 28.12.66

348 "only just short . . .": MP 235

349 "the slightly fleshless . . .": AP/HS, 10.6.89

349 "arguing, delaying . . .": MP 40

349 "three and a half . . . Please amplify . . .": MP 45–6

349 "I felt tempted . . .": A. Dru/AP, n.d. [June 1968]

349 "Dear Tony, I am . . .": J2 50 (the book was *A Love Match*, 1969)

349 one of Barbara's: John Sutro, J2 50

350 A postcard: 13.10.69; information on this lunch from AP

350 by Tony's own account: AP/HS, 26.7.71

350 delivering the manuscript: AP/R. Gant, 20.3.68

350 "Slowdown—illness . . .": Horoscope enclosed in A. Lurie/AP, 19.3.70

350 "I think you . . .": AP/A. Lurie, 22.3.70

350 in Sweden: 5–15 July 1969; AP/R. Gant, 18.7.68

350 Gothenburg to Stockholm: 5–15 July 1969; for Descartes' tomb, AP/A. Dru, n.d.

351 On a Swan tour: 8–22 Aug. 1967

351 "Streaks of sunlight . . .": MD 120

352 "the guide under-estimated . . .": 13.8.67

352 "if you can . . .": AP/A. Dru, 1.10.68

352 "silent as darkness . . .": See Chapter 7, p. 273

352 *I Told You So . . .* : Amis, *Memoirs*, op. cit., 146

352 tour of southern India: 22 Oct.–18 Nov. 1969

352 back streets reminded: VP/A. Dru, 10.11.69

353 "I can't tell you . . .": G. Sitwell/VP, 24.6.70

353 "I've never enjoyed . . .": K. Amis/AP, 19.4.66

353 an addict of the *Dance*: Jilly Cooper, "Start of an Addiction," *Summary*, vol. 1, no. 1, autumn 1970, p. 44.

353 "Like Dr. Barnardo's": AP/A. Dru, 7.6.71

353 "we went anyhow . . .": A. Lurie / HS, 2.1.17

353 "an aspect of myself . . .": A. Lurie/AP&VP, Jan. 1971

353 "fire-air emphasis . . . May be introspective . . .": A. Lurie/AP, 19.3.70

354 "in my usual . . .": AP/D. Higham, 17.1.6

354 "an Homeric . . .": See Duff Hart-Davis, *The House the Berrys Built*, 1990, p. 132; & AP's review, DT, 14.4.90

354 "They held a . . .": Naipaul, *A Writer's People*, op. cit., 68

354 "go bankrupt . . .": J1 244

354 third choice: BDFR 76

354 "who had probably . . .": BDFR 123

354 "it is interesting . . .": H. Goldsmid/AP, 1.3.71

354 "With you, both the horror . . .": A. Mizener/AP, 20.9.60

355 "with precision . . .": SAG 149; AP&VP stayed with him 14–15 May 1966

355 "I seem to have . . .": SAG 148

356 Henry Widmerpool: W. Ketton-Cremer, *Norfolk in the Civil War*, 1969, p. 304; & W. Ketton-Cremer/AP, 27. 10.6

356 "You've gone on . . .": Quoted in K. Amis/AP, 3.6.90

356 "I can't quite . . .": AP/A. Lurie, 13.10.70; the Powells were in Iran 23 Sept.–7 Oct. 1970

356 He consulted: AP/H. Goldsmid, 14.11.70, & H. Goldsmid/AP, 17.11.70

356 two Americans: AP/A. Lurie, n.d. [May 1971], & 17.1.72; A. Mizener/AP, 18.5.71; & AP/Bill Davis, 14.10.71

356 "The roving intelligentsia . . .": TK 26

357 "Miraculous volumes . . .": TK 76

357 "These colours . . .": TK 82

357 "The skill of the . . .": TK 83

358 Dennis Wheatley: AP/D. Wheatley, 21.1.72 & 26.1.72, coll. Jonathan Koop-erstein; see also J1 261 & APSN, no. 35, 1985, p. 34

358 wrote a memoir: AP/Bruce Hunter, 19.8.71, HA; & see Shead, *Constant Lambert*, op. cit., 17–26

358 "In him Powell . . .": D. Piper, *The Times*, 29.11.73

359 "a 23 year long . . .": M. Wood/AP, 29.10.68 (she married Sgt. James Wood)

359 "Rocks of Gibraltar . . .": M. Wood/AP, 2.1.72

359 *Pickle My Bones*: M. Wood/AP, 17.1.79; see MWA under Abbreviations

359 "The way we used . . .": M. Wood/AP, 19.3.88

359 Bobby Roberts: M. Wood/AP, 15.11.68 & 18.11.73; & see MD 97

359 "the particularly helpless . . . mildewed despair . . .": WFC 46

359 "the Derry Mental": J. Heygate/AP, 12.6.69 (City & County Mental Hospi-tal, Londonderry)

359 autobiography of his own: E. Nightingale/AP, n.d. [early 1970s]

359 Maude Ffoulkes: VP, *A Substantial Ghost: The Adventures of Maude Ffoulkes*, 1967

360 "I never heard . . .": Information from JP

360 *"the right arm . . ."* (my italics): TP/HS, 3.2.2000
361 ably assisted by: J. Betjeman/VP, Oct. 1959; & see DP 197–8 & 203–4
361 "the local iconoclast": SiS 79
361 quarry companies: DP 54, 60 & 144; SAG 24; J2 90 & 172
361 "the hypnotised state . . .": AP/D. Higham, HA, 6.12.74
361 "the painter stands . . .": SAG 171
361 "It is a great . . .": N. Poussin/Paul Fréart de Chantelou, 17.1.1649
361 the most pastoral: Grey Gowrie, "The End of the Dance," *Standpoint*, June 2011, p. 71
361 One of them: AP/VP, 16.10.67 (the other two were Sir Mark Palmer & Maldwyn Thomas)
362 "like a footpath . . .": ALM 115
362 "The astonishing thing . . .": A. Mizener/AP, 23.9.75
362 "In the last . . .": P. Scott, "Turning the Full Circle," *Country Life*, 11.9.75
362 "This awful melancholia . . .": AP/A. Lurie, 4.11.77
363 survived a similar crisis: V. S. Naipaul/AP, 18.2.74
363 "which should steady . . .": A. Lurie/AP, 22.12.77
363 the workmen's bucket: HSH 271 & QU 1
363 on 1 December: AP/D. Higham, 1.12.74
363 W. H. Smith Prize: 19.11.74
363 "I can at least . . .": A. Mizener/AP, 18.12.74
363 too dazed: AP/D. Higham, 6.12.74 & 4.9.75, HA
363 "You should . . .": A. Lurie/AP, 24.11.75
363 "My only sadness . . .": O. Lancaster/AP, n.d. [Aug./Sept. 1975]
363 "Will he be . . . I think they will . . .": JH/M. Wood, 23.8.75
363 refused the knighthood: J2 54
364 still too close: AP/D. Higham, HA, 4.9.75
364 "My own guess . . .": P. Scott, "Turning the Full Circle," *Country Life*, 11.9.75
364 "The world remembered . . .": M. Frayn, "The End of the Dance," *Observer*, 7.9.75; republished in APSN, no. 29, winter 2007
364 "like the sadness . . .": K. Amis, *Observer*, 7.9.75
364 almost impossible: AP/D. Higham, 6.12.74 & 4.9.75
364 material in the end controls: AP/J. Brooke, 7.7.60
364 "conscious of an external . . .": SAG 111
364 "One can be classical . . . a way of controlling . . .": T. S. Eliot, "Ulysses, Order and Myth," *The Dial*, LXXV, Nov. 1923

Postscript

365 "Short and slightly . . .": John S. Monagan, "A Visit with Anthony Powell. Time's Musician," *American Scholar*, vol. 65, no. 3, summer 1996, p. 433
365 "It was like discovering . . .": "The End of the Dance," *Observer*, 7.9.75

366 invitation to lunch: 16.9.69

366 *Troubles*: By J. G. Farrell, published Oct. 1970 (Geoffrey Faber Memorial Prize in 1971)

367 on the day: General Election Day, 18.6.1970

367 first biography: H. Spurling, *Ivy When Young. The Early Life of I. Compton-Burnett*, 1974

367 a kind of handbook: AP/HS, 15.4.75; HS, *Handbook to Anthony Powell's Music of Time* (later *Invitation to the Dance*), 1977

367 "*Is* it Ella Wheeler . . .": HS notebook, 26.7.75

368 "tucked away . . .": VP, *Summary*, vol. 1, no. 1, autumn 1970, p. 123

368 John Heygate: J. Heygate/AP, 11.12.75; he died 18.3.76

368 "His energy does . . .": A. Dru/VP, n.d. (Dec. 1976); he died Jan. 1977

368 Reitlinger: Died Clyde Nursing Home, St. Leonards-on-Sea, 8.3.78

368 "it is awfully difficult . . .": AP, "A Day in the Life," *Observer*, 1.4.84

368 "I have absolutely . . .": Interview with Lynn Barber, *Independent on Sunday*, 8.3.92

369 "a band decreasing . . .": OHWB 39

369 one of his own: By David Cheshire for BBC, screened Nov. 1983

369 "His eyes protruded . . .": OHWB 96

369 "*O, How the Wheel* came . . .": V. S. Naipaul/AP, 17.9.83

369 to write no more: J2 69

369 "There is never . . .": MD 108

369 "I am simply . . .": P. Larkin/AP, 7.8.85

369 a last letter: O. Lancaster/AP, n.d. [1985]

370 "eminently respectable . . .": J2 55

370 "the end of a few . . .": WN 142

370 "only too like . . .": J3 210

370 "one of Shakespeare's . . .": J2 223

370 "anyway in his . . .": J3 215

371 "particularly the girls . . .": J3 201

371 sadistic streak: J3 85

371 "War is no strife . . .": J2 135, & see J2 24

371 "Our nearest thing . . . all the theoretical . . .": *Sunday Times*, 1.3.92; & see Jeremy Treglown, "Our Secret Harmonies," *TLS*, 27.1.2006

371 "His review was . . .": Naipaul, *A Writer's People*, op. cit., 71; for Waugh's review: *Sunday Telegraph*, 27.5.90

371 no adverse comment: Sykes, *Evelyn Waugh*, op. cit., 431

371 "the instincts of . . .": Alexander Chancellor, DT, 18.1.2001

371 successive volumes: See Auberon Waugh on BDFR, *Spectator*, March 1971; on TK, *Evening Standard*, 19.6.73; & on HSH, ibid., 9.9.75

371 His autobiography . . . contains: Waugh, *Will This Do?*, op. cit., *passim*; and see Hastings, *Evelyn Waugh*, op. cit., 576–8

371 "Unbalanced though . . .": Naipaul, *A Writer's People*, op. cit., 72; & see Alan Watkins, *A Short Walk Down Fleet Street*, 2000, p. 88

371 Tony resigned: AP/Max Hastings, 28.5.90, & Max Hastings/AP, 30.5.90

372 Shadbold's phrase: OHWB 7

372 the editor agreed: HS/M. Hastings, 6.7.90, & M. Hastings/HS, 29.10.91

372 Rodrigo Moynihan: Portrait of AP at the Chantry

372 so did Henry Mee: Reproduced on dust jacket of AP, UR

372 "Powell undoubtedly . . .": *British Eminences, Portraits by Henry Mee*, ex. cat., Sotheby's, May 1990

372 "as a permanent . . .": D. Holloway/HS, 6.7.90

373 "Some day my plinth . . .": HS/AP, 9.3.93

373 reversed his view: Naipaul, *A Writer's People*, op. cit., 36–41 & 66–7

373 "Anthony Powell was . . .": Tariq Ali, *Guardian*, 26.1.2008 (text of APS annual lecture, 2007)

373 "preceded, accompanied . . .": P. Larkin/AP, 8.8.76

373 "It's elitist . . . Reading it is like . . .": Ian Rankin, *Scotsman*, 17.3.2007; & see APSN, no. 28, autumn 2007

374 "as dim, provincial . . .": Hugh Thomas, *The Times*, 19.1.95

374 like a soldier: AP, interview with Lynn Barber, *Independent on Sunday*, 8.3.92

374 "It's like being . . .": TK chap. 1

374 strongly advised: AP/HS, 3.7.90

374 Humbert trial: See HS, *La Grande Thérèse. The Greatest Swindle of the Century*, 1999, pp. 2, 76–8, 99 & 101

376 "They were obviously . . .": J3 215

376 "I only wish . . .": AP/HS, 22.2.91

376 "a masked and . . .": SAG 194

376 "perhaps my favourite . . .": J3 179

377 "If you subtract . . .": Mount, *Cold Cream*, op. cit., 70

377 passage from the bible: Ezekiel 37:1–3

378 "an extraordinary grasp . . .": SP 54

INDEX

The abbreviation "AP" stands for Anthony Powell. Page references in *italic* indicate illustrations or their captions.

ILLUSTRATION CREDITS

Endpapers: the boiler room collage at the Chantry © The Estate of Anthony Powell. Photographer: Hugh Gilbert

All integrated images from the archives of both Anthony Powell and Violet Powell at the Chantry are used by kind permission of the Powell family © The Estates of Anthony Powell and Violet Powell.

Insert images: *Anthony Powell* by Nina Hamnett, 1927. Image reproduction from *Is She a Lady? Problem in Autobiography*, Nina Hamnett (London, Allan Wingate, 1955); *A Dance to the Music of Time* by Nicolas Poussin © The Wallace Collection, London; *Saturday Market* by Edward Burra. Reproduced by kind permission of the Estate of the Artist, c/o Lefevre Fine Art Ltd, London; *Constant Lambert* by Christopher Wood. Reproduced by kind permission of the National Portrait Gallery; *Anthony Powell* by Henry Lamb. Reproduced by kind permission of the National Portrait Gallery; *Evelyn Waugh* by Henry Lamb. From the collection of Lord Moyne; WA1978.33.1 Eve Disher, Gerald Reitlinger © Ashmolean Museum, University of Oxford. Reproduced by kind permission of the Eve Disher Estate; Portrait of Nina Hamnett by Jacob Kramer. Reproduced by kind permission of Judith Yapp; Painting of Marion and Laura by John Banting. Reproduced by kind permission of Matthew and Susanna Cohn; *Dorothea Varda* by Adrian Daintry. Reproduced by kind permission of Anne Bedish

A NOTE ABOUT THE AUTHOR

Hilary Spurling is the author of five biographies, including *Ivy When Young*, about Ivy Compton-Burnett, and a two-volume biography of Matisse, which won the Whitbread Book of the Year Award and the Los Angeles Times Biography Award. She has been theatre critic and literary editor of the *The Spectator*, and regularly reviews for *The Observer* and *The Daily Telegraph*. She lives in London.

A NOTE ON THE TYPE

This book was sent in Fournier, a typeface named for Pierre Simon Fournier *fils* (1712–1768), a celebrated French type designer. Coming from a family of typefounders, Fournier was an extraordinarily prolific designer of type faces and of typographic ornaments. He was also the author of the important *Manuel typographique* (1764–1766), in which he attempted to work out a system standardizing type measurement in points, a systems that is still in use internationally.

Fournier's type is considered transitional in that it drew its inspiration from the old style, yet was ingeniously innovational, providing for an elegant, legible appearance.

COMPOSED BY
North Market Street Graphics, Lancaster, Pennsylvania

PRINTED AND BOUND BY
Berryville Graphics, Berryville, Virginia